SPECIAL EFFECTS

SPECIAL EFFECTS

NEW HISTORIES/THEORIES/CONTEXTS

Edited by DAN NORTH, BOB REHAK, MICHAEL S. DUFFY

A BFI book published by Palgrave

First published in 2015 by
PALGRAVE

on behalf of the

BRITISH FILM INSTITUTE
21 Stephen Street, London W1T 1LN
www.bfi.org.uk

There's more to discover about film and television through the BFI. Our world-renowned archive, cinemas, festivals, films, publications and learning resources are here to inspire you.

PALGRAVE in the UK is an imprint of Macmillan Publishers Limited, registered in England, company number 785998, of 4 Crinan Street, London N1 9XW. Palgrave Macmillan in the US is a division of St Martin's Press LLC, 175 Fifth Avenue, New York, NY 10010. Palgrave is a global imprint of the above companies and is represented throughout the world. Palgrave® and Macmillan® are registered trademarks in the United States, the United Kingdom, Europe and other countries.

Cover image: Level1studio/Getty Images
Cover design: Liron Gilenberg
Designed by couch

Set by Cambrian Typesetters, Camberley, Surrey
Printed in China

This book is printed on paper suitable for recycling and made from fully managed and sustained forest sources. Logging, pulping and manufacturing processes are expected to conform to the environmental regulations of the country of origin.

British Library Cataloguing-in-Publication Data
A catalogue record for this book is available from the British Library
A catalog record for this book is available from the Library of Congress

ISBN 978–1–84457–517–6 (pb)
ISBN 978–1–84457–518–3 (hb)

CONTENTS

3/SCREENS

ACKNOWLEDGMENTS

This book was put together over a long period, during which we benefited greatly from the unstinting support of staff at the British Film Institute and Palgrave who helped to turn our collected ideas into a cohesive finished product. In particular, we would like to thank Rebecca Barden, Jenni Burnell, Anna Coatman, Sophia Contento and Lucinda Knight. We are also grateful to the anonymous readers who gave us much constructive criticism and encouragement.

We have been delighted with the work of our contributors whose ideas and stories you are about to enjoy. They were diligent in their commitment to making this project happen, and endlessly patient with our suggestions. We are proud to present the essays we have been given to work with, and we grieve those we were unable to include.

Dan North thanks his former colleagues at the University of Exeter for giving him a luxuriant intellectual environment from which to work, singling out the film unit for special mention: Steve Neale, Helen Hanson, James Lyons and Joe Kember. His contributions are dedicated to Tuesday, Evie and Iris, from whom he stole some playtime in order to write them.

Bob Rehak thanks his colleagues and students at Swarthmore College for their support throughout the editing process, along with the participants at the Magic of Special Effects conference which took place in Montreal in November 2013. Their feedback on his work in progress contributed enormously to the chapter that appears in this volume. At home, Katie, Zachary and Trevor provided spiritual nourishment and a welcome absence of shop talk.

Michael Duffy thanks Paul Grainge, Michele Pierson and Greg Faller for their unending support and encouragement, his colleagues at the Electronic Media and Film Department at Towson University for consistently and patiently asking 'How's the book going?', and most importantly, his parents, without whom …

FOREWORD

SCOTT BUKATMAN

That special effects need to be studied hardly needs defending at this point, and surely not to anyone reading this book. The turn to the digital in the world of 'film' production (to say nothing of the world of console games) has seen a proliferation of effects-based entertainment. To the hardy genres of science fiction and fantasy we can now add the superhero film and the action blockbuster as havens of special effects, and there is hardly an aspect of film production that hasn't been affected by the affordances of digital production and manipulation. Effects that were once painstakingly human-labour-intensive, such as animation and work with miniatures, are now at least somewhat achievable by anyone with the right software and processing power. The American blockbuster is increasingly a showcase for ever more realistic effects, whether in the service of reshaping bodies or levelling major metropolitan centres.

Scholarly attention to special effects in all its guises has already generated useful interventions in the world of film theory. That the cinema's central claim to medium-specific profundity rested upon its indexical relation to the real is no longer a given: Stephen Prince has pointed to all the myriad ways that film footage has been manipulated from the medium's inception, while Tom Gunning has argued that we need to reconsider the cinema – the movies, if you will – as primarily a medium of movement rather than a privileged vehicle for truth.[1] (This is not to claim that cinema has lost its referential, indexical power, but it *is* to refute the idea that this is common to all films or modes of production). The ever more pervasive pervasiveness of digital effects (what we might call CGI-tis) lends support to Lev Manovich's contention that cinema was always something of a subset of animation. And the 'special' aspect of the special effect directs viewers' attention to the constructed nature of the image in ways that have little to do with a passive spectator absorbing ostensibly invisible structures. As I've noted before,[2] the cinema itself is, at its core, a special effect, but after the novelty of recorded movement had worn off, new effects needed to be pressed into service, redirecting spectatorial attention to the pleasure of seeing what had never before been so compellingly visualised.

As often seems to be the case within healthy scholarly discourses, an attention to the new has generated an interest in the historical, an interest well documented in this volume. Our engagement with digital effects redirects our attention to effects of all kinds: whether in-camera or optical, mechanical or animated. Bringing Laura Mulvey's concept of the 'clumsy sublime' to bear upon a swath of 'outmoded', and hence no longer 'convincing', effects work, Bob Rehak has demonstrated that even digitial effects have been around long enough to have a history.[3] Continuities, ruptures and hidden histories abound.

But, of course, the rubric of the special effect is increasingly a misnomer in the realm of digital pre-production-post. When I wrote about the work of Douglas Trumbull, whose most significant work occurred on the cusp of the development of CGI, I could concentrate on the special-effects *sequence* – a space that existed apart from human activity (other than cutaways to reaction shots), that returned us to the direct address and spectacular exhibitionism of the cinema of attractions.[4] The limitations of existing technologies made the seamless integration of live action and effects work a nearly insurmountable challenge, although this was not without its benefits. But digital effects, almost from their first deployment, delivered the means of integrating filmed footage with generated effects within a single, often dizzyingly kinetic, shot. The special-effects sequence was absorbed into the diegetic reality of the film; or if you want to look at it another way, entire films became extended special-effects sequences.

It's a truism that the success of the superhero film (beyond the ones about Superman and Batman) had to wait until the world of film technology was adequate to the task of presenting the morphing bodies and alternative physics of the comics, but I can't help but wonder whether the extraordinary, digitally enhanced superhero body represents some kind of acknowledgment of the prevalence of digital technology in our everyday experience. Where, once, a film like *Tron* (1982) needed to insert the human body into those mysterious new data spaces that we engaged with via the new technologies of home computers and ATMs, now technological engagement is played out upon the body in ways that are less abject than in the body-horror films of the 1980s (more films made on the cusp of the digital). Virtual reality, though always, it seems, poised on the edge of a comeback, has been superseded by the augmented reality granted us by the iPhone and its brethren. We don't enter the computer any more, we just bring it with us. We carry it around like *ahem* a secret identity. (Superhero films have yet to make extensive use of the kind of mo-capped performances that marked such films as *Avatar* (2009) and everything that Andy Serkis has appeared in, and so, for me, the integration of human and effect remains, as of this writing, somewhat incomplete and unsatisfying.)

I remain most interested in *spectacular* effects, effects that revel in their own capabilities and that remake our perceptual limits, and still welcome evocations of the sublime, with its literally *awesome* commingling of the sensations of wonder and anxiety. The technological sublime, so fundamental to the special-effects worlds created by Douglas Trumbull, still finds voice in the age of the digital, although the rhetoric may differ.

The technological sublime was manifest in those memorable large-screen optical effects that almost casually redefined notions of scale. The spaceship that fills the screen at the beginning of *Star Wars* (1977), and which keeps on filling the screen as it moves above us, has its analogue in the appearance of the mothership at the end of *Close Encounters of the Third Kind* (1977), dwarfing Devil's Tower and the small group of humans gathered at its base. The digitally produced *Pacific Rim* (2013) similarly plays with scale, as a giant 'Jaeger', a human-controlled giant robot (I know that's an oxymoron but that's what it looks like), rises behind its human operators in an all-too-brief, but still thrilling, shot that owes something, I think, to Jack Kirby's comic book Celestials. While I miss the contemplative mode that Trumbull's work permitted (I miss it a lot, actually), in this case IMAX and 3D effectively give us an experience of the technological sublime. But in some ways, that shift away from normative scale seemed more appropriate to the industrial age: the building of Everytown 2036 in *Things to Come* (1936), for example, or the future Los Angeles, reminiscent of a giant oil refinery, that stretches beyond the screen at the beginning of *Blade Runner* (1982). The technological sublime of the industrial and late-industrial age as presented in *Things to Come*, *Star Wars* and *Close Encounters* was evoked through the presentation of an object or environment with an affective impact familiar to anyone versed in Edmund Burke's writings on sublimity and aesthetics: obscurity, vastness, magnificence and power. And, indeed, despite its digital provenance, *Pacific Rim* is something of a backward looking film: not only did del Toro dedicate the film to monster-masters Ray Harryhausen and Ishirô Honda, but its rusted, mechanical, borderline steampunk environment speaks to an earlier era of industrial might.

Other films evoke the technological sublime differently, and here I'm thinking of what Kristin Whissel has memorably referred to as the 'digital multitude'. The digital multitude is a radically homogeneous mass of digitally generated beings that might take the form of invading armies (be they human-ish, robot-ish, or Orc-ish).[5] They extend to the limits of the frame and presumably beyond, each identical form like all the rest, though there may be some minuscule, randomly generated differences that, Whissel notes, only serve to underscore their overall multitudinous similarity. These figures, this mass, is inevitably set against a far smaller group, a hardy band of rather more heterogeneous humans, who have learned to set aside their differences just enough to beat the digital horde.

The digital multitude shares much with the massive objects of earlier modes of production. The limits of the frame, and by analogy our conceptual frames, are exceeded by a new technological power. The human is dwarfed, if not invisible. Obscurity, vastness, magnificence and power are all in play. But here it would be useful to remember (or learn) that Burke's catalogue also includes the concepts of *succession* and *uniformity.* In its evocation of an infinite number of infinitely repeatable forms, characters and film spectators alike are brought up against new, invasive powers, of whose limits we can scarcely guess. It's digital technology that now overwhelms human scale and sensibility. But it also needs saying that, in its perfect synchronicity and amassed might, the digital multitude is indisputably alluring.

It's been my contention that effects have a pedagogical function, acclimatising us to ideas of technological power, and this remains true here as well. But it's equally true, and I've argued this as well, that effects have an equally important ludic function. Following the static (or slowly moving) shot of massed warriors, digital horde and virtual camera both charge into action. Contemplation yields to participation, giddy kinesis puts *us* in motion. We ride the effects, often first-person-shooter style, but – should we be in the opening-weekend audience – at a scale no big-screen TV can match. Now we *feel* the technologies, and in feeling them we come to understand them both sensorially and sensually. This remains a signal pleasure of these blockbuster movies; perhaps the last remaining one. Even the morphing bodies of the superhero movie, which I like more than I once did, may be helping instantiate a phenomenology of the digital, in which nothing is immutable, nothing is essential. And here mention should be made of the ecstatically plasmatic kaiju of *Pacific Rim*, instantly recognisable as the creations of comic artist Guy Davis, which begin the film as rubberoid homages to Honda but which give way to more sublimely metamorphosing forms that could only be the product of either alternate-dimensional biology or digital effects.

But there is more to effects than pedagogy and playfulness, and this marvellous (to be pithy about it) anthology amply demonstrates the range of ways that scholars have found to engage with effects technologies; the essays here theorise issues of production, representation, reception and history, teasing out the implications not only for the medium of cinema, but also for the corporeal and spatio-temporal imaginaries at work. What was so striking for me in wending my way through its contents was the thoroughgoing and complex hybridity that the essays map so effectively. While the cinema may not ultimately depend for its definition on the indexical relation to the real, rare, it seems, are the works that exist entirely in the immaterial realm of the digital. Digital production techniques coexist rather happily with the ethos and materiality of the handcrafted. The real abides.

This anthology is a testament to the vitality and variegated nature of current scholarship around special effects. Susan Sontag once wrote that, in place of a hermeneutics we need an *erotics* of art, but this volume provides *both* a hermeneutics and an erotics of special effects – no small feat for any area of film studies.

Notes

1. Stephen Prince, *Digital Visual Effects in Cinema: The Seduction of Reality* (New Brunswick, NJ: Rutgers University Press, 2011); Tom Gunning, 'Moving Away from the Index: Cinema and the Impression of Reality', *differences* vol. 18 no. 1 (2007), pp. 29–52.
2. Scott Bukatman, 'The Artificial Infinite: On Special Effects and the Sublime', in *Matters of Gravity: Special Effects and Supermen in the 20th Century* (Durham, NC: Duke University Press, 2003), p. 90.
3. Bob Rehak, 'We Have Never Been Digital: CGI and the New "Clumsy Sublime"', *Graphic Engine*, 24 March 2012, http://graphic-engine.swarthmore.edu/we-have-never-been-digital-cgi-as-the-new-clumsy-sublime/; Laura Mulvey, *Death 24x a Second: Stillness and the Moving Image* (London: Reaktion Books, 2006).
4. Bukatman, 'The Artificial Infinite'.
5. Kristen Whissel, *Spectacular Digital Effects: CGI and Contemporary Cinema* (Durham, NC: Duke University Press, 2014).

NOTES ON CONTRIBUTORS

STACEY ABBOTT is a Reader in Film and Television Studies at the University of Roehampton. She is the author of *Celluloid Vampires* (2007), *Angel: TV Milestone* (2009) and co-author of *TV Horror: Investigating the Dark Side of the Small Screen* (2012). She has written on special effects for *Science Fiction Studies* and has recently edited a special issue of *Critical Studies in Television* on effects and TV. She is currently writing a book on the twenty-first century vampire and zombie in film and television.

TANINE ALLISON is Assistant Professor of Film and Media Studies at Emory University, where she teaches courses on film, video games and digital media. She has published essays on motion capture, digital realism and war video games in the *Quarterly Review of Film and Video*, *Critical Quarterly* and *Literature/Film Quarterly*, and has essays on military science-fiction films and contemporary visual effects forthcoming in edited collections. She is currently completing a book on the aesthetics of combat in American films and video games.

DREW AYERS is an Assistant Academic Specialist in the Media and Screen Studies programme at Northeastern University. His work has appeared in *Film Criticism*, *Configurations*, *Scope* and *In Media Res*, and his essay on the phenomenology of performance capture will appear in an upcoming special issue of *Animation: An Interdisciplinary Journal*. He is currently at work on a manuscript that explores the 'vernacular posthumanism' of film, media and visual culture, and its relationship to the digital logics of contemporary image production.

LISA BODE is Lecturer in Film and Television Studies at the University of Queensland. She has written on synthespians and the digital reanimation of dead actors for *Cinema Journal* and *Animation: An Interdisciplinary Journal*. Lisa is currently writing her first book, titled *Screen Performance and Cinema's Illusions: Technological Trickery, Authenticity, and Value*.

SCOTT BUKATMAN is a cultural theorist and Professor of Film and Media Studies in the Department of Art and Art History at Stanford University. His research explores the ways that such popular media as film, comics and animation mediate between new technologies and human perceptual and bodily experience. His books include *Terminal Identity: The Virtual Subject in Postmodern Science Fiction* (1993); *Matters of Gravity: Special Effects and Supermen in the 20th Century* (2003), the British Film Institute monograph on the film *Blade Runner* (1997) and *The Poetics of Slumberland: Animated Spirits and the Animating Spirit* (2012). His most recent book is *Hellboy's World: Comics and the Adventure of Reading*, forthcoming.

ANDREA COMISKEY is a PhD candidate in Communication Arts at the University of Wisconsin-Madison, where she is also a member of the editorial board of *The Velvet Light Trap*. Her primary research interests are the related histories of US film distribution, exhibition and moviegoing; she also studies animation and film technologies. Among her publications are pieces in *The Classical Hollywood Reader* and the journals *Iluminace* and *Post Script*.

ETHAN DE SEIFE is the author of *This Is Spinal Tap* (2007) and *Tashlinesque: The Hollywood Comedies of Frank Tashlin* (2012). He recently left academia and is now an arts journalist for the Burlington, Vermont, alt-weekly newspaper *Seven Days*.

MICHAEL S. DUFFY is a Lecturer in Film and Media Studies at Towson University in Maryland. He has written and taught on film history, genre, aesthetics, special effects, East Asian cinemas, superhero films, James Bond, 1980s music video and popular/cult television (*Smallville*, *Highlander*), and has contributed to numerous anthologies including Volumes I and II of *Directory of World Cinema: American Hollywood* (2011, 2015). He is currently working on a book exploring the industrial, technological and creative development of Australasian visual-effects companies during the 1990s, and a separate monograph looking at the film and media industry's treatment of the posthumous lives of 'stars'. He holds a PhD from the University of Nottingham and an MA from New York University.

BARBARA FLUECKIGER has been a Professor of Film Studies at the University of Zurich since 2007. Her research focuses on the interaction between technology and aesthetics, especially in the digital domain. She published two standard textbooks, *Sound Design* (2001) and *Visual Effects* (2008), and many articles in renowned books and peer-reviewed journals. In fall 2011 and summer 2012 she was a research fellow at Harvard University, where she explored material and aesthetic aspects of historical film colours, published online as an interactive digital humanities project: *Timeline of Historical Film Colors*: http://zauberklang.ch/filmcolors/. Her current research projects investigate the digitisation of archival film.

OLIVER GAYCKEN is an Assistant Professor in the Department of English and a core faculty member of the Film Studies Program and the Program in Comparative Literature at the University of Maryland, College Park. He is the author of *Devices of Curiosity: Early Cinema and Popular Science* (2015). His articles have appeared in *Historical Journal of Film, Radio, and Television*; *Science in Context*; *Journal of Visual Culture*; *Early Popular Visual Culture*; *Screen*; and the collection *Learning with the Lights Off*.

KATHARINA LOEW is an Assistant Professor in German and Cinema Studies at the University of Oregon. Her research focuses on film technology and special effects. Recent publications include essays on early German film theory, 3D cinema in the 1910s and Fritz Lang's 1929 *Woman in the Moon*. She is currently completing a book manuscript that investigates the impact of special-effects technologies on German film during the silent era.

LEV MANOVICH's awards include a Guggenheim Fellowship, a Digital Cultures Fellowship from UC Santa Barbara, a Fellowship from the Zentrum für Literaturforschung, Berlin and a Mellon Fellowship from California Institute of the Arts. His book *The Language of New Media* (2001) is one of the most significant contributions to the debates around digital technology, and has been translated into more than six languages. He is a Professor in the Computer Science programme at City University of New York.

ANGELA NDALIANIS is Professor in Screen Studies at the University of Melbourne. Her research focuses on entertainment media histories, media and the senses, and the transhistorical and transcultural nature of the baroque. She has published numerous essays in journals and anthologies, and her book publications include *Neo-Baroque Aesthetics and Contemporary Entertainment* (2004), *The Horror Sensorium: Media and the Senses* (2012), *Science Fiction Experiences* (2011) and *The Contemporary Comic Book Superhero* (2008).

DAN NORTH is an independent scholar based in the Netherlands. He is the author of *Performing Illusions: Cinema, Special Effects and the Virtual Actor* (2008), and the editor of *Sights Unseen: Unfinished British Films* (2008). His essays have been published in *Film & History*, *Early Popular Visual Culture*, *Shakespeare Bulletin* and a number of anthologies. He is currently researching the history of puppetry on film.

BOB REHAK is an Associate Professor in the Film and Media Studies Department at Swarthmore College, where his research and teaching focus on animation, video games, fan culture and special effects. His writing has appeared in *Film Criticism*, *Cinema Journal*, several game-studies anthologies and the second edition of the *Cybercultures Reader*.

CHUCK TRYON is an Associate Professor in the English Department at Fayetteville State University. His research focuses on the transformations of movie and television consumption in the era of digital distribution. He is the author of *Reinventing Cinema: Movies in the Age of Media Convergence* (2009) and *On-demand Culture: Digital Delivery and the Future of Movies* (2013). He has also published essays in the *Journal of Film and Video*, *Jump Cut*, *Popular Communication* and *Screen*, as well as in the anthologies *Moving Data: The iPhone and My Media* (2012) and *Across the Screens: Science Fiction on Television and Film* (2011).

JULIE TURNOCK is Assistant Professor of Media and Cinema Studies at the University of Illinois, Urbana/Champaign, in the College of Media. She is the author of *Plastic Reality: Special Effects, Art and Technology in 1970s US Filmmaking* (2015), and has published on special effects of the studio era, the 1970s and recent digital cinema in *Cinema Journal*, *Film History*, *Film Criticism* and *New Review of Film and Television Studies*.

AYLISH WOOD is Reader in Film Studies in the School of Art, University of Kent. She has written articles on visual effects in cinema, animation and games. Her work has been published in *Screen*, *Quarterly Review of Film and Video*, *New Review of Film and Video*, *Film Criticism*, *Games and Culture*, *Journal of Film and Video* and *Animation: An Interdisciplinary Journal*. Her books include

Technoscience in Contemporary American Cinema (2002) and *Digital Encounters* (2007). Her new book *Software, Animation and the Moving Image: What's in the Box?* (2015) has recently been published.

GREGORY ZINMAN is an Assistant Professor in the School of Literature, Media, and Communication at the Georgia Institute of Technology. His writing on film and media has appeared in the *New Yorker*, *American Art*, *Film History* and *Millennium Film Journal*, among other publications. He is also the curator of screening programmes including 'Computer Age', a travelling programme of early computer animations. He is currently completing a book, *Handmade: The Moving Image in the Artisanal Mode*, and is co-editing, with John Hanhardt, *Nam June Paik: Selected Writings*.

INTRODUCTION

DAN NORTH, BOB REHAK, MICHAEL S. DUFFY

The very existence of the anthology you are now reading suggests that special effects are 'things' specific enough to serve as objects of academic study. They are as concrete as any industrial or technological practice, tied to their times like any historical subject and as conceptually layered as any other theoretical focus in film and media studies, such as genre, authorship or narrative form. Indeed, special effects – broadly defined as artificially produced illusions within moving-image media, predominantly cinema – manifest all of these qualities, constituting one of the most energetic and actively discussed areas of film production, marketing and reception since the dawn of the medium. Moreover, special effects have received plentiful attention over the years in popular culture, journalism and fandom, in everything from hostile critiques of story's displacement by empty spectacle to 'behind-the-scenes' materials that pull aside the curtain to reveal the making of 'movie magic' in loving, even fetishistic detail. In popular discourse, then, those who talk about film know what special effects are.

At the same time, special effects present a problem to investigation through their very *lack* of specificity. We might recall Christian Metz's assertion in 1977 that all of cinema could be considered an act of *trucage* or trickery, so no techniques could be singled out as inherently illusory.[1] Especially now, in an era where every image can be retouched if not created from wholly digital cloth, what *is not*, at least potentially, a special effect?[2] We know instinctively how to understand the spectacular illusions at the centre of *King Kong* (1933) or *Close Encounters of the Third Kind* (1977), because marvelling at them is invited by the narrative structures of both of those films. But what of 'invisible' special effects that hide their manipulations, working quietly in the background to stitch together an apparently seamless screen reality? Finally, what about special effects that might have 'fooled' audiences in their time, but became obsolete and all-too-discernible in the years that followed – or, conversely, special effects that once entertained viewers who understood them as pure spectacle, but which current audiences are less likely to recognise because the effects have been subsumed into the larger 'falseness' of black-and-white, silent or early cinema?

The category of special effects, then, is paradoxically slippery and perpetually in prismatic flux, ranging from the 'I know it when I see it' experience of spectators to the 'here's how it was done' of the technical/entertainment insider (or the 'here's how much it cost' of the studio bottom-liner). To study special effects in a scholarly context means first choosing how we should define the concept: are there any essential characteristics common to all special effects, or is the term defined by the very diversity of techniques it covers? Second, it means carefully noting where these very definitions – like the illusory play of special effects themselves – might 'trick' the investigative eye into accepting a stark division between 'special' effects and the rest of cinema, neglecting important aspects of a complicated mix of process, practice and perception.

Consider one of the long-standing distinctions within the special-effects industry: the difference between 'practical' or 'mechanical' effects performed 'live' before the camera while shooting, and 'optical' or 'post-production' effects accomplished, as their name suggests, after shooting has been completed. The latter are also referred to as 'visual' effects, and recent books such as those by Stephen Prince and Shilo T. McClean adopt the premise that everything we once thought of as 'special effects' can now be understood primarily as digital phenomena, fully integrated with the storytelling apparatus of mainstream film-making.[3] This perceived erasure of boundaries between techniques surely attracts scholarship because it gives the impression that studying 'the digital' or 'digitality' can provide an essential understanding of all effects processes. The erasure also brings special-effects studies cosily inside the remit of post-modernist concerns with film's simulationist abilities, because the ease with which images can be manipulated – and the availability of manipulation tools even to amateur users – implies an unregulated proliferation of synthetic imagery, with cinematic visual effects the industrial enclosure for such deceptions. While there are undoubtedly good reasons to study the 'digital turn' (the period when analogue processes were taken over by digital remediations of the same techniques and visual tropes), it should not be at the expense of historically grounded analyses of the multiple, complex and varied ways in which films fabricate and frame their representational terrain. Even though, in many cases, miniatures, puppets, glass paintings and other 'traditional' effects processes *have* been supplanted by digital animation, this should not be seen as an endpoint for cinema's reliance upon and use for the tools of illusion, but one stage in a long historical continuum of adaptation, appropriation (of crafts and techniques) and change.

Perhaps, then, studying special effects in the second decade of the twenty-first century also provides a way of reflecting on the distinctive properties of the digital and how they are remaking cinema in more global terms. In her book *Digital Imaging in Popular Cinema*, Lisa Purse urges spectators to improve their literacy for, and their alertness to, the digital.[4] She presents a series of case studies to demonstrate that viewing and interpreting films is affected in ways both subtle and profound by the digital image's fluid malleability. Most importantly, she focuses on the distinct properties and affordances of digital images, rather than on the ways they replay, accelerate or rectify extant imaging techniques.

These are not merely academic questions – film scholars arguing by simulated candlelight how many analogue 'angels' can dance on the head of a digital 'pin'. The Hollywood visual-effects industry is, at the time of writing, undergoing a very real economic crisis as 'the wonder years of CGI' (as Michele Pierson termed the first years of Hollywood's exploration/exploitation of computer-generated imagery) draw to an end and the pragmatics of wonderment's production line kick in.[5] A number of companies, including Pixomondo and Rhythm and Hues, have found themselves in dire financial trouble, even while, in the case of Rhythm and Hues, producing Oscar-winning work on an international blockbuster, *Life of Pi* (2012); even the makers of otherworldly spectacle have found they are not immune to the mundane challenges of globalisation. In the Classical Hollywood era, special-effects departments, with contracted staff, were held in-house at the studios and allotted work on the studio's own productions. Today, effects houses, which may specialise in very specific types of visual effects (for example, particle systems, virtual actors, matte painting), must bid competitively for the chance to complete certain scenes or even individual shots for films – and they are increasingly likely to be outbid by companies working out of Asia, where labour costs and taxes are significantly lower than in Los Angeles.[6] This need not be an apocalyptic prediction as far as film production is concerned. It may even lead to a democratisation (or internationalisation) of the means of production via the increased availability of visual-effects software. But it is a reminder that special effects, whose greatest moments we tend to remember as sublime bursts of technological exhibitionism, are rooted in the realities of artisanal labour, and however much we might think of mainstream cinema as dependent upon the sugar-coating of visual spectacle, the frangibility of the effects houses that deliver it speaks of the essential separateness of special effects from the central authorities that control studio film-making.

This industrial crisis is mirrored in debates around blockbuster franchises and their seemingly unavoidable 'transmedia' extensions. Within the world of ramifying tie-in texts and product engineering, special effects provide a rhetorical arena for combat between two terms ever more frequently bandied about in public/critical/industry conversation: the distinction between the 'human element' and 'world building'. What do these signify, and why does this distinguishing discussion keep recurring? At what point does the presence of visual effects annihilate the human qualities that have made a mechanical medium so fascinating to audiences for so long, and how might effects creators reinscribe their practice with the markers of human affect and artistry (if it is even desirable to do so)? What does this debate say about how both the industry and the public view effects, spectacle, storytelling, industry/studio mandates and the contemporary Hollywood production process itself? Effects and their creative processes are, like cinema, enveloped in a constant stream of change, and one of the major goals of this collection of essays is to engage with and clarify those changes.

Returning to definitions of special effects, we might think of them as solutions to problems: if a screenplay contains an action or event that cannot be performed on set without specialist assistance, the workaround that enables the scene's completion could be defined as a special effect. Contemporary Hollywood tentpole/blockbuster philosophy privileges a mantra of 'design spectacle sequences first', frequently selecting subject matter, such as superheroes or space travel, for which visual effects will be essential, making the film's actual narrative the workaround to its visual storytelling. These solutions to production problems might include 'practical' or 'physical' effects such as pyrotechnics, stunt wires, rigged vehicles, explosives, animatronic puppetry and miniatures. We might also refer to these as profilmic techniques, since they are achieved live on set in front of the cameras instead of manufactured in post-production. Traditionally, the term 'visual effects' was used to differentiate practical effects from post-production processes that must now include digital animation. Special effects might include in-camera set-design augmentations such as hanging miniatures, glass shots, Schüfftan shots or matte shots, all of which can expand and alter an existing location, fabricate the illusion of a fantastic environment or composite live-action and miniature models in the same frame. Then there are in-camera manipulations such as stop-motion substitutions, dissolves, double exposures, all of which can also be achieved in post-production, and compositing effects such as those achieved with an optical printer that can create screen wipes, on-screen text and composite images. The definitional problem arises not only from the sheer range and diversity of techniques covered under the banner term 'special effects', but from a paradox created by such taxonomies: to define some aspects of film production as 'special', is to assume that the apparatus of the medium of film has some baseline technical properties that are somehow *not* illusionist, *not* extrinsic to reality, *not* special.

Whether at the scale of individual elements and shots or longer segments of film, *special* effects require *specialist* knowledge and equipment for their achievement, and this is largely what confers upon them their 'special' status. See, for example, the sequences supervised by Douglas Trumbull for *Close Encounters of the Third Kind* and *Star Trek: The Motion Picture* (1979). According to Scott Bukatman, these segments of the film – in which spectacular, lingering shots of iconic craft are separated from the films' human protagonists who look on awestruck in reaction shots – can be tied to Trumbull as an effects auteur.[7] Or note the way Ray Harryhausen's animated creatures, however meticulously they may have been composited into the live-action frame, express their ontological separateness in their distinctive movements (consistently authored with Harryhausen's signature style and personality across all of the films to which he contributed), and in their confinement to lairs, temples, caves and lost valleys that isolate them from the main action. The discrete properties of special effects, supplied by their technical idiosyncrasies as well as their diegetic placement as set-pieces or narrative agents, might mark them out as incongruous adornments when they fail to gel with their surrounding *mise en scène*. But noticing this separateness is part of the process of locating and beginning to interpret what it is that special effects contribute to the films in which they appear: it is their separateness, their slight incongruity, that makes them special. The rhetoric of the digital revolution is that all of those incongruities will be obliterated, the joins between composited elements will be made invisible and film-makers will be limited only by their imaginations in what they can put on screen. This revolutionary claim hinges on assumptions that digital technologies do not mediate, but only facilitate and enable representation, and that spectators play no significantly active role as recipients and consumers of special effects.

We should be wary, however, of definitions that depend upon firm distinctions between processes designated as 'effects' and those defined as basic components of the filmic apparatus. The specialist nature of effects might align them with technologies that are not part of the creative, aesthetic or artistic discourses of film production: for example, the makers of the metal armatures inside an animatronic creature need not have any interest in the meaning-making capabilities of the on-screen character they are constructing, and their discipline can exist regardless of whether or not it is used in a film. Similarly, the engineering expertise needed to make us believe that Superman can fly is distinct from the creative exercise that gives the character a personality, dialogue and semiotic significance. But film has always been a mechanical medium whose major attraction was the technological reconstitution of fictional worlds using any available resources. It is a magpie medium, picking up and finding uses for any spectacular opportunity within reach. Moreover, the output of film production (assuming that our subject for the purposes of this discussion is a narrative feature film) ostensibly requires the spectator to focus primarily on the finished images and not on the machines that make them possible: one's enjoyment of a film, at least on first encounter, is likely to be diminished if one is staring at the projector rather than the screen, at the wires rather than the marionette.

Rather than attempting a complete taxonomy of those processes that have been regarded historically as special effects, we can open up the subject by describing the uses to which effects are put in individual films and in their industrial context. We might break down the field as follows:

- TECHNICAL: Special effects are those things produced through particular practices such as stop-motion animation, optical printing, animation, miniature models, compositing, computer graphics. It should be noted that most films that deploy special effects use them in combination rather than in isolation. The eponymous ship in *Titanic* (1997) was visualised using scale models of various sizes, full-size replicas of portions of the vessel and digital substitutes and set extensions for certain sequences.
- ECONOMIC: Effects solve budgetary problems faced by productions in which generating images and sounds indexically would be prohibitively expensive. Building a complete replica of the *Titanic* (and then sinking it) would be a crippling investment, as would a perfect replica of Rome's Coliseum, which was partially built in Malta for *Gladiator* (2000) and then supplemented with digital set extensions and populated with virtual crowds. Visual effects are, in themselves, costly to produce, but elaborate spectacle, incorporated into marketing drives, can be an attraction for audiences, so effects may serve as guarantors of increased box office rather than mere cost-cutting devices.
- NARRATIVE: The best application of special effects is as storytelling agents, conveying narrative meanings and themes. The title character of *King Kong*, a gargantuan ape, was depicted via frame-by-frame animation of miniature figures, and some full-scale partial models of a head and a hand for a few shots. A variety of process shots were deployed, combining studio sets with hanging miniatures and extensive use of glass shots, where scenes are photographed through panes of glass painted with virtual set extensions, to create Kong's jungle home (no location shooting was desired or required). Other processes could have been chosen to visualise Kong, place him in appropriate environments and have him interact with human actors, but these were the methods available and selected at the time. The way in which fantasy worlds, mythical creatures and the historical past are represented depends on how effects artists perform their work, as well as how their work is 'directed' and then incorporated into the final edit, and the meanings they generate will always be inflected by the particularities of those effects. So, the narrative input of special effects to the overall impact and import of a film is never simply the direct transposition of events in a screenplay to images on a screen, but the technological mediation of those events: Kong would have activated a different set of meanings if he had been played by an actor in a gorilla suit. This explains why, even if they are devoted to representing narrative situations, special effects bring with them their own inferences and associations. If *Titanic* was intended as a historical reconstruction of events as faithfully as possible given existing evidence about the disaster, the extensive use of CGI gave the film a subtextual discourse about how history is represented, and how imaging technologies might instead stand in the way of our access to the past by layering it with the distancing effects of simulacra. Encoded in any film is a metanarrative about its own production, but this is rendered more starkly when the material traces of that production are written into the image in the form of ostentatious technique and marketable spectacle.

Beyond these apparently pragmatic categorisations, which note how and why effects are produced, we need to consider how they are to be received, consumed, analysed and evaluated – especially as the interpretation of special effects hinges on what we understand them to be for, their 'how and why'. For example, we assert that special effects 'in their best use' are storytelling agents, but is this necessarily valid from the viewpoint of the producer or studio who desires a revenue-generating spectacle? To clarify the types of frameworks that shape the critical assessment of special effects, we propose an additional set of *discursive* approaches to special effects:

- AESTHETIC/FORMAL: Even though they may be integrated into the workflows of film production (as described above), reducing costs and impracticalities, or achieving narrative goals, special effects possess their own formal properties, their own aesthetic character, their own kind of beauty. Particularly when they are made central to a film's narrative, special effects perform their spectacular function in ostentatious ways: they might be integrated into the narrative and congruent with the film's diegesis, but they can also be bracketed from the main action in showstopping set-pieces that operate equivalently to the song-and-dance routines of the musical genre. That is, plot development can give way to the spectator's contemplation of a spectacular moment of technical virtuosity. The dinosaurs of *Jurassic Park* (1993) are a prime example of a series of effects sequences (the various enclosures that house different species of dinosaur present demarcated set-pieces in which each creature is displayed), where the plot becomes a pretext for the self-reflexive display of technological prowess. Central to the presentation of those dinosaurs is their construction as 'realist' representations distinct from the fantastic or monstrous characterisations in earlier dinosaur films. This impressive realism (the creatures move as we would expect them to move if we encountered them in the real world) doesn't allow them to disappear completely into the fictional space, but simultaneously directs our attention to external points of reference. The very *madeness* of *Jurassic Park*'s dinosaurs, prominently discussed as a key part of the film's promotion, maps onto the debates the film sought to mobilise about genetic engineering, the possibility of *making* dinosaurs. The spectacular effects supported the story, then, but also contributed to the broader making of meaning beyond the diegesis.
- RECEPTION/SPECTATORSHIP: Whatever techniques are used, and however a special effect is contained by a narrative framework, we could argue that effects exist primarily in relation to viewer knowledge and evoke varied responses accordingly. Viewers will have different levels of interest and expertise in how (or even whether) an effect has been achieved when they encounter it on screen. In this sense a special effect is a package containing the filmic incident, the discursive knowledge that that incident has been gimmicked in some way and the bubble of viewer consciousness in which those two things are married. Recognising this fact moves us away from notions of the audiences for special-effects films as passive recipients of stupefying spectacle, towards awareness that any illusion requires investment from its recipient. Audiences have diverse reactions: they may be duped by an effect into believing that Superman can fly, but it is far more likely that their state of (dis)belief is a complex affair whereby they appreciate the effective representation of an impossible event within the context of a consistent and internally logical fictional world.

They may also bring specialist or connoisseurial knowledge to their viewing, and be able to appreciate, enjoy and analyse special effects as technological performances outside of and distinct from the diegetic frame.

- ONTOLOGICAL/PHILOSOPHICAL: Special effects are invariably used to simulate the occurrence of things that never actually happened in front of the cameras, and they therefore interfere with the truth claims of the medium. Whatever privileges were conferred upon the photographic image by its indexical relationship to its subject, its status as a medium of superior evidentiary force has always been undermined by the possibility of manipulations of the profilmic event. This debate has been exacerbated by the ease with which images can be manipulated and faked in the digital realm, but we should not imagine that photography and film were ever available in a pure, honest state free from the spectres of illusion and deception. By decorating a film with markers of manufacture, simulation and manipulation, special effects have always stretched the limits of the representable, and in doing so, they offer points at which to reflect upon the malleability of photographic images, and of media messages more broadly.

Whatever special effects do inside the films that contain them, they are also part of the ways audiences think about the construction of motion pictures. Popular understanding and appreciation of special effects has been moulded by behind-the-scenes information, 'making-of' documentaries and similar disclosures that, however sincerely they might recognise the work of technicians, also serve a publicity function and extend the commercial prospects of a film. As Pierson has shown, 'cultures of connoisseurship' grew up around the technical side of special-effects production, establishing networks of discussion, as well as discourses of spectacle around the production and presentation of special effects in cinema.[8] Pierson recognised special effects as a field of study, the target of fandom and a valid avenue for broader interrogations of film as a medium. By drawing upon the narratives that emerge in the commentaries provided by technical journals, Pierson historicised the discursive networks that met special effects with expert scrutiny, and broke down a prevailing characterisation of this object of study as dumb spectacle, since, 'through the cultivation and popularisation of particular ways of looking at special effects, popular science periodicals made the special effects created for a diverse range of popular amusements identifiable as specifically scientific achievements'.[9] Special effects had been frequently viewed as costly carbuncles grafted onto films as shows of economic and technological prowess, reminding cinephiles of the commercial underpinnings of the medium, but Pierson's historical linkages between nineteenth-century scientific demonstrations, early film, science fiction and contemporary CGI gave them a rich history as the accessible public face of technological experimentation. Dan North's *Performing Illusions* (2008) continued this historical project by modelling the ways in which spectator engagement with special effects was mediated not only by production paratexts, but also by a complex interplay between the viewer's conditioned expectations, and the effects producers' attempts to engage, subvert or meet those expectations. Using the template of magic performance in the nineteenth century, North argued that spectators were always invited to contemplate how a trick was achieved, and played an active role in anticipating, perceiving and reflecting upon the mechanics of the illusions presented to them.

These paratexts of production (the published disclosures that extend the viewer's contemplation of the film text itself) do not just 'add value' to the viewing experience by encouraging repeated, multilevel viewings, nor do they simply 'cash-in' on spectators' interest in 'how they did that' (though both of these factors may be in play). They can actively shape the reception and historical consolidation of a film text as a cultural object. The field of special-effects studies is almost impossible to separate from these paratextual networks; backstage disclosures are the primary points of contact for most people wishing to know more about how effects were produced, and 'making-of' documentaries and featurettes have become an integral part of home viewing (or at least, the marketing of films for home viewers).[10] Accounts of the production of *Jaws* (1975), for example, quickly came to focus on the problems of working the mechanical shark, and on how the *failures* of the special effects caused the film-makers to conceal it from view, incidentally making it a more frightening off-screen threat. Laurent Bouzereau's extensive documentary *The Making of Jaws* (1995), funded by Universal for inclusion on its prestigious laser-disc edition of the film, and since canonised on subsequent DVD and Blu-ray releases, provided extensive interviews with participants backing up this story, thus helping to recover the failures as characteristic virtues of the text, and shaping the way the film should be received as a triumph over the vicissitudes of location shooting. The specialness of *Jaws*'s effects came not from verisimilitude, but from how they changed the tone and impact of several scenes, and how they rerouted the film's representation of its central monster.

Viewers of *The Lord of the Rings* trilogy (2001–3), for instance, can supplement their viewing of the films with many more hours of behind-the-scenes documentaries, visual-effects breakdowns of how individual shots were produced, revealing audio commentaries, plus galleries of props, designs and costumes.[11] These signs of plenitude add to the films' epic status, and are no doubt crucial in encouraging viewers to watch and rewatch, purchase and repurchase various editions of the films, extruding their interest in direct proportion to the lifespan of the franchise. They also mirror the appendices and notes that J. R. R. Tolkien himself added to his original trilogy of books to give a sense of scholarly depth to his fictional Middle Earth. But these supplementary materials, even as they might give the impression of 'access all areas', shape and mediate the films' reception and maintain centralised control over how they are to be interpreted and understood. They build franchise awareness and loyalty.

We should not read the history of cinema uncritically from these paratexts, but we should certainly be sensitive to how they promote and mediate interest in special and visual effects, and how they actively encourage a form of connoisseurship that fosters a certain kind of spectatorial engagement that goes beyond any simple or instantaneous spectacle. For spectators, the lifecycle of a special effect comprises three phases: *construction* (production, pre-visualisation, imaginary), *screen appearance* (diegetic, filmic, narrational, visual) and *discursive* (cultural, appreciation, remembrance). Over the course of these three phases, each effect is thus imagined/planned, visualised/perceived, remembered/interpreted. Therefore, in broad correlation with the three-stage lifecycle of effects, a model of spectatorial engagement with special effects might be divided into three similar phases: *imagination, perception* and *remembrance*.

Potential audiences for a special-effects film (i.e. one where effects feature prominently) are invited to *imagine* how an effect will play out on screen as part of a broader narrative. Promotional materials such as clips and trailers, or publicity images, prime the viewer to expect certain forms of spectacular action. Some narratives and franchises arrive with 'effects potential' built in, so the genre frame can help to shape imaginative expectation. The disaster films of Roland Emmerich, for instance (*Independence Day* [1996], *The Day after Tomorrow* [2004], *2012* [2009]), used excerpts from their extended sequences of mass destruction in their pre-publicity. *Independence Day*'s teaser trailer showed an alien spacecraft obliterating the White House (a combination of CGI, miniature modelwork and explosives), creating an iconic lead-in to the film's wider promise of further detonative spectacle. Emmerich's later films, which could be sold on the strength of *Independence Day*'s success, were able to make similar promises, escalating the scale of the devastation each time. This kind of advance marketing sells viewers what John Ellis calls the film's 'narrative image', 'the cinema industry's anticipatory answer to the question "What is this film like?"', and effects sequences are a key part of building anticipation not only for what will happen, but *how* it will be shown happening on screen.[12] The teaser trailer for *Jurassic Park* withheld all but the slightest glimpses of the dinosaurs promised by the high-concept plot; the poster for *Alien* (1979) showed an alien egg in the process of hatching to unleash its monstrous newborn; the poster for *Jaws* showed a swimmer oblivious to the great white shark surging towards her from below: these examples all make promises upon which their containing films will deliver by filling in a visual absence (revealing the dinosaurs) or completing an action in process (showing us what's inside the egg, or what happens when the shark bites).

In the next phase, while viewing a film, spectators *perceive* special effects by, first, comprehending them as depictions of events inside the diegesis; second, understanding that they were achieved through technical means (the extent of each viewer's knowledge of those means will vary); third, decoding the symbolic, semiotic meanings of the events depicted; and, fourth, by combining these various levels of perception, spectators fourth, decode how the technical composition of the depicted event *affects* those symbolic, semiotic meanings. The perception of a film's effects turns into *remembrance* after the film is over: repeat viewings may be encouraged by DVD/Blu-ray releases with special features that explain in detail how effects were achieved (possibly reshaping the *perception* phase for subsequent screenings), or which may set older films in a historical context that explains the value of their technical achievements. The Universal Blu-ray release for *The Invisible Man* (1933) includes an audio commentary by Rudy Behlmer, and a thirty-five-minute documentary, 'Now You See Him: *The Invisible Man* Revealed', which supply plentiful information on John P. Fulton's groundbreaking photographic effects for the film. This supplementary material helps new viewers to appreciate the historical significance and technical accomplishments of effects that could otherwise seem 'dated', and to view them as both authored by an individual (Fulton), and developed as part of the house style of the Universal monster cycle.

We are not here positing an ideal spectator who obediently and predictably obeys every prompt provided by a film and its advertisers, but mapping the customary exchanges between the makers and the consumers of films. By focusing on how effects are *received* by spectators, we add to existing accounts of how effects are *produced*. In an important way, 'special effects' are industrial/filmic acts – their 'real' exists in balance sheets, shot lists, the plaster lifemasks from which latex appliances are pulled, the animatronic puppets wired to produce movements in mimicry of living creatures, the motion-control rigs and blue/greenscreens, the hard drives and data clouds in which digital animations are stored. But in the broader way that the term is deployed by 'secondary users' (scholars, fans, journalists, audiences), it comprises much more of a blurred and layered composite consisting of the effect 'itself,' a paratextual halo, and the structure of comprehension in the spectator's mind. The latter ranges from recognition of the effect as an effect to the (in)formal research that happens outside the viewing context. Especially in today's 'replay' (Klinger) or 'participatory' (Jenkins) cultures, these acts of 'reading up' on effects involve rewatching them, as well as watching other movies and TV shows to compare.[13] Hence any single encounter with a special effect is convertible into a comparative/researched viewing as when, for example, one replays the end of *Close Encounters* again and again to see precisely how the UFOs have been choreographed.

Amid this welter of perspectives, one consolation offered by the digital is simple consolidation: the only thing all special effects have in common is that they can now be 'performed' digitally. Each of these processes brought its own idiosyncrasies and flaws, and what makes viewers perceive old effects as 'outdated' is precisely their uneasy blend with their diegetic surroundings. By subsuming all effects techniques (this conversion is by no means complete) into the same digital workflow, we can tame the wildness and quirk of the effects landscape – albeit at the risk of smoothing its surfaces to a characterless plain. And in fact the digital turn is not without its own ambivalences: in particular, the line between visual effects and animation (which has also undergone a digital overhaul of its own) has become increasingly indistinct. Several of the essays in this collection stake out territory in just such a categorical gap between film's demarcated zones of form and technique. When James Cameron began a pre-publicity featurette for *Avatar* (2009) by telling us: 'The first thing you have to understand is that this is not an animated picture …', he was speaking to a delineation that is no longer strong enough to aid such understanding. What Cameron presumably did *not* want was for his viewers to approach his film through the paradigmatic frameworks with which they might ordinarily approach an 'animated picture', seeing *through* the process to the diegetic, emotional content, and perhaps even downgrading their expectations, due to some arcane Western associations between animation and children's entertainment. Instead, Cameron was looking to preformat his audience's expectations to receive the film's spectacles as actors' performances mediated by technology, i.e. to view them through a special-effects framework, one that foregrounds process and bolsters its diegetic content through appeals to the technological excellence of the film's production systems.

This book comes out at a moment when the digital 'makeover' of all special effects forces a reappraisal not just of technological evolution/succession, but the very possibility of writing a special-effects 'history' in the first place. Digital production methods have complicated previously distinct categories by blending and blurring the traditional stages of cinematic manufacture, known as pre-production, principal production and post-production. 'The digital' in its very omnipresence and seemingly infinite absorptive powers beckons us to pay special attention to the materiality and specificity of special-effects practices, or even to see special and visual effects as privileged arenas in which the digital now and the analogue past compete for scholarly attention, commercial viability and audience sympathy. Firmly installed now in the workflows of film production, digital technologies have not just brought to bear a new set of tools for making and augmenting images and sounds for films. They have effectively overhauled large parts of the production process at the level of pre-visualisation, cinematography, editing (including sound-effects editing), and post-production (including visual effects), as well as the methods of delivery of films to exhibitors, and the means of projection for audiences. With online content delivery systems, there are also new ways to watch, buy, share, re-edit films at home or on mobile devices, through both legitimate and illicit channels.[14] This all looks like a radical break with the past, sufficient to constitute a 'digital turn' or a fresh start for histories of cinema. But, as suggested by the collective efforts of this volume's contributors, the continuities between what might even be termed analogue and digital eras overwhelm any notion of a rupture with the past. The generic, thematic and formal parameters of the feature-length, narrative-driven, star-led film are remarkably tenacious regardless of the technologies used in their manufacture: mainstream cinema is still pulling the same tricks, but by different means.

One potential problem for historians of older films is that it is impossible to revisualise an effect on behalf of its first viewers. We cannot imagine how the first audiences responded to seeing *King Kong* in 1933, though we might caution against exaggerating the impact or overstating the naivety of those cinema patrons who may have been familiar with stop-motion animation already, and who appreciated the refinement of an old technique rather than being floored by something utterly irruptive and incomprehensible. It is through our esteemed 'disclosure texts' that we can reconstruct a picture of the kinds of knowledge to which they would have had access at the time. We cannot presuppose 'what they knew' or 'how they felt', but we can search for a more accurate idea of how a spectator's tracking of an effect's passage through its three phases might be orientated by supplemental materials. Any teleological history that falls in step with the prevailing sense that newer effects are necessarily refinements and improvements in the naturalism, efficiency or spectacular power of old effects neglects the complex industrial and cultural contexts in which those effects are produced. It may well be the case that faster processor speeds have enabled computer-graphics systems to handle larger amounts of data and thus to feasibly generate more detailed imitations of people, creatures and places. But the more interesting and productive angle from which to come at the study of effects histories would involve attention to the specific circumstances of production that made photorealistic simulation of the minutiae of organic figures a desirable industry goal in the first place. There is no 'natural' or 'evolutionary' explanation for this, only the shared targets of a computer-graphics industry and a film industry, the former the workshop to the latter's showroom, and each of them claiming to fulfil a cultural *wish* for increased photorealism.

Several of our contributors have referred to practical effects as 'handmade'. This syntactical turn might be indicative of their wish to distance their subject from the spreading associations between digitality and *all* effects, or a gauge of a popular nostalgia for 'old' effects (we didn't refer to them as 'analogue' until the digital turn necessitated a separate term to express their shared *difference*). The contrasts are clear: 'Handmade' connotes artisanal, tactile, directly personalised processes, while digital effects speak to us of industrial labour performed at the cool remove of computers and the behest of preformatted software platforms. Special effects are frequently cited as markers of capital – signifiers of studios' economic might, Hollywood studios in particular. It is likely that this association once contributed to critical indifference to the study of effects: they were catalogued separately from those aspects of film production, such as image, sound, performance and narrative, that could be more readily examined using existing analytical models from the humanities, semiology and cultural studies. Recent scholarship has shown that film's hybrid identity as the product of both art and industry demands that we take account of the technical contributories to the semiotic contents of film. This book aims to continue that recovery project without recourse to simple chronologies or technological determinism, but through a collection of discrete case studies that each give detailed consideration to one aspect of the field. We believe these essays collectively constitute a diverse and provocative intervention in the study of filmic special effects. They do not artificially reduce or consolidate the field, but instead show the many directions in which the topic can lead.

Notes

1. Christian Metz, '*Trucage* and the Film', trans. François Meltzer, *Critical Inquiry* vol. 3 no. 4 (Summer 1977), pp. 657–75.
2. Michael Stern poses a similar rhetorical question in his essay, 'Making Culture into Nature', in Annette Kuhn (ed.), *Alien Zone: Cultural Theory and Contemporary Science Fiction Cinema* (London: Verso, 1990), p. 67:

   > What makes an effect 'special'? Everything in a film is an 'effect' – something fabricated, made. No shots compose or photograph themselves. The camera constructs a visual field rather than simply recording what is 'out there' in front of it, and locations are no less producers' artefacts than sound stages. Every frame of film is a product of human labour and intention, however unanticipated the image produced may be. Why are some of the many kinds of effects which constitute a film foregrounded by film makers and audiences as 'special', and others left in the background as ordinary, natural, unworthy of attention?

3. Stephen Prince, *Digital Visual Effects in Cinema: The Seduction of Reality* (New Brunswick, NJ: Rutgers University Press, 2011); Shilo T. McClean, *Digital Storytelling: The Narrative Power of Visual Effects in Film* (Cambridge, MA: MIT Press, 2008).
4. Lisa Purse, *Digital Imaging in Popular Cinema* (Edinburgh: Edinburgh University Press, 2013).
5. Michele Pierson, 'CGI Effects in Hollywood Science-fiction Cinema 1989–95: The Wonder Years', *Screen* vol. 40 no. 2 (1999), pp. 158–76.
6. Ben Fritz, 'Visual Effects Industry Does a Disappearing Act', *Wall Street Journal*, 22 February 2013.
7. Scott Bukatman, 'The Artificial Infinite: On Special Effects and the Sublime', in Annette Kuhn (ed.), *Alien Zone II: The Spaces of Science-fiction Cinema* (London: Verso, 1999), pp. 249–75; revised and expanded in Bukatman, *Matters of Gravity: Special Effects and Supermen in the 20th Century* (Durham, NC: Duke University Press, 2003), pp. 81–110.
8. Michele Pierson, *Special Effects: Still in Search of Wonder* (New York: Columbia University Press, 2002.
9. Ibid., p. 31.
10. See, for example, Barbara Klinger's work on home viewing and what she terms 'digressions', the paratexts (as we call them in this chapter) that shape a viewer's reception of a film on repeat viewings, e.g. 'Digressions at the Cinema: Reception and Mass Culture', *Cinema Journal* vol. 28 no. 4 (1989), pp. 3–18, and *Beyond the Multiplex: Cinema, New Technologies, and the Home* (Berkeley: University of California Press, 2006).

11. For more on the textual operations of *The Lord of the Rings* DVDs, see Jonathan Gray, 'Bonus Material: The DVD Layering of *Two Towers*', in Ernest Mathijs (ed.), *The Lord of the Rings: Popular Culture in Global Context* (London: Wallflower Press, 2006), pp. 238–53.
12. John Ellis, *Visible Fictions: Cinema Television Video* (London: Routledge, 1992) p. 30.
13. Barbara Klinger, 'Becoming Cult: *The Big Lebowski*, Replay Culture and Male Fans', *Screen* vol. 51 no. 1 (2010), pp. 1–20; Henry Jenkins, *Convergence Culture: Where Old and New Media Collide* (New York: New York University Press, 2006).
14. For more on the conversion to digital distribution and exhibition, see David Bordwell, *Pandora's Digital Box: Films, Files, and the Future of Movies* (Madison, WI: Irvington Way Institute Press, 2012); and for an account of movie piracy and file sharing, see Ramon Lobato, *Shadow Economies of Cinema: Mapping Informal Film Distribution* (London: BFI/Palgrave Macmillan, 2012).

1 *TECHNIQUES*

Matte painting, animation, glass shots, CGI, motion capture, puppetry, pyrotechnics, prosthetics, miniatures and many more – these are all practices, some with few material or conceptual similarities to one another, which could be encompassed by the term 'special effects'. Too numerous to explain individually, and too disparate to reduce to a single category, the sheer range of practices covered by the term 'special effects' is met in this section by five diverse essays, each of which deals with a different set of techniques and crafts. Collectively, they provide a partial catalogue of practical and optical-effects methodologies, familiarising the reader with the basic operational procedures of filmic trickery, and troubling the categorical boundaries between those procedures. Film has always picked up and used any available methods to make things happen on screen, giving it an eclectic repertoire of tricks and a collage aesthetic where the affordances of different techniques each contribute to the final mix.

Ethan de Seife's 'Ectoplasm and Oil' examines the use of methyl cellulose, a gelatinous substance that has been employed for decades to simulate everything from ectoplasmic slime to black oil freshly mined from the earth. Because of its chemical properties, de Seife argues, methocel embodies a physical form of special effects that CGI is ill equipped to emulate, suggesting a limit to the representational powers of the digital. In 'Fleshing It Out', Lisa Bode explores a similar divide through her analysis of 'prosthetic performance', or the interaction of special effects and screen acting. Contrasting the rubber suits and latex makeups of the analogue era – creations like the gill-man suit in *The Creature from the Black Lagoon* (1954) – with contemporary computer-generated stars like Gollum in *The Lord of the Rings* (2001–3), Bode maps a continuum of the viewer's consciousness of artifice, and its relation to the other registers of reality and unreality in stardom, whereby our acceptance of a screen performer's identity blends knowledge of the actor with investment in character and story. Just as special-effects performance mixes analogue and digital modes, stop-motion puppet animation has been redefined by the advent of the computer, a topic explored in Andrea Comiskey's '(Stop)Motion Control', which argues that a 'handmade imperative' frames the efforts of digital artists through a sculptural discourse that privileges traces of human manual artistry. Turning from the realm of practical effects to optical processes, Katharina Loew's 'Magic Mirrors' historicises the Schüfftan Process, a common compositing technique in the 1920s and 30s that helped to render some of science-fiction cinema's most iconic images, including the cityscapes in *Metropolis* (1927). A reflection on European effects history as well as on the technical roots of later matte and digital paintings, Loew's essay demonstrates the complex ways in which special-effects techniques mutate, adapt and, in some cases, disappear. Finally, Barbara Flueckiger's 'Photorealism, Nostalgia and Style' looks at the way filmic artefacts – grain, lens flare, motion blur and so on – are strategically remediated in digital imaging as a means of stylisation and of linking contemporary cinema technologies to an authentic-seeming past.

By historicising the multifarious means that have been applied to the task of rendering the impossible visible on screen, we can hold up for inspection the specific qualities of certain techniques before they can be subsumed beneath the catch-all terms such as 'effects' or 'illusions'. Close attention not only to *what* effects do but to *how* they do it will give us a more nuanced understanding of our subject.

ECTOPLASM AND OIL
METHOCEL AND THE AESTHETICS OF SPECIAL EFFECTS

ETHAN DE SEIFE

Methyl Cellulose 101

When the credits for recent, apparently 'all-natural' films such as *The Help* and *Moneyball* (both 2011) list, respectively, twenty-two and sixty-eight digital-effects artists and technicians, one may be forgiven for conflating the terms 'special effects' and 'digital effects'. Yet even in an era when nearly every Hollywood film employs digital compositing, digital colouring, digital rotoscoping and/or several other computer-based processes, a great deal of money and many skilled professionals in the special-effects industry are concerned with practical effects: those made of metal, clay, plastic and other materials. Even though computer-generated imagery (CGI) is shiny and game-changing, the computers used to produce it are simply tools, not unlike like those used to construct models, miniatures and maquettes.

But no special-effects toolkit is limited to conventional tools. There is room in it for far less solid stuff, as well. One of the strangest, most ubiquitous, most versatile and most fascinating of all the devices of practical special effects is a substance called methyl cellulose, far better known by the trade name 'methocel', given it by Dow Chemical, the company whose scientists invented it in the 1930s.[1] A most peculiar kind of goop, methocel has, for several decades, 'played' all manner of viscous substances, from mud in *The Return of the Living Dead* (1985)[2] to demonic slime in *Drag Me to Hell* (2009)[3] to pterodactyl excrement in *The Flintstones* (1994).[4] Even in films heavily dependent on CGI, methocel is a special-effects staple. Scott Heger, head chemist of Blair Adhesives, the largest and most important supplier of methocel to American film and television productions, notes that George Lucas's *Star Wars* prequels (1999–2005), which employ few three-dimensional elements besides actors, used 20,000 gallons.[5] Methocel's remarkable versatility extends to the fact that it often provides a real, physical base for digital augmentation. To cite but two examples: both Ben Stiller's confrontation with a giant octopus in *Night at the Museum: Battle of the Smithsonian* (2009) and Jon Voight's egestion by a colossal snake in *Anaconda* (1997) were rendered on screen with a combination of digital and practical effects. While the octopus and snake were rendered digitally, methocel gives these actors actual coats of cephalopod slime or reptile saliva, as the situation required. Atop those viscous layers of ooze, digital technicians rendered further glisten to enhance the visual force of the scenes. In this way, a practical technology such as methocel complements and combines in complex ways with the latest in digital technologies; these examples point the way toward a more nuanced understanding of the interdependence of analogue and digital special-effects techniques.

As with the advents of colour, sound, 3D, CGI and other technologies that have been folded into moviemaking craft, methocel has generally been used to complement the overarching goal of Hollywood film: clear and coherent narration. In this way, it is just another element of style that – just like three-point lighting, the match on action and the split-field diopter – has served to emphasise and clarify narratively relevant emotions, characters and actions. As David Bordwell writes, every tool and technique of film style has historically been engaged in the Classical Hollywood cinema in order to convey salient narrative information.[6]

Nevertheless, methocel's particular and unusual properties have nudged it into certain types of cinematic functions and meanings, as its properties encourage certain stylistic possibilities and discourage others. Taking two methocel-heavy films – *Ghostbusters II* (1989) and *There Will Be Blood* (2007) – as its chief examples, this essay begins an investigation into the ways in which methocel affects visual style in American film. How does methocel intersect with other elements of *mise en scène*? Does its use open up or close off certain possibilities in editing or cinematography? How, in other words, has methocel been employed not only to achieve the established stylistic and narrative goals of the Hollywood cinema, but to alter them, or to offer novel or creative aesthetic options?

A different, but related, goal of this essay is to use an analysis of the functions of methocel to suggest that the general tenor of scholarship on special effects could benefit from a reorientation. Much extant academic writing on special effects – whether from a practical, 'how do they do it?' perspective, or from a more scholarly purview – is preoccupied with notions of trickery, *trompe l'oeil* and 'unmasking' the deceptive impulses that purportedly undergird the cinema. In this way, the bulk of special-effects scholarship owes a certain debt, acknowledged or not, to apparatus theory, the rather distrustful strain of film theory whose quintessential statement is Jean-Louis Baudry's 'Ideological Effects of the Basic Cinematographic Apparatus'. In that essay, Baudry argues that the very lenses, cameras, projectors and screens involved in film production and exhibition collude to produce an 'illusionistic' effect that, in encouraging us to believe that we are 'inscribed' into a depicted fictional world, is a psychologically and economically repressive system designed to obliterate one's own self and identity.[7] For Baudry, the cinematic apparatus is the logical and most frightening extension of the creation of the 'idealised spectator', a notion that he connects to the establishment of so-called Renaissance perspective in painting. And, indeed, the logical extension of Baudry's own argument is that, if the most fundamental components of cinematic exhibition – lens, projector, screen – all conspire to create an illusion that threatens self-identity, then such further fripperies as special effects are attractive, if redundant, efforts that cement the loss of self. It is a hardline, deeply sceptical view that nevertheless strongly inflects a good deal of scholarship on special effects.

Norman Klein's book *The Vatican to Vegas: A History of Special Effects*, while not the only text to espouse such an attitude, embraces this notion so thoroughly as to be nearly parodic:

> Hollywood f/x have their charm. They are jumbo-sized hoaxes. They are unabashed. They tell you how much fun it is to cheat. They promise you more than your money's worth, every dollar on the screen. They cruise you in their stretch limousine. They know that melodrama looks like a gag. Then they claim that size is everything. So every year they stretch even more, more horizontal, more 'cineramic' (wider, more immersive). … Hollywood f/x is so playfully lopsided, it reveals secrets about the global economy, particularly about production methods.[8]

Klein's take on special effects ignores such historical considerations as craft practices, conventions of cinematic narration and budgetary concerns, opting instead for 'big ideas' about the ways in which special effects must be understood as devices to pull off 'hoaxes' that are somehow linked to economic malfeasance. I submit that there is nothing of the hoax whatsoever in the use of methocel, or of special effects in general, even in Hollywood, that most devious of illusion factories. Methocel, like every other special-effects device and technique, is a tool designed to enhance a film's narrative and emotional content – to present an object or character in such a way as to make it exceptional or unusual. In so doing, methocel renders its object of especial narrative and/or emotional import, and calls visual attention to it for being particularly significant. The mission of special effects in general is not to 'trick' viewers into believing some sort of cinematic hoax. It is to impart visual force to certain elements of fictional narratives.

Chemical and Physical Properties

The particular properties of methyl cellulose are the reasons for its ubiquity in motion-picture special effects, and for its multifarious uses in a great many other industries. Methyl cellulose is a polysaccharide molecule derived entirely from cellulose – generally, wood pulp. In its pure form, it is a white powder; the addition of water turns it into a viscous goop. But adding water to methocel is not a straightforward process, as the compound possesses the unusual property of thickening when heated and thinning when cooled. Once dispersed in water, the resultant goo may be further thickened, thinned, coloured and textured: the special-effects benefits of this manipulation are obvious.

Organic, non-toxic and edible, methocel is nevertheless indigestible, as the human gut does not have the enzymes required to break down its particular family of polymers.[9] For special-effects craftspeople, this quality is a great boon: should the situation require, an actor could ingest methocel with no ill effects – indeed, with no effects at all.

Methyl cellulose is an excellent thickener and emulsifier: a substance that prevents other combined substances from separating. It has been used for decades in many foods, including ice creams, baked goods and a veritable rainbow of condiments.[10] The substance even shows

Mark Wahlberg force-fed crude oil (methocel): *Three Kings* (1999)

Methocel, as crude oil, splattered on the skin of Jake Gyllenhaal: *Jarhead* (2005)

up in the 'Modern Methods of Thickening' chart in *Modernist Cuisine: The Art and Science of Cooking*, the bible of 'molecular gastronomy'.[11] Its other chief ingestive function is as an excipient: an inert substance serving to convey medicine into the body. Methocel is also an excellent laxative, as it attracts intestinal water, thereby producing softer, bulkier faeces. One methocel-based laxative is widely known by the brand name Citrucel.

A database search for the chemical name of this unusual substance turns up a great many scientific papers that discuss its application as a lubricant, a glue, a 'bacterial motility inhibitor' and so forth.[12] Before it became an essential tool of special-effects technicians, methocel insinuated itself, quietly but assertively, into many strata of daily life.

For a special-effects technician, methocel offers many advantages. In addition to being non-toxic, water-soluble and easily altered (thickened, thinned, dyed, textured, bespangled, etc.), it is also biodegradable, a quality that not only reduces disposal costs but gives a production a 'green' sheen.[13] As a physical (i.e. not computer-generated) object, methocel reflects light according to real-world principles of optics – precisely the kinds of visual elements that are among the most difficult things to simulate digitally, and one of the reasons that methocel is used as a substrate on which CGI may be layered: light reflected off methocel provides CGI artists with essential information about the light's intensity, luminosity and directionality.

Additionally, even actors with the fairest and most sensitive of skin types do not generally exhibit any adverse reactions to being slathered in it. A further advantage, noted by special-effects technician Lee McConnell, is that the curve in learning how to use methocel is not steep. Altering the colour or texture of methocel is a simple process; mastery of the material comes quickly.[14]

Most importantly, methocel is inexpensive. In fact, it is inexpensive in several ways. First, the powder itself is cheap. Industrial suppliers of food-grade methyl cellulose powder, such as the e-commerce giant Alibaba, sell it for about $5,000 per metric ton, a quantity that yields thousands of gallons of slime.[15] Furthermore, it is inexpensive to ship. Methocel, in relatively lightweight powder form, can be trucked to even a remote location shoot and mixed on site with local water, thus reducing transportation costs (a single gallon of water weighs more than eight pounds). Inert and non-toxic, methocel staves off any potential lawsuits that might be brought about by performers whose skin or belongings might be stained or ruined by clingier, more corrosive substances. Finally, the labour costs involved in the use of methocel are generally far lower than those needed to generate similar effects digitally. The person-hours involved in the mixing, altering and application of methocel are significantly fewer than those needed by CGI artists to create similar effects. The investment in tools and hardware is similarly smaller: the main costs are buckets, mixers and dyes. In its versatility, nonreactivity and low cost, methocel has long enjoyed the favour not just of special-effects crews, but of performers and of studio accountants.

'He slimed me!'

The most famous line from *Ghostbusters* (1984) refers to the 'ectoplasm' that is ostensibly the residue of supernatural activity. Bowled over and slathered in goop by a mischievous, blobby ghost,[16] Peter Venkman (Bill Murray) utters, 'He slimed me', thereby indelibly linking the film's generic identity (comedy + horror/fantasy) to one of its most conspicuous special effects.[17]

Ghostbusters II massively intensifies the narrative significance – and the volume – of ectoplasm, which is made of methocel. Several of methocel's physical properties are rendered narratively significant in *Ghostbusters II*: its dyeability, its variable viscosity, its nonreactivity, its luminosity, its aeratability and its low cost. According to the film's promotional materials, the production of *Ghostbusters II* required 100,000 gallons of methocel, enough to fill a swimming pool approximately twenty-nine feet wide by fifty-eight feet long by eight feet deep.[18]

The story of *Ghostbusters II* concerns a subterranean 'river of slime' in which all of New York City's 'negative energy' resides. New Yorkers' bad feelings are given material form as a viscous pink ooze that courses through abandoned 'pneumatic transit system' tunnels, and which, when harnessed by the spirit of an evil, long-dead warlord, threaten the city's very existence. The importance of ectoplasm – and the methocel used to signify it – is stressed in the film's very first shot, in which ominous music accompanies an image of ooze burbling up from a crack in a city street.

One hundred thousand gallons is a lot of methocel, but it does not represent a great expenditure. Even though its budget was about $40 million *Ghostbusters II* takes advantage of methocel's inexpensiveness at every turn.[19] The river of slime could have been simulated with

Slimed: *Ghostbusters* (1984)

Tentacles distend viscose methocel: *Ghostbusters II* (1989); the glowing pink hue of dyed methocel: *Ghostbusters II*

models or animation, but methocel's low cost allowed it to be used in great quantity, thus granting the effect the realism of volume.

The first 'set-piece' scene in which methocel plays a major role occurs about twenty-five minutes into the film, in which Ray Stantz (Dan Aykroyd) rappels into a cavernous space beneath New York's streets to find a coursing ectoplasmic river. In this scene, methocel's viscosity and dyeability assume key narrative functions. Because it can so easily be thickened, the surface of the methocel can be significantly distended without rupturing, a property called into service here (in a matte shot) when a tentacle-like object pushes up from the depths of the river. The thickness of the ooze enhances the suspense of the scene, as we are prevented, for a few seconds, from knowing what lurks beneath, thereby linking us with Stantz, who is equally unaware. Notable also in this scene – and across the entirety of the film – is the ectoplasm's distinctive rosy pink hue. This colour is the strongest visual motif of the film: its unusualness – achieved simply by dyeing the methocel – continually alerts us to the presence of supernatural elements. In this scene, the same pink shade features in the gel of the light that illuminates Aykroyd, thereby confirming for us the fact that he is dangerously close to a paranormal entity so energetic that it actually glows. The pink ectoplasm seems to have served to establish a 'colour baseline', its pinkness the basis of the entire film's colour palette. No other objects in the film are of the same colour; indeed, many items seem to have been selected in part because their own colourings are noticeably altered when splattered by or reflecting the pink ectoplasm. The fact that methocel could be readily dyed facilitated its adoption as a stylistic/narrative reference point: the film is *about* the paranormal, and the methocel's colouration unfailingly indicates the presence of the supernatural in the narrative.

Just as there is no such thing as ectoplasm, there is no direct connection between the use of methocel and the presence of the supernatural in the story of *Ghostbusters II*. *Any* special effect – lighting, composited animation, mechanised puppets – could have been employed by the film-makers to suggest the presence of a supernatural force or entity; yet it is methocel that fills this narrative need, precisely because it is readily adaptable to a variety of narrative situations: it can be made in small or large quantities, thicker or thinner, more or less reflective and so forth, while still possessing the essential quality of *unfamiliarity*. With the exceptions of a few children's toys, as well as certain exudations by such organisms as moulds, snails and the bizarre hagfish, few earthly substances possess methocel's peculiar physical properties. Its inherent oddness and its remarkable versatility made methocel ideally suitable for the cinematic representation of the presence of the paranormal.

The story of the film is strongly linked to its Manhattan location; it was shot in part in New York City. The nonreactivity of methocel permits certain shots and events that might otherwise have added time and expense to the production. One brief, two-shot scene, filmed on location, shows Aykroyd ladling up ectoplasm from a building's exterior stairway, a shot made possible by methocel's nonreactive nature. The film's climax has actor Peter MacNicol absolutely drenched in the stuff; unharmed, no treatment beyond hot showers was required to render MacNicol methocel-free.[20]

In both of these scenes, the use of methocel affords the film-makers another, less obvious benefit. The stairway scene consists of two shots: the medium close-up of the ladle, and a long shot of Aykroyd and Harold Ramis crouched down to collect the goop. Markings on the stonework indicate that both shots were filmed in the same location – which is to say that, because methocel is inert and cannot damage the stonework of even a historic building, it was unnecessary to film either of these shots in a studio, thus saving the expense of constructing an elaborate mockup of a particular staircase.

In the *Ghostbusters* films (1984–), most of the actors eventually come into contact with methocel, but none quite so extravagantly as Peter MacNicol. Were methocel corrosive or toxic, MacNicol would surely never have agreed to appear in such a scene.[21] On a visit to the set of *The Sorcerer's Apprentice* (2010), I interviewed a number of special-effects technicians, one of whom, Lorenzo Hall, neatly summarised why digital technology will never fully supplant practical special effects. To paraphrase him: 'When CGI can make it rain *and* make the actor appear to be wet, that's when I'll quit my job.' Hall's observation is germane to the climactic scene of *Ghostbusters II*: even if digital animation (which did indeed exist at the time of the film's production) had been used to create the slime that drenches MacNicol, some other substance would have been necessary to make him appear to have been slimed. He would have required drenching with *something*, so why not drench him with the slimiest, least expensive, most visually striking substance available? These properties have made methocel one of the most essential tools of practical special effects, and one of the most striking *mise en scène* elements of

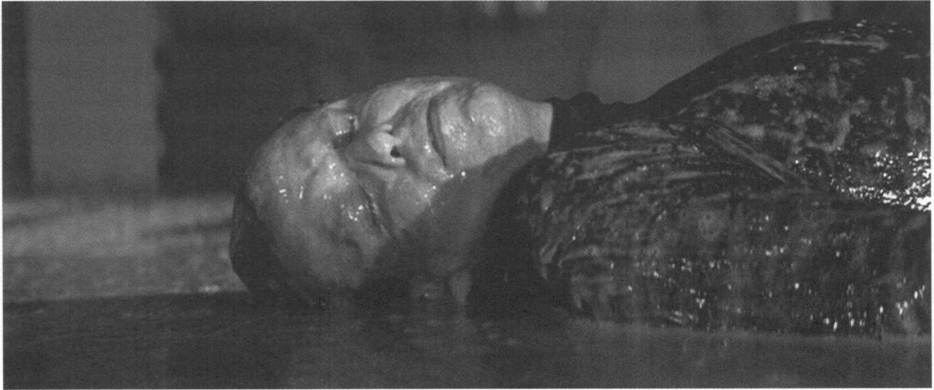

Nonreactive methocel on a stone stairway in Manhattan: *Ghostbusters II*; Peter MacNicol slimed: *Ghostbusters II*

countless genre films. And yet – like its relatives foam latex and spirit gum – it is *so* ubiquitous that its contributions to cinematic special effects have gone largely unnoticed.

Additional properties of methocel help to clarify the narrative import of the ooze. In a courtroom scene, a judge becomes irate over the Ghostbusters' seemingly ludicrous claims about paranormal activity. A nearby jar of ectoplasm, brought to the courtroom as evidence, bubbles noisily in response to the judge's anger. This event is of crucial narrative importance: the judge, in his rage, unwittingly confirms the Ghostbusters' theory that the ectoplasm responds strongly to 'negative energy'. Alternating shots of the judge and the jar indicate the causal link between 'bad vibes' and ectoplasmic activity, but it is methocel's physical properties that confirm this narratively vital point. The ooze is, as always, dyed pink, and is therefore the most vivid object in the drab courtroom, thus imbuing it with particular visual importance. This importance is emphasised by methocel's translucence: the jar is lit from beneath, so the ectoplasm appears luminous. Methocel, as a thick liquid, can be aerated to produce bubbles, and this capacity of the material is especially salient to the courtroom scene. The air bubbles that gurgle upwards through the jar (accentuated by blooping noises on the soundtrack) are visual evidence of the fact that negative energy excites the ectoplasm, the single most important narrative conceit of the film.

A jar of methocel set aglow and a-bubble by anger: *Ghostbusters II*

When the judge blows his top, so does the jar of ectoplasm. His anger so riles up the ooze that from it burst two bizarre figures: the ghosts of the Scoleri brothers, a pair of murderers whom the judge had, years previously, condemned to the electric chair. The appearance of these spirits confirms the fact that the ectoplasm possesses supernatural powers. The very strangeness of methocel – its viscosity, colour and dissimilarity from the materials of daily life – is the key physical link between the real world and the supernatural world. The ectoplasm's unusual physical properties – which are identical to and dependent on methocel's unusual physical properties – are narratively analogous to the bizarre, paranormal world from whence it comes.

Methocel is the single most important visual effect in this effects-heavy film. Its low cost, dyeability, nonreactivity, viscosity and aeratability play important roles not only in the visual style of *Ghostbusters II*, but in its narrative. The most important quality of methocel, in this case, is its *strangeness*. Methocel is unlike any substance with which human beings regularly interact (even though, ironically, it is a component of many everyday items). Its odd physical qualities are the reason that it is so often used to indicate otherworldliness. *Ghostbusters II* seizes on those odd qualities: methocel is *the* strangest and most unmistakable sign of the supernatural: the film's very subject matter.

There Will Be Methocel

Not all films that feature methocel take advantage of its inherent strangeness. *Ghostbusters II* opts for one of the two most typical general strategies when using methocel as a special-effects tool: as an otherworldly or bizarre substance, in common with many science-fiction and horror films. The other general strategy takes advantage of methocel's ability to mimic real-world substances. The same qualities that allow methocel to stand in for ectoplasm in *Ghostbusters II* have often been exploited to make it look like bodily fluids (blood, mucus, vomit, excrement) or large quantities of familiar substances: water, paint, lava, the onion dip in *Honey, I Shrunk the Kids* (1989), the chocolate river in *Charlie and the Chocolate Factory* (2005); with the addition of grey, gritty clay, methocel easily plays unset cement.[22]

Methocel has also often stood in for crude oil, perhaps never so notably as in Paul Thomas Anderson's *There Will Be Blood*. Though the volume of methocel utilised in the film's production

Bizarre Mogwai cocoons glisten and ooze with methocel: *Gremlins* (1984)

is not entirely clear, special-effects coordinator Steve Cremin notes that 'up to 53,000 gallons' were concocted at a single time on location at the film's set in Marfa, Texas.[23] In depicting the explosive oil gushers central to its story, the film may have used more methocel than even *Ghostbusters II*. Chosen in part for its biodegradability, methocel makes an excellent oil substitute, as its viscosity and colour are so easily controlled. The narrative of *There Will Be Blood* calls for, at various times, both small and large quantities of oil. Smaller quantities of actual crude oil are different in colour, viscosity and opacity from large quantities, facts that further favour the use of methocel. Notes Cremin, 'You can take the same substance that looks perfect in a pool, but when you squirt it out of a tube, it may take on a brownish tinge. We had to adjust viscosity and colour.'[24] Lee McConnell, special-effects rigging foreman for the film, makes the related observation that, while water dyed black might be similar in colour to a puddle of oil on a cement floor, it will neither reflect light nor undulate like oil; methocel replicates these behaviours far better. Dyed water, McConnell notes, has neither the viscosity nor the slimy look of methocel, especially when a performer interacts with it; these are the very qualities that enable methocel to emulate oil so successfully.[25]

The wordless opening scene of *There Will Be Blood* depicts oil prospector Daniel Plainview (Daniel Day-Lewis) and his roughneck associates operating a primitive drill and, at long last, striking oil. The two most important events of this complex scene are emphasised by the use of methocel, its visually striking qualities put in the service of clarifying the narrative importance of certain actions.

The first such event is when Plainview's rig first strikes oil, a fact illustrated by black methocel burbling up from the depths; moments later, when a workman descends into the well, the oil is thicker, blacker and more voluminous. When the drill bit is pulled up, methocel provides further visual confirmation of the strike: it is sufficiently viscous to adhere to the bit. Its dyeability and nonreactivity offer even more iconic visual confirmation of the oil strike in staining Day-Lewis's outstretched palm with an inky smear.

There Will Be Blood **(2007): a methocel-coated drill bit; the mark of oil; baptism by oil**

The scene's other central narrative event is also rendered clearer by the use of methocel. In a medium close-up, one of the workmen 'baptises' his son with a smear of oil to the forehead, a moment that links 'family' and 'oil', two notions relevant to the film's central narrative tensions. The anointed child is unofficially adopted by Plainview, when the boy's father, standing waist-deep in oil, is killed by a falling wooden beam, an event that spurts a red jet of blood into the lens. Thus is oil/methocel linked not only with family, but also with blood, wealth and death.

A glob of methocel on the camera lens: *There Will Be Blood*

Such associations do not specifically follow from any of methocel's physical properties, but the narrative significance of oil is accomplished in part by the substance's versatility.

Just as *Ghostbusters II* is 'about' ectoplasm, *There Will Be Blood* is 'about' oil; in both films, these narratively vital substances are portrayed by methocel, as evident in both films' first scenes. In the same opening scene, Anderson provides the first hint that *There Will Be Blood* will use methocel in less conventional ways: a dollop of it falls onto the camera lens, where it thus somewhat jarringly emphasises the visual and narrative importance of oil. This shot could easily have been cut from the film, but clearly Anderson found in it a striking, iconic visual quality.

In some cases, the versatility of methocel can obviate the need for other, costlier effects. About twenty minutes into the film, Plainview's success as an oilman is confirmed by the incredible force of the gusher tapped by one of his rigs. So powerful is the blast of oil that it dislodges several wooden boards from the roof of the drilling shed. This effect was achieved by a column of thinned methocel under great pressure: the boards really are dislodged by the blast, just as the shed's swinging electric light is really displaced by the gusher, just as the actors and props inside the shed are genuinely coated in methocel. *There Will Be Blood* was released in 2007, at a time when digital effects were not only possible but ubiquitous (the film's credits list about twenty digital-effects artists). Both the geyser and the subsequent displacement and splattering of objects by jets of oil *could* have been achieved digitally, but not without complex and time-consuming work, not to mention significant expense. Furthermore, the eruption of the gusher is filmed uninterruptedly, in a single, fluid tracking shot of about twenty-two seconds. The use of methocel does not guarantee long takes, but may facilitate them, since it is a practical effect whose reactions with people and objects occur and may be filmed in real time. Methocel thus assists Anderson in maintaining the moving-camera, long-take aesthetic that he has cultivated across his career. It is not a stretch to consider the substance as one of the tools with which the director enhances his reputation as an auteur.[26]

The single scene in *There Will Be Blood* that features the greatest volume of methocel occurs around the film's midpoint, when another of Plainview's rigs strikes a gigantic gusher. In this scene, oil (and the methocel that stands in for it) is again linked to danger, as well as to the unusual relationship between Plainview and his adopted son, H.W. (Dillon Freasier). The blast of oil – more specifically, the rush of pressurised air that precedes the oil up the pipe – ruptures H.W.'s eardrums, causing the deafness that is one of the sources of the two characters' estrangement. Though this narrative linkage has nothing specifically to do with methocel's qualities as a device of special effects, its importance to visual storytelling merits remark.

This same scene, though, *does* take advantage of several of methocel's physical properties, some of which again obviate the need for costlier and more labour-intensive CGI, even as digital effects enhance the substance's behaviour. When the oil blasts forth from the rig, it soon blankets the earth, the drilling shack and the nearby rigging gear. To make these objects appear slathered in oil, they were *actually* slathered with methocel: it adheres to and drips from surfaces, reflects light and intensifies in opacity as more of it falls – all in almost exactly the way oil would do if it were not too toxic to employ on a film set. Light pine boards are stained dark brown; white shirts turn instantly black; droplets of liquid drip from actors' brows, noses and chins; performers slip and skid as they run through the stuff, since methocel is nearly as lubricious as crude oil. While the waft of fine black mist was partly generated digitally, the great majority of the gushing oil is composed of methocel.

The transformations described above – objects darkening, liquid coursing over performers and props – are far more easily and cheaply (if messily) accomplished by such practical effects as methocel. The digital simulation of fluid dynamics remains one of the most difficult tasks for a CGI artist; methocel has the advantage of flowing like a fluid because it *is* a fluid – one whose viscosity may be adjusted to suit visual and narrative needs.

A less obvious way in which methocel can confer a potential advantage to *mise en scène* also has to do with visual authenticity, albeit of a different stripe. Methocel as a substance can intersect meaningfully with performance, one of the aspects of film style that has been most dramatically affected by the digital revolution. Actors such as Bill Nighy have remarked that acting in CGI-heavy films is often a liberating experience. Nighy, whose performance is the basis for the all-digital character Davy Jones in *Pirates of the Caribbean: Dead Man's Chest* (2006) and *Pirates of the Caribbean: At World's End* (2007), posits that such digital techniques as 'performance capture' 'can enlarge an actor's experience. … I see no reason why actors and CGI can't work hand in hand. There's no reason one should threaten the other.'[27]

Nevertheless, when actors do not interact with physical costumes, sets and/or props, they are deprived of objects around which to tailor their performances. There may well be an ontological difference between the two performances that might result from, for instance, an actor stroking the soft fur of a real, live poodle and that same actor miming both the action of petting the dog and simulating the fur, its texture *and* his haptic and mental responses to that imagined surface. I do not necessarily wish to take a stand on this matter, which is beyond the purview of this essay. Nevertheless, the issue is germane to the analysis of performative responses to a practical effect like methocel, the use of which persists despite plausible digital substitutes.

Had the oil in *There Will Be Blood* been digitally simulated, an actor as accomplished as Daniel Day-Lewis would likely not have had difficulty 'pretending' that he was coated in oil. Still, all other things being equal, *actually* drenching an actor in goop allows for certain performative gestures that might be difficult or impossible for actors had the goop been strictly digital. In the gusher scene, for instance, Day-Lewis, Freasier and one other actor (the torrent of methocel makes it nearly impossible to identify this performer) perform physical actions that appear to be involuntary responses to their dousing in syrupy goo. All three actors slip on slick surfaces, lose their grips on grabbed objects, wince as they are hit by jets of methocel, jerk their heads in response to splatters, gasp as if they were coming up for air after a long swim and squint constantly. While none of these gestures is impossible on a methocel-free shoot, the use of methocel provides both physical and metaphorical lubrication for the actors' performances: the fact that they can physically respond to a narratively relevant device lends their actions a degree of authenticity – perhaps intangible – that may be more difficult to simulate in a digital environment.

Methocel and Film Style

I hope to have suggested that this kind of analysis – a study of how a certain device encourages and discourages certain stylistic and/or narrative uses and meanings – may be applied to any device of special effects. Methocel is strange, versatile stuff. In its unusual properties and appearance, methocel – whether playing an actual substance or an otherworldly one – behaves like most other devices of cinematic special effects: it adds visual and/or narrative force to people, objects and events. Film-makers as dissimilar as Ivan Reitman and Paul Thomas Anderson have realised that methocel's properties open up a wide range of stylistic options. Its use meaningfully informs many other areas of film style, production and history: editing rates, actors' performances, location shooting, production design, even authorship. Like any other prop or effect, methocel can serve to create narrative meanings of all kinds, but its inherent strangeness, its ability to mimic other substances and its low cost encourage its use in narrative situations like the ones described in this essay.

It may be tempting to conclude that special effects are tools of deception, but I would like to argue that they are no more deceptive than other cinematic tools. In viewing *Ghostbusters II*, we are not 'fooled' into thinking that there is a river of ectoplasm surging below Manhattan; we are not 'tricked' into believing that it is crude oil that coats people and objects in *There Will Be Blood*. Rather, we are asked to entertain the notions that these situations obtain in their respective fictional texts – a response of an entirely different order, and one no different from entertaining the notion that Dan Aykroyd plays Ray Stantz or that Daniel Day-Lewis plays Daniel Plainview. It is 'make-believe', yes, but it is not deception. The study of special effects need not encourage the application of apparatus theory; conducted in a historical-stylistic-economic context, such analysis may instead reveal a great deal about the intersection of style and narrative.

For their assistance with this essay, I would like to thank Richard Barratta, Mark Bero, Dan Forrest, Lorenzo Hall, Scott Heger, Bethany Kormos, Lee McConnell, Josh Miller and Michael Singer.

Notes

1. For an account of Dow's fascinating explorations into methocel's uses and properties, see Susan Warren, 'Why Dow Chemical Finds Slime Sublime: From Monster Slobber to Soup, Some Gooey Stuff Named Methocel Has Many Uses', *Wall Street Journal*, 15 November 1999, p. B1. Dow capitalises the name of the substance, but this essay does not.

2. Robert E. McCarthy, *Secrets of Hollywood Special Effects* (Boston, MA: Focal Press, 1992), p. 52.
3. Tom Huddleston, 'The Make-up Guru from *Drag Me to Hell* on Blood, Guts and That Prosthetic Penis', *Time Out London*, n.d. www.timeout.com/film/features/show-feature/7835/.
4. Interview with the author, 15 July 2009.
5. Ibid.
6. See David Bordwell, *Narration in the Fiction Film* (Madison: University of Wisconsin Press, 1985), p. 162.
7. Jean-Louis Baudry, 'Ideological Effects of the Basic Cinematographic Apparatus', *Film Quarterly* vol. 28 no. 2 (Winter 1974–5), p. 46 (translated by Alan Williams).
8. Norman Klein, *The Vatican to Vegas: A History of Special Effects* (New York: New Press, 2002), p. 236.
9. Bethany Kormos, Senior Scientist in Computational Chemistry, Pfizer, Inc., email to the author, 16 June 2009.
10. Dow's website boasts, 'To add volume, outstanding crumb structure, and moistness to baked goods, nothing performs like METHOCEL™ Food Gums. They're excellent film formers and binders that homogenize mixes.' See http://www.dow.com/methocel/food/index.htm. A long list of this substance's applications may also be found at http://www.dow.com/methocel/other/index.htm, *et seq.*
11. Nathan Myhrvold, Chris Young and Maxime Bilet, *Modernist Cuisine: The Art and Science of Cooking: Volume 4: Ingredients and Preparations* (Bellevue, WA: Cooking Lab, 2011), pp. 18–19.
12. A quick search on Google Scholar for 'methyl cellulose' reveals an abundance of such clinical and experimental uses for the substance.
13. Environmental awareness – or at least the name-checking thereof – has become an important public-relations strategy in Hollywood. The credits of such recent films as *There Will Be Blood* and *Bridesmaids* (2011), for instance, proudly proclaim that measures were taken to balance out the productions' carbon footprints. More anecdotally, on a recent visit to a large Hollywood set, I was told that the recycling bins that dotted the hallways were a recent – and grudging – concession on the part of the film's studio.
14. Interview with the author, 24 August 2011.
15. See http://www.alibaba.com/product-gs/460963994/carboxyl_methyl_cellulose_CMC_powder.html.
16. In the animated television show *The Real Ghostbusters* (1986–91), among other texts, this ghost is known as 'Slimer', another reminder of the importance of slime/methocel/ectoplasm to the *Ghostbusters* universe.
17. The slime in this shot was not its *only* special effect; it also employs puppetry, compositing and bluescreen technologies, to name a few.
18. See http://www.sonymoviechannel.com/movies/ghostbusters-ii/details, a document that appears to be simply a digital version of the film's original presskit.
19. See http://www.imdb.com/title/tt0097428/business.
20. The transcript of an online interview with MacNicol may be found at http://www.oocities.org/televisioncity/6025/pmchat2.txt.
21. I cannot confirm it, but I suspect that clear methocel also plays the part of the mucus that coats the nose and upper lip of an infant actor in the film.
22. Scott Heger, interview with the author, 15 July 2009.

23. David S. Cohen, 'Unsung Heroes: Steve Cremin', *Variety*, 12 February 2008, available at http://www.variety.com/index.asp?layout=awardcentral&jump=features&id=oscarwrap&articleid=VR1117980841.
24. Ibid.
25. Interview with the author, 24 August 2011.
26. Scholar James Udden has recorded a 13.7 Average Shot Length (ASL) for *There Will Be Blood*, 19.5 seconds for *Punch-Drunk Love* (2002), 10.8 seconds for *Boogie Nights* (1997) and 11 seconds for *Magnolia* (1999). See James Udden, 'Child of the Long Take: Alfonso Cuarón's Film Aesthetics in the Shadow of Globalization', *Style* vol. 43 no. 1 (2009), p. 42.
27. Bill Nighy, quoted in David S. Cohen, 'New Techniques Make Visual Effects More Actor-friendly', *Variety*, 11 December 2006, available at www.variety.com/article/VR1117955526/.

FLESHING IT OUT
PROSTHETIC MAKEUP EFFECTS, MOTION CAPTURE AND THE RECEPTION OF PERFORMANCE

LISA BODE

The Region 4 Blu-ray release of *Rise of the Planet of the Apes* (2011) contains the featurettes 'A New Generation of Apes' and 'The Genius of Andy Serkis'. These showcase the processes involved in bringing the film's main character, an unnaturally intelligent and empathetic chimpanzee called 'Caesar', to the screen, disassembling him into components that make different calls on our attention. According to Weta Digital Creatures Supervisor Simon Clutterbuck, Caesar's body is informed by an in-depth study of ape anatomy. Digital musculature and nerve bundles, although unseen on screen, were attached to digital ape skeletons in order to 'fill the inside of the creature with the stuff that drives it'.[1] The visible layers of the character are also framed with recourse to biological science: micro-physiognomy in the wrinkling on faces and hands; the characteristics of ape hair; and ophthalmologic information about the muscles and surfaces of the eye. 'Fleshing out' our impression of Caesar's body with biological detail, it is also the film's major technological and aesthetic point of departure from the earlier films in the *Planet of the Apes* franchise: Caesar and his simian peers are digital to the bone – there are no actors in monkey-suits and rubber masks here.[2]

However, this explanation of Caesar's digital nature also displaces the actor, Andy Serkis, whose motion-captured performance drives the character. So, asserting Serkis's on-screen presence, the various featurettes are peppered with splitscreen footage of him on set, crouching in a grey unitard covered in sensors, his face scrunched in a snarl or lit in a wide-mouthed cackle, juxtaposed alongside footage of the rendered Caesar appearing to mirror his expressions. Moreover, we find that Serkis and the other ape actors had to wear structural prosthetics in the forms of fangs to distort their faces, and limb extensions that allowed them to approximate the loping four-limbed gaits of chimps and orang-utans. This knowledge challenges the spectator to find the actor in the digital character, and disarticulate acting from the work of animators. Promotional interviews tell us that Caesar is a hybrid of computer-generated flesh and actor-generated 'soul'. But the soul is a nebulous idea. So at the same time, using terms that might be more easily imagined spatially by film audiences, Serkis rhetorically dons the mask and monkey-suit, and speaks in the featurette of his amazement at recognising himself on screen in the role, 'cloaked in this digital chimpanzee skin'.[3]

Scott Balcerzak, Jessica Aldred, Barry King and Tanine Allison note the lengths taken in the promotion of recent films like *Avatar* (2009), *Beowulf* (2007) and *King Kong* (2005) to re-synthesise the unseen actor's physical presence.[4] There is a consensus that this is, in part, a discourse of reassurance, bent on injecting 'humanity' into the digital body, or grounding it in a tangible physical universe. King points also to the institutional interests at stake, as Hollywood still depends on the marquee value of the actor's name for promotion and to attract production investment. Certainly, the promotion of Serkis as a performance-capture star and the emphasis on his physicality in the featurettes for *Rise of the Planet of the Apes* chime with these arguments. But at the same time, in their call on different modes of attention (to the achievement of visual effects; to the location and work of acting), and in their assertion that performance capture represents both a break from and continuity with prosthetic makeup effects, the featurettes and critical reviews point in complex ways back to an analogue past. This essay will follow some of these trails back, examining the ways that similar modes of attention for special-effects makeup and acting have operated in very different pre-digital film-making contexts.

Through three case studies – Lon Chaney Sr in *The Phantom of the Opera* (1925), John Hurt in *The Elephant Man* (1980) and Andy Serkis in *Rise of the Planet of the Apes* – I will argue that, like performance capture currently, prosthetically augmented performance has also presented challenges to ideas of actorly achievement and excellence. My aim here is not just to extend our understanding of the actor's location and function in film-making contexts in which they seem to disappear, eclipsed by animation or special effects. As there is little scholarship on prosthetic makeup apart from the 'how-to' books, showcases of individual artists, and the histories which frame it as a series of incremental advances in material science and simulated flesh, I hope also to expand our knowledge of how makeup effects work on screen in synergy with performance, how their reception shifts and what import they may have for film meaning.[5]

Digital Prosthetics

The term 'digital prosthetics' has been pushed by actors and directors in the commercial film industry seeking to frame performance capture as a form of legitimate acting, by referencing selective examples from cinema's analogue past. It was first raised by Peter Jackson in an interview with *Entertainment Weekly* in 2002. Arguing in support of Andy Serkis's Oscar nomination bid for his motion-captured/digitally animated role as Gollum in *The Lord of the Rings: The Two Towers* (2002), Jackson said:

> I think that what Andy has ultimately achieved with Gollum is as relevant an acting performance as *The Elephant Man* with John Hurt. Hurt's buried beneath inches of rubber, but he has to use his acting skills to push this prosthetic around and fuel the character.[6]

Hurt, performing inside Christopher Tucker's elaborate latex appliances, gained a Best Actor Oscar nomination playing real-life nineteenth-century sideshow exhibit and medical curiosity, Joseph Merrick – a man hideously deformed by neurofibromatosis – in David Lynch's 1980 film.[7] Jackson's argument about Hurt as unseen but driving the expressivity of a synthetic face has become the prototype for arguments made by Serkis himself; *Rise of the Planet of the Apes* director, Rupert Wyatt; Tom Rothman, head of Twentieth Century-Fox (the studio releasing the film); and co-star James Franco.[8] This raises the question: what continuities and breaks actually exist between digital performance capture and practical prosthetic makeup?

In ontological terms alone, the prosthetic makeup analogy is fairly easy to dismiss. As Balcerzak observes, 'Heavy makeup alters the appearance of the body while mo-cap removes the physical reality of the body and replaces it with something or someone digital.'[9] With digital screen characters like Caesar or Neytiri (Zoe Saldana) in *Avatar*, we can only take on faith (and with the assistance of the behind-the-scenes documentation) that what we see on screen has a direct transcriptional relationship to the gestures and expressions performed by the actor, whereas we know (from deduction or promotional information) that there has to be *someone* inside the rubber suit or behind those grotesque layers of latex pushing it around. This dichotomy is admittedly complicated by cases where practical prosthetics are worn by an actor but then digitally animated or composited with digital body parts.[10] Nevertheless, in recent critical reviews an ontological distinction appears to hold.

For instance, Michael O'Sullivan in his review of *Rise of the Planet of the Apes* compares 'Andy Serkis, in motion-capture CGI [and] rendered by computer animation' to the earlier actors in makeup, such as Roddy McDowall in Franklin J. Schaffner's original 1968 film. While conceding that the digital apes here are 'frightening – and believably emotive [...] they're less than fully present', McDowall was 'paradoxically, more real, even in his stiff rubber mask'.[11] O'Sullivan's belief that computer animation rather than an actor in a mask is largely responsible for what he sees seems to block his engagement with the character as diegetically 'real'. For him, belief in the actor's profilmic presence is more important to the construction of cinematic reality than how expressive or 'realistic' the end result may be.

However, the mere physical presence of someone inside the suit or behind a mask does not entail a *performance*, or mean that what the hidden actor does on screen will be easily evaluated as such. For some critics, the use of artificial methods to transform an actor's appearance is read as a distraction or a visual crutch that means the actor has less to do in signifying character. We see an instance of this in an article from 1991 about a then-new stage version of *The Elephant Man*, in which the actor playing Merrick wore no makeup, but instead suggested Merrick's deformity through bodily contortion and voice alone. In praising the actor, Stan Barouh disparages Hurt's performance in the earlier film with the line: 'a few pounds of latex, a mouth full of marbles, a burlap cap and your aunt could play the Elephant Man'.[12] A focus on ontological differences or technical processes alone, then, while a useful starting point for analysis, does not necessarily give insight into how and why modes of viewing and evaluation persist or shift, and what kinds of contextual factors may be in play.

The reviews for *Rise of the Planet of the Apes* suggest that the prosthetic makeup analogy has gained traction with some critics, who, trying to understand performance capture in relation to what is familiar, locate Serkis on screen 'underneath'[13] Caesar or as providing Caesar's 'skeleton and soul'.[14] As with the promotional interviews, the analogue reference points drawn upon to praise Serkis are selective, excluding not just rubber-suited creature or alien performances but also the ape performances from earlier films in the franchise. When Schaffner's 1968 or Tim Burton's 2001 versions are mentioned, they are compared more in terms of their special-effects achievements or their overall success or failure as cinematic experiences, rather than on the grounds of performance.

This may be because the dominant critical paradigm privileges realism and verisimilitude, and films with a seriousness of tone. The earlier prosthetic ape makeup, while winning an honorary Oscar for John Chambers in 1969, is now received through the lens of nostalgia as charmingly camp. As Rick Baker pointed out in 2001 when promoting his updating of the makeup for Burton's reboot, the stiff rubber muzzles designed by Chambers allowed little expressivity compared to the ways real chimps use their lips and bare their teeth.[15] The heightened artifice of what now resemble 'dime-store masks'[16] do not encourage us to take Roddy McDowall and Kim Hunter's performances seriously, and indeed the anthropomorphised ape characterisations strive less for realism than just credibility within the bounds of that film's world. Rather than an updated McDowall, then, Serkis is labelled a 'CGI Streep',[17] 'the modern Lon Chaney, a man of 1,000 faces grafted on digitally',[18] and 'the Lon Chaney Sr of CGI', grouping him with well-respected actors known for 'disappearing' into a role.[19]

The most persistent overall comparisons to Serkis are then instances of pre-digital prosthetically augmented performance where the actor's own face is covered: John Hurt in *The Elephant Man*, and Lon Chaney Sr, whose best-remembered character face is that of Erik, the hideously deformed, masked composer in *The Phantom of the Opera*. Although produced in very different historical and film-making contexts, many decades apart, there are some obvious similarities between the films. In each case, Chaney, Hurt and Serkis are playing a character trapped in a body that is visually at odds with its interior self. Because of the connotations of their appearance – whether freakish monster, or subhuman beast – each character faces persecution from their broader communities, with tragic narrative results.[20] To varying degrees, each film asks for our empathy for this character (albeit for Chaney's Phantom, Erik, this appeal is more muted, as through his vengeful actions of kidnapping and murder threats he is turned into a figure of horror). This interrelation between interior and exterior is communicated through performances of very different kinds that, as we shall see, inflect the interior/exterior interrelation, and therefore the makeup or CGI, differently. The reception materials for each film in turn furnish us with clues as to how modes of attention are activated, the evaluative frameworks they refer to and the challenges that are negotiated in promotional materials, interviews and subsequent films. Looking at these provides us with something of an outline of how shifting ideas about verisimilitude, acting and selfhood have impacted upon special-effects makeup, and continue to have import for performance capture.

Chaney as the Phantom: Grimacing through Makeup

The way each character's appearance is first shown – our first invitation to look – cues our initial responses. As the Phantom, Chaney spends the first part of the film hidden behind a benignly smiling creepy mask that resembles the face of a plump shop-window dummy. The mask, along with whispers from characters about the extent of the Phantom's true hideousness, build anticipation for what we shall eventually see. At the same time, the blatant artifice of the mask enhances the impression that by comparison, what lies beneath is authentic flesh. The unmasking scene is presented as a set-piece of spectacular horror. In this scene, the achingly curious Christine (Mary Philbin) creeps up behind Erik while he faces the camera in medium shot, playing the organ. To their mutual shock, she removes his mask to reveal a cadaverous face beneath: with a shining dome of a forehead, tombstone teeth and staring eyes. To create the face, Chaney built up his forehead and cheekbones with layers of morticians' wax. Fish-skin and wire insertions turned up his nose and gaped his nostrils, and he used black greasepaint in his eye sockets to suggest a frightening skull-like visage.[21] As something cued by the film as a special effect and as Chaney's latest self-transfiguration, the makeup invites evaluation of its claims to spectacular cadaverousness within the generic boundaries of the film, and its credibility as artificial flesh.

Retrospective reviews of the film tend to universally praise both Chaney's makeup and find his performance easy to locate in 'languorous' hand gestures.[22] But they are viewing through the lens of an accrued hagiography that ossified Chaney's reputation as special-effects makeup pioneer and self-transforming 'man of 1,000 faces', and links his abilities as a 'powerfully expressive mime' to his childhood as the son of two deaf mutes.[23] The 1925 reception, by contrast, reveals uncertainty about the efficacy of the makeup, and the value and location of Chaney's performance in relation to it. An unnamed reviewer from the *Washington Post* compares the makeup favourably to that employed for Chaney's previous role in *The Hunchback of Notre Dame* (1923), and claims that this one 'eclipses his weird disguise as Quasimodo in the Hugo classic'.[24] Others, demonstrating a greater level of detached scrutiny, question whether the unmasking of Erik's face is quite as frightening as promised in the film's buildup. Mordaunt Hall says, 'He is by no means beautiful, but he is not as hideous as one anticipated', and refutes the claim by a character in the film that the Phantom has no nose: 'he has a nose, with long straight nostrils'.[25] Hall apparently does not see character but instead Chaney attempting an artifice that does not quite succeed.

While retrospective reviewers praise Chaney's skills as a mime and attend to his hand gestures in the role, reviewers in 1925 seem unsure as to whether he is overacting or not acting at all. Hall concedes in his 7 September review that, while Chaney's performance is 'compelling', it is 'a little exaggerated at times' – something he forgives as a requirement of the film's genre as 'ultra fantastic melodrama'.[26] However, a week later he reconsiders, deciding that Chaney 'overdoes it' to the point of absurdity.[27] The reviewer from *Variety* is not highly impressed either but, rather than accusing Chaney of overacting, seems to find performance difficult to locate, expressing a disappointment that Chaney was throughout 'either behind a mask or grimacing through his fiendish makeup'.[28] This view was echoed a few years later upon the film's re-release in 1930 with some added soundtrack, when a reviewer from *The Times*, while conceding the makeup was 'startling', opines that Chaney 'has few opportunities to act'.[29]

The divergences in the 1920s and 30s reviews can be partly explained in relation to then-emerging valorisation of the actor's face as the most inherently cinematic site of acting. European film-makers Jean Epstein and Béla Balázs saw the cinematic close-up as revealing the micro-physiognomy of the human face, cuing viewers to search for signs of psychological interiority in the twitch of a lip or an eyelid.[30] Roberta Pearson's work on early popular ideas about screen acting in North America similarly finds that trade opinion from 1908 in *Moving Picture World* emphasised the desirability of moving the camera closer to actors to show facial expressions as indicators of thought. The use of the eyes and the face, she argues, were coming to be seen as 'perhaps the crucial component of the verisimilar code'.[31] She identifies the verisimilar code of performance as one that tended towards subtlety and bodily containment, and was valued above an earlier 'histrionic' or more excessively gestural mode of performance, criticised in trade and industry discourse during the 1910s.[32] This provides some contextual explanation for why critics ranked Chaney's facial transformations fairly low on a hierarchy of cinematic aesthetics. The Phantom's mask and the disfiguring makeup are read as obstructions that put limits on facial movements, or form a barrier that he must 'grimace through'. Of course the actor's face continues to be considered the primary locus of performance; the developmental telos of performance capture is often framed in industry press as a movement towards registering increased facial-motion data and the expressivity of digital eyes.[33] However, in the 1920s the emerging cinematic emphasis on the face was not the only contextual factor Chaney had to negotiate.

The 1920s also ushered in a mass cosmetics industry and a corresponding development of highly feminine connotations around makeup.[34] There is evidence to suggest male actors distanced themselves from makeup as a result. An interview with romantic leading man John Gilbert, for example, reported that male actors were increasingly abandoning makeup for screen roles, finding with new lighting techniques that 'a man's face is more efficient without it', whereas 'a woman's features are more delicate and her colouring has to be more even to register properly, so that powder and a little rouge are a real necessity before the camera'. The article speculates that soon the only man on screen still wearing makeup would be Chaney.[35] Similarly, a 1925 article labels Chaney as 'unquestionably the screen's most adept manipulator of the brush and the powderpuff',[36] aligning his tools with feminised cosmetics rather than the more craft-oriented make-do materials his biographers have foregrounded, such as gutta percha, greasepaint, fish-skin and morticians' wax.[37]

In this context of makeup effects' dubious critical status in the 1920s as feminised artifice, Chaney sought to promote their value and relationship to his performances, emphasising realism and structural depth. In a key interview from 1927, Chaney takes the reader through his process of preparing for a role by linking it to the emulation of everyday, lifelike verisimilitude, highlighting time, effort, creativity and tremendous bodily discomfort, while positioning himself somewhere between an experimental chemist, a student of facial structures and a keen observer of people. He stresses that his transformations are never simply about the mimicry of outward appearance, or the surface of things. Rather, his synthesis of makeup and acting for each role relies on 'a knowledge of human anatomy and the observation of human characters in action'.[38]

Such discourses of realism and structural depth appear to shape the aesthetic aims of realist prosthetic makeup design and acting, countering their artificial foundations. As the paratexts for films like *Avatar* and *Apes* indicate, they have been rearticulated for digital-creature design and performance-capture contexts seeking validation. But they had also been developed further in the context of sound film and biography by Hurt and Tucker for *The Elephant Man*. Examining this film illustrates shifts both in the cultural status of prosthetic effects makeup and in the interplay between makeup and performance in the connection of character interiority to exteriority.

Hurt: The Elephant Man's Breath

The Elephant Man emerged in the very different performance context of sound film. Moreover it was produced at a time when the generic connotations of makeup effects had been shaped since the 1930s Universal horror-film cycle by decades of monster movies and creature features, lending such effects dubious aesthetic value. For at least one reviewer at the time of *The Elephant Man*'s release, the science-fiction and fantasy connotations of the makeup were inescapable, and pushed the appearance of Merrick into absurdity by heightening awareness of artifice. Painting Hurt as a rather laughable figure 'encased in layers of foam laytex (sic) to approximate Merrick's enlarged head', the anonymous writer was reminded of other 'fondly recalled movie monsters' such as the cantina aliens in *Star Wars* (1977) or the monster in *The Creature from the Black Lagoon* (1954).[39]

To an extent, the film also cued these generic reference points, as Merrick's appearance is only gradually revealed through the murky visual register of horror. We are led to his on-screen revelation from behind the craning necks of gasping nineteenth-century gawkers and grubby freakshow exhibit curtains; a distorted silhouette behind a medical screen exhibited to bearded respectable scientists; and finally a meek-voiced figure, his face hidden by a burlap sack. As with Chaney's Phantom, we hear of his monstrosity from others before we see him for ourselves. What is suggested but not shown incites our dread, and frames our first encounters with the makeup as monstrous.

Once fully revealed, what we see is a misshapen figure, and the faint glimmer of a wary eye from deep within rubbery masses of tumorous flesh. *New York Times* reviewer Vincent Canby, a persuasive advocate for the aesthetic recognition of makeup effects in the context of historical biography and biological realism, praised the film, actors and makeup artist, but also acknowledged the potentially problematic status of elaborate disfiguring makeup, based on generic associations:

> John Hurt, as John Merrick, is a monster with a bulbous forehead, a Quasimodo-like mouth, one almost obscured eye, a useless arm, and crooked torso. It's to the credit of Christopher Tucker's makeup and to Mr. Hurt's extraordinary performance deep inside it, that John Merrick doesn't look absurd, like something out of a low-budget science-fiction film.[40]

Canby moves beyond the fantasy connotations of Tucker's appliances to remind us to read them in relation to an actual historical personage, of whose physiognomy, photographic, skeletal and lifecast evidence exists. Moreover, the film moves us spatially and emotionally from being a voyeur of Merrick's almost faceless exterior to understanding something of his interior, bringing us inside Merrick's experience of his own body, and attempting to conjure unseen anatomical and psychological depths.

Tucker used the remains of Merrick's body to provide structural information for the prosthetic design. He found reference in late nineteenth-century photographs of the real Joseph Merrick, written testimony from medical journals, as well as Merrick's skeleton and plaster lifecast of his face and torso (with Merrick's hair still embedded in the plaster), borrowed from the London Hospital Museum. From this he discovered the extent of Merrick's visible and invisible deformities. Protuberances (impacted wisdom teeth, a bone projecting through his jaw into the back of his spine) obstructed the man's breathing, speaking and eating while painfully twisting his torso. Tucker constructed an elaborate set of prosthetic appliances comprising twenty-two different pieces which had to be built up on Hurt's body and face, section by overlapping section, from a teeth plate worn inside the actor's mouth, to the liberal use of foam latex in the simulation of the 'large warty, smelly masses of flesh' encasing his cranium.[41]

The knowledge of Merrick's interior deformation also informed Hurt's performance. Hurt's viscous snuffles, groans and wheezes, his excruciating pauses and inhalations, his audible exertions to breathe and speak, give a fleshy, suffering materiality to rubber, a sense of mouth and airways obstructed by wayward growths and bony protrusions. When he does speak, the timidity of his voice suggests he has spent a lifetime in this body. Fittingly, Roger Ebert, although disliking the film's shift from framing Merrick as object of horror to object of sentimentality, singled out Hurt's performance as 'remarkable for somehow projecting a humanity beyond the disfiguring makeup'.[42] The unnamed reviewer for the *Guardian* also commended Hurt for being 'never quite without breath' despite being 'smothered in makeup'.[43]

These views have some continuity with recent attempts to legitimate digital bodies and performance capture, and to encourage viewer evaluation of both the separate processes involved and their synergy in the character. Chaney, Tucker and Hurt's evocation of the biological and behavioural 'real' in their character designs foreshadows the ways 3D character designers (such as Weta for *Rise of the Planet of the Apes*) use detailed anatomical knowledge and models in the service of verisimilitude. It also parallels stories of the time spent by the motion-capture performers, who were largely ex-gymnasts and circus performers, in 'ape school'. There, according to Terry Notary (the ex-stuntman who plays two ape characters), they learnt the principles of ape locomotion – allowing the front limb to absorb one's weight and squaring the shoulders before moving the back limb – and the ways apes focus intently on one object at a time.[44] So we begin to see where some of the continuities – and distinctions – between digital and practical prosthetic performances lie.

From Suffering and Constraint to Physical 'Empowerment'

Since Chaney, physical discomfort under rubber has been a key authenticator for prosthetic makeup performances. For any such role we read about what the actor had to endure in terms of physical constraints on movement, vision, eating, drinking, bathroom breaks and hours of boredom and waiting. For instance, *The Elephant Man*'s publicity emphasised John Hurt's daily seven hours in makeup for the role. References to the discomfort endured by his body in the service of transformation remind us that beneath the foam latex is a man who for six weeks during filming could only eat 'two eggs beaten in orange juice [...] sipped through a straw', and could not lie down while in makeup, so would have to nap, sitting up, 'exactly like Merrick'.[45] It makes little difference whether the role in question is for serious drama or fantasy: the emphasis on actor suffering remains the same. Michael Chiklis, complaining about the sixty-pound latex suit he wore to play the Thing in *The Fantastic Four* (2005), says 'it was excruciatingly hot and heavy and ironically gave me everything I needed to play the role. I'm playing a guy who's trapped in a body he doesn't want to be in [...] my interior monologue was fulfilled.'[46] Hurt and Chiklis both draw attention to the weight and pressure of prosthetics on their bodies, constraints that help them get into the right frame of mind for the role.

By contrast, performance capture is, according to *Iron Man 2* (2010) visual-effects supervisor Janek Sirrs, like post-production-applied prosthetics 'but without the suffering'.[47] Physicality and labour are still stressed, but now this is consistently framed as 'empowering' and 'liberating'. Stripped of costume, wigs, masks and the extra burden of suits and rubber that may itch, constrict their movements or give them debilitating excess weight to carry, the actor in the lightweight grey performance-capture suit has more physical freedom, and therefore, arguably, more responsibility for communicating their character's embodiment through their own contortions and movements.[48] From this perspective, at least, performance-capture acting can claim a greater level of actor autonomy than does prosthetic makeup.

Serkis and the 'Thinking' Ape

But what difference does performance capture make to the expression of interiority in relation to exteriority? If Chaney as the Phantom could, for retrospective reviewers at least, use his languorous hand gestures to indicate an inner melancholic grace at odds with the appearance of his face, Hurt used vocalisation to give a sense of not just a timorous and gentle personality inside horrific deformed features, but also an extra dimension that 'fleshes out' the image and the interior of the body. In the case of Serkis's Caesar, gesture and voice are of course present but, rather than compensating for what the actor's hidden face cannot show, these performance elements supplement a digital conveyer (not a mask) of facial expression. According to reviews, Caesar's face brings us the uncanny sight of a fully sentient animal, silently observing, calculating and strategising, that expresses largely without words a character arc from trust to bewilderment to anger and resolve.[49] The visibility of recognisable thought processes on the creature's face recalls Balázs and Epstein's reveries on the close-up in the 1920s, and are perhaps what Serkis, Wyatt and Franco elsewhere call the character's 'soul'.

Thus many reviewers praise Caesar for his unprecedented levels of 'expressivity', in comparison to previous motion-captured performances.[50] But this comparison also means that digital effects become the point of evaluation for the film, giving technology credit for the character: as Manohla Dargis says, 'When Caesar scowls, as he increasingly does, you don't see just digital wizardry at its most expressive; you also see a plausible, angry, thinking character.'[51] Reading Dargis's review I am reminded of Dan North's analysis of Gollum's facial expressions in *The Lord of the Rings: The Two Towers* where he observes that 'the computer's ability to convey these effects is what renders them spectacular'.[52]

North foregrounds the extent to which we are encouraged to wonder at the technical apparatus that 'conveys' the character's emotional states, wherever their originating point. So too, the spectacular value of Caesar's face for Dargis is that his expressivity is generated by computers rather than recorded by a camera. But other reviewers like Peter Travers and Dana Stevens, determined to give Serkis credit for Caesar, use his previous role as Gollum as a legitimating reference point: if that character and Caesar are both so compelling on screen compared to the performance-capture characters in *Beowulf* or *Avatar*, then Serkis, as the common denominator between the two, must be responsible.[53] Moreover, he must be an actor of extraordinary expressivity for his performance to register through so many mediating and potentially manipulated layers of digital muscle, skin and eyes. Nevertheless, as Ebert says, 'one never knows exactly where the human ends and the effects begin'.[54]

In the face of such doubt, 'fidelity' becomes a key if problematic term – for fidelity is relative rather than absolute – used repeatedly by Serkis and in some industry articles to frame both the performance-capture apparatus, and the relationship between Caesar and Serkis.[55] The character rig is seen not as a mask, or even just a conveyer of character expressivity but, importantly, as a conveyor of human performance. This also means that, as a visual effect, Caesar functions very differently from Chaney or Tucker's prosthetic faces. Prosthetic makeup, due to its direct physical contact with the actor's body and face, gathers part of its spectacular value from the way it transfigures actors and makes them unrecognisable, even when they are on screen. Images of the actors both in and out of prosthetic makeup invite us to marvel at the points of difference between Chaney or Hurt's real physiognomy and that of their characters. In contrast, the digital character, being already a wholesale replacement in screen space of the actor's body and face, gathers its spectacular value from the ways it appears to *retain* a recognisable connection to the actor. The splitscreen footage that pits Serkis against the final rendered Caesar invites us to marvel at the ability of the technical apparatus to convey or remain faithful to the performance, no matter whether this is directly and automatically informed or animated from reference footage. Performance, then, is conceptualised in some reviews not as something 'beneath' or 'inside' the digital character, but as the actor's kinaesthetic trace, through which Serkis 'invests' or 'imbues' Caesar with personality, 'life' or 'soul'.[56]

Conclusion

Grappling with continuities and discontinuities between digital motion-capture performance and practical makeup effects requires attention to reception and paratextual information as well as ontological questions. One point of continuity is that acting and special effects have so often been perceived as demanding divergent modes of evaluation, dividing viewership between attention to artifice and authenticity, interiority and exteriority, craft or technical apparatus and emotion. The history of prosthetic makeup effects has been written as a teleological one of advances in material science, technique, and lighting, pushing towards greater powers of astonishing simulations of the flesh. But omitting a consideration of the actor and their place in reception misses the importance of contextual factors, such as how the status of makeup effects shifts in relation to dominant paradigms of 'good' cinematic acting. This illuminates the industry discourses emerging around performance capture, which stress actor autonomy and 'empowerment' as well as the 'fidelity' of the process. The discourse of 'fidelity' encourages us to see performance capture as 'conveyance' rather than 'mask' even as the prosthetic appliance or rubber creature suit is used as the legitimating connection to cinema's analogue past.

More important than the light it sheds on the interrelations between prosthetic makeup and the location of the actor's work, however, is the way this comparison frames the role of physical and digital prosthetics for film meaning. From Chaney to Hurt and Serkis, such analogies negotiate the critical status of makeup or performance capture while helping us to locate the actor's performance, labour and skill. But they also suggest some of the differences that developments in special-effects makeup and cinema technologies have made to the way we express and imagine the relationship between character interiority and bodily exterior.

Notes

1. Simon Clutterbuck; Joe Letteri; Keven Norris (interviews), 'A New Generation of Apes', *Rise of the Planet of the Apes* (Blu-ray), dir. Rupert Wyatt, Twentieth Century-Fox Corporation, 2011.
2. The earlier films are: *The Planet of the Apes* (1968); *Beneath the Planet of the Apes* (1970); *Escape from the Planet of the Apes* (1971); *Conquest of the Planet of the Apes* (1973); *Battle for the Planet of the Apes* (1974); followed by the TV series *Planet of the Apes* (1974); *Return to the Planet of the Apes* (1975); *Farewell to the Planet of the Apes* (1981); *Back to the Planet of the Apes* (1981); and the reboot directed by Tim Burton, *Planet of the Apes* (2001).

3. Andy Serkis (interview), 'A New Generation of Apes'.
4. Scott Balcerzak, 'Andy Serkis as Actor, Body and Gorilla: Motion Capture and the Presence of Performance', in Scott Balcerzak and Jason Sperb (eds), *Cinephilia in the Age of Digital Reproduction* (London and New York: Wallflower Press, 2009); Jessica Aldred, 'From Synthespian to Avatar: Reframing the Digital Human in *Final Fantasy* and *The Polar Express*', *Mediascape* (Winter 2011) (online); Barry King, 'Articulating Digital Stardom', *Celebrity Studies* vol. 2 no. 3 (2011), pp. 247–62; Tanine Allison, 'More than a Man in a Monkey-Suit: Andy Serkis, Motion Capture, and Digital Realism', *Quarterly Review of Film and Video* vol. 28 no. 4 (2011), pp. 325–41.
5. Thomas Morawetz, *Making Faces, Playing God: Identity and the Art of Transformational Makeup* (Austin: University of Texas Press, 2001); Richard Rickett, *Special Effects: The History and Technique* (New York: Billboard Books, 2007).
6. Peter Jackson (interview), quoted in Adam Duerson, 'Hobbit Forming', *Entertainment Weekly*, 18 December 2002 (online).
7. Merrick's first name was changed to 'John' for Bernard Pomerance's stage play and Lynch's film.
8. Rebecca Keegan, 'Andy Serkis of "Apes" Being Promoted for Oscar', *LA Times*, 5 November 2011 (online); James Franco, 'On Why Andy Serkis Deserves Credit from Actors', *Deadline*, 8 January 2012 (online).
9. Balcerzak, 'Andy Serkis as Actor, Body and Gorilla', pp. 195–6.
10. See for instance the Sacrificial Engineer in *Prometheus* (2012) played by Daniel James who wore fifty-five pounds of silicon. According to Joe Fordham in *Cinefex* vol. 130 (p. 36), Weta Digital animated rapid decay on the prosthetic body before quickly transitioning to a fully CG figure.
11. Michael O'Sullivan, 'The Humans Play Second Bananas' (review), *Washington Post*, 5 August 2011 (online).
12. Stan Barouh, 'Elephant Man's Mental Makeup', *Washington Post*, 16 August 1991, p. 31.
13. Michael Phillips, '"Apes" Prequel Stands Alone, Upright' (review), *Chicago Tribune*, 4 August 2011 (online).
14. Ty Burr, 'Beastly Good: Newest "Apes" a Compelling Sci-fi Story of Injustice' (review), *Boston Globe*, 5 August 2011 (online).
15. Rick Baker (interview), John Calhoun and Scott Essmann, 'Show Me the Monkey', *Entertainment Design* vol. 35 no. 8 (2001), p. 28.
16. Rick Pinkerton, 'The Making of a Monkey Activist in *Rise of the Planet of the Apes*' (review), *Village Voice*, 3 August 2011 (online).
17. Joe Neumaier, 'Rise of the Planet of the Apes' (review), *New York Daily News*, 4 August 2011 (online).
18. Steve Persall, 'Did a Chimp Write This Screenplay?' (review), *Tampa Bay Times*, 4 August 2011 (online).
19. Pinkerton, 'The Making of a Monkey Activist'.
20. Caesar is confiscated from his human 'father' and mistreated with other apes in a shelter, before escaping and wreaking havoc on the city; Merrick, rescued from a freakshow by a surgeon, finds he still cannot escape cruelty, and takes his life; Erik the Phantom, a hideously deformed but brilliant composer infatuated with a beautiful opera singer, terrifies her with his appearance and takes revenge before being chased by a mob into the river where he drowns.
21. Robert G. Anderson, *Faces, Forms, Films: The Artistry of Lon Chaney* (New York: Castle Books, 1971), p. 110.

22. Roger Ebert, 'The Phantom of the Opera' (review), *Chicago Sun-Times*, 19 December 2004 (online).
23. Mark Bourne, 'Phantom of the Opera: The Ultimate Edition' (review), *The DVD Journal*, 2003 (online).
24. 'Lon Chaney in "Phantom of the Opera"', *Washington Post*, 18 October 1925, p. B2.
25. Mordaunt Hall, 'The Opera Phantom', *New York Times*, 13 September 1925, p. X5.
26. Mordaunt Hall, 'The Screen' (review), *New York Times*, 7 September 1925, p. 15.
27. Hall, 'The Opera Phantom', p. X5
28. Variety Staff, 'The Phantom of the Opera' (review fragment from 1925), variety.com.
29. 'The Phantom of the Opera' (review), *The Times*, 22 July 1930, p. 12.
30. Jean Epstein, 'Magnification' (1921), in Richard Abel, *French Film Theory and Criticism: A History/Anthology, 1907–1939* (Princeton, NJ: Princeton University Press, 1988), vol. 1, pp. 235–41; Béla Balázs, 'The Close-up' (1924), in *Béla Balázs: Early Film Theory*, trans. Rodney Livingstone, edited by Eria Carter (Germany: Bergahn Books, 2010).
31. Roberta A. Pearson, *Eloquent Gestures: The Transformation of Performance Style in the Griffith Biograph Films* (Berkeley and Oxford: University of California Press, 1992), p. 127.
32. Pearson, *Eloquent Gestures*, p. 124.
33. See for instance Michael Ordoña, 'Eye-popping 'Avatar' Pioneers New Technology', *San Francisco Chronicle*, 13 December 2009; and Dave Kehr, 'Duplicate Motion, Then Capture Emotion', *New York Times*, 18 November 2007.
34. Michael Carter, 'Facials: the Aesthetics of Cosmetics and Makeup', *Literature and Aesthetics* vol. 8 (August 1998), pp. 97–112.
35. 'This Plan Won't Work for Women', *Washington Post*, 25 December 1927, p. F3.
36. 'Lon Chaney Determined to Film Self as Made', *Washington Post*, 23 August 1925, p. A2.
37. See Michael F. Blake, *A Thousand Faces: Lon Chaney's Unique Artistry in Motion Pictures* (Lanham, MD, New York and Oxford: Vestal, 1995); and Anderson, *Faces, Forms, Films*. Chaney asserted his physical authenticity in the publicity for his first and only sound film, Jack Conway's *The Unholy Three* in 1930. In this remake of the Tod Browning film of 1925, he reprised his role as a ventriloquist conman. Against apparent scepticism around the five voices his character produces in the film, Chaney publicised his signing of a deposition that all five voices were his own and none were dubbed ('Lon Chaney's Five Voices', *New York Times*, 6 July 1930, p. 90). In this way Chaney's negotiation of the manipulating potential of technology to invalidate his work is an early forerunner to the kinds of performance-authenticating strategies used by Serkis in the context of performance capture.
38. 'Mr Chaney Studies Human Nature', *New York Times*, 21 August 1927, p. X3.
39. '"Elephant Man": A Beastly Cinematic Tease' (review), *Washington Post*, 17 October 1980, p. C4.
40. Vincent Canby, 'Film: "Elephant Man" Study in Genteelness' (review), *New York Times*, 3 October 1980, p. C8. See also Canby, 'A Bow in the Direction of the Makeup Artists', *New York Times*, 23 November 1980, pp. 15, 33.
41. 'The Elephant Man Revealed' (featurette), *The Elephant Man* (1980) dir. David Lynch, DVD Region 1 Release, 2001.
42. Roger Ebert, 'The Elephant Man' (review), *Chicago Sun-Times*, 1 January 1980 (online).
43. 'The Mask of Sorrow' (review), *Guardian*, 9 October 1980, p. 11.
44. Terry Notaro (interview), 'A New Generation of Apes'.
45. John Hurt (interview), Tom Buckley, 'At the Movies', *New York Times*, 26 September 1980, p. C12.

46. Michael Chiklis (interview), Reed Tucker, 'Q +A with Michael Chiklis', *Esquire*, July 2005, p. 36.
47. Janek Sirrs (interview), David S. Cohen, 'F/X Chief Helps "Iron" Out the Kinks', *Variety* 3–9 May 2010, p. 17.
48. This is of course complicated by the use of structural prosthetics for limbs and teeth in *Rise of the Planet of the Apes*, albeit these were ones that enabled ape motion rather than disabling the actors.
49. Rick Groen, 'Rise of the Planet of the Apes: The Ape Movie has Evolved' (review), *Friday's Globe and Mail*, 5 August 2011 (online).
50. David Denby, 'Noble Creatures' (review), *New Yorker*, 5 September 2011 (online); Kenneth Turan, 'Rise of the Planet of the Apes' (review), *LA Times*, 5 August 2011 (online); Michael Phillips, '"Apes" Prequel Stands Alone, Upright' (review), *Chicago Tribune*, 4 August 2011 (online).
51. Manohla Dargis, 'Looking Apocalypse in the Eye' (review), *New York Times*, 4 August 2011 (online).
52. Dan North, *Performing Illusions: Cinema, Special Effects and the Virtual Actor* (London: Wallflower Press, 2008), p. 175.
53. Peter Travers, 'Rise of the Planet of the Apes' (review), *Rolling Stone Magazine*, 4 August 2011 (online); Dana Stevens, 'Rise of the Planet of the Apes' (reviews), *Slate.com*, 4 August 2011 (online).
54. Roger Ebert, 'Rise of the Planet of the Apes' (review), *Chicago Sun-Times*, 3 August 2011 (online).
55. Andy Serkis (interview), 'The Genius of Andy Serkis' (featurette), *Rise of the Planet of the Apes* Blu-ray (2011); Andy Serkis (interview), David S. Cohen, 'Capture Suits Serkis Just Fine', *Variety*, 25 November 2011 (online); Barbara Robertson, 'Chimp Change', *Computer Graphics World* vol. 34 no. 7 (August/September 2011).
56. Todd McCarthy, 'Rise of the Planet of the Apes' (review), *Hollywood Reporter*, 3 August 2011 (online); Mark Mohan, 'Rise of the Planet of the Apes' (review), *Portland Oregonian*, 4 August 2011 (online).

(STOP)MOTION CONTROL
SPECIAL EFFECTS IN CONTEMPORARY PUPPET ANIMATION

ANDREA COMISKEY

Prior to the 1990s, investment in stop-motion puppet animation on the part of major film studios was largely relegated to the realm of visual (and especially 'creature') effects in live-action films. Full stop-motion works were most often found in other media, including theatrical short films, commercials, children's TV specials and the avant-garde. Indeed, stop-motion features were for decades essentially absent from the production rosters of US studios as well as the domestic theatre screens. In 1993, two films signalled a change in this industrial configuration. One was Steven Spielberg's *Jurassic Park*, which was heralded as a paradigm-shifting triumph of computer-generated creature effects (despite relying heavily on 'old-fashioned' animatronics). The other was Henry Selick's *The Nightmare before Christmas*, which demonstrated that highly sophisticated, big-budget feature-length puppet animation was feasible as well as potentially lucrative. Although still a niche option, stop-motion features have in the ensuing two decades continued to maintain a visible and commercially viable presence within contemporary theatrical animation. And they have flowered at the same time that CGI has both rendered stop motion obsolete as a visual-effects medium and usurped cel animation as the dominant mode of feature-length animation production.

Contemporary stop-motion animation is in fact tightly imbricated with digital technologies and aesthetics, but this relationship is contradictory. On the one hand, digital technologies have provided a new set of craft tools that have helped puppet animators solve many of the most daunting challenges posed by stop-motion production (especially at feature length). But on the other hand, the digital serves as a computerised 'other' against which stop motion is frequently positioned, thereby affirming the medium's cultural and economic value – and indeed its ontological status – as a material, tactile and *handmade* medium. Thus, while the increasing integration of digital technologies has in some ways proven a boon to stop motion, it also threatens to erode what are perceived to be essential tenets of the medium's 'analogue' craft practices and aesthetics. This contradiction results in a kind of double erasure in which animators use digital technologies to efface certain artefacts of the stop-motion process while at the same time attempting to minimise markers of the digital.

This study examines the role of the digital in eight major Anglo-American stop-motion features produced since 1993: *Nightmare*, *James and the Giant Peach* (1996) and *Coraline* (2009), all directed by Henry Selick; Aardman Animations' *Chicken Run* (2000), *Wallace and Gromit: The Curse of the Were-Rabbit* (2005) and *The Pirates! In an Adventure with Scientists* (2012); Tim Burton and Mike Johnson's *Corpse Bride* (2005); and Wes Anderson's *Fantastic Mr. Fox* (2009). I begin by drawing on trade journals, craft manuals and popular criticism to survey the ways puppet animators have integrated digital technology into their craft practices. I go on to consider these innovations in light of what I identify as an enduring 'handmade imperative' that circulates within stop-motion production cultures. That is, I examine the ways in which the craft of puppet animation is increasingly reliant on the logics of the digital (e.g. modularity, automation and variability),[1] even as practitioners and observers posit an antithetical relationship between stop motion and the digital (and especially between stop motion and computer animation). Next, I take a closer look at the range of approaches taken toward effects work in recent puppet animation features in order to show how these competing logics of the handmade and the digital play out in the texts themselves. Finally, I offer some conclusions on the contradictory practical and discursive roles of digital effects in puppet animation – and on the value of stop motion as a case study in contemporary cinematic 'workflow'.

Stop-motion Craft Practices

The aura of stop-motion animation is often figured in terms of intangibles. Film-makers and other commentators frequently ascribe to the medium qualities like warmth, magic and charm. Israeli animator Tatia Rosenthal attributes to stop motion a paradoxical quality, in that it features 'real' objects but virtual movement: 'stop motion creates an alternative world where realism and magical realism can live together cohesively'.[2] This paradox is sometimes described in terms of the uncanny, an inherent 'creepiness' deriving from the animation of physical, inanimate objects (this sense is one factor contributing to the medium's relative edginess).[3] But to understand more precisely the aura that stop motion has cultivated – the ethos of its practitioners and enthusiasts, the factors shaping its aesthetics and the tensions it faces in the digital age – we need to consider the tangibles of stop-motion craft practices, which have changed significantly over the past several decades.

Stop-motion puppet animators face numerous logistical and aesthetic challenges beyond the obvious problem of the time and labour required to make a stop-motion film. All of these obstacles are compounded by the demands of feature-length production. L. Bruce Holman identifies many of these challenges in his 1975 book *Puppet Animation in the Cinema: History and Technique*, one of the earliest histories of stop motion.[4] A major difference between the organisation of movement in puppet and traditional cel animation relates to the more linear workflow necessitated by the former medium. While cel animators typically begin by establishing key poses that occur at distinctive moments within a movement or series of movements, leaving 'breakdowns' and 'in-betweens' to be completed by assistants, puppet animators cannot similarly articulate a character's movements out of order and assemble a fluid, sequential whole later. Rather, they must map out the movements in advance and execute each increment consecutively. They have traditionally had little or no ability to check and revise their work as they progress; as Holman puts it, 'at the time of filming the puppet's previous movements exist only in the animator's memory and as an invisible latent image of the film'.[5] Puppet animators nonetheless commonly think in terms of 'key poses', especially when preparing test animation runs to check movement, lighting, decor and other elements before committing to full animation on ones or twos.[6]

The puppets themselves must be sufficiently strong, and their armatures' degrees of tolerance sufficiently calibrated, so that they will not sag or move unintentionally. Even the finest puppets typically do not survive more than a few scenes, requiring a fleet of identically constructed, painted and costumed replacement puppets. Because the stop-motion process requires absolute rigidity of sets, props and non-moving puppet parts, these elements must be sturdily built and securely fastened down (via screws, bolts, magnets, etc.). Puppets commonly need to be fastened and unfastened to the set every few frames, adding to the production time (and increasing the risk of unintentional disturbances). While some animators, like Jiří Trnka, use puppets with unchanging faces – largely eschewing dialogue and evoking emotion via other forms of movement – others have sought ways to enhance facial expressivity and produce plausible lip-synching via replacement heads and mouths, mouldable faces or other techniques.

Puppet animation also poses cinematographic challenges. Performing camera movement is arduous because it requires minute measurement and planning to generate incremental frame-by-frame movements that appear smooth and natural in projection. The small, cramped nature of most stop-motion sets, along with the need to give animators room to work, can preclude camera movement. Even when the camera is static, it is often necessary to build sets with trapdoors or removable walls, or to use periscopic/snorkel lenses, to allow animators the access they require. Maintaining constant light and exposure values is also difficult when shooting frame by frame. Light bulbs can vary significantly in intensity, whether on a moment-to-moment basis due to fluctuations in electrical currents or over longer periods due to natural changes in a bulb's filament over its lifespan.[7]

Over the past two decades, engineers and craftspeople have developed a number of innovations – most of them involving digital technology – to alleviate these problems and many others. Some are available only to top animation studios, while others can be obtained by independent animators and even amateurs. What follows is a survey of these innovations and their uses in recent stop-motion features. It draws largely on 'semi-public craft trades' like *American Cinematographer* and *Cinefex*, which are the best available sources for reliable information about the technologies and working methods utilised in recent stop-motion features.[8] But, as their coverage prominently features interviews with crew members, these journals are also valuable sources of what John Caldwell calls 'production talk' and 'lay theorizing' – reflexive and critical industrial discourses through which practitioners make sense of, and perform, their roles within the culture of media production.[9] The ways in which craftspeople frame and editorialise their explanations of the technologies and processes involved in stop-motion film-making are rhetorically rich; these instrumental narratives tacitly or overtly conceptualise and position the medium within the broader sphere of media production. The role of digital technologies – and particularly the potential tension between digital technologies and traditional stop-motion working methods – figures prominently in this discourse, which strives to uphold the status of stop motion as an essentially handmade medium.

Motion-control Devices

Most camera movement in stop-motion features is achieved via motion-control technology, which ensures that a camera adheres strictly to a pre-programmed incremental motion path. It thus allows a camera to make multiple passes along exactly the same trajectory. Though motion control was developed in the late 1960s for special-effects work in live-action films, it became clear that the technique could be used in stop motion to create fluid, natural camera movements; to generate multiple takes with identical movements for seamless compositing work; and to give animators greater access to sets by allowing the camera to be moved out of the way entirely, then moved back to its exact previous position (or to the next position in a programmed camera movement) for shooting of the next frame. Referring to the production of *The Nightmare before Christmas*, cinematographer Pete Kozachik quipped, 'When we get into a major flying camera move, it's really a lot more expeditious to let the robot do it. It's just not as likely to screw up.'[10] Motion control can also be enlisted to move other elements, including lights or large props, at regular intervals. A sizeable portion of *James and the Giant Peach* takes place at sea, and film-makers developed a custom motion-control rig to calibrate the bobbing of the peach (at twenty feet in diameter and 2,000 pounds, an unusually large prop for a stop-motion film) on the water. To coordinate with the Sony technicians who did the film's digital compositing, the *Peach* camera team sent discs of motion-control data files that the computer's virtual camera could then match.[11] The team behind *Coraline* used motion-control rigs to coordinate group movement in a scene featuring 450 identical terrier dogs.[12]

Lighting and Other Image Controls

Numerous innovations have helped stop-motion animators regulate lighting effects within a shot or scene as well as across an entire film. This level of control is especially important for features, which typically involve dozens of units working simultaneously, some on sets representing different parts of the same diegetic space. Special electrical generator-regulators that supply consistent power to a set (or to an entire studio) are commonly used in conjunction with a computerised master light board that allows centralised manipulation of any lighting element on the production. These systems also allow the immediate and precise recreation of a previous setup.[13] Toby Farrar, a gaffer for *Fantastic Mr. Fox*, described the film's lighting setup as follows:

> Sometimes we would automate the lighting so that if they needed a fixture to gradually brighten over 20 or 30 frames, they could set it to increase by 4 percent every time a frame was taken. The other way is to use an old-school Variac dimmer, mark out the positions and let the animator get on with it. Each of the three stages had a centralised dimmer rack, which was networked over an Ethernet to a simple DMX converter board at every unit. It was a very clever system built to our specifications.[14]

Lighting systems can be linked with motion-control systems as well as the camera motor. Stop-motion productions tend to organise and execute this highly complex, networked automation in a manner that interferes minimally with animators' ability to perform their work as they have traditionally. A technical director at Aardman claimed that

> animators often prefer things to be a bit less automated. This is particularly important because the motion-control, lighting setups and everything else are done before the animator moves on set, where he's left in isolation and takes charge of the pre-set camera moves.[15]

Stop-motion features were early adopters of the Digital Intermediate (DI) process, which involves creating a full digital scan of a film so that the image, and especially colour, may be manipulated within the computer. As storage capacity increased and scanners and image-manipulation software improved throughout the 1990s, the use of DI technology on a piece-meal basis (i.e. for individual shots or scenes) grew steadily. In 2000, *Chicken Run* became one of the first two films to employ a full digital intermediate.[16] The process is now standard for works shot on film as well as digitally (though the scanning process is more straightforward for the latter).[17] *Corpse Bride* and *Fantastic Mr. Fox*, both shot digitally, used the digital intermediate process to achieve distinctive looks beyond what set design, lighting and filters could imbue. *Corpse Bride* employs a markedly desaturated and limited colour palette for sequences that take place in the 'Land of the Living', while the 'Land of the Dead' is brighter and more garish.[18] The latter is cast throughout with a warm and slightly dark autumnal glow that accentuates the ambers, reds, browns and yellows that dominate the *mise en scène*.

CGI Work

Closely related to Digital Intermediate work is CGI, which has been employed in stop-motion puppet features to a variety of ends. Among the first – and still one of the most popular – uses for CGI in this context is the digital erasure of rigging systems that help support puppets in challenging poses. This process requires frame-by-frame scanning of the footage and removal of the rigging; *Nightmare* required wire removal, cleanup and other effects on about 100 shots.[19] Selick's next stop-motion feature, *James and the Giant Peach*, required such fixes on over 350 such shots.[20] David Lawson, head of puppet rigging on *Coraline*, reported,

> Ninety percent of our puppets needed to be rigged. We really went for it on the character designs: we had huge-breasted women with tiny ankles, we had Bobinsky with his huge belly and the longest, thinnest legs you could imagine.[21]

The Bobinsky puppet for *Coraline* (2009)

Digital bunnies for *Wallace and Gromit: The Curse of the Were-Rabbit* (2005)

Also relevant in this regard is the role of computer-aided drafting (CAD). Now commonly used in the design and machining of puppet armatures, CAD has facilitated the development of extremely stylised puppet forms.

CGI can also be engaged in conjunction with chroma key compositing to add to stop-motion footage expansive backgrounds that are hard to achieve on miniature sets – in particular, elements like sky and detailed landscapes. It is also used for effects that are simply not well suited to puppet animation. The crew of *Wallace and Gromit* turned to CGI to create the Bun-Vac 6000, a suction device employed by the title characters to capture bunnies from their clients' lawns; the creatures float and spin inside the Bun-Vac's clear chamber. According to Aardman founder Steve Box, the crew attempted to develop a traditional solution: 'We had these twelve rabbits on sticks, but we couldn't achieve that smoothness of rotation which is the perfect thing for CGI.' Aardman animators had tested the mimicking of Plasticine objects via CGI on an earlier project and judged that 'you couldn't tell the difference'.[22] Although many film-makers prefer to find traditional, low-tech solutions to the perennial challenge of animating effects like smoke, fog, fire and moving water via stop motion, others have eagerly adopted CGI to create more sophisticated and realistic effects, as I will later discuss.

Replacement Facial Parts

The desire to create expressive and physiognomically convincing puppets for recent stop-motion features (all of which, unlike much Eastern European and avant-garde puppet animation, are dialogue-centred and thus reliant on precise rendering of mouths and other facial features) has spurred a variety of innovations. Productions typically rely on a mixture of replacement heads, faces and facial parts as well as the increasingly sophisticated machining of puppet heads. The makers of *Nightmare* created a digital database of major characters' replacement heads and expressions so that the proper lip-synch could be worked out precisely before shooting. A video frame-grabber system ensured 'exact casting replications' during the production of clay replacement heads.[23] For *Coraline*, 3D computer modelling was used in conjunction with rapid prototype machines and stereolithographic printers to generate major characters' replacement faces. That is, after being designed digitally, 3D replacement parts were printed in resin, which 'circumvented hundreds of man-hours of sculpting replacement faces in clay'.[24] Because the major characters' faces comprised top and bottom halves that could be magnetically mixed and matched (with literally hundreds of thousands of possible expressive combinations for the character of Coraline), a seam laterally bisected these faces. Most of the film's shots therefore required digital erasure to remove this bifurcation and produce smooth faces.

Video Taps and Instant Replay

For decades, stop-motion animators faced what Holman describes as a kind of 'Zeno's Paradox':

> The animated puppet ... can only be seen in the position which he is occupying at any given moment. The puppet animator may refer to notes, script or storyboard to keep track of a puppet's actions, but at the time of filming the puppet's previous actions exist only in an animator's memory and as an invisible latent image in the film.[25]

Thanks to digital technology, this dilemma no longer obtains for most professional as well as amateur animators – unless they choose to retain the constraint. During filming of *Nightmare*, animators had access to a video tap that allowed them to compare a frame they were working on with the one shot previously. Although the setup was far from foolproof, some animators abandoned their surface gauges entirely in favour of the video assist. The film-makers also noted that the video tap was more helpful in detecting frame-to-frame changes in lighting than their light meters.[26] Since *The Nightmare before Christmas*, this technology has evolved into a full-scale computerised instant-replay system, through which animators can view the entire sequence of frames for the shot they are working on – or any other shot from any of the production units. Combined with the switch to digital photography discussed below, this new paradigm gives the animator more to rely on than simply creative intuition. In so doing, it can radically transform the work process, threatening to collapse some of the basic distinctions between stop motion and other forms of animation. According to Kozachik,

> all that reviewing access comes with a catch: it is seductive and easily abused in an endless shoot-view-tweak loop, quite similar to the tweak cycle many CG animators decry. To make the best use of digital photography, we had to consciously practice the self-discipline that is naturally imposed by shooting film. I found that the most productive crews continued to use skills from their film backgrounds, trusting their light meters and contrast glasses and visualizing how a shot would cut in ... the quickest turnaround in frame finding, move programming and set dressing was a result of using the viewfinder or video tap, saving digital stills for less frequent checks.[27]

The CG 'tweak cycle' refers to computer animators' practice of executing and previewing a movement or other task(s) – then undoing and reattempting the original action(s) and repeating the cycle until satisfied with the result. Of all the digital innovations surveyed here, it is this approach that is perhaps most profoundly at odds with the traditional logics of stop motion.

Digital Still Photography

Feature-length stop-motion animation has transitioned from 35mm film photography to digital still photography. All of the stop-motion features since *Corpse Bride* were shot with digital still single-lens-reflex (DSLR) cameras. The *Corpse Bride* production went digital relatively late in pre-production, when director of photography Kozachik purchased thirty-one consumer-grade Canon DSLRs and gathered a team of data wranglers to manage the files generated.[28] The *Coraline* production used forty-six cameras, thirty-eight of which were high-end, state-of-the-art Machine Vision devices.[29] Film-makers cite a number of advantages to this method, including the lower cost of still cameras, the cameras' manoeuvrability and small size, the ease of creating video taps and instant-replay feeds and the elimination of costly and time-consuming film processing and scanning prior to manipulation in the digital intermediate phase. For *The Pirates! In an Adventure with Scientists*, which relied heavily on CGI for backgrounds and water effects, Aardman Animations retired its storied fleet of thirty-five custom-fitted Mitchell cameras (most of them dating to the 1930s) in favour of Canon EOS-1Ds.[30] (Director Peter Lord attested, 'the digital pipeline has been liberating for me'.)[31]

The switch to digital photography and the accompanying development of an immediately available bank of (virtual) footage, uploaded to a dedicated Ethernet, has also enabled remote micromanagement of stop-motion productions. In a widely publicised example, Wes Anderson performed most of his directorial duties on the London shoot of *Fantastic Mr. Fox* from his Paris apartment, where he could use the Internet to access any material from the shoot, from any production or post-production unit. Anderson exchanged over 65,000 emails with crew members.[32] This approach to coordinating the production dovetailed smoothly with Anderson's auteur persona. In a promotional featurette, producer Jeremy Dawson deemed the project 'perfect for someone like Wes, who loves to direct every detail ... animation, in some sense, is a natural extension of that kind of work, because he really can plan almost every detail'.[33] But the distinctive appeal and discursive ethos of stop motion goes beyond this opportunity for from-scratch world-building. More specifically, the idea that it is a handmade medium dominates the discursive construction of stop-motion animation.

The Handmade Imperative

Despite the extensive integration of CGI and other digital technologies into contemporary stop-motion animation, film-makers, critics and other commentators typically figure stop motion as an old-fashioned and hands-on medium – opposed and superior to the digital. Central to the handmade ethos are the tactile interactions of craftspeople with tangible materials, the most privileged instance of which is the animator's manipulation of the array of physical objects within an actual profilmic space (in contrast to the virtual profilmic space of CGI). In this discourse, the labour involved in computer animation is characterised as artless, depersonalised, boring and even deskilled, in contrast to the 'painstakingly precise artistry' of stop motion.[34] Henry Selick suggested that stop motion 'is a lot more challenging than sitting at a computer all day'.[35] *Coraline*'s effects supervisor Brian Van't Hul recalled how the film's in-house compositing team 'could go downstairs and be right there where the movie was being made' if they 'became frustrated working in a bunch of *Dilbert*-like offices'.[36] Similarly, another crew member, Brian McLean, insisted that he 'always needed something to hold onto. I felt CG was a little sterile and I didn't like being in front of the computer screen.'[37] Stop motion's minority status within commercial, theatrical animation gives it an instant distinctiveness. Ramin Zahed declared *Fantastic Mr. Fox* 'nothing like the crop of CG-animated features that arrive with regular predictability in theatres these days', while to Marian Quigley, Aardman 'avoids the smooth perfection of those made by Disney and DreamWorks'.[38] By this logic, some irregularities and artefacts of the hands-on production process are not mistakes to be rejected or hidden but virtues central to the medium's appeal.

The handmade imperative is evident in technical trade discourse, which readily acknowledges the increasing role of digital technologies in stop motion. But it is even more prominent in explicitly promotional discourses such as official making-of featurettes, distributed online and/or on home video releases. Some of the motifs of stop-motion making-ofs are similar to those of computer animation and other effects-heavy films (making 'magic', being transported to another world, etc.). But stop-motion promos heavily emphasise the films' 'handmade' status and rarely if ever highlight the role of digital effects.[39] In a *Coraline* promo titled 'The Biggest Smallest Movie Ever Made', one sequence begins by showing various arrays of puppet hands, with superimposed text reading 'Thousands of hands'. Soon after, we see one of the puppet hands resting in a human's palm, with text reading 'made by hand'.[40] Two other *Coraline* featurettes highlight the 'quirky' jobs of two craftswomen, one who knitted tiny puppet clothing and another who built custom puppet wigs; both shorts prominently feature close shots of the women's hands.[41] These promos are available on the film's official website, which greets visitors with a screen reading 'You're about to enter a world where everything you see is made by hand.'[42] The promotional campaign for the 2014 stop-motion feature *The Boxtrolls*, directed by Graham Annable and Anthony Stacchi, also produced by the studio Laika, adopts similar rhetoric. One of the film's main trailers begins with a one-minute montage of behind-the-scenes footage – mostly close-ups of crew members working with their hands – accompanied by a simple arrangement of 'They've Got the Whole World in Their Hands' (a slight variation on the traditional spiritual). The sequence ends with title cards reading, 'From the hands that made *Coraline* and *Paranorman* …'. Making-ofs, which are designed to be accessible to general audiences and typically avoid heavy technical detail, can serve a number of critical-rhetorical functions beyond simple advertisement – in this case, distinguishing (and celebrating) stop motion for its tangible, hands-on approach.[43]

Discourses of stop-motion animation also hold that it is a more 'immersive' and emotional medium than either CG or cel animation due to its origins in physical reality – that is, its indexicality. Merlin Crossingham, an Aardman director, claims that stop motion sparks 'an instant connection with people … even if they are not necessarily consciously thinking about it … because the characters really do exist in the world and have been photographed'.[44] This vaguely Bazinian line of reasoning is echoed in a 2006 piece in *Adweek* about the increasing use of stop motion in commercials. The author states (as a trade fact),

> stop motion also has a cinematic and nostalgic look to it, which often packs more of an emotional wallop than the use of computer-generated imagery. The viewer can more readily immerse himself into a world where the characters seem to be more real and feel like they've been touched by the film-makers.[45]

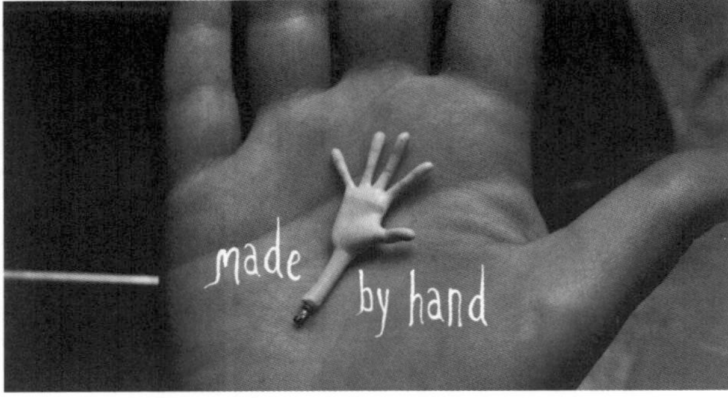

A promotional trailer for *Coraline*

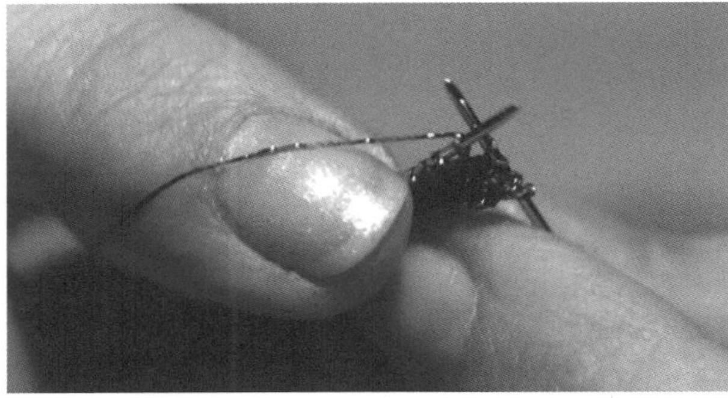

Behind-the-scenes features promoting *Coraline*

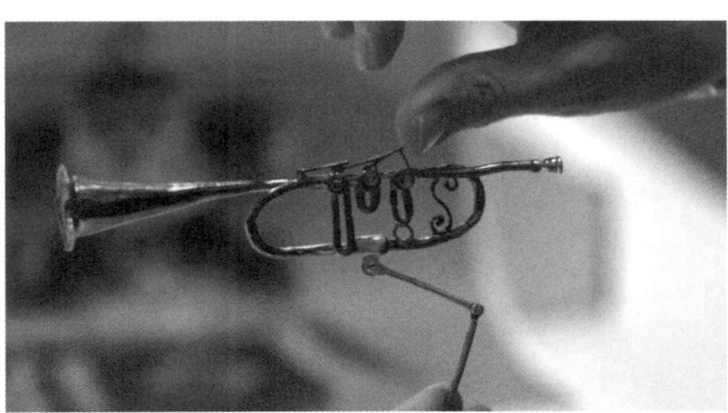

Promotional trailer for *The Boxtrolls* (2014)

The distinctiveness of stop motion, however, is most commonly figured in terms of its 'human' qualities. Eric Anderson, brother of Wes and a voice actor in *Fantastic Mr. Fox*, describes the medium's appeal in this manner:

> There's a little personality in there that's just, maybe it's a little warmer than something that is made by a computer ... like, if it's the [P]lasticine stop motion, you'll see a thumb print on one of the characters. I'm not saying that's why you like a thing, but that might be part of the life of the thing that's so handmade, and we are currently in a drought of handmade-feeling things.[46]

The handmade imperative functions not just to distinguish stop motion from other forms of animation – to carve out its niche – but also to situate it oppositionally. Similar reactions against the rise of digital media and the presumed dematerialisation of culture can be found among contemporary advocates of vinyl records. Though not handmade, these objects are valued for their nostalgic appeal, their physicality/tangibility and their purportedly 'warmer', richer sound than that of digital formats like CDs or mp3s. Stop motion thus occupies a curious position within cinema's ongoing digital transitions in image capture, post-production and distribution/exhibition. On the one hand, the medium is being transformed by these developments. On the other, it is widely championed as a bastion of the 'aura, magic, and humanity' that are ostensibly being lost with the decline of 35mm film stock.[47]

Though the notion of the 'handmade' dominates the public narrative of stop-motion animation, there is already a perception among some practitioners that the medium is at risk of over-relying on digital technology. This perception holds, for one, that the digital threatens certain essential craft practices, as suggested by Kozachik's cautionary account of the impacts of video assist and digital photography. Another risk is an undesirably 'slick' look that undermines the handmade qualities of stop motion. According to Australian animator Adam Elliot, director of *Mary and Max* (2009), 'it's kind of counterproductive because their films end up looking like CGI movies'.[48] A *Coraline* artist revealed that there was disagreement among the crew over digital removal of the puppets' bilateral facial seams (artefacts of the complex replacement-part system). He reported that 'the hardcore stop motion animators wanted to keep the crack to preserve the handcrafted feel'.[49]

Test Cases: Approaches to Effects Work

Digital technologies offer myriad new opportunities for the integration of environmental effects like water, smoke and fire, which have been notoriously difficult to achieve via stop motion. Film-makers have taken advantage of these technologies in different ways, but most profess to have established a 'best practice' of pursuing traditional methods whenever possible. In many cases, they strive to generate effects by shooting 'real', i.e. physical, live-action elements, even if these elements require extensive digital compositing to be rendered as part of the finished film. The films thus try to different degrees to efface their digital manipulations, in some cases showcasing an overtly traditionalist or retrograde aesthetic. These strategies seem to bespeak stop-motion animators' wariness of the 'slippery slopes' to which Kozachik and Selick allude in their testimonies above, as well as the premium placed on asserting – extratextually as well as textually – their commitment to, and the distinctiveness and integrity of, stop-motion animation.

What follows are a few examples of the range of options now available for stop-motion effects work, which demonstrate these strategies for navigating the integration of the digital in terms of craft practices as well as filmic discourse.

As mentioned earlier, *James and the Giant Peach* required extensive CGI work for the scenes at sea – in particular, the 'shark attack' that prompts the heroes to yoke their peach to a passing flock of seagulls. Due to the logistical problems of integrating a rapidly moving shark puppet with the (also rapidly moving) computer-generated water, film-makers elected to do the entire shark apparatus as CGI. However, they attempted to give these effects a stop-motion quality. According to visual-effects supervisor Scott Anderson,

> Animation-wise, we didn't want this to come off as a computer graphics sequence in a stop motion film. We wanted it to be another stop motion sequence that just happened to be done on the computer ... we really wanted to capture the nature of stop motion. The water had to have a hand-constructed and animated feel.[50]

The 'shark' is a highly stylised brown metallic creature, with visible bolts and a body that expands and collapses in sections, accompanied by loud metallic creaks and groans. By hard-wiring into the creature a jerky, mechanical form, the film-makers ensure that, despite its glossy and distinctly computerised surface features, the computer animation will render a type of movement broadly compatible with the stop-motion enterprise. If anything, it is excessively so; there is nothing else so overtly mechanical in the rest of the film, and the sequence retains an odd quality, perhaps due to its combination of competing animation styles and production strategies. One shot, for example, shows the shark, framed diegetically in an eyepiece held by James; of particular note is the contrast of the waxy, lo-fi look of the hand at the edge of the frame and the CGI shark with which it is composited.

The mixture of digital and 'traditional' effects can be seen explicitly in a scene from *Coraline* in which the heroine, having just arrived in a parallel world, eats a magical dinner with her parents' doppelgängers. The sequence begins with shots of the elaborate spread on the dinner table, including several lit candles and pale wisps of steam rising from dishes of food on two Lazy Susans. Other Mother rings a bell to summon the gravy train – a miniature steam locomotive, carrying a gravy boat, that winds its way around the table to Coraline's place setting. The flames, along with the steam over the food, were live-action elements shot with a motion-picture camera at 100 frames per second, while the puffs of smoke from the locomotive were created digitally using Side Effects (a standard 3D animation software suite). These elements were digitally matched and composited with the stereoscopic stop-motion footage, with additional effects applied to render the live-action footage in stereo. The resulting composite is apparently seamless.[51] However, when the train stops, an old-fashioned accordion-style

CGI shark in *James and the Giant Peach* (1996)

A combination of stop motion and digitally animated elements in *Coraline*

metal contraption raises the gravy boat and pours gravy onto the mashed potatoes on Coraline's plate. The glistening gravy has a distinctively irregular and sculpted quality; even when viewed at regular speed, one can see minor variations in its shape, colour, texture and gloss from moment to moment. These overt imperfections clearly mark the substance as 'real' stop-motion gravy that has been moulded frame by frame, sometimes appearing in the same shot with digitally generated and composited elements such as puffs of smoke from the train.

Fantastic Mr. Fox is perhaps most resolute in its commitment to the overt traditionalism of the handmade imperative. Wes Anderson's films are highly recognisable in part due to their decorative intricacy and rich texturing – e.g. the meticulous selection and patterning on signage and letterheads. He suggested that stop-motion animation appealed to him in part because 'you have the chance to invent every detail of this world' (and indeed, *Fox* involved the construction of over 4,000 props). Cinephilic motivations were also salient. Anderson has often professed his admiration for early-to-mid-twentieth-century puppet animators such as Ladislaw Starewich and Willis O'Brien, whose works frequently betray the processes behind them (e.g. the 'boiling' of fur, or minor shifts in the positioning of fabrics from frame to frame):

> the whole magical aspect of stop motion was one of those things where you can see the trick – I mean, you know the Cocteau movies? The visual effects in *Beauty and the Beast*, for instance, are things where you can really see that a person is behind this wall sticking their arm through it, holding a torch, and the film is running backwards, and so that is how this light is coming on, or the mirror is actually water. You know, those kinds of effects, where you can see what it is, have always been the most fascinating and mesmerizing and moving to me.[52]

To achieve this aesthetic, which 'favours tactility over realism', Anderson eschewed the compositing of live-action effects (as seen in *Coraline*), instead favouring effects created via stop motion.[53]

This approach can be seen most clearly in the film's 'fire-bombing' sequence, in which Mr. Fox and his animal allies in the sewer do battle with villains Boggis, Bunce and Bean (and other humans) above ground. They throw into the street fiery pine cones, whose flames were animated not via CGI or composited live-action flames, but with pieces of translucent orange soap that were backlit and carved frame by frame. The pine cones ignite many additional fires on the street, producing great plumes of smoke that were created by stretching and shaping tufts of dyed cotton and wool.[54] The resulting movement is, like the gravy in *Coraline*, not smooth and seamless but distinctly irregular and jerky. Elsewhere in the film (for example, when Mr. Fox's son Ash dives into a kiddie pool), water effects were achieved with plastic wrap for a similar aesthetic. Not only did the animators embrace the boiling of fur that typically accompanies creature animation, they reportedly blew on the puppets as the camera captured the frames

Stop-motion animation of fire and smoke in *Fantastic Mr. Fox* (2009)

'just to keep it alive'.[55] This rejection of a 'smooth' look, and the overt display of traditional, low-tech methods (in a production that, like all stop-motion features, was nonetheless heavily reliant on digital technologies) is one expression of a broader cultural ambivalence toward the digital.

Conclusions

The dramatic changes in stop-motion craft practices are part of a broader reorganisation of analogue cinematic workflows. In addition to making us ask 'what, now, is cinema?', the digital transition has muddied traditional distinctions between concepts like 'shooting' and 'editing', 'production' and 'post-production'.[56] Stop-motion film-makers have grappled with the logics of the digital in a variety of ways. These logics open the door to radically different craft practices – practices that both make feasible large-scale, highly sophisticated stop-motion productions and threaten to collapse many of the ontological tenets and practical constraints that have long shaped puppet animation as a distinct artistic form. Stop-motion film-makers (from directors to photographers to scores of below-the-line craftspeople) have thus sought a balance between innovation and tradition. They value, and strive to make visible, certain traces of the earlier medium – particularly the 'handmade' and sculptural qualities that are connected to materiality and indexicality – while repressing other, undesirable, artefacts of these processes, typically through the use of digital effects. Yet they also seek to efface or limit the incursion of the digital in order to uphold the computerised/handmade binary that is central to both their professional identities and the medium's cultural cachet.

Notes

1. Lev Manovich, *The Language of New Media* (Cambridge, MA: MIT Press, 2001), pp. 27–48.
2. Rodney Appelyard, 'The Revival of Stop Motion', *Inside Film*, September 2009, p. 41.
3. See, for example, Joe Fordham, 'A Handmade World', *Cinefex* no. 117 (April 2009), p. 51.
4. L. Bruce Holman, *Puppet Animation in the Cinema: History and Technique* (South Brunswick, NJ: A. S. Barnes, 1975).
5. Ibid., p. 51.
6. Animating on 'ones' involves articulating a new movement for each frame, while animating on 'twos' involves shooting each drawing/pose for two frames. See Ken A. Priebe, *The Art of Stop Motion Animation* (Boston, MA: Thomson Course Technology, 2007), pp. 187–90; Ron Magid, '*James and the Giant Peach* Grows on the Big Screen', *American Cinematographer* vol. 77 no. 5 (May 1996), pp. 54–64.
7. Holman, *Puppet Animation in the Cinema*, pp. 64–9.
8. John Caldwell, *Production Culture: Industrial Reflexivity and Critical Practice in Film and Television* (Durham, NC: Duke University Press, 2008), p. 284.
9. Ibid., pp. 14–18.
10. Frank T. Thompson, *The Nightmare before Christmas: The Film, the Art, the Vision* (New York: Hyperion, 1993), p. 149.
11. Mark Cotta Vaz, 'A Giant Peach in the Big Apple', *Cinefex* no. 66 (June 1996), pp. 90–109.
12. Fordham, 'A Handmade World', p. 58.
13. Magid, '*James and the Giant Peach* Grows on the Big Screen', pp. 55–6; Pete Kozachik, 'Stop Motion without Compromise: *The Nightmare before Christmas*', *American Cinematographer* vol. 74 no. 12 (December 1993), p. 40.
14. Mark Hope-Jones, 'An Exceptionally Sly Fox', *American Cinematographer* vol. 90 no. 12 (December 2009), p. 78.
15. John Gainsborough, 'Flying the Coop', *American Cinematographer* vol. 81 no. 8 (August 2000), p. 59.
16. Rachael K. Bosley, 'A Model Thriller: Directors of Photography Tristan Oliver and Dave Alex Riddett Crack the Stop Motion Mystery', *American Cinematographer* vol. 86 no. 10 (October 2005), p. 34.
17. Stephen Prince, *Digital Visual Effects in Cinema: The Seduction of Reality* (New Brunswick, NJ: Rutgers University Press, 2012), pp. 70–80; John Belton, 'Painting by the Numbers: The Digital Intermediate', *Film Quarterly* vol. 61 no. 3 (Spring 2008), p. 58.
18. Mark Salisbury, *Tim Burton's* Corpse Bride: *An Invitation to the Wedding* (New York: Newmarket, 2005) pp. 68–71.

19. Mark Cotta Vaz, 'Animation in the Third Dimension', *Cinefex* no. 66 (June 1996), p. 53.
20. Vaz, 'A Giant Peach in the Big Apple', p. 93.
21. Fordham, 'A Handmade World', p. 50.
22. Andy Lane, *The Art of Wallace and Gromit: The Curse of the Were-Rabbit* (London: Titan, 2005), pp. 118–21.
23. Vaz, 'Animation in the Third Dimension', p. 40; Thompson, *The Nightmare before Christmas*, pp. 158–60.
24. Vaz, 'Animation in the Third Dimension', p. 45.
25. Holman, *Puppet Animation in the Cinema*, pp. 50–1.
26. Vaz, 'Animation in the Third Dimension', pp. 44–8. The history of video assist is discussed in Jean-Pierre Geuens, 'Through the Looking Glasses: From the Camera Obscura to the Video Assist', *Film Quarterly* vol. 49 no. 3 (Spring 1996), pp. 16–26.
27. Pete Kozachik, 'Renanimated Romance', *American Cinematographer* vol. 86 no. 10 (October 2005), p. 55.
28. Ibid., p. 52.
29. Pete Kozachik, '2 Worlds in 3 Dimensions', *American Cinematographer* vol. 90 no. 2 (February 2009), pp. 26–39.
30. John Gainsborough, 'Aardman Animations: A Perpetual Stop Motion Machine', *American Cinematographer* vol. 77 no. 3 (March 1996), p. 82; James Silver, 'How Aardman Is Embracing the Digital Age', *Wired*, 2 November 2010, http://wired.co.uk/magazine/archive/2010/12/features/aardman-morphs.
31. Bill Desowitz, 'Immersed in Movies: Aardman's Peter Lord Talks "Pirates"', *Indiewire*, 26 April 2012, http://blogs.indiewire.com/thompsononhollywood/immersed-in-movies-aardmans-peter-lord-talks-pirates.
32 Hope-Jones, 'An Exceptionally Sly Fox', p. 72; Richard Brody, 'Wild, Wild Wes', *New Yorker*, 2 November 2009, pp. 48–58; Michael Specter *et al.*, *The Making of* Fantastic Mr. Fox (New York: Rizzoli, 2009), p. 104.
33. 'Still Life (Puppet Animation)', *Fantastic Mr. Fox*, DVD (Twentieth Century-Fox, 2010).
34. Vaz, 'A Giant Peach in the Big Apple', p. 100. Of course, other discourses position the digital differently – as hyperrealistic, nonrealistic, uncanny, etc. See Prince, *Digital Visual Effects in Cinema*, for more on discourses surrounding digital effects.
35. Andy Rose, 'Stop in the Name of Animation', *Moviemaker*, n.d.
36. Fordham, 'A Handmade World', p. 50.
37. Renee Dunlop, 'One Step at a Time for the Puppet of a Thousand Faces', *CGSociety*, 12 February 2009, http://www.cgsociety.org/index.php/CGSFeatures/CGSFeatureSpecial/coraline.
38. Ramin Zahed, 'The Fantastic Retro *Fox* Rewrites the Rules', *Animation Magazine*, November 2009, p. 20; Marian Quigley, 'Poultry in Stop-motion: the Challenge of Technology in *Chicken Run*', *Australian Screen Education*, Summer 2008, p. 117.
39. These promos do not fully efface the digital; they leave it largely unaddressed. For example, in the DVD bonus feature 'Behind the Scenes of *The Curse of the Were-Rabbit*', computers and video-assist monitors can frequently be seen but are not discussed by interviewees or the narrator. Acknowledgment of digital-effects work in stop-motion features appears more often in a different form of promotional discourse: video portfolios created by effects artists themselves to showcase

their work. Two such videos are 'Now You See It, Now You Don't', which shows Jerry Svoboda's rig removal work on *Coraline*, and 'Coraline – Visual Effects Reel', on compositor Adam C. Sager. See http://www.steamcontroller.com/coraline_effects_rigging.html and http://www.dailymotion.com/video/x90f32_coraline-visual-effects-reel_shortfilms, respectively.

40. '*Coraline* – The Biggest Smallest Movie Ever Made', Focus Features/Laika, 2009, https://www.youtube.com/watch?v=cayVMHSRHZI&feature=plcp.
41. '*Coraline* – Knitting Itty Bitty Outfits', Focus Features/Laika, 2009, https://www.youtube.com/watch?v=K5VTE9MZzlw&feature=plcp; '"Coraline"– Really Small Hair', Focus Features/Laika, 2009, https://www.youtube.com/watch?v=FCDOs5DxJPY&feature=plcp.
42. See www.coraline.com.
43. Caldwell presents an informal 'Taxonomy of DVD Bonus Track Strategies and Functions' in Appendix 2 (pp. 362–7) of *Production Culture*.
44. Appelyard, 'The Revival of Stop Motion', p. 42.
45. Teresa Piti, 'Stop Motion Gains Speed', *Adweek*, 27 March 2006, pp. 22–3. Tim Burton describes his own nostalgic affections for the medium in Salisbury's *Tim Burton's* Corpse Bride, p. 13.
46. Specter *et al.*, *The Making of* Fantastic Mr. Fox, p. 87.
47. Gerald Sim, 'When and Where Is the Digital Revolution in Cinematography?', *Projections*, Summer 2012, pp. 87–8.
48. Appelyard, 'The Revival of Stop Motion', pp. 39–40. Some animators, including Tatia Rosenthal, are more sanguine, citing digital technologies' capacity to aid independent/small-scale film-makers.
49. Fordham, 'A Handmade World', p. 50.
50. Vaz, 'A Giant Peach in the Big Apple', pp. 102–5.
51. Fordham, 'A Handmade World', pp. 50, 54–5.
52. Specter *et al.*, *The Making of* Fantastic Mr. Fox, p. 31.
53. Hope-Jones, 'An Exceptionally Sly Fox', p. 78.
54. Zahed, 'The Fantastic Retro *Fox* Rewrites the Rules', p. 21.
55. 'Still Life (Puppet Animation)'.
56. Ignatiy Vishnevetsky, 'What Is the 21st Century?: Revising the Dictionary', *Mubi.com*, 1 February 2013, http://mubi.com/notebook/posts/what-is-the-21st-century-revising-the-dictionary.

MAGIC MIRRORS
THE SCHÜFFTAN PROCESS

KATHARINA LOEW

In the history of special effects, the 1920s represent a key transitional period. The decade saw a steady proliferation of cinematic illusions in both the United States and in Europe. Simultaneously, the dominant function of 'tricks', as special effects were known throughout the silent era, changed as well. In early cinema and into the 1920s the vast majority of tricks depicted supernatural events or impossible physical feats. During the 1920s, however, cinematic illusions were increasingly employed for practical (usually financial) reasons. Pricey location shoots or extravagant sets were now inexpensively faked in the studio. By the time sound was introduced, the main purpose of trick technology had become the discreet imitation of physical reality.

Paramount to this functional change was the standardisation of trick techniques. In early cinema, film-makers devised tailormade solutions for trick shots that were expectedly far more troublesome and expensive than conventional scenes.[1] During the 1910s, producers of slapstick comedies and sensational melodramas in the US made important advances in trick technology, frequently to facilitate stunts. Respectable film-makers with artistic aspirations, however, often dismissed such devices as inauthentic and deceitful. Special-effects pioneer Norman O. Dawn, for example, failed to convince D. W. Griffith to let him create glass paintings for *Intolerance: Love's Struggle throughout the Ages* (1916). According to Dawn, 'Bitzer [Griffith's cinematographer] said he didn't want any of that fakey stuff.'[2] And so, Babylon was built full-scale. Since the late 1910s, however, versatile compositing procedures such as glass paintings, foreground miniatures and matte paintings became popular with film-makers and producers. Effective and economical, they began to be utilised routinely to imitate physical reality. In 1926, cinematographer and special-effects expert Carl Louis Gregory recalled how special effects took root in the American film industry:

> For a long time [trick photography] was the step-child of the legitimate producers. The comedy producers, however, have always regarded it as one of their strongest allies. It is, in fact, mainly due to the patient research of serious workers on the slapstick lots that the credit for the present perfection of trick effects is largely due [sic]. Farsighted producers have awakened to the money savings that may be effected by the use of trick photography and now all the larger companies retain the services of high salaried experts who are specialists in the business of artistic photographic trickery.[3]

In European film-making, standardised, inconspicuous and economical special effects started gaining traction in the mid-1920s. This novel approach was epitomised in the much-publicised commercial launching of the Schüfftan process in Germany in 1925–6 and in Britain in 1927. In contrast to previous practices, the Schüfftan process was not conceived to solve one specific problem. Applicable in a variety of contexts, it embodied the burgeoning European trend towards utilising special effects for practical purposes. The Schüfftan process economises space and time on location and requires little equipment. Only small portions of the set have to be built in full size since all purely scenic décor can be provided by reflected images. Although the arrangement of live-action and complementary sets demands considerable talent, the final composite can be monitored directly and does not rely on costly and time-consuming laboratory work. Although many contemporaries perceived the technique as an emblem of modernisation, 'Schüfftan's magic mirrors'[4] were still very much grounded in nineteenth-century traditions of handicraft and optical illusions. Inventor Eugen Schüfftan's main motivation in creating a universal, cost-efficient special-effects technique was to facilitate previously unattainable representations of the unreal and impossible; in his own words, he sought to 'visualise the imagination'.[5] Yet the potential of Schüfftan's invention to depict the fantastic was seldom realised: the most widely employed method for rendering synthetic images in European film-making from the 1920s to the 40s was predominantly used for set extensions. The fate of the Schüfftan process highlights how, in the 1920s, the standardisation of special effects changed their principal function. Compared to the total film output, 'fantastic effects' receded while 'invisible' uses prevailed. In time the Schüfftan process was marginalised in favour of high-tech processes such as rear-projection or travelling mattes. Nonetheless, due to its capacity to generate striking effects on a shoestring budget, it continued to play a role in film-making. Eventually, it became a nostalgic icon for a time in film history when film-makers were simultaneously craftsmen, artists and magicians.

How the Schüfftan Process Works

The basic principles of the Schüfftan process are simple. A model is set up to one side of the camera while a live-action scene is staged straight ahead of it. A front-silvered mirror is placed at a forty-five-degree angle directly in front of the camera and parts of the mirror's reflective surface are removed.[6] The model is reflected in the mirror's remaining silvered portions and replaces parts of the live-action scene. The mirror is positioned quite close to the camera's short focal (wide-angle) lens, which is focused on infinity. As a result, the reflection of the model is in focus, whereas the mirror's surface itself is blurred. Optically, the two scenes merge and are recorded simultaneously.

The Schüfftan process facilitates the combination of live-action scenes with a variety of visual components, both still and in motion, including photographs, models and projected images. The transition between the Moloch miniature and the full-size stairs in *Metropolis* (1927) is remarkably difficult to spot. This is a result of Schüfftan's broad jagged zones where the reflective surface gradually peters out.

The Moloch-scene in *Metropolis* (1927)

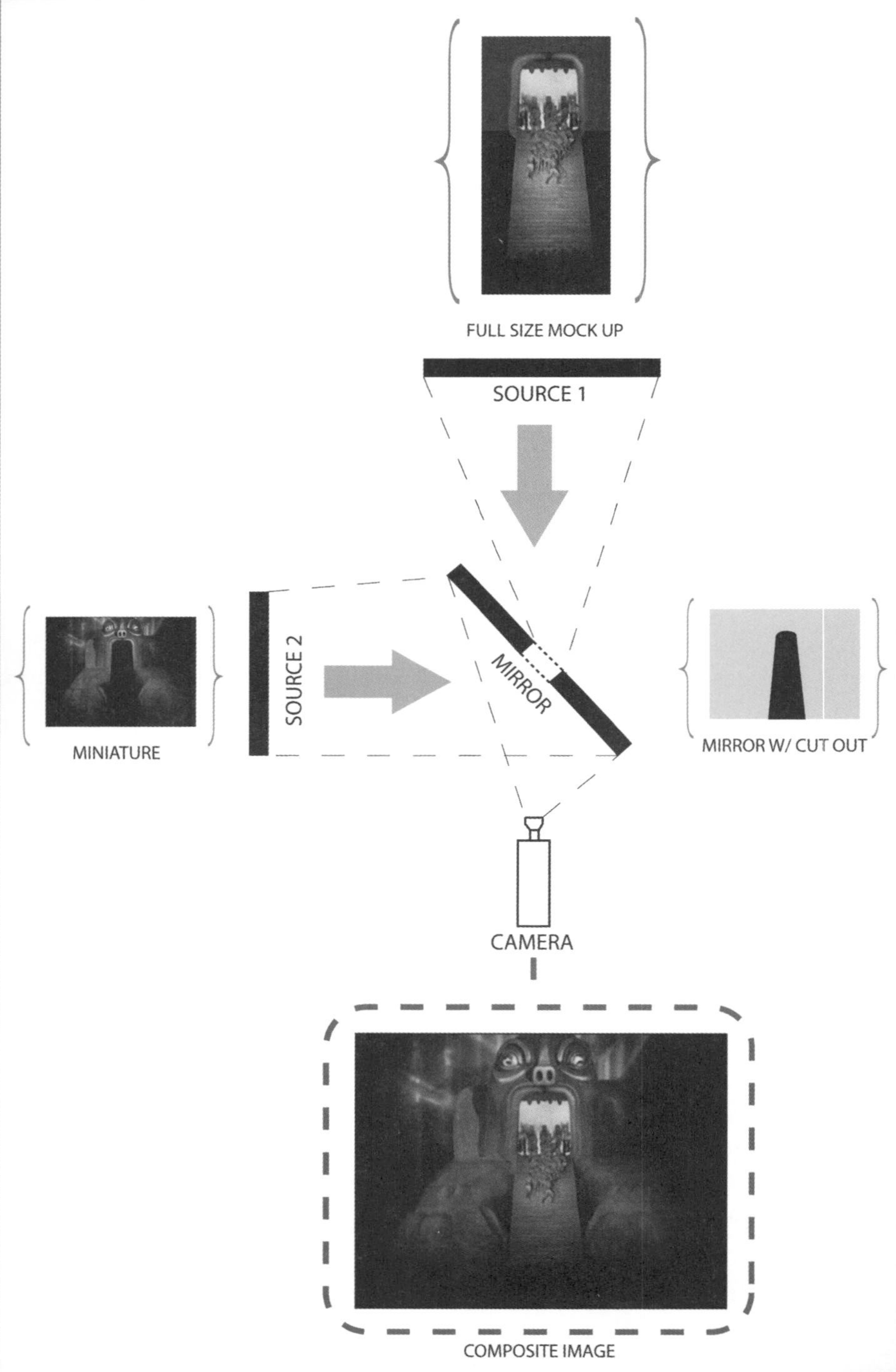

The Moloch-scene in *Metropolis*, created by means of the Schüfftan process

These transitional areas, which render objects indistinct and partially transparent, help to conceal dissimilarities in lighting between image components, but can also be revealing. Apart from minor defects, i.e. their soft image quality and blurry transition zones, Schüfftan shots have few unique visual features. Instead, they reproduce those of the image components involved. When employing models, for instance, Schüfftan shots exhibit the advantages and disadvantages of conventional miniature shots: the Moloch appears relief-like, but its face lacks aerial perspective. Similarly, when mobile models are being used, miniatures in Schüfftan shots often seem to be moving at an accelerated pace.

The Schüfftan process opened up great new possibilities for film-makers. To begin with, it could render transformations unattainable by any other analogue technique. This is particularly apparent from its first application in Fritz Lang's *Die Nibelungen: Siegfried* (1924). Here, the eponymous hero slays Alberich (Georg John), king of the Nibelungs, whereupon the dwarfs who are chained to the king's treasure basin turn into stone. The execution of the dwarfs' petrifaction remains impressive today. To achieve this shot, two treasure basins were constructed, one in front of the camera for the live actors and a replica, complete with petrified dwarfs, situated beside the camera. Because it would have been exceedingly difficult to create a mirror-inverted mould of the live-action scene, two mirrors were used: one fixed and fully reflective and one that was partially transparent and could slide up and down. Initially, the live-action scene was shot through the transparent part of the sliding mirror. At the moment of petrifaction, the mirror slowly moved up, allowing the reflective part to replace the live actors with their plaster copies.[7] Conventionally, this effect could have been realised by means of a dissolve from the live actors to their stone replicas. It would have been impossible, however, to represent the dwarfs' transformation from the bottom up and it is precisely this aspect that gives the shot such an eerily realistic quality.

The dwarfs' petrifaction in *Die Nibelungen: Siegfried* (1924)

Before the major problems of rear-projection could be addressed satisfactorily, the Schüfftan process was the only feasible single-exposure technique for rendering previously recorded moving images.[8] In addition, the Schüfftan process allowed for the integration of moving models with live-action footage. Finally, 'Gulliver' effects, i.e. the rendition of extreme size differences between living things, became convincing and flexible enough to sustain a feature film. Although *Gulliver's Travels*, one of Schüfftan's pet projects and a main selling point of his invention, was never realised with its help, the Schüfftan process was used to achieve 'Gulliver' effects for instance in *Knock, ou le triomphe de la médecine* (1925)[9] and *Das kalte Herz* (1950).

Eugen Schüfftan: The Man behind the Process

Born in Breslau in the German empire (today: Wrocław, Poland), Eugen Julius Schüfftan (1886–1977) was trained as a painter, architect and set decorator at the reputable Königliche Kunst- und Gewerbeschule (Royal Art and Vocational School) in Breslau. In 1912, he applied for his first film technological patent, a motorised projector that could alternately display two reels of film. During the early years of World War I, Schüfftan was wounded in France and subsequently honourably discharged.[10] After having unsuccessfully attempted to commercialise his projector patent,[11] he began collaborating with his former teacher, architect Hans Poelzig[12] and contributed to Poelzig's acclaimed renovation of Max Reinhardt's Großes Schauspielhaus (1919) in Berlin.[13] Around the same time, Schüfftan started to work as an animator for the studio Deutsche Lichtbild-Gesellschaft and devised the trick technique that would become known as the 'Schüfftan process'. Having spent the 1920s refining and promoting his invention, Schüfftan grew frustrated that the technique was mostly used for set extensions. He consequently launched a career as a cinematographer with *Menschen am Sonntag* (1930). Forced into exile by the rise of the National Socialists in 1933, Schüfftan went to France where he photographed several masterpieces of poetic-realist cinema, most notably *Drôle de drame* (1937) and *Le quai des brumes* (1938). The German invasion of France in 1940 forced him to flee once again, this time to the US, where his career came to a virtual standstill. Because of Hollywood studios' closed-shop labour environment and the rigid protectionism of the American Society of Cinematographers (ASC), Schüfftan, 'the master and patriarch of German cinematographers at the time',[14] was only able to find sporadic and mostly uncredited employment as a cameraman or special-effects supervisor. In the 1950s and 60s, he worked primarily in Europe, but could never revive what had once been a distinguished career. Despite his major accomplishments as a cinematographer, Schüfftan's name is now mainly associated with his early trick technological invention.

Old and New Mirror Magic

Mirrors have constituted the single most important tool in optical illusions for centuries and the Schüfftan process is just one in a multitude of mirror-based effects. Mirrors are integral to optical toys like the Praxinoscope and to fairground attractions like halls of mirrors and mirror mazes. Nineteenth-century magicians relied on mirrors for various levitation, vanishing, decapitation and multiplication acts. The best-known trick for combining visual components live on stage makes use of a partially reflective mirror (i.e. a pane of glass) and is commonly referred to as Pepper's Ghost. This effect is based on the simple fact that glass can both reflect and transmit light and had already been described by Giambattista della Porta in 1558. The more

Pepper's Ghost on the nineteenth-century stage

the lighting conditions vary on both sides of a pane of glass, the more pronounced are the glass's reflective qualities: Objects on the lighter side of the pane appear 'superimposed' onto the objects on the darker side. Around 1863 John Henry Pepper and Henry Dircks adapted this phenomenon for the theatre stage and popularised it under the name of 'Pepper's Ghost'. An invisible glass plate in front of the stage reflects the image of a hidden and brightly illuminated actor, which the audience perceives superimposed onto the stage.

As Sidney W. Clarke concluded in 1926, it was Pepper's Ghost that for the first time 'brought home the immense possibilities of glass, plain or silvered, in the production of magical illusions'.[15] Its principles were subsequently utilised in a variety of theatrical illusions, in cinematic 3D performances since the 1910s[16] and also in conventional film.[17] Because the Schüfftan process also involves a mirror at a forty-five-degree angle, it is distantly related to Pepper's Ghost. However, in contrast with Pepper's Ghost, the Schüfftan process does not create superimposition effects. What is more, it is a technique that relies on monocular vision and cannot be implemented on stage.

While partially reflective mirrors such as those used in the Pepper's Ghost illusion confronted early film-makers with severe lighting problems,[18] fully reflective mirrors became a standard tool for creating image distortions, duplications and composites early on in film history. Widely publicised, for instance, was the mirror trick behind the confrontation between a human-sized smoker and live-action miniature fairies in the most celebrated trick film of its day, *Princess Nicotine; or, The Smoke Fairy* (1909).[19] Here, a conventional mirror that reflected actors performing next to the camera was integrated with a black backdrop.

This type of mirror composite differs significantly from Schüfftan's, which not only utilises reflected images but is also related to foreground model techniques like glass paintings and hanging miniatures. Indeed, the important innovation of the Schüfftan process lies in the fact

Mirror composite in *Princess Nicotine* (1909)

that the mirror is placed in the foreground rather than background of the scene without creating superimposition effects *à la* Pepper's Ghost. The use of reflected images compensates for problems with lighting, focus and depth of field and thus allows for a smoother integration of the additional image components with the live-action scene.

However, given the tradition of foreground models and reflected images in film-making, the novelty of the Schüfftan process was called into question, particularly in the US. Norman O. Dawn asserted that he had employed the same technique as early as 1912.[20] Carl Louis Gregory also raised objections to Schüfftan's originality: 'This method has lately been heralded as a wonderful German invention under the name of the Schuefftan process but is antedated by several American uses, among whom are David Horsely [sic], J. Searle Dawley, and myself.'[21] There is no doubt that mirrors, glass paintings and hanging miniatures had featured in single-exposure composites prior to Schüfftan. However, there is no evidence that others anticipated Schüfftan's specific approach with partial foreground mirrors. In addition, regardless of whether individuals previously experimented with similar setups or not, Schüfftan won all patent litigations and it was undeniably his specifications that established mirrors as standard tools for producing composites in film.[22]

Illusions Become Products

As the demands of an international and profit-oriented entertainment industry prevailed during the 1920s, film-making in Europe became progressively rationalised and globalised. At the same time, as long-established, popularly held aesthetic ideas would have it, art had to originate in the imagination, in subjective experience and in the mysterious, intangible and magical. The Schüfftan process can be understood as an attempt to reconcile these opposites and integrate prevalent romantic ideals with the realities of a modern film industry. On the one hand, the Schüfftan process harks back to earlier traditions. Its reliance on mirrors and the laws of optics echoes a nineteenth-century fascination with optical illusions and stage magic. The ardour of German film pioneers like Max Skladanowsky and Oskar Messter resonates in the dedication with which Schüfftan refined his process over a decade, developing complex modifications with a variety of mirrors, lenses, prisms and projectors. On the other hand, Schüfftan's commitment to trick technological innovation was also driven by commercial considerations. In fact, Schüfftan envisioned his process as a worldwide marketable product, which was both ambitious and highly unusual at the time. Until then, trick techniques were commonly seen as a cinematographer's personal assets and constituted closely guarded secrets. Schüfftan, in contrast, turned special effects into a commodity. Between 1922 and 1930, Schüfftan was granted over forty patents in at least eight countries for variations of his process and embarked on an unprecedented international business scheme. Ultimately, however, Schüfftan's attempts to establish his invention as a global brand proved barely profitable.

Ufa, Spiegeltechnik and the Menace of Modernity

After Schüfftan had demonstrated the great potential of his invention in *Siegfried*, Ufa acquired the licence to commercialise the patents in April 1925. However, rather than exploiting further the technique's capacity for realising fantastic scenes, the studio became interested in the Schüfftan process as a means to lower expenditure on set design.[23] Ufa set up an in-house mirror-trick department that was subsequently outsourced and merged into the specialised company Spiegeltechnik GmbH & Co. (roughly 'Mirror Technology Ltd').[24] Founded in September 1926, Spiegeltechnik GmbH & Co. produced made-to-order Schüfftan shots for Ufa and other German studios. In 1927, one out of every ten German films contained Schüfftan shots.[25] As one of Spiegeltechnik's shareholders, Ufa had an exclusive contract that entitled the studio to 1,000 metres of Schüfftan footage per year for an annual guarantee sum of 100,000 Reichsmark (equivalent to £5,000 or $25,000 in 1927). All 'external' licensees were charged per metre of Schüfftan footage produced. Rates were negotiated on an individual basis and covered the licence, rental fees for mirrors and cameras, salaries for the technicians and expenses.[26] Spiegeltechnik GmbH & Co. turned out to be a disappointment, mostly due to exaggerated expectations on the part of Ufa. In order for the contract with Spiegeltechnik GmbH & Co. to be profitable, approximately two-thirds of Ufa's total feature-film production would have had to include an average of more than three minutes of Schüfftan footage. In actual fact, however, in 1925 only about one minute of Schüfftan footage was used in one-quarter of Ufa's feature films.[27] Strangely, the use of Schüfftan process at Ufa almost ceased after Spiegeltechnik GmbH & Co. had been established: during the 1926–7 season, only one Ufa production featured Schüfftan shots.[28]

To be sure, other studios took advantage of the Schüfftan process and commentators were enthusiastic about the technique's allegedly unlimited possibilities. They even associated it with utopian ideas of artistic renewal. Art director Walter Reimann, for instance, envisioned:

> The film of the future will no longer need huge studios and warehouses full of props. The moving camera, the mirror image, the painted backdrop, veils, smoke, pyrotechnics, curtains and a few rags – and in between human beings, real human beings, with incredible expressivity and light in all nuances.[29]

In addition, the promotion of the Schüfftan process as the hallmark of German technological excellence also inspired national pride. Schüfftan shots featured prominently in Ufa's prestigious flagship productions such as *Varieté* (1925), *Metropolis* and *Die Liebe der Jeanne Ney* (1927). In the majority of smaller-scale Ufa films, however, where first-level management had greater bearing, negative attitudes towards the Schüfftan process adversely affected its use. Many film-makers saw it as a threat to their artistic freedom. Cinematographers, for instance, felt limited in their creativity: '[T]he cameraman has to content himself with turning his handle in the usual way. His personal skills come less into their own, because the process … already prefabricates everything before the take.'[30] Fearful for their livelihood, set designers and set decorators viewed the Schüfftan process with trepidation, as it was supposedly 'a cinch to predict that the future belongs to this invention [the Schüfftan process] and that the set designer and the huge set will be ousted with its help'.[31] In view of the fears the Schüfftan process raised, it is not surprising that a 1927 report concluded that

> [c]ertain circles within [Ufa's] production departments are sabotaging the Schüfftan process. Despite the sympathetic support from the head of production, Dr. Grau, it has not been possible to obtain orders from directors or set designers, even though there had been plenty of opportunities to shoot scenes using the Schüfftan process.[32]

Given Ufa's substantial financial investment in Spiegeltechnik and the Schüfftan process's capacity to reduce production costs, the senior management was understandably interested in employing the technique. However, they evidently overestimated the studio's demands and also staff acceptance. Ufa ended up severely underutilising the Schüfftan process, thus incurring significant losses and withdrawing from the partnership in February 1928.[33] After Ufa's withdrawal, Spiegeltechnik continued to exist into the 1930s. At this point, however, Schüfftan no longer attended to his invention.

From Lilliput to Hitchcock

When travelling in Europe in August 1925, Carl Laemmle became aware of the Schüfftan process and secured Universal Pictures a two-year licence for commercialising the patents in North America, 'primarily to film *Gulliver's Travels*', as the *New York Times* reported.[34] Several other studios had previously considered adaptations of *Gulliver's Travels*, but none of these projects had been realised on account of the technological obstacles involved.[35] However, the scenes from *Gulliver's Travels* featured in Schüfftan's showreels apparently convinced Laemmle that the project had become feasible.[36] Starting in late 1925, Schüfftan and his collaborator Ernst Kunstmann spent about ten months in Hollywood where they refined the process while working on several low-profile Universal productions, as well as E. A. Dupont's first American film, *Love Me and the World Is Mine* (1926–7). Schüfftan's invention was met with considerable resistance in Hollywood and, compared to the media buzz in Europe, drew little public response in America. According to Schüfftan's observations, American directors and producers were more open to innovation than their German colleagues.[37] Cinematographers, on the other hand, were far less accommodating and, as mentioned above, accused Schüfftan of taking undue credit for a well-known technique. Universal eventually abandoned both the *Gulliver* project and its licence to the Schüfftan patents. In 1930, a second attempt was launched to promote the Schüfftan process in Hollywood. Now the technique's main selling point was its ability to resolve sound-related issues: large settings could be staged in intimate studio contexts where the sound was more easily controllable. As *Popular Science Monthly* reported,

> synthetic sets have become a vital problem. Thus it is expected that the Schufftan unit which arrived in the movie colony the other day will prove the nucleus from which will grow the general adoption of the system in this country.[38]

However, these hopes never materialised and the Schüfftan process failed to establish itself in America.

In contrast to its fate in Hollywood, the Schüfftan process prospered in Britain. In January 1927, British National Pictures acquired the world rights (except for Germany and North

Schüfftan shots in *Blackmail* (1929)

America) as part of a major endeavour to modernise and expand the studio.[39] Replicating Schüfftan's German business strategy, a subsidiary company, the British Schüfftan Process Co. Ltd,[40] was formed, to which, as the *Kinematograph Weekly* reported, 'other production companies will be invited to subscribe … [making the invention] available on license to all interested'.[41] Schüfftan and other Spiegeltechnik personnel travelled to London where they promoted the process, trained British staff and worked on British National's *Madame Pompadour* (1927). In the following decades, numerous British productions utilised the Schüfftan process, including several Hitchcock films such as *The Ring* (1927) and *The Man Who Knew Too Much* (1934). In *Blackmail* (1929), the climactic final sequence includes nine Schüfftan shots. As Hitchcock explained to François Truffaut and Peter Bogdanovich, the lighting conditions inside the British Museum precluded shooting on location. Using photographs that had been taken with exposure times of thirty minutes, the film-makers created backlit transparencies that were combined with the live action by means of Schüfftan mirrors.[42]

In each case, only a small fraction of what is visible in the frame was built to size. As Hitchcock recalled, 'there was barely any set that could be seen on the stage'.[43] Although two-dimensional photographs were used, the shots convey a sense of depth and the transitions between the photograph and the stage are difficult to spot, which renders these composites quite convincing.

With the coming of sound, the Schüfftan process became even more popular with European film-makers. Mirrors could charm away microphones positioned above actors' heads and, as Hans Nieter, staff member of British Schüfftan Process Co. Ltd, pointed out, 'the "Talkies" had increased the demand for the process tremendously, because it was possible to portray large scenes in a small compass and defeat the bugbear of echo in the microphone'.[44] The requirements of sound equipment also accelerated the ongoing shift in the dominant function of special effects, which were now primarily used to recreate physical reality.

Niches for Schüfftan's Mirrors

In the early 1930s, Hollywood and subsequently European studios began investing in high-tech composite systems. Although the Schüfftan process appeared painstaking and antiquated in comparison, it continued to play a considerable role in European film-making into the 1950s. Being cheap, low-tech and unobtrusive, it proved advantageous for production companies on tight budgets. By the mid-1940s, only studios that had Schüfftan experts on staff or were unable to invest in high-tech systems continued to employ Schüfftan shots. The technique remained in use where resources were scarce, most notably in television, low-budget film production and amateur film-making.

The studio that utilised the Schüfftan process most consistently after World War II was the publicly owned East German DEFA (Deutsche Film-Aktiengesellschaft). Established in 1946, DEFA acquired a reputation for productions with fantastic subject matter. Given the studio's limited resources, the realisation of spectacular scenes in fairy-tale films like *Die Geschichte vom kleinen Muck* (1953) and *Das singende, klingende Bäumchen* (1957) called for inexpensive yet sophisticated trick technological solutions. Head of the studio's special-effects department between 1947 and 1963 was Schüfftan's former associate Ernst Kunstmann. He perpetuated Ufa's trick tradition and repeatedly reverted to solutions that had served him well thirty years earlier. The petrifaction of the wicked miller in *Der Teufel vom Mühlenberg* (1955), for example, was evidently modelled after the dwarfs' petrifaction in *Siegfried*. In comparison with their colleagues in the West, Kunstmann and his successors Kurt Marks and Erich Günther took an anachronistic approach to special effects that was consistent with the somewhat outmoded style of DEFA's fairy-tale films.[45] DEFA surely valued the Schüfftan process for its affordability, but also employed it more than any other studio to fulfil the inventor's original objective, namely to visualise the unreal and impossible.[46]

The Schüfftan process continued to be used in the West as well, albeit more sporadically. Film-makers working with small budgets like Mario Bava in *Terrore nello spazio* (1965) and Roberto Rossellini in *La Prise de pouvoir par Louis XIV* (1966) and *Socrate* (1971) deployed Schüfftan shots for set extensions. Remarkable post-war depictions of fantastic subject matter include Ulysses' confrontation with the giant Cyclops in *Ulisse* (1954), which was created under Schüfftan's personal supervision.

One of the technique's rare forays into magical effects in American film-making was Darby's (Albert Sharpe) visit to the Leprechaun cave in *Darby O'Gill and the Little People* (1959).[47] Indeed, the rendering of extreme size differences is one of the most striking applications of Schüfftan shots. Even in the late 1950s, the Schüfftan process was therefore considered an attractive option to cost-efficiently realise *Gulliver's Travels*. In 1958, writer-director Jack Sher

Darby entering the Leprechaun cave in *Darby O'Gill and the Little People* (1959)

expressed an interest in engaging the technique for his Gulliver project at Universal. On 23 May 1958 he wrote to Schüfftan:

> our script involves split-screen work, miniatures, the use of mock-ups and other standard tricks that are extremely costly. If your process can eliminate the necessity for six months of special printing after the picture is photographed, I know that we will be extremely interested.[48]

Unfortunately for Schüfftan, however, Universal backed out of the project and Sher signed with producer Charles H. Schneer, whose long-term partner Ray Harryhausen was entrusted with the special effects for *The 3 Worlds of Gulliver* (1960).[49]

Although the Schüfftan process only played a minor role in post-war special effects, it continues to inspire film-makers and technicians. It was influential in the development of front-projection systems, including Introvision.[50] In the digital age, film-makers like cinematographer Henri Alekan in *Der Himmel über Berlin* (1987) put the Schüfftan process back on the map. Special-effects supervisors Robert and Dennis Skotak, who enlised the Schüfftan process in *Aliens* (1986),[51] value traditional in-camera effects for their immediacy and excellent image quality: 'Even in the digital age, these techniques still work perfectly, and you can get your shot done in one take without any additional processes.'[52] The Skotaks as well as other film-makers like Niklaus Schilling in *Der Atem* (1989) have successfully experimented with hybrids of Schüfftan shots and digital technologies.[53]

Like no other phenomenon in the European context, the Schüfftan process highlights a crucial transition in the history of special effects: the shift from one-of-a-kind, eye-catching tricks to standardised, economical and imperceptible special effects. Simultaneously, it embodies a key feature of European silent cinema, namely the attempt to reconcile ideals of artisan film-making with the realities of the motion-picture business. While Schüfftan's idealistic project of promoting fantastic film art could not ultimately succeed in a modern entertainment industry, the versatility and cost efficiency of the Schüfftan process as well as its capacity to produce high-quality composites have ensured its continued survival. To this day, the Schüfftan process epitomises the legendary ingenuity and creativity of German film technicians of the 1920s. As an icon for the inseparability of craftsmanship and film art, Schüfftan's magic mirrors persevere in the digital age.

This article is dedicated to Helmut G. Asper and Rolf Giesen, who prepared the ground for my work on Eugen Schüfftan and provided invaluable assistance during my research. Many thanks to David Degras, Yancey Clayton and Leigh Ann Smith-Gary for their generous help with completing it.

Notes

1. Talbot for instance writes:

> In common with other producers of trick films, Paul found that the time involved in their production was out of all proportion to the financial results. It was no uncommon circumstance for a subject approximating 100 feet in length to absorb a week or more of continuous work.

See Frederick A. Talbot, *Moving Pictures: How They Are Made and Worked* (London: William Heinemann, 1912), pp. 205–6.

2. Quoted in Mark Cotta Vaz and Craig Barron, *The Invisible Art: The Legends of Movie Matte Painting* (San Francisco, CA: Chronicle Books, 2002), p. 41.
3. Carl Louis Gregory, 'Trick Photography', *Camera* vol. 33 no. 1 (July 1926), p. 58.
4. –y, 'Die Wunder des Spiegels', *Film-Kurier*, 6 November 1926.
5. Gertrud Isolani, 'Gespräch mit Eugen Shuftan', *Basler Nachrichten*, 19 October 1965, p. 9.
6. Alternatively, a two-way mirror and masks can be used.
7. Erich Kettelhut, *Der Schatten des Architekten*, Werner Sudendorf (ed.) (Munich: Belleville, 2009), p. 93.
8. See Carl Louis Gregory, 'Trick Photography Methods Summarized', *American Cinematographer*, June 1926, p. 21.
9. For the use of the Schüfftan process in this film, see 'Tricks und Vorspiegelungen: Das neue Schüfftan-Verfahren – Wie ein Trickfilm entsteht', *Scherls Magazin* vol. 1 (1927), pp. 2–7, 5.
10. Helmut G. Asper (ed.), *Nachrichten aus Hollywood, New York und anderswo: Der Briefwechsel Eugen und Marlise Schüfftans mit Siegfried und Lili Kracauer* (Trier: Wissenschaftlicher Verlag, 2003), p. 4.
11. Eugen Schüfftan, 'Mein Verfahren', *Kinotechnische Rundschau des Film-Kurier*, 18 November 1926.
12. Hans Poelzig was president of the Royal Art and Vocational School in Beslau, Schüfftan's alma mater, between 1902 and 1916. Apart from his art deco design for the Großes Schauspielhaus, Poelzig is best known for his sets in *Der Golem, wie er in die Welt kam* (1920) and the IG Farben building in Frankfurt am Main (1928–30).
13. According to Asper and Giesen, Schüfftan was in charge of the colour design of the prominent cascading 'limestone cave' dome. See Asper, *Nachrichten aus Hollywood, New York und anderswo*, p. 4;

Rolf Giesen, 'Eugen Schüfftan', in Hans-Michael Bock (ed.), *CINEGRAPH: Lexikon zum deutschesprachigen Film*, vol 7 (Munich: edition text-kritik, 1984–present), p. B1.

14. Max Ophüls, *Spiel im Dasein: Eine Rückblende* (Stuttgart: Goverts, 1959).
15. Sidney W. Clarke, 'The Annals of Conjuring', *Magic Wand* vol. 14 (1926), p. 91.
16. See Katharina Loew, 'Tangible Specters: 3-D Cinema in the 1910s', *Film Criticism* vol. 3 no. 2 (Spring/Fall), pp. 87–116.
17. See Guido Seeber, *Der praktische Kameramann*, vol. 2, *Der Trickfilm in seinen grundsätzlichen Möglichkeiten* (1927) (Frankfurt am Main: Deutsches Filmmuseum, 1979), p. 132; George E. Turner, 'The Evolution of Special Effects', in Linwood G. Dunn (ed.), *The ASC Treasure of Visual Effects* (Hollywood, CA: American Society of Cinematographers, 1983), pp. 15–82, 45.
18. Before the 1910s, emulsions and lamps were not capable of rendering dim and extremely bright illumination levels simultaneously.
19. J. Stuart Blackton and Albert E. Smith revealed the secrets behind *Princess Nicotine* in 'Some Tricks of the Moving Picture Maker', *Scientific American*, 26 June 1909, p. 476. Books and journals worldwide subsequently took up the story in remarkable detail. See for instance Talbot, *Moving Pictures*, pp. 242–53.
20. Dawn referred to a mirror shot in an unidentifiable production. Other details provided are questionable as well. See 'Inventory List', *Norman O. Dawn Collection of Special Effects Cinematography*, Henry Ransom Center at the University of Texas at Austin.
21. Gregory, 'Trick Photography Methods Summarized', pp. 21–2.
22. For the patent litigations, see Giesen, 'Eugen Schüfftan', p. E2.
23. See 'Bericht über Zwischenrevision der Geschäftsbücher und der Bilanz per 28. Februar 1927', *Files of the Deutsche Spiegeltechnik GmbH & Co. K.-G. Berlin* (R109/I2455), Bundesarchiv Berlin.
24. Confusingly enough, Spiegeltechnik GmbH & Co. was a joint venture between Ufa and a separate company, the open corporation Spiegeltechnik AG. See 'Angebot der Universum-Film AG an die Deutsche Spiegeltechnik GmbH &Co, Berlin W9, Köthenerstrasee 1/4 vom 15. September 1926', *Files of the Deutsche Spiegeltechnik GmbH & Co. K.-G. Berlin* (R109/I2070), Bundesarchiv Berlin; 'Auflösungsvertrag vom 28. Februar 1928', ibid.
25. See 'Bericht über Zwischenrevision'; 'Bericht über Revision der Geschäftsbücher und der Bilanz für das am 30. September 1927 abgelaufene Geschäftsjahr', *Files of the Deutsche Spiegeltechnik GmbH & Co. K.-G. Berlin* (R109/I2456), Bundesarchiv Berlin; Giesen, 'Eugen Schüfftan', pp. F1–F2; Alexander Jason, *Handbuch der Filmwirtschaft: Filmstatistiken und Verzeichnisse der Filmschaffenden, Filmfirmen, der Filme und der Tonfilmkinos*, vol. 2, Film-Europa (Berlin: Verlag für Presse, Wirtschaft und Politik, 1931), p. 17.
26. Having initially aimed at a flat fee of 200 Reichsmark (£10 or $50 in 1926) per metre, the price actually averaged around 125 Reichsmark ($31.25 or £6.25 in 1926) per metre in 1926. See 'Bericht über Zwischenrevision'.
27. The total German feature-film production in 1925 amounted to 253 titles, including Ufa's twenty-nine titles. See Kinemateksverbund, Arbeitsgruppe Deutsche Filmografie, 'Deutsche Spielfilme 1925: Jahresproduktion und Filmbestand Bundesarchiv', Bundesarchiv-Filmarchiv, October 2007. Even before Spiegeltechnik GmbH & Co. was established, doubts were raised regarding the specific terms of the contract. A memorandum in the Ufa files at the Bundesarchiv Berlin deemed the annual guaranteed purchase quantity of 1,000 metres of Schüfftan footage grossly exaggerated.

See 'Notiz vom 4. August 1926', *Files of the Deutsche Spiegeltechnik GmbH & Co. K.-G. Berlin* (R109/I 2070), Bundesarchiv Berlin.

28. See 'Bericht über Zwischenrevision'.
29. Walter Reimann, 'Filmarchitektur – heute und morgen', *Filmtechnik*, 20 February 1926. Similarly, cinematographer Karl Freund expressed his hopes that the Schüfftan process would eliminate monumentalism in German set design. See A. Koslowski, 'Die Männer der Kurbel IV: Karl Freund', *Film-Kurier*, 30 May 1925.
30. Seeber, *Der Trickfilm in seinen grundsätzlichen Möglichkeiten*, pp. 141–2.
31. 'Das Ende der Dekoration', *Kinematograph* vol. 950 (3 May 1925).
32. See 'Bericht über Zwischenrevision'.
33. See 'Auflösungsvertrag vom 28. Februar 1928'. See 'Bericht über Zwischenrevision'.
34. See Frederic Wynne-Jones, 'When the Camera's Eye Lies for Entertainment', *New York Times*, 2 May 1926, p. X5. Laemmle announced that *Gulliver's Travels* was to become one of three Universal 'Super-Jewels' for 1926 via cable from Europe in September 1925. See Grace Kingsley, 'Flashes', *Los Angeles Times*, 17 September 1925, p. A11. Swift's work celebrated its bicentenary in 1926.
35. Edwin Schallert, 'Fantasy Again in Foreground', *Los Angeles Times*, 15 February 1925, p. D19.
36. See Moulton, 'Magical Effects Brought to Screen by Unique Process', *Los Angeles Times*, 18 April 1926, pp. C25–6.
37. Schüfftan, 'Mein Verfahren'.
38. Michael Mock, 'New Ideas Sweep Movie Studios', *Popular Science Monthly*, May 1930, p. 144.
39. 'British National Strengthened', *Kinematograph Weekly*, 13 January 1927, p. 56.
40. Hans Nieter, 'The Schüfftan Process of Model Photography', *Photographic Journal*, January 1930, p. 16.
41. 'Schüfftan Process Acquired', *Kinematograph Weekly*, 13 January 1927, p. 56.
42. François Truffaut, *Hitchcock* (New York: Simon & Schuster, 1967), p. 64; Peter Bogdanovich, *Who the Devil Made It* (New York: Alfred A. Knopf, 1997), p. 495. According to Hitchcock, the transparencies were about twelve by fourteen inches in size. Considering that BIP held the world rights (outside Germany and North America) of the Schüfftan process, Hitchcock's claim that he had to employ it behind the backs of the studio heads is certainly incorrect. See also Tom Ryall, 'Blackmail', in Rob White and Edward Buscombe (eds), *British Film Institute Film Classics*, vol. 1 (London: BFI, 2003), p. 99.
43. Hitchcock in Bogdanovich, *Who the Devil Made It*, p. 495.
44. Nieter, 'The Schüfftan Process of Model Photography', p. 18.
45. This conservative stance had not only financial but also technical reasons. The colour print materials used in the East German film industry (ORWO) prohibited chroma key compositing and special-effects artists had to make do with rear-projection and traditional techniques.
46. At DEFA, the Schüfftan process was routinely utilised into the 1980s. In addition to those mentioned above, the Schüfftan process was employed in the following fantastic GDR productions: *Das Feuerzeug* (1958); *Vom König Midas* (1962); *Spuk im Hochhaus* (TV, 1982); *Die Geschichte vom goldenen Taler* (TV, 1985).
47. The unusual resurfacing of the Schüfftan process at a major Hollywood studio possibly traces back to special-effects artists Peter Ellenshaw and Albert Whitlock, both of whom had worked on several British films that had utilised Schüfftan shots.

48. 'Letter from Jack Sher to Eugene Schüfftan', Eugen Schüfftan file in the Paul Kohner archive, Deutsche Kinemathek, Berlin.
49. See Giesen, *Special Effects Artists: A Worldwide Biographical Dictionary of the Pre-digital Era with a Filmography* (Jefferson, NC: McFarland, 2008), p. 144.
50. Les P. Robley and John W. Eppolito, *Front Projection Composite Photography System Combing Staged Action with Two Projected Images*, United States Patent 5,061,061, filed 14 June 1988, and issued 29 October 1991. Front-projection as a method of composite photography was pioneered by Walter Thorner, who had previously patented an improvement of the Schüfftan process. See Walther Thorner, *Verfahren und Vorrichtung zur Herstellung kinematographischer Kombinationsaufnahmen*, Deutsches Reichspatent 598,712, filed 19 May 1932, and issued 18 June 1934. The trailblazers of the modern Scotchlite system were Will Jenkins, who references Schüfftan in his patent application, and Schüfftan's former assistant Henri Alekan. See Will F. Jenkins, *Apparatus for Production of Light Effects in Composite Photography,* United States Patent 2,727,427, filed 3 March 1952, and issued 20 December 1955; Henri Alekan, *Procédé et dispositif de prise de vues combinées*, République Française Brevet d'invention 1,098,128, filed 7 January 1954, and issued 2 March 1955. Schüfftan himself patented a number of front-projection improvements. See for instance Eugen Schüfftan, *Photocomposition System*, United States Patent 2,857,806, filed 26 July 1954, and issued 28 October 1958.
51. Sheldon Teitelbaum, 'Special Effects: Aliens', *Cinefantastique* vol. 16, October 1986, p. 122.
52. Quoted in Richard Rickitt, *Special Effects: The History and Technique* (New York: Billboard Books, 2007), p. 91.
53. 'Der Atem der Geschichte: Niklaus Schilling im Gespräch mit Mareike Sprengel', http://www.visualfilm.de/texte.htm.

PHOTOREALISM, NOSTALGIA AND STYLE
MATERIAL PROPERTIES OF FILM IN DIGITAL VISUAL EFFECTS

BARBARA FLUECKIGER

With the introduction of smartphone apps such as Hipstamatic (2009) and Instagram (2010), the rendition of instant snapshots in the style of old photographs has recently spread in amateur photography. These apps recast even the most mundane scenes in a lovingly nostalgic light, giving them a romantic touch and evoking memories of family albums packed with faded pictures from a time before the 'digital natives' were even born.

In fact, the popularity of these apps turned a strategy for the production of professional visual effects into a tool of mass entertainment. Starting in the 1990s, computer scientists began to develop algorithms to enhance sterile and naked-looking computer-generated imagery with material properties initiating those that could have emanated from either the photographic apparatus or the photochemical stock, such as motion blur, depth of field, film grain, scratches and dirt. These simulations of analogue artefacts were more than embellishments of early renderings. Connecting these images to the long-established traditions of photography and film meant they became a cornerstone of the now-established concept of 'photorealism' in computer graphics and animation. Only in recent years, however, has CGI acquired such a high degree of sophistication that it has become barely distinguishable from imagery captured with an analogue or digital camera.

From the 1990s on, there has been a growing tendency to showcase these artefacts to the point of exaggeration, not only evoking the loving memories of faded photographs, but also commenting on them in an ironic fashion. One of the most striking examples in this vein is Baz Luhrmann's *Moulin Rouge!* (2001), which depicts turn-of-the-century Paris in the style of Georges Méliès' silent films, combined with the frantic movement and speed of a virtual camera that rushes through the narrow streets, and other stylistic properties of contemporary filmmaking; Luhrmann termed this combination 'artificial reality'.[1] There is a tension in the computer-generated imagery of the 2000s between achieving a higher degree of photorealism by appropriating the cultural rules and mechanical properties of photography and at the same time marking these images as utterly artificial through a stylised rendition of such distortions.

This article draws upon my analyses of this phenomenon in two earlier texts.[2] It starts with an investigation of a variety of the most common analogue artefacts added computationally to CGI and digital compositing. Based on this primary description, I will then develop a functional typology to describe and analyse different strands of their uses and functions in movies. Finally, I will contextualise these findings in a broader cultural discourse surrounding the concepts of nostalgia, postmodernism, pastiche and authenticity.

There is, however, an urgent need to clarify one of the most important issues when we talk about digital images, namely that there is no such thing as *the* digital image, but only a variety

Moulin Rouge! (2001): Baz Luhrmann's artificial reality

thereof. Between a computer-generated image and an image captured with a digital camera, there is a fundamental difference with regard to their technical and epistemological foundations and aesthetics. While CGI has to be built from scratch based on mathematical models or on image data collected in the real world, digital photography stands by definition in the tradition of its analogue predecessor and shares with it more common features than it does with CGI. In contrast to digital photographs, computer-generated imagery struggles to achieve full photorealism. A further variety of digital imagery is compositing that combines images from various sources into a seamless or even heterogeneous-looking whole. With the latest developments in image-based techniques and even more so with computational photography,[3] the gap between CGI and digital photography is becoming more and more irrelevant. Still, it remains necessary to keep the different evolutionary, epistemological and aesthetic strands in mind when we discuss phenomena and problems associated with digital images.[4] Most of the imprecision in studies of digital images stems from the overlap of different concepts in the genesis and critique of digital images. In this essay, I will focus on the combination of CGI with live-action footage in digital visual effects.

Since William J. T. Mitchell's diagnosis of a post-photographic era there has been a mostly dystopic discussion of digital image processing, frequently explained in terms of forgery and manipulation.[5] However, there is a notable difference between the covert manipulation of a documentary image and a computer-generated or processed image as part of a movie's fictional world. Therefore, we should embed the discussion in a contextual field defined by institutional and cultural factors.

Photorealism and Analogue Artefacts

In his observations on the use of blurred images in historical and contemporary photography, Wolfgang Ullrich reports an early experiment by art historian Charles H. Caffin to evaluate the impression of reality in photographs.[6] In this experiment, performed with people who were not accustomed to perceiving photographs, Edward Steichen's photo entitled 'The Pond' was deemed the most realistic one.

This is surprising because Steichen's photo is a typical example of the pictorialism that emerged in the early twentieth century to establish an artful and painterly style in photography.

'The Pond – Moonlight', Edward Steichen, 1904

Furthermore, it is processed in a three-colour technique that applies layered bichromate gums in different colours during printing, and contains a fair amount of optical diffusion. Instead of being a direct record of the scene in front of the camera, this photograph transforms its subject significantly. It renders a mood and an atmosphere rather than a detailed depiction. In opposition to this atmospheric style in photography, an early rendering in computer graphics, such as the first example of raytracing by its inventor Turner Whitted in 1980, evokes a rather different impression but, at the time of its introduction, it was considered photoreal.[7]

While it certainly shares some aspects with a photographic image, we would hardly agree any more that this image is photoreal, because it lacks features found in the real world. The refraction in the glass sphere looks too clean; the shadow is sharp, but grey, due to the ambient term in the Phong shader.[8] In sum, the lighting situation doesn't seem very natural since there are no indirect reflections, no refractions and no caustics.[9] Apart from these features, which we can attribute to the very limited calculation of physical properties of light propagation in early computer graphics, we also notice a lack of depth-of-field. As a result, the image looks too sharp and sterile.

From this comparison we can conclude that photorealism is a highly debatable and historically variable concept. In the theories of representation proffered by philosophers such as Nelson Goodman,[10] Max Black, Noël Carroll and others, it is not granted – as realists such as André Bazin, Roland Barthes or Siegfried Kracauer have suggested – that the basic photographic or cinematographic apparatus automatically provides a faithful representation of the real. In order to explore and fully understand this mode of representation we have to explore the basic assumptions already present in this apparatus. These assumptions are themselves rooted in insights from psycho-physics into the physiology and processing of human perception as performed in the nineteenth century by Thomas Young, Gustav Theodor Fechner, Johannes von Müller or Hermann von Helmholtz. In addition to this bias already present in the theoretical underpinnings of the technological apparatus, there is a culturally determined variability associated with notions of style and fashion that influences the concept of (photo)realism. These surrounding elements establish certain conventions that inform our perception of any depiction in a given historical moment in a certain culture. It is always our contemporary mode of depiction that seems the most transparent to us, as Nelson

Raytracing by Turner Whitted

Goodman has pointed out in his reflections on the ideological influences on any form of representation: 'Realism is relative, determined by the system of representation standard for a given culture or person at a given time. ... This relativity is obscured by our tendency to omit specifying a frame of reference when it is our own.'[11]

Grain, Scratches, Dust and Noise

In conjunction with cultural influences on contemporary styles, one of the most important factors in the formation of conventions are technical limitations and choices made in the production of films. Throughout the history of film, the photochemical composition of film stock has been a major influence on the look of filmed images. While there have been shifting preferences and tolerances in the sensitivity and contrast rendition of film stocks, especially in the domain of black-and-white film and to a lesser degree in the chromogenic multilayered colour film stock that has proliferated since the 1950s, one of the most typical elements in the aesthetics of film has been its grain, produced by the silver halide crystals present in the filmic emulsion. In contrast to the fixed orthogonal pattern provided by the pixels in a digital image, this grain is randomly distributed. In projection this produces a pseudo-movement from frame to frame, and these micro-movements designate the temporality of the film; even if we watch a still image recorded on film, the movement of the grain evidences its temporal unfolding.

Furthermore, the grain endows the surface of the film with a specific texture that we associate with the cinematic. Thus the grain is attributed with something like the essence of the filmic experience, as expressed by cinematographer Janusz Kaminski:

> To me, movies are a social event ... . They don't necessarily help us escape reality, but they offer us a reality that is different from what we see at home. If you can't see or sense grain in the image, you're not experiencing the magic of movies.[12]

Many contemporary film-makers and cinematographers choose a stock or a processing that enhances the graininess of the film, while suppliers of stock have constantly evolved it to produce ever-finer grain, even to the point where it is hardly noticeable due to the T-Grain introduced in modern Kodak stocks.[13] Kaminski, for example shot on the super-sensitive Kodak Vision 800T and applied the so-called bleach-bypass process to *Minority Report* (2002), enhancing the dark atmosphere of the film's dystopic vision with a gritty-grainy effect.[14]

Heavily visible grain, preferably in connection with black-and-white or sepia-toned cinematography, has become a marker of historicity in films, either to denote an earlier period in the narration or the memory of a character in a flashback. In films that combine historical footage with CGI or live action in compositing, as in *Forrest Gump* (1994), the grain has to be added evenly to the new elements to grant aesthetic coherence. To achieve this effect – which was first applied digitally in Woody Allen's *Zelig* (1983), albeit only to still images – one has first to filter the grain out of the original footage, only to add it again after the compositing is completed. Similar aesthetic effects can be found in the works of Guy Maddin or in the Swiss production *Terra Incognita* (2004).

Like grain, scratches and dust are directly associated with the materiality of the film stock: as markers of its repeated use, they communicate the age of the material. In the opening

Grain in *Terra Incognita* (2004)

sequence of *The Curious Case of Benjamin Button* (2008) we are presented with the story of a clockmaker who – after he lost his son in the war – constructs a clock that runs backwards. This short allegorical episode is enhanced by scratches, dirt, diffusion and a seemingly historical colour scheme. This strategy has a long-standing tradition. Seventy years earlier, in Orson Welles's *Citizen Kane* (1941), scratches marked a staged newsreel entitled *News on the March* that summarised Kane's life. Even the unstable handling of the camera mimicked the perspective of a clandestine paparazzo who had shot some footage from behind a fence with the camera on his shoulder. In Michel Gondry's *Be Kind, Rewind* (2008), such fake footage is shot with a VHS camera in front of which a fan produces the flicker and real threads add the scratches to the low-resolution video when the protagonists stage the life of a famous former member of their neighbourhood, musician Fats Waller. In her reflections on 'cinephilia without film', Caetlin Benson-Allott describes scratches added to the HD digital video as a 'new mode of digital nostalgia' in a 'transhistorical, simulacral moment' that marks the universe of *Grindhouse* (2007) by Robert Rodriguez and Quentin Tarantino.[15] Both *Be Kind, Rewind* and *Grindhouse* are similar instances of a low-tech approach to the rendition of film's historical past, located somewhere between parody and sincere homage.

Another genre to enlist simulated scratches and noise is the fake documentary or 'mockumentary'. These films often formulate a critical stance toward documentaries by provoking a vigilant mode of perception in the viewer. The ambiguous status of these films will be the topic of the final two sections of this essay. Many of them apply traces of wear and tear, such as scratches and dirt, as in *Zelig*. More recently, Neill Blomkamp's *District 9* (2009), a mockumentary about a slum in South Africa populated by aliens, featured footage with a worn-out look, fraught with evidence of use and degraded by poor resolution. By referencing different kinds of materials, ostensibly produced by embedded journalists who give a firsthand account of the wretched situation of the aliens at the borders of civil society, he establishes a web of allusions to media representations.

Depth-of-field

With the virtual camera in CGI, no lens configuration transforms the profilmic scene in the rendering process, so there are several optical effects that can be applied separately, either by a camera shader or in post-processing.[16] One of them is depth-of-field, others are lens distortion, chromatic aberration, lens flare or vignetting.

In practical photography – both analogue and digital – depth-of-field is intrinsically connected to the aperture, the focal length of the lens and the diameter of the image plane. Wide-open aperture, telephoto lens and large diameter tend to produce shallow depth-of-field. From the perspective of aesthetics there have been several historical periods where either shallow depth-of-field or deep focus were fashionable. In early film, with its frontal staging and lack of montage, deep focus was necessary to depict the whole image space. In the later teens and especially from the mid-1920s on we can notice a trend towards shallow depth-of-field. Famously, this development was inverted in the late 1930s with the deep-focus style of films such as *The Grapes of Wrath* (1940) and later *Citizen Kane*, both photographed by cinematographer Gregg Toland. These films reference the growing social awareness in photography in the wake of the economic decline in the 1930s with the reportages for the Farm Security Administration by Walker Evans or Dorothea Lange. The deep-focus style stresses the relationship between the individual and his environment. Thus these developments were only partly the result of technical limitations such as the low speed of early film stock. My own investigations have shown that cultural movements had a bigger impact, not least for the development and implementation of certain technological advancements.

In CGI, however, it was impossible until the late 1990s to even render depth-of-field (DOF), because it requires not only the blurring of certain parts of the image, but a systematic relationship between focus and depth. Moreover, DOF is not only a critical issue in CGI but also in compositing where, since the different elements are initially shot or rendered in focus, the compositors have to carefully establish a relationship between the different image planes and their rendition of focus.

In his standard textbook *The Art and Science of Digital Compositing*, Ron Brinkmann shows an important difference between the photographic quality of out-of-focus areas – called bokeh – and a simple Gaussian blur, that is, the computational averaging of adjacent pixels according to Gaussian distribution.[17] Bokeh refers to a pleasing quality of the out-of-focus area where, due to spherical aberration, the circles of confusion create shiny spots of light. Many lens manufacturers take great care in designing their lenses to deliver beautiful bokeh. As Brinkmann points out, there are digital tools to render bokeh but they are still seldom applied. For *Wall-E* (2008), the producers consulted with cinematographer Roger Deakins, who taught the CGI professionals how to successfully convey the impression of DOF and how to apply it sensibly both with regard to narration and style. In fact, Deakins's lessons pay off visibly in *Wall-E*. Not only does the application of DOF enhance the photographic quality of the renderings, but it

Rack focus in *Wall-E* (2008)

makes it appear organic and convincing, with objects out of focus acquiring a transparent quality with a pleasingly glowing translucent effect. Even rack focus is engaged as a means of storytelling, for instance in a scene when the robot protagonist discovers the last plant on earth. Rack focus operates to align the spectator with the heightened attention *Wall-E* bestows on his discovery. Rack focus, then, is a further strategy engaged to transform the visual space by optical means and to use depth-of-field to shape the point-of-view structure of the narrative.

Motion Blur

In his reflections on filmic artefacts in digital video, Stephen Prince states that 'film has motion blur, video does not'.[18] In fact, the situation is a bit more complex. In video we must distinguish between two modes, one being the *interlace mode*, whereby the even and odd lines of an image are generated alternately, a technique that dates back to analogue electronic video; and the *progressive mode*, whereby full frames are captured as on film. In the most recent generation of digital video cameras, the CMOS (complementary metal-oxide superconductor) sensors apply a third kind of movement artefact connected to the rolling shutter, which moves vertically from top to bottom. In the progressive mode, there is no visible difference in the production of motion blur of digital video compared to film. This mode was introduced to HD video in the early 2000s to generate a 'film look'.

'Plastic Synthesis of Movements of a Woman', Luigi Russolo, 1911

In CGI, on the other hand, there is no motion blur at all. Like depth-of-field, motion blur is an artefact that has to be assigned arbitrarily to the images, ideally in conjunction with an evaluation of both the camera's and the object's movements. Motion blur is, in addition to grain, probably the most typical artefact of film recording. Classical stop-motion animation therefore had a different quality because it lacked motion blur. Only when go motion was introduced in the 1970s could motion blur be integrated into stop-motion animation.

In the history of art, a form of motion blur was introduced in Italian futurism of the 1910s, for instance in a painting by Luigi Russolo. The Italian futurists were concerned with depicting modern urban life, and were especially fascinated by its dynamics. They adopted a mode of representation which was connected to the emergence of cinema, in that they mimicked the sequential unfolding of still images. Thus motion blur had already been used to express speed and dynamics early in the twentieth century. Also, the German painter Gerhard Richter incorporated many analogue artefacts into his photorealist paintings – especially the portraits – to reflect the differences between painting and photographic images. In combination with depth-of-field, motion blur was one of the most pervasive of these artefacts in Richter's work. In visual effects, this tradition has been resurrected, for instance in some shots of *The Matrix* (1999) to depict the extreme agility of the virtual agents.

The situation is somewhat different in *Fight Club* (1999), where another traditional strand of motion blur can be observed. In late nineteenth-century photography, motion-blurred

Superhuman speed in *The Matrix* (1999)

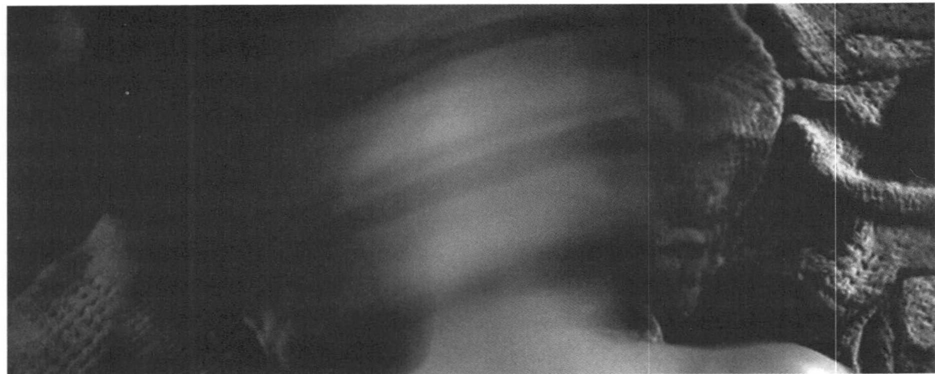

Motion blur in *Fight Club* (1999)

images were connected to ghostly apparitions. The sex scene with Marla Singer (Helena Bonham Carter) refers to this mode and generates a dreamlike quality. A similar use of extreme motion blur was implemented in *What Dreams May Come* (1998), where it alludes directly to the iconographic tradition of ghost images. In many images, figures and objects are subject to such a high degree of motion blur that their contours are completely dissolved in blurred, painterly lines associated with the brush strokes of the protagonist's wife, a painter. In addition, motion blur can serve to soften an image by adding diffusion.

Diffusion, Lens Flares and Vignetting

Diffusion is one of the pertaining features in the photographic pictorialism associated with the journal *Camera Work*, funded by Alfred Stieglitz to establish photography as a fine art. In the 'soft style', the blurred image quality soaked the photographs in a dreamlike, surreal bath of heavily diffused light. Diffusion was introduced in photography and especially in portrait photography before the advent of film to emulate a painterly style, which was deemed more artistic, and to enhance the beauty of the women portrayed.

Starting with films like *Broken Blossoms* (1919), this style was embraced by cinematography. In Classical Hollywood, even in movies featuring a crisp deep-focus style, the close-up of the female star was usually embellished with soft diffusion, which could be produced by placing a special type of silk stocking in front of the lens or by applying thin layers of grease directly to it. Cinematographer Henry Alekan kept his black Dior silk stocking for decades, because he relied on its especially beautiful diffusion capabilities, up until the shooting of one of his last films, *The State of Things* (1982).

Most often, diffusion was combined with a blooming highlight produced by backlighting and with shallow depth-of-field. A scene from Josef von Sternberg's film *Blonde Venus* (1932), photographed by Bert Glennon, is emblematic of this style. It is no coincidence that the star, Marlene Dietrich, had to smoke to enhance the diffusion effect. Costume designers and art directors chose fabrics and materials with a beautiful shimmery look such as the sequins on Dietrich's fan. Diffusion has a long-standing tradition in painting to which the pictorialists were referring. For instance, Leonardo Da Vinci invented a certain kind of diffusion called *sfumato*, achieved by adding thin layers of whitish glaze to oil paintings. This technique had a softening

Shallow depth-of-field and diffusion in *Blonde Venus* (1932); the soft look of *Sky Captain and the World of Tomorrow* (2004)

effect and lent depth to the landscape by creating a hazy, misty atmosphere. At the same time, the figure in the foreground is separated from the background and thus gains more presence, with the viewer's gaze directed to the more detailed and sharper areas of the image.

Like the randomly distributed grain, diffusion works against the overly sharp look of CGI. With photochemical stock there is, intrinsically, a slight diffusion. It stems from the silver halide

Vignetting with matte in *Das Cabinet des Dr. Caligari* (1920)

crystals in the emulsion. When the light enters the film stock, it gets more and more diffused, primarily in the red-sensitive layer at the bottom. *Sky Captain and the World of Tomorrow* (2004), a film shot in a completely computer-generated environment, establishes a phantasmagoric 1940s look. In the history of film, this combination of soft style, colours and diffusion never existed, since Technicolor – the dominant colour system at the time – strictly avoided optical diffusion, but nevertheless it is beautiful and perfectly serves its purpose in evoking a period style.

Lens flares are surely the most widespread analogue artefact in CGI. As early as 1999, author Terence Masson called them a cliché in computer graphics. In fact for several years, they acted like flags, indicating the computer origin of the images, which seems ironic given that they were introduced with the opposite effect in mind. When utilised carefully, lens flares can contribute to the aesthetics of CGI in a convincing fashion; they imply the presence of a camera because lens flare originates from internal reflections in the lens. On the image's surface they act as a suturing device which fuses different image parts in compositing. And finally they can trigger associations either with a sunny, southern feeling or with a dark noir style when created by head- or searchlights.

The term vignetting describes the decrease in brightness towards the edges of the frame. It is an effect that formerly occurred with the use of mainly wide-angle lenses and is therefore associated with older films. In a still from *Das Cabinet des Dr. Caligari* (1920), the vignetting effect is enhanced with a matte. As cinematographer Tom Fährmann reported in an interview, vignetting is now routinely added to films because modern lenses are so even in their rendition of brightness that it has become necessary to guide the viewer's gaze towards the centre of the frame, and also to add to the cohesive impression of an image. For his 'artificial reality' in *Moulin Rouge!*, Baz Luhrmann combined vignetting with dust and scratches. Together with the breathless moves of the virtual camera, these artefacts contributed to an ambiguous effect situated somewhere between historicity in a style inspired by Georges Méliès, and an aesthetics of postmodern pastiche.

Functional Typology of Analogue Artefacts in VFX

To adjust CGI to the viewer's expectations in the cinema – or in short to emulate a film look – is certainly the primary reason for the incorporation of analogue artefacts into CGI and compositing. Often CGI is perceived as too 'perfect', but instead of labelling it as perfect, I would rather discuss the topic from the perspective of complexity. For a long time, images tended to seem too carefully composed, and this lack of complexity threatened and continues to threaten their aesthetic value. In 1974, the psychologist D. E. Berlyne conducted an empirical study to investigate the relationship between complexity and a viewer's appreciation based on the hedonistic value (the measurable pleasure felt by the spectator) of an artwork. When an artwork lacks complexity, it evokes – according to Berlyne – little hedonistic value. However, this value increases with complexity up to an optimal point. When the complexity is experienced as being too dominant – or to put it differently, confusing and chaotic – the hedonistic value decreases. These results explain why CGI is expected to offer a certain amount of complexity.

Art historian Gottfried Boehm introduced the term 'aesthetic density' to describe a similar concept. Imperfections, based on analogue artefacts, enrich the image with textures and deviations, thus densifying the visual impression. As I have noted in my reflections on a theory of representation of CGI, model-building based on mathematical algorithms leads to a lack of randomness in compositions. Obviously many practitioners – directors and visual-effects artists – are aware of this interrelation. Among others, James Cameron advised his visual-effects team during the production of *Terminator 2: Judgment Day* (1991): 'Don't think of yourselves as Industrial Light and Magic, think of yourselves as Industrial Light and Dirt.'[19] On *Moulin Rouge!*, Baz Luhrmann 'wanted the visual effects to have a handmade feel, to hark back to those olden days rather than be seamless in terms of their digital perfection',[20] while Lars von Trier, according to his long-term collaborator Peter Hjorth, had the label 'Make mistakes!' attached to his monitor.[21] Wherever possible, these film-makers were trying to work against the cleanliness and orderliness of CGI.

In addition to these basic explanations, my research has identified the following functions of analogue artefacts in visual-effects-driven movies:

/// They help to create *aesthetic coherence* in compositing, integrating the image parts from different sources seamlessly and in a convincing way.

As mentioned above, when in *Forrest Gump* the protagonist had to be inserted into pre-existing historical documentary footage of famous figures from art and politics, it was necessary to eliminate the artefacts before the compositing could be performed, and reintroduce them afterwards. If these differences between the various image elements were not ironed out, the aesthetic incoherence would attract attention to itself, leading to a change in the mode of perception whereby the image composition would become the subject of reflection. According to the rules of the continuity system in Classical Hollywood film, it was imperative to avoid this kind of inconsistency. Much of the fascination elicited by the playful ironic mode present in *Forrest Gump* can be attributed to the double consciousness at work. The seamlessness of the compositing acts like a perfect magician's trick, where we know that we are viewing an illusion, but are unable to locate the deception, however much we scrutinise the performance. Paul Grainge used the term 'eclectic irony' suggested by Jim Collins to contextualise this effect. These films 'utilise the sophistication of media culture ... greeting new forms of textuality by reworking traces of the "semiotic array" in hybrid and ironic combinations'.[22]

As we have seen, attempts to evoke a historical period or indicate a flashback by reproducing earlier technical or aesthetic standards and/or wear and tear like scratches and dirt, date back several decades. Such techniques are often associated with the genre of biopics, and helped to underscore the public significance of the person portrayed, as in Martin Scorsese's *Raging Bull* (1980). In *Le fabuleux destin d'Amélie Poulain* (2001), this tradition is once again inverted to ironic effect when the protagonist watches her own funeral on TV. Such an ironic distancing effect had been lacking in Oliver Stone's *JFK* (1991), where staged footage was introduced side by side with historical sources. While Robert Burgoyne attributes the 'ferocious controversies' surrounding *JFK* and *Forrest Gump* to the use of CGI and 'the seamless splicing together of fictional scenes and archival footage ... blurring the boundary between actuality and fiction', I would argue for strict distinctions between these two films.[23] In *Forrest Gump*, as in *Zelig*, there is a comedic element at work that instructs the viewer to doubt the documentary status of the hybrid images.

Due to the lack of such internal inconsistencies as well as of any markers to flag the staged footage as fictitious, such guidelines are missing from *JFK*.

/// They mark different narrative strands in complex patterns to support the viewer's orientation.

The Matrix is the best-known example of a narrative structure that implies a double diegesis differentiated by various degrees of a supposed reality effect. Colour codes and differences in *mise en scène* helped the viewer recognise the different worlds, within and without a computer-simulated reality. With a similar pattern, Mamoru Oshii's *Avalon* (2001) established a scheme based on analogue artefacts in combination with colour codes. At first, the game world is toned in sepia and indicated by heavy diffusion, in part as black halo. Black halo had been a fashion in a certain kind of art reportage photography of the 1970s whereby light diffusion was added in the printing process. However, starting with *Tron* (1982), many films with a narrative scheme similar to that of *The Matrix* exposed the digitality of the alternative, simulated world, thus generating a difference to the filmic material, even when a major part of the simulated world had been shot on film, as with *Tron*, *Virtuosity* (1995) and *Johnny Mnemonic* (1995).

/// They enhance a film's style for artistic reasons, either to deepen the expressiveness of the film or to comment on the film-making process in a self-reflexive manner.

In this case, the CGI emulates the look of analogue film in order to deliver something the viewer would perceive as familiar as well as a filmic experience conspicuously different from his or her everyday perception. It is no coincidence then, that this strategy is mainly applied to science-fiction or fantasy films to underscore their autonomous fictional worlds. A typical example is *Sky Captain and the World of Tomorrow*, which combines a lovingly devised pastiche of film noir elements with a romantic soft-focus style to produce a filmic representation soaked in nostalgia and cinephilia. The sheer quantity of analogue artefacts establishes its postmodern stylisation in creating a fairy-tale world full of mythic allusions. We could relate this strategy to Victor Shklovsky's call for alienation in the representation of an art work. In mockumentaries, a similar style serves another purpose, namely to introduce a different quality in a self-reflexive manner with an ironic or even sarcastic tone.

/// They reinforce the illusion of authenticity by emulating low-resolution footage or blurred and shaky images like those an amateur witness might produce when capturing a scene.

Analogue artefacts have long become markers of authenticity, especially when they involve noise and the breakdown of signals as in a famous scene from *Wag the Dog* (1997). On a blue-screen stage the two protagonists produce a fake documentary about an alleged war in Albania to divert attention from a sex scandal involving the US president. In this satirical tale about media manipulation, artefacts such as screen-lines, noise and dropouts are incorporated to denote a tradition of war reportage in an attempt to simulate authenticity.

Simulation of an 'amateur' look in *War of the Worlds* (2005)

There are a vast number of such emulations of amateur or documentary footage. They are often connected to the framed representation on a television screen such as the surveillance footage in *Enemy of the State* (1998) or the previously mentioned shots gathered by the journalists in *District 9*. By displaying certain clusters of distortions commonly associated with stressful situations or clandestine operations where cameramen risk their lives to shoot the material, they enhance the reality effect. *War of the Worlds* (2005) is a case in point. Its overt allusions to media representations of 9/11 recall a feeling of paranoia. As Bill Desowitz noted of the film: 'The gritty look was inspired by amateur 9/11 footage, with dust and debris falling from the sky, and hand-held shots of pandemonium. ... The vfx shots occur behind smoke, ambience and camerawork.'[24]

Nostalgia, Style and Authenticity

Such widespread replication of the characteristics of film and electronic video stands in sharp opposition to the assumption that media develop towards a completely transparent representation of reality. And I would even contest D. N. Rodowick's assertion that 'technological and creative innovations in digital image synthesis have been driven by a single, though somewhat paradoxical goal: the achievement of "photographic realism"'.[25] First of all, the phenomena analysed here are highly mediated transformations of the current state of the art in photography. They do not aspire to the standards of professional technologies, but rather display earlier or low-tech approaches to photography. Second, there have always been different strands in computer-generated imagery such as non-photographic renderings in animated films, computer games and many more applications outside the entertainment industry, i.e. scientific visualisations. In turn, such visualisations can become part of fictional narrations to denote a scientific approach to fictitious objects or events, as in science-fiction films where imaginary inventions are rooted in some pseudo-scientific explanations. For instance, in *Avatar* (2009), not only the world in Pandora, but the function of the Avatars themselves is explained and backstoried, or in *Inception* (2010), where the highly subjective experience of the protagonists is continually explained to the audience.

Photorealism is but one possible outcome in this development and a majority of the several hundred films that I have analysed in the course of my research show a variety of strategies, even to the point where discontinuities are deliberately highlighted rather than subsumed in seamless integration. Generally, technological developments tend to seek to showcase their achievements. If these achievements were dissolved in perfect photorealism, so that the viewers would no longer notice them nor distinguish them from ordinarily captured film, much of the fascination would be lost. Many of my investigations into technological changes have shown that this downplaying of innovations only happens when a new technology is fully mastered. Based on my analyses, this phase began only recently, with films like *The Kite Runner* (2007), *United 93* (2006) or *Children of Men* (2006).

Apart from the functions described in the preceding pages, there are more general aspects located in culture and society to discuss to eventually explain the phenomena of exposed cinematic artefacts in CGI. In the wake of Fredric Jameson's critical notions of postmodern culture in late capitalism, nostalgia and pastiche were two of the most debated concepts in the last decade. In Jameson's reflections – that are by themselves highly nostalgic for a bygone era – he contrasts the sincerity of high-modernist culture to the 'waning of affect in postmodern culture', in which 'modernist styles … become postmodernist codes' and produce 'a field of stylistic and discursive heterogeneity without a norm'. He associates the 'nostalgia film' with the concept of '"historicism" … the random cannibalisation of all the styles of the past, the play of random stylistic allusion'.[26] Jameson's highly influential analysis concludes that nostalgia is yet another commodity governed by capitalist laws.

In his investigations into the use of black-and-white cinematography in contemporary films, Paul Grainge identifies the 'retro style' that 'has become a term used to describe the past as it is figured within style narratives of the chic and trendy … playful, ironic, and where the past is a storehouse of fashion'.[27] It is a mode infused with an atmosphere of 'pastness'. Many scholars associate this resurgence of pastness with the 'death of cinema', a cultural change from the once analogue mode of production, with the cinema as the locus of exhibition, to a hybrid or fully digital version of 'what was cinema',[28] with a multitude of scattered displays now replacing what had been the cinematic experience. The currently fashionable retro mode in the smartphone apps, Hipstamatic and others, fit into this explanation in that they connect a vernacular culture of easy snapshot photography to a tradition that was once charged with a higher value reserved for special moments in family life such as holidays and weddings. Moreover, in the case of cinema, there is the specific cultural tradition of fandom, termed cinephilia, which, as Benson-Allott suggests, is at the very foundation 'to create a transhistorical cinematic mythology' and 'a celluloid affect'.[29]

Pastiche, however, is not a practice restricted to postmodernism, nor to cinema, nor to nostalgia. As Gérard Genette in *Paratexts*[30] and Richard Dyer in *Pastiche* point out, it has a long-standing tradition in art, literature and in many other cultural practices. 'The word itself comes from Italian "pasticcio" … which, in its earliest recorded use, meant a pie … . The idea of a mixed dish – meat and/or vegetables plus pastry – was then applied to art.'[31] Based on this etymological definition, Dyer differentiates between 'pasticcio-pastiche' to denote a combination of means[32] and pastiche in the sense of imitation which is 'unconcealed',[33] 'textually signalled' and 'evaluatively open'.[34] Genette refers only to the latter meaning, but distinguishes it from parody, travesty and persiflage in assigning the pastiche the role of a more lovingly playful form of imitation restricted to style.

Style in this conception can be considered as independent of the content, that is, as an intertextual and transtextual tool to tell or show something new in a fashion borrowed from earlier artworks. With the concept of pasticcio-pastiche we have a theoretical framework to understand the highly hybrid mode that characterises the strategies described and analysed in the previous sections.

Beyond being a purely transtextual strategy, the dislocation and reappropriation of stylistic features across historical and medial boundaries creates a specific form of meaning. It is with (semio-)pragmatics, established by Roger Odin[35] and further developed by Frank Kessler and William Uricchio, that we can investigate this transformation of style from an autonomous feature of filmic artworks to a signifier in its own right. In his reflections on a definition of the documentary, Odin elaborates how the documentary is essentially a mode of communication highly informed by the institutional framing both of the production and the sociocultural space of consumption which informs the spectator how to 'read' a film. This entails extratextual information as well as internal signals such as credits, but also stylistic features that call upon the spectator's intertextual knowledge to interpret specific bundles of textual properties as indicating a nonfiction film. Noël Carroll defines this extratextual framing as index: 'When a film is indexed as nonfiction then we know that it is appropriate to assess it according to the standards of objectivity of the field of which it is an example.'[36] In the words of Odin, the documentary mode produces an 'authentic effect'.[37]

Following this line of theoretical reasoning, we can understand the reappropriation and recontextualisation of material and stylistic properties from historical, documentary or amateur footage in fiction films as a transposition from style to meaning. The style references a specific production/consumption mode and transposes it onto a different film. A typical case of this strategy is the mockumentary, where the stylistic features of a documentary are applied to a fiction film. It is precisely the accumulated, exaggerated and exposed artificiality that is typical of all the films discussed here, that provokes an ironic, self-reflexive stance and enables this playful merging of a variety of allusions and quotations. 'Authenticity' in this context is not meant to be a category to be evaluated in the framework of truth or fakery, but a sheer effect that puts any reality represented in the media into question.

Acknowledgment: I would like to thank Dominik Schrey for his valuable suggestions.

Notes

1. Baz Luhrmann, quoted in Joe Fordham, 'Paris by Numbers', *Cinefex* no. 86 (2001), p. 16.
2. Barbara Flückiger, 'Zur Konjunktur der analogen Störung im digitalen Bild' [On the Boom of Analogue Imperfections in Digital Images], in Alexander Böhnke and Jens Schröter (eds), *Analog/Digital – Opposition oder Kontinuum? Beiträge zu Theorie und Geschichte einer Unterscheidung* (Siegen: Transcript, 2004), pp. 407–28; *Visual Effects: Filmbilder aus dem Computer* (Marburg: Schueren, 2008).

3. Computational photography captures images in connection with data that allow their transformation based on a series of images or on the recording of a light field.
4. See D. N. Rodowick, *The Virtual Life of Film* (Cambridge, MA and London: Harvard University Press, 2007), p. 94.
5. William J. T. Mitchell, *The Reconfigured Eye: Visual Truth in the Post-photographic Era* (Cambridge, MA: MIT Press, 1992).
6. Wolfgang Ullrich, *Die Geschichte der Unschärfe* (Berlin: Klaus Wagenbach, 2002).
7. Turner Whitted, 'An Improved Illumination Model for Shaded Display', *Commun. ACM* vol. 23 no. 6 (1980), pp. 343–9.
8. A shader describes a surface's reaction to incident light. The Phong shader was an early example. It was comprised of a term for the colour of an object, one for the glossy reflection and another one for ambient light. With these properties it generated the look of plastic.
9. Caustics are a pattern of light as seen on the bottom of a swimming pool or below a glass. It is created by internal reflection and refraction.
10. Nelson Goodman, *Languages of Art* (Indianapolis, IN: Hackett Publishing Company, 1976 [1968]); *Ways of Worldmaking* (Indianapolis, IN: Hackett Publishing Company, 1990 [1978]).
11. Goodman, *Languages of Art*, p. 37.
12. Janusz Kaminski, quoted in Jay Holben, 'Criminal Intent', *American Cinematographer* vol. 83 no. 7 (July 2002), p. 35.
13. See http://store.kodak.com/store/ekconsus/en_US/html/pbPage.termsT/ThemeID.16765600.
14. Kaminski, in Holben, 'Criminal Intent', p. 36.
15. Caetlin Benson-Allott, '*Grindhouse*: An Experiment in the Death of Cinema', *Film Quarterly* vol. 62 no. 1 (Fall 2008), pp. 20–6.
16. Post-processing is applied to CGI after the rendering.
17. Ron Brinkmann, *The Art and Science of Digital Compositing* (San Diego, CA: Morgan Kaufmann, 1999), p. 233.
18. Stephen Prince, 'The Emergence of Filmic Artefacts: Cinema and Cinematography in the Digital Era', *Film Quarterly* vol. 57 no. 3 (Spring 2004), p. 32.
19. James Cameron, quoted in Jody Duncan, 'A Once and Future War', *Cinefex* no. 47 (1991), p. 33.
20. Joe Fordham, 'Paris by Numbers', *Cinefex* no. 86 (2001), p. 16.
21. Peter Hjorth, 'The Development of Shooting Concepts from *The Celebration* to *The Boss of It All*', in Andreas Kirchner *et al.* (eds), *Abschied vom Zelluloid? Beiträge zur Geschichten und Poetik des Videobildes* (Marburg: Schueren, 2008).
22. Paul Grainge, *Monochrome Memories: Nostalgia and Style in Retro America* (Westport, CT: Praeger, 2002).
23. Robert Burgoyne, 'Memory, History and Digital Imagery in Contemporary Film', in Paul Grainge (ed.), *Memory and Popular Film* (Manchester and New York: Manchester University Press, 2003), p. 222.
24. Bill Desowitz, 'War of the Worlds, A Post 9/11 Digital Attack', *VFXWorld*, 7 July 2005, http://www.awn.com/articles/production/iwar-worldsi-post-911-digital-attack-0.
25. Rodowick, *The Virtual Life of Film*, p. 101.
26. Fredric Jameson, *Postmodernism, or, the Cultural Logic of Late Capitalism* (London: Verso, 2001), p. 17.
27. Grainge, *Monochrome Memories*, p. 54.

28. Rodowick, *The Virtual Life of Film*, p. 25.
29. Benson-Allott, '*Grindhouse*', p. 22.
30. Gérard Genette, *Paratexts* (Cambridge: Cambridge University Press, 1997).
31. Richard Dyer, *Pastiche* (London: Routledge, 2007), p. 8.
32. Ibid., pp. 9–21.
33. Ibid., pp. 21–5.
34. Ibid., p. 24.
35. Roger Odin, 'For a Semio-pragmatics of Film', in Warren Buckland (ed.), *The Film Spectator: From Sign to Mind* (Amsterdam: Amsterdam University Press, 1995 [1983]).
36. Noël Carroll, *Theorising the Moving Image* (Cambridge: Cambridge University Press, 1996), p. 232.
37. Odin, 'For a Semio-pragmatics of Film', p. 221.

2 *BODIES*

At the 86th Academy Awards, Sandra Bullock was nominated for Best Actress in a Leading Role for Alfonso Cuarón's space disaster movie *Gravity* (2013). A couple of weeks prior to the announcement of the Academy Awards winners, the Visual Effects Society held its own awards, at which Bullock's character in *Gravity*, Ryan Stone, was nominated as an 'Outstanding Animated Character in a Live Action Feature Motion Picture', alongside the digital dragon Smaug from *The Hobbit: The Desolation of Smaug* (2013) and one of the gargantuan *kaiju* from Guillermo del Toro's *Pacific Rim* (2013). How could the same performance be celebrated both as a triumph of human physicality and of technologised simulation? Most of the coverage of Bullock's performance drew attention to the gruelling process she had undergone to simulate the appearance of weightlessness on screen, and the isolation she endured as the only actor for most of the film, held up by props, wires and harnesses, and probed by a camera at the end of a robotic arm: it was a poignant picture of how something as human and delicate as 'acting' can be utterly modified by new technologies.

But technology has always mediated our view of the filmic body. From the multiple exposures that helped Georges Méliès to clone his screen self indefinitely and allowed Buster Keaton to play every instrument in the band for *The Playhouse* (1921), through John P. Fulton's dazzling process shots to 'disappear' Claude Rains in *The Invisible Man* (1933), to the contemporary motion-capture studios that turn human performance into just one stage in the production of augmented images of corporeal movement, special effects have made the body a site of ontological contest, and a testbed for imaging technologies.

The essays in this section examine the issues raised when special-effects processes are unleashed upon human, animal and supernatural bodies. As a site for the inscription of power and the signifiers of identity, the body has long been a particularly malleable variable for use in special effects that warp, disguise and transform human limbs and visages into abject monstrosities or godlike superheroes. The warrior body as agent of labour is the subject of Drew Ayers's 'Bleeding Synthetic Blood', which analyses the 'simulated space' of *300* (2006) as a staging ground for tensions between the analogue and digital, and the materialisation of information itself. If *300*'s Spartan bodies are particularly productive of meaning in their muscular visibility, the penguin bodies of *Happy Feet* (2006) enact the inverse, eliding and warping the signifiers of race to selectively deny facets of the original performer's identity: Tanine Allison's 'Blackface, *Happy Feet*' contrasts the motion capture of Savion Glover for *Happy Feet* with the rotoscoping of Cab Calloway seventy years earlier for *Betty Boop* cartoons, demonstrating a continuity not just between methods of transferring performance attributes from human to animated bodies, but the selective filtering and whitewashing of race. In 'Being Georges Méliès', Dan North explores the filmic body of an auteur, reconsidering the legacy of the French pioneer of cinematic special effects through a discussion of how he has been represented across a range of feature films, TV shows and artworks, up to and including his latest incarnation in Martin Scorsese's *Hugo* (2011). Finding similar bridges between analogue and digital eras, Stacey Abbott's 'The Battlefield for the Soul' examines the changing terms of body horror in demonic-possession films, from *The Exorcist* (1972) to recent films such as *The Last Exorcism* (2010), where production technologies, as well as supernatural forces, vie for control of (invariably female) bodies. In 'Baroque Façades', Angela Ndalianis uses the digital reconstruction of the youthful face of Jeff Bridges in *Tron: Legacy* (2010) to answer 'an effects-driven metaphysical question'.

Ndalianis uses theories derived from baroque architecture to interrogate the complex play with interior and exterior, old and new, that occurs in the film's reconstructions of the actor's face. The spectacular revivification of Bridges's image is an invitation to contemplate the broader science-fictional territory of artificial bodies and the ontological conundra they push upon us. Rounding out this section, Michael S. Duffy's 'Guillermo del Toro's Practical and Digital Nature' illustrates how director Guillermo del Toro takes a multifaceted approach to conveying unnatural phenomena on screen, utilising complex combinations of practical and digital-effects techniques in a bid to consistently and categorically inform how his often gruesome and grotesque bodies and creatures can be made both forensically astute and hauntingly beautiful.

The digital turn brought with it a teleological myth of human replacement, positing the convincing simulation of human existence and expression as a 'holy grail' for the industry. But as these essays show, the role of special effects in screen performance has a long and varied history, their illusionistic interventions marked by a *dramatis personae* of altered and artificial bodies whose vivid mutability goes hand in uncanny hand with their familiarity.

BLEEDING SYNTHETIC BLOOD
FLESH AND SIMULATED SPACE IN *300*

DREW AYERS

Blood does not merely flow in Zack Snyder's *300* (2006). It sprays, spurts and spatters, gushing forth from severed limbs and eviscerated torsos. Blood reminds us of the physicality of the body and the ease with which the boundaries of the flesh might be breached. Blood offers evidence of life, and its seeping from the body offers evidence of death. Blood is a material thing, and it contains the stuff from which we are made: the biological 'code' of DNA. Blood is life. In *300*, however, blood is also something else. Here, blood is lifeless. It is synthetic and simulated, an expression of a very different kind of code. *300*'s blood is the expression of binary computing code. It flows not from the biological body but from a particular interpretation and visualisation of numerical information. This blood, like almost all blood in mainstream narrative film, is a special effect, an enhancement and approximation of biological blood.

The simple fact of this blood's provenance, however, makes it no less visceral than its biological counterpart. In much the same way as a false alarm nevertheless stimulates and calls the body into action, so too does the synthetic blood of *300* index the viscerality of the living body. In his reading of C. S. Peirce, Brian Massumi argues that an indexical relationship exists not only between an object or event and the signs it produces – the fire and the alarm – but also between the sign and its effect on the perceiving body – the alarm and the body's jolt into action.[1] Thus, even if there is no fire and the alarm has sounded in error, the result is the same: the body perceives the alarm and experiences a jolt. The sign has produced its event. Regardless of whether or not there is actually a fire, the effect of the alarm on the body remains real and produces real effects.

The same applies to *300*'s blood. Whether or not the blood exudes from a biological body, its visualisation within the film registers in our perception, indexing the tangled relationship between physical bodies, computer simulations and visual perception. The visceral simulation of *300*'s blood functions as a test case for the interaction between living flesh and computer-generated imagery in the film as a whole. *300* is a confused – and confusing – visual object, both in terms of its own hybrid analogue/digital ontology, as well as in terms of our perception of its aesthetic appearance. On the one hand, the film confidently espouses a technological fantasy of the easy merging of flesh and informational patterns: the fleshy bodies and simulated spaces they inhabit are almost indistinguishable from each other. On the other hand, the film fetishises the 'hardbodies' of the Spartans, which creates a disconnect between their hyper-physicalised presentation and the glossy, simulated environment in which they reside. This mismatch is simultaneously foregrounded and elided, made uncanny and mundane.[2] *300* is a film that wants it both ways: it desires the affective impact of analogue bodies while at the same time presenting an image whose digital components undermine the physicality that the bodies

Blood: *300* (2007)

represent. *300*'s deployment of visual effects – most notably the almost exclusive use of simulated space – aims to fold the analogue into the digital and the digital into the analogue.

In his analysis of digital processes of image compositing, wherein photochemically based and computer-generated components are combined in a single image, Lev Manovich writes that the fundamental challenge of digital realism is

> no longer how to generate convincing individual images but how to blend them together. Consequently, what is important now is what happens on the edges where different images are joined. The borders where different realities come together is [sic] the new arena where the Potemkins of our era try to outdo one another.[3]

Elsewhere Manovich argues that digital compositing, which relies on an image composed of discrete units that can be easily exchanged and combined in myriad permutations, draws on the logic of our contemporary remix culture. This remix culture is itself founded in an 'information aesthetics' that is indicative of the flexibility and portability of data in the information age.[4] The intermingling of flesh and simulated space in *300* is symptomatic of this mode of informationalism, and the translation of flesh and blood into informational patterns – as well as the translation of informational patterns into material images of space – reflects on a desire of an informationalist cultural logic to attribute a fundamental flexibility and exchangeability to both flesh and computer code. At the same time, however, there is something *too* perfect about the images in *300*, something *too* mannered about the interaction between the bodies and the space they inhabit. *300*, therefore, becomes less about producing a photorealistic image (though, as I will later discuss, realism is a concern of the film-makers) and more about the effects of the interaction between its digital and analogue components. Or, to put it another way, *300* is worried about the indexicality of synthetic blood.

To the extent that *300* simultaneously fetishises the physical and the simulated, the analogue and the digital, it serves as an exemplar of the relationship between indexicality, photography and the digital image. As Michele Pierson argues, the reception of special effects, at least among connoisseurs and active fans, has always occupied a liminal space, and viewers take pleasure both in assessing the quality of the effects as well as in discovering how the film-makers achieved them. The primary mode of viewing for effects connoisseurs is not one of passive belief in the image but rather one of active critique of the film's techniques of visualisation. In discussing the period from 1989–95, a time she calls the 'wonder years' of digital visual effects, Pierson identifies two aesthetic strategies deployed by digital effects: simulationist and technofuturist. The former describes the attempt to render digital effects as an unnoticeable simulation of the physical world while the latter describes the development of a unique and specific digital aesthetic.[5] In these years, audiences developed a relationship of wonderment to digital effects, which was accompanied by a burst of paratextual material discussing the production history and context of the effects. This relationship, claims Pierson, has conditioned our reception of contemporary digital effects as well as the scepticism and speculation with which audiences approach the interaction between the digital and the analogue.

300's synthetic blood aims to mimic biological blood (simulationist) while at the same time possessing a computerised glossiness and digital aesthetic (technofuturist). Like the use of corn syrup, red paint, chocolate or ketchup to imitate biological blood, the digital blood of *300* is an effect aimed at simulating an indexical relationship with the body. This indexicality is largely affective, and it is achieved, in part, by relying on the presence of hyperphysicalised bodies in order to ground the simulation through its affective ties to the physical. Tom Gunning posits that much of what has been theorised as photographic indexicality is better understood not in terms of photography's relationship to a particular object in the world but rather in terms of our affective and phenomenological investment with the photographic image and the discourses that establish the photographic process as having the ability to put us in the presence of something absent.[6] Similarly, Alessandra Raengo, in her affective reading of Barthes's notion of the reality effect, argues that it is a sustained 'photochemical imagination' that produces an 'a(e)ffect of indexicality'.[7] Lev Manovich, explaining how photographic and photochemical attitudes persist in digital images, writes that 'at present our visual culture is characterised by a new computer "base" and an old photographic "superstructure"', indicating that, while film-making production practices may now be largely digital, their expression is framed within a photographic understanding of aesthetics.[8] Echoing this idea, Deborah Tudor, in her analysis of the nostalgia wrapped up in digital simulations of photographic processes, terms the imbrication of digital and photochemical processes as '"looking for Bazin" in that the certainty of an image's indexical relationship to actuality slips into the symbolic space of the real when photochemical images are placed in dialectic with digitised images produced solely within the computer'.[9] The synthetic blood of *300* is the point at which the film pivots between the affective registers of indexicality, and its allegiances are both to the physical bodies from which it flows as well as to the processes of simulation from which it emerges.

As a result of *300*'s desire to have its indexicality both ways, connoisseurship of the film's visual effects becomes difficult, as the analogue and the digital infect and bleed into each other, rendering their production difficult to assess without significant paratextual information. This confusion is also reflected in popular coverage of the film, which seems similarly mystified as to which elements are analogue and which digital. In particular, commentators were concerned with establishing just how fleshy the bodies of the actors really were, whether their muscular physiques were a product of gym labour, digital touchups, old-fashioned movie magic or a composite of all of these techniques. The uncertainty surrounding the live-action and simulated components of the film – as well as their interaction with each other – points to a larger concern of our networked, digital cultural logic: the desire to conceptualise all entities – human, animal, machine – as fundamentally translatable in terms of code or information. Digital visual effects function as one method by which we imagine, visualise and make material the possibility of this utopic informationalism. In the remainder of this chapter, I will explore how fleshy bodies might bleed synthetic blood – and how they might inhabit a simulated space – by thinking through the interaction between flesh and information in terms of their material basis in the abstraction of labour. The physical bodies of *300* are folded into the virtual spaces of the film, providing a visualisation of the materiality of information and the ways in which the virtual and actual become enfolded into each other. The conflicted perspective of *300*, which refuses to relinquish the physicality of the body while simultaneously imagining an environment in which flesh becomes part of a larger informational pattern, is symptomatic not only of contemporary approaches to image production but also indicative of our increasingly networked, informationalised and digital cultural logic.

Creating the Synthetic Fleshiness of 300

300 recounts the events of the Battle of Thermopylae, which took place in 480 BC when the Persian forces, led by Xerxes I, battled 300 Spartan warriors, led by King Leonidas. Originally recorded by the Greek historian Herodotus in his *Histories*, the story of the 300 Spartans has been retold in several contemporary incarnations, the most recent of which is the film *300*. *300* is based on a graphic novel of the same name by Frank Miller and Lynn Varley,[10] which in turn is based on the 1962 film *The 300 Spartans* (directed by Rudolph Maté). Snyder's 2006 retelling of *300* strives to maintain much of the visual style of Miller and Varley's book and, according to one interview, Snyder set out to make the book into a movie rather than make a movie of the book.[11] As a consequence of Snyder's commitment to staying faithful to the book's style, much of the *300* film had to be created digitally. Except for a single shot of a rider on horseback, the film was shot exclusively against bluescreen sets in a Montreal studio,[12] and the guiding directive of shooting, according to Snyder, was that 'whatever actors touched, or walked on, we should build. Everything else was going to be CG.'[13] In other words, aside from the actors and props, almost everything seen on screen is a digital simulation of space and materiality.

With such an effects-heavy production, it is easy to lose the tether to the materiality of live-action film-making– the sense that things are happening on a scale of human size and vision. A simple statistic will put things in perspective: out of 1,500 shots in the film, 1,306 of them involve digital effects,[14] and four different studios were tapped to handle each of the four battles that comprise the central action pieces of the film: Animal Logic, Hybride Technologies, Hydraulx and Pixel Magic.[15] According to Lisa Purse, a film like *300*, which is composed of almost completely digitally created environments, arouses materialist-based anxieties surrounding the compositing of digital effects and live action. For Purse, the presence of the profilmic (i.e. 'live-action') body in films like *Sky Captain and the World of Tomorrow* (2004) and *Sin City* (2005) bestows upon the image a material verisimilitude and integrity, even when those bodies are surrounded by digital visual effects and environments.[16] J. P. Telotte echoes Purse's claims, and he argues that hybrid films like *300* are in the process of working out the

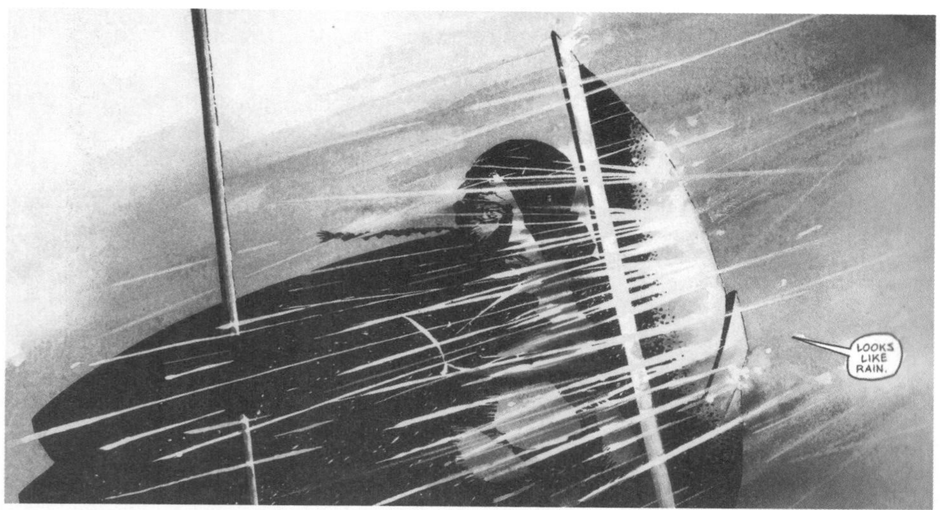

Book ... and movie

visual cultural problematic of the relationship between animated and live-action images.[17] The physical bodies in *300* thus serve to link the film both to the material basis of its production and filming as well as to larger anxieties about the informationalisation of the self and the body.

As a result, establishing the live-action and digital elements of the film became a preoccupation of popular coverage of the film, especially in the context of the muscular physiques of the film's actors. Lev Grossman, writing in *Time Magazine*, claims that 'with so much computer-generated make-believe going on, the actors' physicality is the movie's only link to the real world'.[18] However, because of the placement of material bodies into a digital space, the physicality of the actors' bodies is called into question. Michael Williams argues that, even though the musculature of the actors was achieved through a strict exercise regime and traditional Hollywood tricks of lighting and makeup, audience awareness of the pervasiveness of digital trickery fostered a distrust in the authenticity of the actors' bodies.[19] Creating additional confusion is the fact that, for the battle scenes requiring multitudes of soldiers, the film-makers used

MASSIVE software to fill out the ranks with computer-generated crowds, further blurring the line between live action and simulated bodies.[20]

To combat this confusion, press coverage and promotional materials made much of the physical transformation and muscularity of the actors in the film, specifically highlighting the fact that the bodies were indeed real and not the product of digital visual effects. Because so much of the film was created through the labour of computer coding and animation, doubt was cast on the veracity of the labour expended to sculpt the bodies of the actors. In response to allegations that the actors' physiques were the product of computer trickery, Mark Twight, proprietor of Gym Jones[21] and lead trainer of the *300* cast, used his blog to vigorously defend the authenticity of the actors' bodies and the efficacy of his workout regime.[22] Twight, of course, has a personal stake in maintaining the perception of authenticity of his trainees' bodies, but other accounts of the actors' training confirm Twight's claims, though they admit that traditional aspects of Hollywood magic – makeup and lighting – highlighted the appearance of the actors' bodies.

More specifically, lighting, shadows and makeup – achieved both through digital, as well as traditional, means – emphasised what the actors 'already had', rather than adding any muscle mass.[23] Prosthetic attachments were only used for scars and injuries, not to enhance the Spartans' physiques, and resin-based paints were applied directly to the actors' bodies to create shadowing effects and make the muscles 'pop'.[24] Gerard Butler (King Leonidas) denies taking any steroids, but admits that his body was enhanced with makeup: 'I had spray-on abs as well ... but I could also stick my finger up to almost the second knuckle – that's how deep in my hands could go. You use make-up on your face. That doesn't mean you're an ugly fucker.'[25]

Popular press accounts of the film fetishised the muscular physiques of the actors in *300* as well as the brutal training regimen they endured to achieve those bodies. These accounts stress the labour of the actors – in particular, that of the lead, Gerard Butler – and they take pains to emphasise that the sculpting of the actors' bodies was the product of hard work and weeks in the gym, rather than CGI magic. As Mark Twight puts it:

> The typical interviewer wants to know about the 'magic' workout the cast did to make them look so good. Some were disappointed to learn that hard work is magic, while others marvelled – as did we some days – that the actors would work so hard.[26]

According to coverage in publications such as *Men's Health*, *GQ* and *WebMD*, the actors trained ninety minutes to two hours a day, five days a week – plus an additional ninety minutes to two hours of fight training – for eight weeks, and, everyone was put on a calorie-restricted diet.[27] (The stunt crew trained the same way, with an additional two to four hours of fight training per day.)[28] The centrepiece of the training regime was the intense '300 Workout', which was a one-time, invitation-only challenge for those actors and stunt crew who felt up to the task.[29]

I have recounted the workout and diet regimes of the actors and stunt crew in detail in order to illustrate the extent to which these popular discussions work to sediment and reinforce the distinction between CGI and gym magic, virtuality and actuality, digitality and materiality. The excessiveness of this rhetoric functions as an overcompensation, stressing how much 'sweat' went into the production in order to alleviate any anxieties that might be attached to the idea of a fully digital body,[30] as well as serving to differentiate further the physical and simulated elements of the film image.

The fact that *300* was shot on traditional film stock provides an additional example of the oscillation between the worlds of digital visual effects and live-action film-making within the film. According to visual-effects supervisor, Chris Watts, *300* was filmed 'the old-fashioned way' on high-speed film stock.[31] At the time of production, digital video speed was limited to sixty frames per second, so Watts decided to shoot everything on photochemical film in the interests of giving the film 'a consistent look'.[32] The use of such high-speed cinematography was necessitated by Snyder's penchant for extreme slow motion and nested zooms. An example of the use of both can be found in the first major battle scene, during which Leonidas, in a seventy-second tracking shot, charges the field first with a spear and then with a sword. During this sequence, the film alternates between extreme slow-motion, standard-speed and fast-motion photography. Additionally, the camera seemingly zooms between three levels of the action: long, medium and close-up shots. These effects were created through a combination of high-speed photography, technological ingenuity and digital trickery, stitching together the perspectives of multiple cameras in post-production.[33]

Despite the reliance on 'old-fashioned' film-making techniques or the digitally assisted emulation thereof, as well as the rhetorical work of commentators in the press to delineate clearly the analogue and digital elements of the film, the visual effects and almost completely simulated space of *300* create an image that attempts to upset easy distinctions between live-action and digital film-making. The hyperphysicality of the actors serves to offset this tension and provide a material grounding for the images created by the film. What all of these production stories, anecdotes and interviews add up to is a sense that the boundaries between the analogue and the digital, as established within the context of *300,* are perceived as being quite porous, and each side requires advocates in order to establish its ontology. The contradiction between physical bodies and simulated space – between flesh and information – as pictured in *300,* rather than illustrating the failure of the film's visual regime to visualise adequately the relationship between digitality and materiality, instead provides a metapicture of the tension in contemporary visual culture's transition into digitality.

A Metapicture of Fleshy Information

Two key images from *300* will serve as guides through the thorny terrain between flesh, synthetic blood and simulated space. These images function as metapictures – visual illustrations of a concept – and they picture the theory of the relationship between flesh and information posited by *300.* According to W. J. T. Mitchell, metapictures are 'pictures about pictures', pictures that theorise their own existence.[34] They are material objects that claim to 'show themselves in order to know themselves'.[35] In that *300* pictures a kind of informationalist utopia, where flesh and information can freely intermingle regardless of medium, the film functions as a metapicture of the cultural technofantasies of exchangeability between the physical body and information networks. Within this fantasy, all that is required for translation is a general equivalent – in this case code – and I trace this fantasy through a lineage of theories of labour and materialism.

Bodies and simulated space; Leonidas and simulated architecture

The first image provides a thesis for the operating logic of visuality presented in *300*. In this image we see Leonidas, accompanied by his wife and son, inspecting his 300 troops before heading out to the Hot Gates. This image is particularly striking for the way in which it creates a dialogue between the physicality of the bodies and the simulated space in which those bodies reside. If we follow the rule of thumb established by Snyder, that everything except what the actors touch is CGI, then only the ground, the actors and perhaps the stalks of wheat closest to the actors are non-simulated within this image. Despite the differing production methods of the pieces of the image, the resulting composite image presents itself as a unified whole, the flesh and information interacting with each other without disrupting the visual integrity of the image. Through the excessive composition and posing of the image, the digital and analogue elements find a way to dialogue with each other without losing their pictorial verisimilitude.

The second image continues the visual logic of the first, and it adds the element of simulated architecture. The close-up of Leonidas's upper torso and face, directly juxtaposed with the simulation of Sparta in the background, highlights the way in which the visual regime of the film conceives of the digital and the analogue as exchangeable and conversant with each other. Along with their exchangeability within the visual scheme of the film itself, Leonidas and Sparta share a similar foundation in their expression of human labour. Both digital and analogue images in *300* occupy the position of abstract human labour, though they differ in the ways in which they foreground their embodiment of that labour. As Marx argues, 'The body of the commodity, which serves as the equivalent, always figures as the embodiment of abstract human labour, and is always the product of some specific useful and concrete labour.'[36] While they are visual equivalents within the diegesis of the film, the abstract labour congealed in the 'bodies' of the digital and analogue images is founded on different forms of concrete labour. The bodies of the Spartan warriors depicted in the film can be conceptualised as a form of abstract human labour rooted in the concrete labour of physical/bodily exertion. Each Spartan body represents not only the work, suffering, sacrifice and dedication needed to create it, but also, by proxy, the work, suffering, sacrifice and dedication of the entire Spartan army. The Spartan army is a single unit, fighting together in a phalanx and relying on each other to survive a battle. As such, the strength of the individual becomes the strength of the group, obscuring the singular labour required to form each physical body. The Spartan bodies thus come to represent labour in the abstract. Within the film, the men are not seen training (except as children), nor are they seen engaging in any sort of physical activity except waging war. Like the commodity in capitalism, these bodies arise in fully formed perfection, denying the labour needed for their creation and serving as a sign of abstract human labour.

These bodies function as complex sign systems, fetishising the affect of indexicality associated with the physicality of the analogue image. The actors playing the Spartans *really* had to submit themselves to the pain, toil and dedication of sculpting their physiques. They *really* had to train themselves to perform the stunts and other physical feats of the film. They *really* had to engage in mock fighting. The hyperphysicality of the actors' bodies creates their hyperpresence in the film and, in comparison to the simulated environments that surround them, the bodies of the Spartans are truly, emphatically *there*. The fictional filmic images of the Spartan warriors serve as indexes to the real bodies of the actors playing the Spartans, 'proving' that the representation of those bodies reflects a real body behind that representation.

The simulated images in *300*, on the other hand, are grounded in a seemingly less physical form of concrete labour, namely that of mental and technological labour.[37] Just as the physical images in *300* serve as forms of abstract labour, hiding the concrete labour behind their existence, so too do the simulated images in the film obscure their foundations in the concrete labour of mental exertion.[38] Unlike the overdetermined indexicality of the bodies in *300*, the simulated environments exist within a virtuality. That is, they have no concrete referent in reality and exist only as the result of the mental exertions of their human creators, giving them an ephemeral quality that the ostentatiously physical bodies of the film strive to offset. However, like their analogue counterparts, the simulated images of *300* strive to embody a kind of visual perfection. Both types of image are presented in a highly stylised manner, and both are presented as 'perfections' of their respective ontological positions. As such, both images are subject to the same kind of commodity fetishism that occludes the concrete labour that goes into their production, resulting in their integration into the cinematic whole of *300*.

The general equivalency between the digital and analogue modes of representation in *300* – the equivalency between information and flesh – results from an abstraction of their forms of materiality into the equivalent of code, and this abstraction also expresses itself as an *aesthetic* equivalency of form. While the fantasies of translation, abstraction and equivalence I have thus far been discussing happen beneath the surface, as a kind of cultural imaginary, this fantasy is also visible on the surface of the images. Between the flesh and simulated space of *300* there exists a sensorial equivalence, a sameness of form and expression. The digital and the analogue infect each other, and their ontological reciprocity within the image results in a certain affective stickiness that bleeds between the analogue and digital components of the image. As a result, the simulated images of space attract some of the phenomenological weightiness of the fleshy bodies, and the fleshy bodies attract some of the smoothness, glossiness and 'perfection' of the simulated environments. The sensorial circuit established between flesh and information creates an aesthetic and sensorial equivalency of digital and analogue forms. In other words, the digital and analogue pieces of the film look and feel like each other, which reinforces the fantasy that flesh and information can be easily exchanged.

The materiality of the digital image is one of the more pressing concerns of contemporary media studies, and I follow Deleuzian scholars in thinking through the 'digital turn' in terms of the ways in which the digital visualises a particular attitude toward the relationship between the actual and the virtual. In his *Cinema* books (specifically in *Cinema 2*), Deleuze theorises the relationship between the virtual and the actual and how a particular mode of cinema – the time-image – visualises this relationship.[39] What is most relevant to my own discussion concerning the ways in which the relationship between the actual and the virtual can be applied to the relationship between the analogue and the digital is Deleuze's formulation of how the actual and the virtual interact. Rather than acting dialectically, as opposing sides of the same coin, the actual and the virtual appear as reflections of each other, one inhabiting the image of the other.[40] Deleuze mobilises another set of metaphors – the crystal and the baroque fold – to make more vivid the confusion of inside and outside, which are in continual exchange, occurring within images that open up into the space between the actual and the virtual.[41] While Deleuze probably did not have visual effects (or *300*) in mind, his discussion of the relationship between the actual and the virtual can fruitfully be applied to issues of CGI and the relationship between analogue and digital modes of film-making.

For Deleuze, the actual and the virtual are co-constitutive of each other, and they form a circuit of sensation within the image. In the context of *300*, we can see the interaction between the actual and the virtual as well as the folding of flesh into the code of the digital environments. However, rather than opening up a new form of perception *à la* the time-image film, *300* strives to elide the crystalline structure of the actual and the virtual, presenting instead a flat movement image that imagines a utopia of informationalism. The bodies of the actors merge into the simulated environments that surround them, producing a whole that emphasises continuity rather than discontinuity, harmony rather than tension. Despite its insistence on presenting a cinematic world that refuses to differentiate between the analogue and the digital, *300* nevertheless acts as a metapicture of a particular kind of pervasive thinking about the relationship between flesh and information, one that reduces physical materiality to a kind of signifier of presence rather than something that is grounded in ontological difference.

The synthetic blood of *300* crystallises the relationship between the analogue and the digital, and it offers a location where we might see the actualisation of the affects of indexicality that influence the film. Sensation, for Massumi (as well as for Deleuze), is a key for understanding the ways in which images might open up new forms of perception, and this sensation is able to travel across different mediums.[42] *300*'s synthetic blood is an object that allows us to see how sensation might be translated between the physical and simulated components of the film. This idea of translation can also be applied to the relationship between the analogue and the digital, since both are expressions of similar sensational and representational desires. The act of sensation is fundamentally analogue – the example Massumi uses is the transformation of one medium (e.g. words) into another (e.g. thought) – and thus the digital must always first pass through the analogue at the moment of production and back through the analogue at the point of consumption. Thus, if we follow Massumi, every piece of digital media is also intrinsically analogue, in that in order to produce and consume that media, the world must first be translated, coded and then sensed by an observer.

In the context of *300*, Massumi's formulation allows us to reconcile some of the seeming contradictions in the film's approach to its analogue and digital pieces (though I would maintain that the contradictory nature of the film's imagery is what makes it such a valuable specimen for studying the role of actors, CGI and visual effects in today's media industries). Following a Deleuzian framework, the actual and the virtual must be thought of as pieces of the same crystal, folded into each other in a perpetual recursive circuit. The flesh of the bodies in *300* is folded into the digital environments of which they are a part, while at the same time, the digitality of the environments is folded into the flesh of the bodies. Each is granted some of the qualities and sensations of the other, and they share an aesthetic equivalency of form and appearance. Much of the difficulty in delineating the physical from the simulated in the film can be attributed to this exchange between digital and analogue. The film's synthetic blood, flowing digitally from the characters' physical bodies, evokes the sensations of real blood and violence. Regardless of its digital provenance and its ephemeral, stylised appearance, the potential effects this synthetic blood produces act on the viewer's physical body, creating stubbornly analogue sensations. The blood is of two worlds, much like the film itself. It is impossible to separate the virtual and the actual, the digital and the analogue, since they are pieces of the same whole.

With a foot placed firmly in both camps of analogue and digital film-making, *300* stands on the precipice of a shift in mainstream forms of media production, and it is representative of contemporary media in that it leans heavily on digital technologies while not being quite willing to completely forgo its ties to physical reality. Even with the rise of films like James Cameron's *Avatar* (2009) and Rupert Wyatt's *Rise of the Planet of the Apes* (2011), the motion-capture technology on which the animation of the characters is based still relies on the presence, during production, of living, breathing human actors. My goal in describing the dual (and often contradictory) nature of these hybrid, composite digital/analogue images is not to argue that there will ever be a 'pure' media of either completely analogue or completely digital production. Rather, my intent has been to argue that the analogue and the digital will always be present together, whether it be during production or consumption, and as such the digital and the analogue will be travel companions through various states of actuality and virtuality for as long as bodies engage with media.

Notes

1. Brian Massumi, 'The Future Birth of the Affective Fact: The Political Ontology of Threat', in Melissa Gregg and Gregory J. Seigworth (eds), *The Affect Theory Reader* (Durham, NC: Duke University Press, 2010), pp. 64–5.

2. Dan North argues that part of the enjoyment of special effects derives from 'spotting the joins' where live action meets special effect. As I will soon discuss, much of the extratextual 'are they real or aren't they' rhetoric surrounding the muscular bodies of *300* demonstrates a working through of North's process of 'spotting the joins'. See Dan North, *Performing Illusions: Cinema, Special Effects and the Virtual Actor* (London: Wallflower Press, 2008), p. 2.
3. Lev Manovich, *The Language of New Media* (Cambridge, MA: MIT Press, 2001), p. 155.
4. Lev Manovich, 'Image Future', *animation: an interdisciplinary journal* vol. 1 no. 1 (2006), pp. 39–40.
5. Michele Pierson, *Special Effects: Still in Search of Wonder* (New York: Columbia University Press, 2002), p. 101.
6. Tom Gunning, 'What's the Point of an Index? Or, Faking Photographs', *NORDICOM Review* vol. 25 nos 1/2 (2004).
7. Alessandra Raengo, *On the Sleeve of the Visual: Race as Face Value* (Hanover, NH: Dartmouth College Press, 2013).
8. Manovich, 'Image Future', p. 28.
9. Deborah Tudor, 'The Eye of the Frog: Questions of Space in Films Using Digital Processes', *Cinema Journal* vol. 48 no. 1 (2008), p. 92.
10. Frank Miller and Lynn Varley, *300* (Milwaukie, OR: Dark Horse Books, 1999).
11. I interpret Snyder's statement as indicating that he wanted to translate the poetics of the graphic novel to film, rather than try to impose the poetics of film onto the story of the graphic novel. A similar approach was taken in Robert Rodriguez and Frank Miller's *Sin City*. According to Snyder, '*300* – like *Sin City* – was story-based, presenting the point of view of a graphic novelist. I felt it was my job as a director to present that on screen'. Quoted in Joe Fordham, 'A Beautiful Death', *Cinefex* no. 109 (2007), p. 66.
12. Barbara Robertson, 'The Art of War', *Computer Graphics World* vol. 30 (2007), p. 20.
13. See also David E. Williams, 'Few against Many', *American Cinematographer* vol. 88 no. 4 (2007), p. 55.
14. Ron Magid, 'A Spartan Effort', *Animation* vol. 21 no. 4 (2007), p. 28.
15. Robertson, 'The Art of War', p. 21.
16. Lisa Purse, 'Digital Heroes in Contemporary Hollywood: Exertion, Identification, and the Virtual Action Body', *Film Criticism* vol. 32 no. 1 (2007), p. 16.
17. J. P. Telotte, *Animating Space: From Mickey to Wall-E* (Lexington: University Press of Kentucky, 2010), p. 241.
18. Lev Grossman, 'The Art of War', Time Inc., http://www.time.com/time/magazine/article/0,9171,1595241,00.html.
19. Michael Williams, 'The Idol Body: Stars, Statuary and the Classical Epic', *Film & History* vol. 39 no. 2 (2009), p. 46.
20. Robertson, 'The Art of War', p. 26. MASSIVE software (short for 'Multiple Agent Simulation System in Virtual Environment') is used to generate virtual crowds. MASSIVE was originally developed to generate the crowds in the battle scenes of Peter Jackson's *Lord of the Rings* trilogy (2001–3).
21. The reference to cult leader Jim Jones is intentional. According to Gym Jones co-owner Lisa Twight, they 'knew some people would call [them] a cult so [they] decided to own the joke'. Quoted in Brooks Barnes, 'The Cult of Physicality', *New York Times*, 11 September 2011.
22. Mark Twight, '300 Opinions: Everyone Has One', http://www.gymjones.com/knowledge.php?id=36.

23. Daniel Foggo, 'Those Spartan Guys Sure Knew How to Work up a Six-pack', *Sunday Times (London)*, 25 March 2007, p. 12.
24. Fordham, 'A Beautiful Death', p. 68.
25. Mickey Rapkin, 'Gerard Butler's Just Desserts', 6 January 2010, http://www.gq.com/blogs/the-q/2010/01/gerard-butlers-just-desserts.html.
26. Mark Twight, '"300" The So-called Program', http://www.gymjones.com/knowledge.php?id=35.
27. Gerri Miller, 'Inside "300"', HowStuffWorks, Inc., http://entertainment.howstuffworks.com/inside-3004.htm.
28. Kathleen Doheny, 'The *300* Workout: Can You Handle It?', WebMD, LLC, http://www.webmd.com/fitness-exercise/features/the-300-workout-can-you-handle-it.
29. According to Twight, around half of the cast and crew successfully completed the 300 Workout. See Jeff O'Connell, 'The Gerard Butler Workout: The 300 Fitness Plan', Rodale Inc., http://www.menshealth.com/celebrity-fitness/gerard-butler-300-workout.
30. For further discussion of the digital body, see Tanine Allison's chapter in this collection.
31. Magid, 'A Spartan Effort', p. 29.
32. Ibid.
33. Williams, 'Few against Many', p. 63.
34. W. J. T. Mitchell, *Picture Theory: Essays on Verbal and Visual Representation* (Chicago, IL: University of Chicago Press, 1994), p. 35.
35. Ibid., p. 48.
36. Karl Marx, *Capital: Volume 1: A Critique of Political Economy*, trans. Ben Fowkes (New York: Penguin Classics, 1990), p. 150.
37. As theorists of phenomenology point out, the mind/body duality is untenable if one conceives of consciousness as an embodied process that arises from an interaction with the world. My use of abstract labour as a means to integrate the digital and analogue components of the image is an attempt to move beyond such dualities.
38. For a discussion of the perceived 'effortlessness' of animation, see Vivian Sobchack, 'Animation and Automation, or, the Incredible Effortfulness of Being', *Screen* vol. 50 no. 4 (2009), pp. 375–91.
39. In short, the time-image is the logic that governs post-World War II art cinema, and as opposed to the movement-image, which follows a logic of action and reaction (as in Classical Hollywood cinema), the time-image follows a logic of duration and focuses on the space between perception and action. The time-image confuses past, present and future, and through its presentation of duration, it opens up a space of perception whose concern is perception itself.
40. Gilles Deleuze, *Cinema 2: The Time-Image*, trans. Hugh Tomlinson and Robert Galeta (Minneapolis: University of Minnesota Press, 1989), p. 68.
41. Ibid., p. 70.
42. Brian Massumi, *Parables for the Virtual: Movement, Affect, Sensation* (Durham, NC: Duke University Press, 2002), p. 135.

BLACKFACE, *HAPPY FEET*
THE POLITICS OF RACE IN MOTION CAPTURE AND ANIMATION[1]

TANINE ALLISON

Described by one critic as 'a mash-up of *March of the Penguins* and *Moulin Rouge*', the animated film *Happy Feet* (2006) features photorealistic Emperor penguins singing and dancing in Antarctica.[2] Acclaimed by critics and moviegoers alike, *Happy Feet* won the Academy Award for Best Animated Feature and was successful enough to spawn a sequel, *Happy Feet Two* (2011). Although both films were largely financed by Warner Bros., the first film in particular highlights its Australian roots: George Miller, known for the *Mad Max* films (1979–), served as director and shared writing and production credit; Australian actors Hugh Jackman, Nicole Kidman, Anthony LaPaglia, Hugo Weaving and even Steve Irwin (the 'Crocodile Hunter') performed voices; and the Sydney-based company Animal Logic created the animation and visual effects. But despite their Australian origins, the *Happy Feet* films are obsessed with American popular culture, especially music and dance.

Happy Feet and *Happy Feet Two* take the form of jukebox musicals, filled with snippets of American pop songs mixed together into toe-tapping medleys. In the first film, Hugh Jackman, playing a penguin named Memphis, impersonates Elvis Presley and, as Norma Jean, Nicole Kidman emulates the breathy voice of Marilyn Monroe. The film's narrative revolves around the tribulations of their son, Mumble, who prefers dancing to singing and is thus ostracised from the penguin community, which believes that each penguin must find – and sing – his 'heartsong'. Mumble, unlike the other penguins, speaks primarily through his body, instead of through his voice. The second film features Mumble as an adult, but focuses more on the efforts of his young son, Erik (voiced by Ava Acres), to discover his own special talent. Both films problematise issues of communication, particularly in relation to how the body acts as a conduit for or barrier to personal expression.

These problems are also apparent at the level of production. The division within the character of Mumble between voice and action, mind and body, reflects the technologies that were used to bring the character to life. Mumble, the imaginary offspring of American pop culture's two most iconic figures, is also an amalgam of performances representing distinct aspects of American culture. For both films, Elijah Wood – known in 2006 for just having starred as the Hobbit Frodo in *The Lord of the Rings* films (2001–3) – provided the voice for Mumble, while through the process of motion capture, famed tap dancer Savion Glover lent Mumble his distinctive movement and dancing. At its unacknowledged core, therefore, *Happy Feet* is not only about American pop culture, but also American race relations, narrating, however indirectly, the white appropriation of black culture, through both its voices and its songs. In addition to the fictional narrative, this appropriation takes place behind the scenes, with motion capture enabling a fusion of black and white performers. Utilising the recognisable voice of a white actor and the equally distinctive movements of an African American dancer to create the character of Mumble highlights the inherent hybridity of motion capture, which transposes human performances onto computer-generated models. It is the goal of this essay to explore the implications of this hybrid technology for the representation of race and ethnicity in contemporary animated film.

On the one hand, motion capture acts as a medium through which African American performance can be detached from black bodies and applied to white ones, making it akin to digital blackface. Moreover, *Happy Feet* perpetuates the association of blacks with music and corporeality, whether through a perceived gift for singing and dancing or an excess that needs to be contained (because of the black body's supposed strength or sexuality).[3] On the other hand, by severing performance from bodies with particular racial, ethnic and gender identifications, motion capture might hold open the promise of a truly post-racial form of representation. More than a coincidence, then, the black-and-white penguins may act as symbols of interracial harmony. To investigate these two possibilities, I will perform an historical comparison between Glover and jazz singer Cab Calloway, whose rotoscoped performances appeared in a series of Fleischer Studios Betty Boop cartoons in the early 1930s. While both rotoscoping and motion capture conceal and transform the performer's body, the context of Calloway's performances allows a critical assessment of the technology, while Glover's performance remains relatively invisible and thus unavailable for critical reflection. Rather than heralding a post-racial age, therefore, *Happy Feet*'s de-racialised characters ultimately make possible the regressive representations of ethnic minorities on the film's soundtrack, particularly in the voice acting of Robin Williams. Instead of transcending race, motion capture, in this instance, perpetuates the white appropriation of black culture.

Motion Capture as Special Effect

As with most contemporary animated features, the opening credits of *Happy Feet* and *Happy Feet Two* list the names of the stars who provided voice acting for the film: Elijah Wood, Robin Williams and so on. For both films, however, Savion Glover's name is nowhere to be found in the initial titles or in any of the trailers or ads; the film texts do not acknowledge his contribution as performer or choreographer until the closing credits – where it is not particularly prominent, wedged somewhere between the music arranger and the supervising sound editor. While not as famous as Williams or Kidman, Glover is widely regarded as the best tap dancer of his generation and has starred on Broadway and in numerous films and television shows, from *Tap* (1989) to *Bamboozled* (2000) to *Sesame Street* (1969–). And although he supplies just one piece of a character, this piece – like the voice, the one part the other top-billed performers provide – is essential, especially in these movies that take dancing as one of their central themes. So, why isn't Savion Glover's name more prominent?

John Bell explains film publicity's oversight of motion-capture performers, even famous ones like Glover, as a reluctance to update common assumptions about the nature of performance in the digital age. According to Bell, popular American culture 'lacks the language, concepts, or interest to fully come to terms with mediated performing object forms'.[4] As a form of 'digital puppetry', motion capture involves a human actor making a series of movements in order to enact a performance, but this performance only becomes visible through another form – the

CG model or digital puppet.[5] To some advocates of motion capture, like actor Andy Serkis and director James Cameron, the actor's performance comes through the mo-cap process unadulterated, ensuring enhanced realism and emotional authenticity for digital characters.[6] However, in the world of animation, many deride motion capture as 'Satan's rotoscope', an illegitimate shortcut replacing the artistry of the animator with a computer program.[7] The end credits of Pixar's *Ratatouille* (2007), for instance, take a crack at *Happy Feet* with a line that reads, '100% Genuine Animation! No motion capture or any other performance shortcuts were used in the production of this film.'[8]

These two camps disagree on whether motion capture should be artistically valued as 'real' acting or disparaged as computer-automated cheating, but they agree that motion capture has the ability to create unprecedented realism in animation. However, the 'realism' at stake in many discussions of motion capture may be a red herring. Instead of 'blending in', mo-cap animation stands out because of the distinctive quality of the movement, whether realistic or uncanny. The popular press articles and behind-the-scenes extras that explain and promote the technology play into viewers' awareness of the technique, so audiences are even more likely to regard the technique *as* a technique and not just as an immersive illusion of life. As Paul Ward argues of rotoscoping, technological innovations meant to produce increased mimesis can still be used

> as a kind of *special* effect, while simultaneously playing on the increased sense of realism they provided. ... [T]here is a sense that they are augmenting the naturalistic look of the films while also *drawing attention* to the naturalism they are engendering.[9]

More than other special effects, though, which revel in their visibility, motion capture first involves an act of erasure, grounding itself in invisibility. The movements of the motion-capture artist may be recorded optically, but the visual aspects of the performance are often ignored in favour of the spatial arrangement of the performer's body. The motion-capture apparatus transforms this visual and spatial performance into data – now only legible as code by the computer – until it is revisualised and applied to a computer-generated model. The extent to which the human model's performance is perceptible in the finished product is thus a constant, and fraught, question.

Yet to downplay the impact of the mo-cap performance, to consider it invisible or under erasure, has significant consequences for our evaluation of performance in the digital age. Already, the film actor exists as part of a vast image-making machine; digital technology just heightens this state of affairs. Motion capture – by challenging contemporary notions of stardom and performance – brings this mechanisation to the fore. The image of the mo-cap performer as machine differs from the image evoked earlier by John Bell of the performer as puppeteer. While the puppeteer connotes artistry, mastery and control over the technologies (the puppets) that visualise the performance, the mo-cap performer can be derogated as merely a movement generator providing the raw material for subsequent technological processes.

Indeed, mo-cap artists are often treated as such by the industry: paid little and uncredited, even as they create performances (or at least movements) that can potentially be used over and over again, attached to different digital characters. Despite lip service from the likes of Andy

Serkis, one of the very few to have gained some amount of fame for this kind of work (as Gollum in *The Lord of the Rings* films or Caesar in *Rise of the Planet of the Apes* [2011], for instance), motion capture has more potential to instrumentalise filmic performance than to innovate and reinvigorate it. This view of the mo-cap artist as a mere cog in the larger digital animation machine may have played a part in Savion Glover's neglect in *Happy Feet*'s credits. The film-makers may have considered Glover a technician rather than a performer – something akin to a glorified Foley artist, paid to create realistic tap sounds and movements. In this view, his contribution would pale in comparison to that of Elijah Wood or Robin Williams; unlike the voice actors, he would not be perceived as having interpreted the character or expressed his thoughts and feelings.

Race, Expression and the Rotoscope

To understand Savion Glover as merely a highly skilled movement-generator, however, fails to take into account the fact that his unique dance style *is* a form of expression, just as subtle and revealing as acting or speaking. Although he does not appear in *Happy Feet*'s opening credits, Glover is featured in two paratexts related to the first film, both of which emphasise dancing as communicating. On the DVD release, he appears in a special feature titled 'Dance like a Penguin: Stomp to the Beat', addressing a basic tap-dancing lesson to kids. He reiterates the dancer's ability to express him- or herself through movement. 'Like all art forms', he begins, 'dance is a form of communication.' In addition, a behind-the-scenes featurette produced for television, '*Happy Feet*: Creating the Tap', focuses primarily on the motion-capture process, the penguin choreography and Glover's contribution to the film. Cutting back and forth between Glover in an interview and shots of him dancing in the mo-cap suit, the film emphasises the commonalities between Glover and the character of Mumble. Glover explains, 'I'm best expressed through the feet, just like Mumble.' George Miller, interviewed for the featurette, remarks, 'we wanted [Glover's] very distinct style to mark Mumble out as an individual and as an artist'. Beyond merely dancing instead of singing, Mumble stands out from the penguin society because his dancing is particularly expressive.

Throughout *Happy Feet*, Mumble dances seemingly involuntarily to express emotion – love, frustration, joy and so on. Soon after he emerges from the egg (feet first, of course), he begins tapping, skittering across the ice. When Memphis, embarrassed at his son's odd behaviour, asks him what he's doing with his feet, Mumble replies, 'I'm happy, Pop. They're happy too'. Later, he dances to the singing of Gloria (voiced by Brittany Murphy), conveying through movement that he is falling in love with her. But beyond personal communication, dancing becomes a way to unite the community of penguins in a way their individual heartsongs cannot. After Mumble undergoes a quest to determine why the penguins' supply of fish has dried up,

Tap dancer Savion Glover provided the dancing for Mumble through motion capture. *Happy Feet* DVD special feature, 'Dance like a Penguin: Stomp to the Beat'

he leads humans back to the penguin colony. When the penguins discover the effect their dancing has on the humans, the penguin elders finally accept Mumble and the whole community adopts his dancing. A montage sequence shows the world uniting to finally curb overfishing and pollution once a video of thousands of penguins dancing goes viral.

Like Mumble, Glover has used dance to express not just personal emotions, but communal experience. His work has sought to convey the history and experience of African Americans. As a young dance prodigy, hailed as 'a saviour of tap dance – the ultimate copier and absorber of tradition', Glover had the opportunity to work alongside such tap legends as Charles 'Honi' Coles, Sammy Davis, Jr and Howard 'Sandman' Sims.[10] The tradition he absorbed and sought to preserve was explicitly linked with the black experience. His second appearance on Broadway at age fifteen in the dancehall revue *Black and Blue* celebrated the elegance and style of black music and dance, 'reject[ing] an earlier minstrel-show image of ragged self-deprecation'.[11] Further, Glover's first featured role on Broadway, as the young jazz great Jelly Roll Morton in *Jelly's Last Jam*, was in 'a show in part about what it means to be African-American ... an attempt to remake the Broadway musical in a mythic, African-American image'.[12]

Glover's magnum opus, *Bring in 'da Noise, Bring in 'da Funk*, for which he served as both choreographer and star, relates black history from slavery to the present through music and dance, giving it a contemporary, hip hop-infused slant. It was 'Glover's artistic manifesto on the lives of young black men like himself – misunderstood, taken for granted, and burning with purpose tinged with anger'.[13] Glover furthered his personal association with the history of black entertainment by starring in Spike Lee's *Bamboozled*. Glover plays a street performer, Manray, who is coaxed by a white executive to perform in a new television show reviving blackface minstrelsy.

In both dance style and persona, then, Glover evokes the history of black performance in America, from its regrettable beginnings (the minstrel show) to its most culturally important moments (jazz, dancehall revues, funk). Glover embodies this history, lending corporeal form to a palimpsest of contributions from a long lineage of black dancers. Explaining his work on *Happy Feet* to *Jet* magazine, Glover said, 'I did routines or steps that were recognisable to and from my pioneers', listing Gregory Hines, Jimmy Slyde and Chuck Green as some of these influences. He continued, 'I had fun just watching their moves on a penguin.'[14] But what are the implications of this transformation, when motion capture decorporealises the performance, eliminating its physical body and applying it to some other, virtual body – in the case of *Happy Feet*, that of a penguin? Is this racially specific dance history – so apparent in Glover's live performance – eliminated by digital technology? Or does it come through in the ones and zeroes, imbuing the CG character with a realism that is in turn founded on a sense of racial authenticity? Furthermore, what are the ramifications of the conglomeration of these ethnically meaningful movements with a character voiced by and identified by the credits 'as' Elijah Wood? Could this be considered the digital equivalent of a minstrel show, in which a white actor 'puts on' the performance of an African American?

To shed light on the above questions, I turn to a similar historical example: Cab Calloway's rotoscoped appearances in Betty Boop cartoons in the early 1930s. Motion capture is often understood as 'a modern form of rotoscoping', an early animation technique that allowed artists to trace over live-action footage frame by frame.[15] In the early 1930s, Fleischer Studios tapped the jazz musicians of the Harlem Renaissance to provide music for and (sometimes) appear in, its animated shorts. By depicting performers like Cab Calloway and Louis Armstrong, the Fleischers were the first to create animated characters based on specific African Americans.[16] Avoiding the stereotypes from minstrel shows that frequently appeared in cartoons – the tribal savage, happy slave or lazy nitwit with thick lips and wide eyes – the Fleischer cartoons that featured Calloway forged an alternative, if still negative, iconography based in urban life. Matching the lyrics of the songs, which often discussed drug use and crime, the grim imagery included speakeasies, gambling, guns and money. While not all jazz musicians appeared within the cartoons, Cab Calloway, with his distinctive dance moves and energetic stage persona, was a good candidate for the rotoscope, a Fleischer invention. His animated alter egos appear in three Betty Boop cartoons: *Minnie the Moocher* (1932), *Snow White* (1933) and *The Old Man of the Mountain* (1933). Instead of a savage or slave, Calloway, through the technology of the rotoscope, metamorphoses into a dancing walrus, a ghostly KoKo the clown and a lecherous old hermit.

In *Minnie the Moocher*, Calloway's ghostly walrus double appears in a puff of smoke to sing the title song and perform his signature moves: slow-drag walking (which has been compared to Michael Jackson's moonwalk), spins, rhythmic footwork and expansive arm movements with fingers waggling. Each of the films presents the space in which Calloway appears, usually a dark cave, as an alluring draw to Betty, but ultimately it is dangerous and frightening, driving her to return to a familiar space. As Christopher P. Lehman explains,

> These African American performers and the surreal dwellings of their caricatures in the 'Betty Boop' series represent an 'other' that provides an appealing sense of liberation for whites but contains a threat of miscegenation via Betty's presence in their part of town.[17]

Although, of all of the Calloway characters, only the Old Man of the Mountain demonstrates lustful interest in Betty, her overt sexuality, along with lyrics about urban plagues like drug abuse and prostitution, lends each of these cave scenes a sense of sexual threat undergirding potential anxieties about racial integration.

The figure of the ghost, also present in *Snow White*, refers not only to the threat of death lurking in urban spaces, but also to the process of rotoscoping. The spectral walrus in *Minnie the Moocher* challenges the boundaries between animal and human, life and death. Like mo-cap-based digital characters, Calloway's animated apparition is 'a cinematic figure whose very ontology challenges us to rethink the limit between the animate and the inanimate, the human and the synthetic'.[18] The phantom also reflects the technology behind rotoscoped animation, combining the human model with the animated recreation. Calloway, though physically absent, maintains an unmistakable, if ghostly, presence in his cartoon depictions. Mark Langer and others observe in rotoscoped animation 'a *simultaneous presence* of the drawn and the photo-indexical, in which the rotoscoped or Rotoshopped body is not so much fused with the human body as it is *mapped over* it'.[19] Therefore, in rotoscoping, the performer's body remains a palpable spectre within the animation, making any sense of realistic movement uncanny.

Although the cartoons do not depict or reference racial identity directly – none of the animated versions of Calloway is dark-skinned, for instance – there are other ways they represent race. Two of the cartoons, *Minnie the Moocher* and *The Old Man of the Mountain*, begin with live-action shots of Calloway with his band playing the music that will be heard later in the film. In these short scenes, Calloway performs his trademark dancing and the scat and call-and-response singing for which he was known. While the rotoscoped portions later in the films do not appear to be taken directly from these shots, Calloway dances many of the same steps and kinds of movement that are so prominent in the rotoscoping later on. By synchronising the voice of Calloway – already familiar to audiences through the radio – with his distinctive dancing, the live-action scenes prompt viewers to recognise Calloway in the rotoscoped sections later. Thus, the aural representation of black jazz music is particularised in Calloway's body and bodily movements.

As Joanna Bouldin points out, the films thus posit an unambiguous racial authenticity to the performer's rotoscoped body. This sense of authenticity – beyond just the perceived realism of rotoscoped movement – is grounded in the live-action scenes, but continued into the animation through the use of the rotoscope. Bouldin argues that, by depicting performers identified as 'primitive', the Betty Boop cartoons tap into a sense of realism associated with ethnographic documentation. Pointing to the theories of French anthropologist Felix-Louis Regnault, Bouldin notes the propensity to see movement as the essence of race.[20] By transferring authentic movement from the 'ethnographic body' (of the jazz musician) to that of the animated character, the rotoscope thus 'allows the animated body to become legible as authentically and actually racialised'.[21] The authenticity bestowed upon the animated image because of its relation to a 'real', racialised body helps to calm the 'ontological ambiguity' caused by the dual body in the first place.[22]

As a consequence, the original performance becomes generalised into an authentic expression of race, rather than being particularised to the performer. Even as unique a performer as Calloway could then be taken to express the excess, exoticism and sexuality associated with the black body, playing into the 'nativist perception of black rhythm and excessive energy'.[23] Dance, in particular, is often considered to be 'natural' to the black body. In transferring racially 'authentic' movement from the performer's body to the animated body, the rotoscope makes the original, racialised body invisible. This kind of erasure naturalises such racial assumptions, making movement the ultimate mark of racial identity so that race becomes perceptible in the animated characters even if they fail to conform to visual expectations of blackness. Denying the visible specificity of one performer's body, rotoscoped animation allows movement to become generalised as a racial essence that can be employed like a costume, attached to various characters in specific situations to lend a particular, if unspoken, racial meaning. Rotoscoping in this instance could then be read as a form of temporary blackface – but instead of the physical process of blacking up, the imitation takes place immaterially through movement. Furthermore, this imitation takes its authority and authenticity from the apparent truth value of ethnographic film, making it appear authentic and natural, rather than a parody or critique.

However, according to Arthur Knight, certain blackface films 'draw attention to blackface as a process', showing scenes of performers putting on the mask; thus, the minstrel tradition 'is opened for question or at least explicit view, and a space … is made for examining and perhaps altering the ways in which racialised identities are delimited and maintained through sight and sound'.[24] With its 'ontological ambiguity', the rotoscope may play a similar role, even if the technology (the 'process' that creates a kind of virtual blackface) is less visible. It has the power to portray the instability of corporeal categories, breaking down binaries between fleshy body and animated body, animate and inanimate, black and white. While the rotoscope can also end up reinforcing such binaries by using non-white bodies to ground colonial fantasies of exoticism in bodily reality, the visible duality of rotoscoped animation – as the animated body is mapped over the performer's moving image – opens up the possibility of critical distance on the part of the viewer.

In the case of Cab Calloway, this critical awareness had both positive and negative consequences. The cartoons led to increased appreciation and promotion of his talents, particularly among white audiences. But they also drew criticism from conservative cultural voices, for whom the animations reinforced a link between the black body and excessive sexuality. When Catholic and other conservative groups put pressure on Paramount, distributor for Fleischer Studios cartoons, to tone down representations of sexuality, they censored not only Betty – clothing her in a more demure dress and eliminating sexual innuendos – but also the black jazz musicians. After the institution of the Production Code, the Fleischer cartoons never again featured African American musicians or jazz music: 'In dispensing with the African American entertainers and their music after limiting the "Betty Boop" series' sexual references, Fleischer thus acknowledged the widely assumed connection between raciness and blackness.'[25] By self-reflexively making audiences aware of the process of rotoscoping – showing live-action footage and synchronising sound – the cartoons acknowledged the racialised body behind the animated movement, leading in this case to censorship.

Capturing Motion, Appropriating Race

Whereas the Fleischer–Calloway films give audiences something like a knowing wink by providing live-action footage of Calloway dancing, letting audiences in on the origin of the illusion, modern motion-capture animations tend to relegate these inter- (or intra-) textual references to behind-the-scenes documentaries or special features. By more seamlessly joining motion capture and keyframe animation, contemporary films may not prompt the viewer to contemplate the production process, denying them the critical distance necessary to deconstruct the illusion. Does a film like *Happy Feet* then lose its opportunity to use digital technology to make a critical statement about bodies and race? Is it possible to use motion capture to effect cultural critique?

Certainly in its explicit content, *Happy Feet* has been deemed a progressive film openly critical of certain aspects of human society. Its major cultural critique is scathing and overt, casting humans as 'aliens' (in the point of view of the penguins), whose gluttony and enormous technological contraptions drive them to desecrate the oceans and starve the wildlife. Toward the end of the film, a huge fishing ship inadvertently captures Mumble in its nets, and he ends up in a zoo in a small, artificial enclosure. The film utilises live-action footage effectively in these scenes, showing actual humans staring dumbly at the penguins, unmoved by Mumble's cries for help, which to them (as we learn in a moment of subjective sound) resemble incoherent squawking. Instead of enhancing familiarity and identification, these photographically captured images of humans distance viewers from them, turning the depicted humans into aliens and indicting the audience by extension for failing to understand the consequences of their actions.

Ultimately, it is only when Mumble begins to tap dance out of frustration that the zoo patrons begin to take notice of the penguins' plight.

As in the Betty Boop cartoons, these scenes combine live-action shots of people with animated creatures adopting the movements of human performers. However, while in the Cab Calloway depictions the live-action shots work self-reflexively to reference and acknowledge the source of the rotoscoped performance later in the film, there is no such link between live-action and motion-capture performances in *Happy Feet*. Beyond creating Mumble's dance moves, Savion Glover does not even appear in a cameo in the film; more importantly, his voice is not heard on the soundtrack. If bodily presence can be inferred in part from the sounds of that body – both in movements (like tap dancing) and in language – Glover is further effaced by his vocal silence. His manifestation becomes even more ghostly, a set of movements divorced from body and voice. The lack of transparency regarding Glover's role in the film suggests that, while *Happy Feet* stridently critiques human society for its environmental destruction, it avoids critical consideration of corporeal categories such as race, particularly as they are implicated by the motion-capture process.

One might argue in response to this that *Happy Feet* is itself committed to representing a world untainted by such cultural categories. It represents humans as other, thereby explicitly distancing itself from concerns like race that would only apply to humanity. By presenting an animal world in which almost all members look more or less identical (Mumble stands out from the others only by continuing to sport infantile, downy feathers into his adulthood), the film aims to avoid the portrayal of discrimination based on physical appearance. Instead, penguin society in the film hierarchises individuals based on ability – specifically, singing ability. Since Mumble cannot sing, he is ejected from society, until that society learns the value of his particular talent, dancing, in making the humans sympathetic to their needs. By showing society's eventual embrace of Mumble and his dancing ways, *Happy Feet* broadly endorses a tolerance of difference that is compatible with a politically correct discourse of multiculturalism.

One could argue further that the use of motion capture reflects this particular discourse of tolerance. In erasing, and 'e-race-ing', the visual appearance of the mo-cap performer, motion capture renders racial difference irrelevant. One might claim that mo-cap de-essentialises race by making possible the performance of a character of one race by someone of another race without any of the mockery and scorn implied by 'blacking up', or otherwise changing one's appearance to look like (a stereotype of) the other. By capturing performance that is then divorced from an actual body – with its racial identities visible on the surface – motion capture creates the possibility of true colour-blindness in cinematic representation.

One might make this case – and perhaps in some other film, the argument would work – but, looking at the example of *Happy Feet*, I am led ultimately to reject this line of reasoning. Putting aside for the moment the issue of whether or not a post-racial society would actually be desirable, the above argument treats race as a visual trait that would easily disappear if the image were not captured. However, the example of Cab Calloway's rotoscoped performances shows that, even if movement is divorced from corporeal reality, it can be used in such a way to essentialise and reify racial identity. Furthermore, Savion Glover's repertoire trades on the idea that racial identity can be expressed through movement, though he demonstrates how it can be done in a variegated and complex way, as opposed to the simplified and crude representations of the minstrel show or colonialist ethnography.

In casting Elijah Wood and Savion Glover to provide incomplete parts of the Mumble whole, I am not proposing that the film-makers were consciously motivated by racism. I imagine that the decision to split the performance between two people was made for promotional reasons and to craft a performance out of the best of both worlds: a skilled voice actor, on the one hand, and a brilliant tap dancer on the other. New media technologies make such a design option not only possible, but also increasingly prevalent. No longer must only one person – such as a highly paid star – create a whole performance. Already, digital technology and editing techniques permit performances to be tweaked at every level. Motion capture allows performances to be divided from the start, with multiple performers creating only fragments of the whole. This piecemeal characterisation flies in the face of those – like Serkis, Cameron or director Peter Jackson – who would like to see the digital character as a direct extension of the human performer, transmitting every nuance of expression and intention.

I do not want to essentialise conventional film acting, since it has never been a seamless whole either, but the patchwork nature of performance with the use of motion capture entails additional consequences for the representation of race and other qualities specific to performers' bodies. Despite the film-makers' presumed intentions, the schism within the performance of Mumble reduces Glover's performance to corporeal movement, perpetuating the association of African Americans with the body while the white actor provides the language, usually associated with the mind. Motion-capture technology could have split the performance in any number of ways, but it still managed to reproduce the mind/body dualism along racial lines. As Mumble tries to reason through his feelings with language, the performance is dominated by the white actor, but when his emotions take over, Mumble is compelled to dance to express frustration, anger, joy or anxiety, connecting the African American performer to the non-rational experience of the body.

Moreover, *Happy Feet*'s racially divided hybrid performance of Mumble mirrors the film's seemingly uncritical thematisation of the usurpation of African American musical styles by whites, for either parody or profit (or both). This can be seen clearly in Hugh Jackman's vocal performance of Mumble's father, Memphis; his Southern drawl and quotations from 'Heartbreak Hotel' intentionally evoke Elvis Presley, an early adopter (thief, to some) of black music. The songs selected for inclusion in the medleys throughout *Happy Feet* are also dominated by those written and/or performed by African Americans: especially Stevie Wonder and Prince, but also Earth, Wind & Fire, TLC, Lionel Richie, Salt-N-Pepa, Clifton Davis, Sylvia Robinson, Kenneth 'Babyface' Edmonds and Sir Mix-a-Lot, among others. Despite this overwhelming reliance on African American music, there are almost no African Americans in the main vocal cast. The character of Seymour (voiced by rapper Fat Joe and, in the second film, rapper/actor Common), whose 'heartsong' is rapped rather than sung, seems to be a lone representative of African American hip-hop culture. Initially a rival to Mumble's affections for Gloria, Seymour does not have a major part in the plot, but he is also associated with music and corporeality – he is a music teacher, and his character is distinguished from the other penguins by being fatter. Seymour seems to be the films' 'token' black character, possibly included in order to disarm challenges to the film's racial politics in Savion Glover's and Robin Williams's performances.

Williams's contributions to the films are even more symptomatic of their uncritical racial appropriation. Williams performs a kind of 'aural blackface'[26] through the voices of two characters: Ramon, an Adelie penguin with a Latino accent, and Lovelace, a Rockhopper penguin who evokes a number of African American caricatures. These characterisations align ethnic difference in humans with species difference in the animal kingdom, perhaps naturalising those categories. The character of Ramon plays into ethnic stereotypes by being part of a rabble-rousing gang of Latino penguins known as 'the Amigos'.[27] Filled with a Latin passion that drives him to dance – the Mambo, of course – Ramon gives Mumble romantic advice about winning over Gloria. In a moment of potential self-reflexivity about ethnic drag,[28] Mumble lip-synchs to Ramon's Spanish version of the Frank Sinatra classic 'My Way' in order to woo Gloria. Gloria discovers the ruse, however, and rejects Mumble's attempt to be someone else. The film displays little self-awareness, though, of this scene's implications for the inauthenticity of Williams's own impersonation of a Latino.

Williams's vocalisation of Lovelace tends closer to blackface specifically, as this penguin is aurally coded as African American. Lovelace acts as a sort of guru for the Adelie penguins, collecting stones in exchange for dispensing wisdom and advice. Despite being short and fat, he also collects the attentions of the female penguins, exploiting the ladies' man caricature that matches his vocal impression of Barry White. He intones, 'Ladies, please avert your eyes … 'cause I've been known to hypnotise.' In other scenes, Williams adopts the didacticism and cadence of a black preacher, calling to the heavens, 'Speak to me, O Mystic Being', and referring to others as 'my brother'. Williams also mixes in a little of the exuberance of James Brown and the eccentricity of George Clinton, with the bright yellow plumes on his head and a funky necklace made of plastic six-pack rings adding to the impersonation of the latter. Although Lovelace claims that the rings were bestowed on him by the 'Mystic Being', he is in fact being slowly suffocated. Lovelace, in other words, suffers from excessive corpus – like the other black performers he impersonates who are also associated with surplus bodily size, sexuality, energy or dance.

It is important to note that *Happy Feet* did not use Glover's movements to animate a penguin with Williams's ersatz African American voice. The combination of the two may have thrown into sharp relief the inauthenticity and offensive parody of Williams's performance, while also highlighting motion capture's complicated relationship to race. The sidelining of Glover – in both the film's credits and the reduction of his contribution to Mumble's movements only – has the effect of shoving these questions of racial representation aside, allowing Williams's caricature to stand unquestioned.

If Glover's movement does represent a substantial link to the black experience, then it is isolated by remaining just a piece of the character of Mumble, rather than being integrated into his character. But his movement is also widely appropriated since it is later adopted by the whole society. While this results in the unification of the Emperor penguin society, this union is predicated on the invisibility of race. The history of African American dance is then treated as an individual quality (Mumble's unique form of personal expression), rather than a channel for cultural meaning and communal experience. If the film acknowledged how the adoption of difference often necessitates the erasure of its origins – as whites have often made black culture their 'own' by creating alternative histories of its birth – this knowledge would risk fracturing such unity.

Ultimately, the de-racialisation of *Happy Feet*'s main character attempts to cover over the film's use of racial stereotypes, 'e-race-ing' the histories of inequities behind the film's music and dance. Motion capture and other digital techniques are therefore implicated in this process of naturalising racial discrimination, by making it, like Glover's body, invisible. Instead of overtly telling the story of racial appropriation, the film relegates it to the musical subtext and in the stereotyped vocal performances of Robin Williams. This ends up concealing the histories of racial tensions, negotiations and appropriations that subtend the music and dance comprising the film. Therefore, negative racial representations – such as the mind/body split between white and black – appear natural, a state that is only exacerbated by motion capture's apparent realism. While Cab Calloway's overt representation in the live-action scenes of the Betty Boop cartoons gave audiences the potential for critical distance, Glover's relative invisibility means that the film can keep under wraps its racial politics of the body. Motion capture may promise an authentic and realistic performance for animated characters, but, in *Happy Feet*, this authenticity comes at the expense of racial invisibility, turning it into a tool of racial appropriation rather than post-racial representation.

Notes

1. This research was assisted by a New Faculty Fellows award from the American Council of Learned Societies, funded by the Andrew W. Mellon Foundation.
2. Chris Hewitt, 'Tap-dancing Penguins, Heaped with Indignities, Leave This Filmgoer Cold', *St. Paul (Minnesota) Pioneer Press*, 17 November 2006, p. 1E.
3. While the scholarship on the topic of racial representation and colonialist stereotypes of African Americans is voluminous and multifaceted, a good overview and history can be found in Jan Nederveen Pieterse, *White on Black: Images of Africa and Blacks in Western Popular Culture* (New Haven, CT: Yale University Press, 2006).
4. John Bell, *American Puppet Modernism: Essays on the Material World in Performance* (New York: Palgrave Macmillan, 2008), p. 165.
5. Ibid., p. 161.
6. For more on how Andy Serkis and others adopt the language of Method acting to justify the artistic validity of motion capture, see Tanine Allison, 'More than a Man in a Monkey Suit: Andy Serkis, Motion Capture, and Digital Realism', *Quarterly Review of Film and Video* vol. 28 no. 4 (2011), pp. 325–41.
7. References to the use of the phrase 'Satan's rotoscope' by animators can be found in Maureen Furniss, 'Motion Capture: An Overview', *Animation Journal* no. 8 (2000), p. 68; and in Alberto Menache, *Understanding Motion Capture for Computer Animation*, 2nd edn (New York: Morgan Kaufmann, 2010), p. 47.
8. Steve Pond, 'The Fine Lines of Motion-capture Animation Films', *Reuters*, 6 October 2011, http://www.reuters.com/article/2011/10/06/us-motioncapture-idUSTRE7957AY20111006. For more on the film industry's struggle to define animation in relation to motion capture, see Yacov Freedman, 'Is It Real … or Is It Motion Capture? The Battle to Redefine Animation in the Age of Digital Performance', *Velvet Light Trap* no. 69 (Spring 2012), pp. 38–49.
9. Paul Ward, 'Rotoshop in Context: Computer Rotoscoping and Animation Aesthetics', *Animation Journal* no. 12 (2004), pp. 32–52.

10. Constance Valis Hill, *Tap Dancing America: A Cultural History* (New York: Oxford University Press, 2010), p. 307.
11. Anna Kisselgoff, 'Elegant Ghosts Haunt "Black and Blue"', *New York Times*, 21 May 1989, http://www.nytimes.com/1989/05/21/theater/dance-view-elegant-ghosts-haunt-black-and-blue.html?src=pm.
12. Frank Rich, 'Jelly's Last Jam; Energy and Pain of a Man Who Helped Create Jazz', *New York Times*, 27 April 1992, http://theater.nytimes.com/mem/theater/treview.html?res=9E0CEED6133EF934A15757C0A964958260.
13. Karyn D. Collins, '*Bring in 'da Noise, Bring in 'da Funk* [review]', *Dance Magazine*, April 2003, p. 75.
14. Quoted in 'Savion Glover: The Man behind the Moves of *Happy Feet*', *Jet*, 25 December 2006, p. 62.
15. J. P. Telotte, *Animating Space: From Mickey to Wall-E* (Lexington: University Press of Kentucky, 2010), p. 226.
16. Christopher P. Lehman, *The Colored Cartoon: Black Representation in American Animated Short Films, 1907–1954* (Amherst: University of Massachusetts Press, 2007), p. 31.
17. Ibid., p. 33.
18. Tom Gunning, 'Gollum and Golem: Special Effects and the Technology of Artificial Bodies', in Ernest Mathijs and Murray Pomerance (eds), *From Hobbits to Hollywood: Essays on Peter Jackson's* Lord of the Rings (Amsterdam: Rodopi, 2006), p. 324.
19. Mark Langer, 'Issue Introduction', *Animation Journal* no. 12 (2004), p. 6.
20. Joanna Bouldin, 'Cadaver of the Real: Animation, Rotoscoping and the Politics of the Body', *Animation Journal* no. 12 (2004), p. 23.
21. Ibid., p. 24.
22. Ibid., p. 14.
23. Alison D. Goeller, Dorothea Fischer-Hornung and Dorota Janowska, 'Black Bodies in American Dance: Reflections on Aesthetics, Representations, and the Public Performance', in Fischer-Hornung and Goeller (eds), *EmBODYing Liberation: The Black Body in American Dance* (Hamburg: Lit Verlag, 2001), p. 18.
24. Arthur Knight, *Disintegrating the Musical: Black Performance and American Musical Film* (Durham, NC: Duke University Press, 2002), p. 52.
25. Lehman, *The Colored Cartoon*, p. 35.
26. 'Aural blackface' is a term used by Barbara Savage to describe the white performers parodying black dialect in the radio programme *Amos 'n' Andy*. See Barbara Dianne Savage, *Broadcasting Freedom: Radio, War, and the Politics of Race, 1938–1948* (Chapel Hill: University of North Carolina Press, 1999).
27. The other 'Amigos' are played by Latino comics Carlos Alazraqui, Lombardo Boyar, Jeffrey Garcia and Johnny A. Sanchez.
28. 'Ethnic drag' is Katrin Sieg's term. See her *Ethnic Drag: Performing Race, Nation, Sexuality in West Germany* (Ann Arbor: University of Michigan Press, 2002).

BEING GEORGES MÉLIÈS

DAN NORTH

The protagonist of Martin Scorsese's *Hugo* (2011) is a young orphan boy who lives in the Gare Montparnasse, Paris in 1931. To avoid the orphanage, Hugo (Asa Butterfield) hides inside the workings of the station's clocks, all the while secretly attempting to restore an automaton left incomplete by his father, a master horologist, which he believes contains a message for him. He runs into conflict with a toy seller, Papa Georges (Ben Kingsley), and the fates of these two figures, along with those of the people around them, become intertwined. When Papa Georges is later revealed to be the former owner of the automaton, the forgotten film pioneer Georges Méliès (1861–1938), Hugo's healing of his own trauma is effected simultaneously with the restoration of a neglected artist to the popular history of cinema, in a romantic dramatisation of Scorsese's passion for film preservation.

According to certain of its reviewers, *Hugo* is 'a great director's greatest love story' that was 'guaranteed to make all true cinephiles go misty-eyed'.[1] Many critics gave thanks for this 'immaculate present to film lovers everywhere',[2] which Kristin Thompson called 'Scorsese's birthday present to Georges Méliès' (*Hugo* was released within days of the 150th anniversary of his birth).[3] Others noted the significance of an 'important director' working in the still disreputable territory of stereoscopic 3D,[4] drawing a connection between Scorsese's film preservation/conservation efforts and the content of *Hugo* itself, 'a fable for film restoration and film history'.[5] Todd McCarthy in particular linked Scorsese to film history, with Méliès as his spirit guide to the past:

> A passionate brief for film preservation wrapped in a fanciful tale of childhood intrigue and adventure, *Hugo* dazzlingly conjoins the earliest days of cinema with the very latest big-screen technology … the obvious expenditures of time, care and money would seem to have been devoted to matters directly connected to Scorsese's overriding obsessions with film – the particulars of its creation, manner of presentation, the nature of the people who make it, its importance to the inner lives of those who love it and preservation both of film itself and the reputations of its practitioners.[6]

For Roger Ebert, the film was 'a mirror of [Scorsese's] own life', due to its

> parallel with the asthmatic Scorsese, living in Little Italy but not of it, observing life from the windows of his apartment, soaking up the cinema from television and local theatres, adopting great directors as his mentors, and in the case of Michael Powell, rescuing their careers after years of neglect.[7]

Even when critics were scathing, they opted for this preservationist angle; for David Sexton, *Hugo*'s self-reflexive excurses on film history represented 'cinema shining a light reverently up its own fundament'.[8]

Most significantly, many reviews claimed that Scorsese was not just commenting upon the history of early cinema, but actively picking up its spectacular project from where the 'Cinema of Attractions' left off. Ebert stated that *Hugo*'s 3D conversion of the Lumières' *Arrival of a Train* (1896) 'is a shot which demonstrates the proper use of 3D, which the Lumières might have used had it been available'.[9] Robbie Collin justified the use of 3D on the grounds that 'if the technology had been available to Méliès, he would have almost certainly used it himself'; the film was thus 'an attempt to impress modern audiences in the same way Méliès's work impressed turn-of-the-century Parisians'.[10] Similarly, for Kim Newman, '*Hugo* finds Scorsese ... wholly embracing the possibilities of contemporary film technology in the way Méliès did in his day.'[11]

The reviews coalesced, then, into a set of connective threads between artist and subject; this was about Scorsese, cinema, childhood. Scorsese was in the paradoxical position of being presented as an advocate both for the preservation of old films,[12] and the proliferation of modern digital 3D processes.[13] In *Hugo*, the automaton represents Méliès, broken and yearning to speak to us from the past; Méliès represents the dream of cinema, thwarted by cynical commerce; cinema represents machinery, regulated movement and modernity, the codependencies of people and the city. The film's narrative and thematic structure builds a network of interconnections that function together like the very machines/people that Hugo is hoping to 'fix'. The construction of Méliès as a lost pioneer is central to the correlative construction of Scorsese as a collector, archivist and historian, with *Hugo*/Hugo as the reconciliatory balm that can soothe the rupture between early and contemporary film's technological histories by blending digital aesthetics and historical narrative.

For Scorsese, Méliès was the perfect conduit for themes and interests that spoke to his own profile as an auteur-historian, and allowed him to inscribe his authorial trace onto the surface of a narrative property that might ordinarily have evaded his association or alienated his core audience. But Scorsese is by no means the first to deploy the cultural memory of Méliès in this way. More than any other film-maker pre-Chaplin, Méliès has inspired popular and artistic references to his work. He is, with little doubt, the most famous of all early film-makers, and his legacy the most amenable to rediscovery and reinvention.

The reviews of *Hugo* demonstrate the extent to which Méliès has been canonised as a metonymic placeholder for an ineffable 'fantastic' in cinema history, or even for the whole of cinema history itself. He is rarely allowed his own legitimate biography, and this has sometimes served to neutralise his work, to enshrine it as timeless, magical, thus disengaging it from its sociohistorical/political contexts. This essay will examine the figure of Méliès, as he is represented in a variety of films and other media. Rather than attempting a biography, or even a subjective historical analysis of Méliès' life and work, these films tend to use his image as a cypher for a range of responses to film technology and special effects. Méliès has been 'traditionally identified as taking the first step from the cinematograph as scientific curiosity to the cinema as spectacle and narrative entertainment'.[14] Most commonly, he is given the status of 'father of special effects', a paternalistic moniker that is doubtless high praise, but which ironically extracts him from his historical context to stress instead advances in the state of the art. At the same time, contemporary imaging technologies are not necessarily best served by being framed as 'magical', rather than sociohistorically significant phenomena. What follows is by no means an exhaustive tour of homages to Méliès, but it should be indicative of the variety of uses to which his memory has been put, as well as an index of some of the more common ways in which Méliès has come to represent all of early cinema.

Dreams of Artists

Méliès himself crafted an autobiography of sorts by continually acting in his own scenarios, giving himself the role of conjuror, devil, scientist, inventor. In *Le Mélomane* (1903), he plucks his own head from his shoulders and tosses it upwards, where it lands on overhead power cables; immediately sprouting a new head, he repeats the process until there are six decapitee doppelgängers arrayed on the cables like musical notes on a stave.

As well as offering this cumulative treatise on the malleability of the body, Méliès repeatedly depicts the life of the image. Living portraits, spirit photographs and duplicates of his own image are shown to move, live and sometimes respond to the artist's bidding, at other times expressing naughty independence.[15] The matte black backdrop that fills portions of the frame in *The Man with the India Rubber Head* (1901), *The Dancing Midget* (1902) and *An Impossible Balancing Feat* (1902, in which he replicates himself to perform a four-man acrobatic act), is the blank canvas of Méliès' imagination, the readied space into which he can project, thanks to expertly calibrated multiple exposures, any objects or figures. In *Spiritualistic Photographer* (1903), Méliès begins by stepping in front of the camera carrying two signs, announcing (in French *and* English, a marker of the director's commercial acumen and international outlook) that the film will contain a 'Dissolving effect obtained without black background. Great Novelty'. This tells us that the existence of a black background was common knowledge among audiences, and that this was central to the working of many of the tricks in his previous films. Méliès announces this as an advance on the previous technique. The joke is that he uses a *white* background, a canvas placed centre-stage, rather than a 'hole' in the set, to effect a minor variation on what is otherwise an old trick: such engagement with audience expectations is all part of an ongoing dialogue with the spectator that takes the form of authored mediation of spectacular moments.[16]

In the interstices of his stop-action substitutions, Méliès perfected both the match-cut and its subversive double, the transformation, as his on-screen magician avatar instantly metamorphosed his own and others' bodies. In *The Shadow Girl* (1902), a man jumps through a paper hoop and Jeanne D'Alcy, Méliès's lover throughout his film-making career (and his second wife from 1926 until

Georges Méliès multiplies his own body to perform *An Impossible Balancing Feat* (1902)

his death) appears on the other side.[17] He had already made her disappear in *The Vanishing Lady* (1896), bathe near-naked in *Après le Bal* (1897) and burned her at the stake in the title role of *Jeanne d'Arc* (1899); his playful but compulsive mastery over the female body has energised several feminist readings of his work,[18] but may also be a more direct and personal enactment of his feelings for D'Alcy, however covert they might be. The biographical record is not complete enough for us to do anything other than read *into* the films for clues, seeking personal and aesthetic details in the kinds of techniques and ideas to which he returned again and again. Stan Brakhage once gave Méliès a 'fictional biography', a psychoanalytic reading in which the artist creates a 'demon-self' to battle the heroic magician persona he has created for his films.[19] The idea of a Mélièsian surrogate self, made visible through the cinematographic apparatus, is an attractive metaphor for the way screen personae become unmoored from their harbouring bodies and take on an independent, imagistic life.

Repeatedly destroying, erasing, transmogrifying, multiplying then annihilating, before reassembling his own body, Méliès fabricated a screen self that was as demonstrative in its gestures as it is today opaque in its motives. The suspicion that he was acting out *something*, compounded by the fact that he is often gesticulating towards the viewer directly, urgently trying to direct our gaze and show/tell us something, tempts us to knit together a coherent biographical portrait from the fragments scattered across his oeuvre. He wrote his memoirs in the third person, 'as if actualities, the brass tacks of daily life, coffee cups and ashtrays, belonged to someone else',[20] or as if he was already accepting his separation from the filmic proxy he had spawned, but they were written in old age, the memories already decomposing like old nitrate film, scattered with apocrypha and exaggeration.[21] This story was picked up and calcified by the protective arms of the Malthête-Méliès family, who were largely responsible for collecting and buying back the films,[22] but who also tightly controlled distribution rights until they entered the public domain in 2008, seventy years after Méliès' death. Out of this irresistibly fantastic, phantasmal backstory, inscribing technological history with the markers of magic, it has fallen to a succession of artists to extrapolate some ideas about what the Méliès legacy might come to mean.

The most sustained filmic depiction of Méliès' career has come from Georges Franju's *Le Grand Méliès* (1953).[23] Franju knew Méliès personally, and in 1937 had appointed him as the first curator of the Cinémathèque Française, which Franju had co-founded with Henri Langlois that year. Franju's film consists of biographical reconstructions interspersed with clips from Méliès films, and it offers imprimaturs of authenticity by including shots of Jeanne D'Alcy, narration by one of Méliès' collaborators (François Lallement, who performed in *Le Voyage dans la Lune* [1902]), and footage from Méliès' retirement home, while Georges' own son, Andre, is cast as the elderly magician. The film works backwards from his final years. We are shown Méliès in the Gare Montparnasse toy store where he came to be working by the mid-1920s. We see a conjuring trick performed at the Théâtre Robert-Houdin, but Franju uses camera tricks that could not possibly have worked on stage, as if attempting to finesse the equivalences between stage and screen magic.[24] We see Méliès innocently happening upon the first Cinématographe Lumière shows.[25] Here then, are all the foundational myths of the Méliès story: he worked as a magician; stumbled across the cinema; accidentally discovered special effects through a technical glitch while filming at Place de l'Opéra; failed to modernise with the film industry; and ended up selling toys in a train station. The toy store is a crucial part of the Méliès mythos. It captures not just the lowly status to which the man was reduced (he is selling, not making, props for imaginative play), but also the ludic terms of his retirement: he was still in a playful role. This narrative suggests innocence and accident as major contributories to his career, even as it paints him as a genius ignored by a malevolent, commercialised film industry. Knowing that this purveyor of fantastic stories of flights to the heavens and trips to the Moon was eventually marooned on the peripheries of a more mundane mass transit system lets us congratulate ourselves for recovering an underappreciated virtuoso from the ignorant disregard of his contemporaries. Méliès' body of work, and his position as a trickster pioneer of cinematic illusionism, has inspired many artists not necessarily to reenact scenes from his life, but to evoke some of his essential or aesthetic characteristics. I want to mention several examples of this, before returning to more direct representations of Méliès' most famous film, *A Trip to the Moon.*

Pierre Etaix's *Le Cauchemar de Méliès* (1988) was made as part of '*Méliès 88*', a project conceived by Bénédicte Lesage and Christian Janicot to mark the fiftieth anniversary of Méliès' death. A number of film-makers were invited to make a new short film based on a scenario from one of the more than 150 films lost from Méliès' oeuvre.[26] Etaix, an accomplished clown and collaborator with Jacques Tati, updates the trick effects to what were then quite novel wire-frame computer graphics to depict Méliès' studio. The artist (Christophe Malavoy) paints for the viewer an outline that becomes a frame of Fay Wray in *King Kong* (1933). When the artist falls asleep, the image flickers into life on the easel. The insinuation that Méliès' imagination begat the special effects of *Kong* (not to mention the paintbox effects used in this film) is clear, but this is Méliès' *nightmare* of a degraded consumer culture, not his aspiration towards a glorious and erotic future of special effects, so just as his screen self was frequently bedevilled by changeable imps, spirits and demons, this scene is interrupted by garish advertising that snaps the artist out of his reverie.

Peter Tscherkassky's *Coming Attractions* (2010) is assembled, like all of his work, from manipulated found footage, in this instance outtakes from advertisement shoots. In a series of eleven vignettes, Tscherkassky repurposes the footage to compare its mode of direct address to that suggested by Tom Gunning's concept of the 'cinema of attractions'. In *La Femme à la tête de caoutchouc,*[27] a woman's face is framed in close-up; she wears an inflatable hood dryer on her head: it looks both retrofuturistic, and slightly ridiculous. The shot moves away from her to try out different framings. In *La Femme orchestre*, the same model repeats the action of raising and lowering a saxophone to look at it. No doubt this footage was intended to be cut into a longer sequence, and would make sense when contextualised in the finished advertisement, but Tscherkassky gives it a new set of rhythms and significances. He reworks detrital fragments of film into something independently beautiful, even as he foregrounds the monotony of modelling merchandise. If Tscherkassky's aim is to reinscribe the footage with a sense of fresh wonder, it also points up the bonded relationship between film and commerce. A highly attenuated sense memory of Méliès' work is detectable in the direct address to the camera and Tscherkassky's mischievous intertitles, serving to contextualise even these degraded scraps of film as offshoots of the same impulse to make strange the perceptible world that drove Méliès' magical cinema.

A similar motive inspired South African animator William Kentridge's *7 Fragments for Georges Méliès* (2003), a compiled sequence of tricks played out in his own studio.[28] In the first, for instance, by playing backwards footage of himself destroying a self-portrait, the artist appears to produce this self-image quite magically. Kentridge uses what might by now be considered rudimentary special effects such as substitutions, multiple exposures, reversed or accelerated footage: if these are implicitly attributed to Méliès' invention (the origin of each of them is too complicated to be claimed by any single inventor), they are also in-built capabilities of the camera that summarise for Kentridge Méliès' search for 'a whole different world that was possible with the technology of cinema that wasn't about naturalistically recording the world'.[29]

Having spent his life filming human processes of construction and destruction, industries and wars, Dutch documentarian Joris Ivens's extraordinary final film, *A Tale of the Wind* (1989, co-directed with his partner Marceline Loridan) is a metaphysical attempt to 'film the invisible wind' in China. Instead, he films the wind's effects, or earthly things that interact with it, such as Tai-Chi practitioners demonstrating how they control their own breathing. *A Tale of the Wind* is a collage of fact and fiction, documentary, drama and spectacular tourism that, with its questing, ambivalence and nomadic structure, casts doubt upon the ideological certainties that had made his earlier work (on Maoism or Stalinism, for instance) so controversial in the West.[30] One scene reenacts a heart attack Ivens, now frail and severely asthmatic, suffered during filming. When Ivens was hospitalised, Loridan took up a much bigger role as co-director of the film, and restructured it around a self-reflexive vision of the artistic process. The Monkey King, a Peking-operatic trickster visits him in hospital and, spreading out a sheet covered with Méliès-style cartoons of a dragon, summons the creature to come and take Ivens away. Following a brief excerpt from *A Trip to the Moon*, Ivens emerges from the mouth of the Man in the Moon (a painted backdrop based on Méliès' original designs for his film) on an artificial set hung with paper stars. He sees a vision of a legendary 'rebellious poet' who drowned reaching for the Moon's reflection in a lake, and meets the lunar deity Chang'e, who tired of life and Earth and flew to the Moon (which also bored her). This is Ivens's hallucination *through* cinema history, and an encounter with the fictional aspects of his own practice.

Sylvain de Bleeckere suggests that the wind in the film represents 'mankind's free, collective imagination, which again and again escapes everything that wants to lock it up. Some party or group may own the film studios, but ultimately, the film belongs to life itself.'[31] Ivens had frequently used techniques from fiction film-making in his documentaries, such as scripted dialogue and post-synched sound, but *A Tale of the Wind* is a more liberal blend of fantastic and prosaic elements. Méliès is the portal through which he must pass to make that transition from documentary to

Joris Ivens travels to the surface of the Moon in *A Tale of the Wind* (1989)

fantasy. For André Stufkens, the film sees Ivens entering 'a no man's land between the documentary and the feature film – an innovation with which he embraced the avant-garde again with a film that drew lines to the next century'.[32] In Tom Gunning's analysis, this sequence is part of a broader quest for revolution and social justice on the part of Ivens, who 'uses Méliès's film as a fragment of modern mythology, a viewpoint from which the utopian ideal of a single world can still be envisioned'.[33]

Méliès undergoes a kind of apotheosis in the film, becoming not an aesthetic influence, but an icon of transcendent poeticism, but if Ivens is romantic in his picturing of China as a land of ancient wisdom and colourful tradition, he is realistic about its practical obstacles. A lengthy sequence shows him and Loridan negotiating with Party officials to shoot at the site of the terracotta warriors that guard the Emperor's tomb. Finally frustrated by the bureaucratic restrictions on filming, he buys a collection of souvenir models of the warriors and uses them to shoot a miniature tableau instead, a testament to film's fabricating power when the real world will not cooperate. For Jonathan Rosenbaum, the resulting sequence is an 'instance of folklore and technology, archaeology and fantasy being brought into sublime proximity, even a communication with each other'.[34] It is poetic because it uses mythical visions to speak of lived experience (the wind is invisible, but still a demonstrable fact of nature), and technical because the film uses its apparatus to make concrete pictures of metaphysical things.

By making himself the subject of his own film, one which is 'simultaneously a documentary *and* a fantasy',[35] Ivens poeticises his film-making process in much the same way as Méliès might have done: Méliès' demonstrative magician figures are a fictional proxy for the more prosaic work of crafting filmic fantasy, and his on-screen presence a marker of the overlap between fantasy and reality, between (auto)biography and performance.[36] All of the artists discussed in this section have invoked this Mélièsian proxy to varying degrees as a way of reflecting upon their own practice. But one Méliès film in particular has enjoyed a more prominent place in popular culture, and has served as the recognised brand of the artist and the promise of early film.

Round-trips to the Moon

A Trip to the Moon, with its indelible image of the Man in the Moon with a rocketship lodged in his eye, is Méliès' insignia, the film that makes him recognisable to a much wider audience than is enjoyed by any other early film-maker. It has been referenced in two separate episodes of *The Simpsons*;[37] it serves as the logo for both the Visual Effects Society (and the trophy for the annual VES Awards) and the European Fantastic Films Federation; the Smashing Pumpkins award video for 'Tonight, Tonight' (1996, directed by Jonathan Deyton and Valerie Faris) recreates scenes from a range of Méliès films including *A Trip to the Moon*, deploying similar backdrops and special effects. It forms part of a prologue to *Around the World in 80 Days* (1956), where Edward R. Murrow delivers a to-camera monologue (thus investing the sequence with some of the gravitas he brought to his news and current-affairs broadcasts), presenting Jules Verne and Méliès as prophets of a long-imagined Moon mission. We are then shown an abbreviated, sped-up version of Méliès' film, narrated by Murrow. This prologue serves the purpose of introducing the author of the novel on which the film is based, positioning him as a pioneer of imaginary space travel. Méliès is bundled into that picture of Verne, creating the genealogical bond between Verne's book and Michael Anderson's film. At the time of the embryonic US space programme, then, spectators were being told that their imaginative investment in dreams of space travel were an important part of the process of pre-visualisation and thus ultimate realisation of a Moon landing.

The HBO TV series *From the Earth to the Moon* (1998), executive-produced by Tom Hanks (following his lead role in *Apollo 13* [1995]), similarly appropriated *A Trip to the Moon* as the ideational bedrock for its larger narrative. Over the course of twelve hour-long episodes, the series, HBO's most expensive production at that time, reconstructs moments from the twelve-mission Apollo space programme of the 1960s and 70s. While these are all told in chronological sequence, with great focus on technical detail, internal debates at NASA and character studies of the astronauts, the final episode applies a different structure. Intercut with scenes of the Apollo 17 Moon landing and exploration (the last moonwalk to date) are recreations of the shooting of *A Trip to the Moon*. The reason for the parallel editing is unambiguous – the end of the Apollo programme is viewed through its opposite bookend of an imaginative 'beginning' seventy years earlier.

Tchéky Karyo plays Méliès as a passionate taskmaster on set, gesticulating wildly and talking his actors through scenes as they play out, semi-improvised but always emphatically directed (thus capturing that contrast in Méliès' work between meticulous control of technique and rather chaotic crowding in the busier scenes). There are some direct comparisons between these two distinct timespaces: the making of *A Trip to the Moon* is juxtaposed with the broadcast of the Apollo 17 mission, showing in the twinkling of a match-cut the disparity between the wonderment of first imaginings to the bored, overfamiliar indifference of sated audiences; the rehearsal of a volcanic eruption on the 1902 film set is followed by the search for evidence of previous volcanic activity on the Moon's surface in 1972, playing off a pyrotechnic fantasy against the long-form legwork of full-on geological investigation; a shot of sleeping astronauts is matched to the scene of Méliès' moonwalkers dreaming of stars.

Positing *A Trip to the Moon* as the pinnacle of a film-making career that was to be cut short by industrial expansion makes for a convenient parallel with the close of the Apollo space programme – both events are made to seem like wasted opportunities, thwarted by executive interference. Méliès is a useful icon for the show's rhetoric of progress and glorious exploration, ignoring the possibility that his intentions might have been satirical, mischievous, less starry-eyed. Aligning one's enterprise, whether it's a space programme or a TV programme about space, with one of cinema's greatest pioneers is the quickest route to romanticising it by claiming that you yourself recognised the importance of fantastic cinema all along.

A Trip to the Moon was future-ready in another sense. Its brevity, levity and novelty value have made it a fixture on YouTube (dubbed by Teresa Rizzo, among others, as 'the new Cinema of Attractions'):[38] it has been uploaded in dozens of different versions and received millions of views. It is also freely available in various formats from the Internet Archive. Its prominence and newfound digital shareability grant it ambassadorial status as a metonymic representative of *all* early cinema history. In 1993, the only known surviving hand-coloured print of *A Trip to the Moon* was discovered among a collection of 200 early films donated to the Filmoteca de Catalunya in Barcelona.[39] It served as a poignant reminder of the material basis of cinema history, and of its pitiable frailty. Too greatly deteriorated to be screened, it was painstakingly restored by an alliance of archives led by Lobster Films, and the result finally unveiled at the Cannes Film Festival, 11 May 2011. *A Trip to the Moon* had to be digitally scanned frame by frame, the image stabilised, missing or damaged shots or portions of the frame replaced with sections taken from other prints, which in turn needed colouring. So much digital cosmetic work has been performed on the colour print that one might wonder whether the restoration, which has since been screened all over the world and released internationally on Blu-ray and DVD, is a cleansed picture of Méliès' film, or its palimpsestic afterimage, overhauled using the very techniques of digital image manipulation that today make Méliès' work seem so historically distant.

It now seems apt that *A Trip to the Moon* should be put back together using the same visual effects that conventional film histories would have us believe it set in motion. By the same token, this reconstruction work should cause us to reflect on the status of 'originals' and 'copies', something which Méliès frequently toyed with in his films: those multiplied screen selves were not biological clones, but photographic duplicates, layered into the frame in prodigious displays of recombination, superimposition. The simulation of wholeness in the restored film effaces the story of its neglect, and camouflages its materiality. Such is the archivist's dilemma: rescuing a film from deterioration (both physical decay and cultural obscurity) always alters the relationship between the object and its history. Similarly, our picture of Méliès is always changed in the process of historical recovery and appropriation.

In the documentary *Le Voyage Extraordinaire*, produced to accompany screenings of the restored *A Trip to the Moon*, HBO's reconstruction of the film's production serves to illustrate a history of Méliès' career and working methods. In an interview excerpt, Tom Hanks tells us that 'Méliès and his voyage to the Moon, was [*sic*] the first draft of the Apollo space program'. It fits with the series' position that dreaming of travel to the Moon was the first step towards its achievement. It shields Méliès from his own oppositional heritage by labelling him a paternalistic children's entertainer. If we're positing Méliès as forefather of science fiction on the back of *Le Voyage dans la Lune*, we should at least note that the film is not set in 1902, and is certainly not set in the future. Rather, it reclaims space *from* scientific speculation by encrusting it with the markers of Méliès' own bag of tricks, his preoccupations and his ideational template. He didn't make a Moon mission look gloriously plausible: he made it look silly, vandalous. Another commentator in *Le Voyage Extraordinaire* describes *A Trip to the Moon* as 'the *Avatar* of its day', but Méliès used the same equipment that the Lumières used for their actualities. His tricks were drawn from his repurposing of the extant capabilities of the apparatus, not developed from external technologies and brought into the studio.

We tend to think of today's special effects as part of film production's workflow rather than something personalised or artistic. Special effects have always explored the ways new technology can mediate representation, but this is perhaps why we often find Méliès taken as a reference point for special-effects histories: his work is colourful, artisanal and boisterously disruptive, while later special effects became industrialised, folded into the Classical cinema's project to make spatiotemporal unity of composited elements and shots. His is the image of a prelapsarian zone of spectacular display.

Ending

Méliès did not destroy all his films in a fit of rage at his neglect by an industry and an audience that had lost interest in his innocent fantasies, as suggested in *Hugo*. The actuality was probably less tragic-heroic, a little more mundanely fiscal: his company offices were commandeered by the military in 1914 and, rather than pay the expenses of relocating the copies of the films and building a new vault to house them, he sold the films, probably for industrial celluloid. The most blatantly 'old-fashioned' thing now about Méliès is that he was able to destroy most of his body of work by disposing of the negatives. It seems unthinkable in the digital age that disposing of a film's negative would put it permanently out of circulation.

One of the problems with *Hugo*'s vision of Méliès is that it paints him as a benevolent patriarch, when recent Méliès scholarship has been more interested in how his films don't coddle, they bite; they are satirical and subversive, not dreamy flights of escapist fantasy. He was not restored to prominence by a grateful film industry, but by surrealists who saw him offer an oneiric alternative to mainstream narrative cinema. Especially cumulatively, when you see how obsessively he dismembers bodies or replicates himself, they have a persuasive power to disrupt expectations, not flatter imagination. Was Méliès a subversive who mocked the powerful, as Jack Zipes suggests?[40] In *The Colonel's Shower Bath* (1902) the eponymous authority figure, whom we have just seen acting bluff and strict with his soldiers, sits down to read a message, while two men, one of them played by Méliès, are painting an archway. Méliès trips, and spills the bucket of paint over the colonel, who storms off screen while everyone else laughs uncontrollably. This is the filmic remnant of his time as a political cartoonist for *La Griffe*, and a small indicator of his mockeries of authority. Méliès is often cited as some kind of forwardlooking technologist, but mechanical transportation, in particular, is repeatedly portrayed as reckless and combustible. See, for example, *An Adventurous Automobile Trip* (1905), in which a king claims he can drive from Paris to Monte Carlo in two hours. He makes the deadline, but demolishes houses and flattens pedestrians in the process.

We have been invited to consider Méliès as the farsighted pioneer of cinema rather than its spiky critic; those substitution cuts he engages so deftly might prefigure the mastery of editing, the syntax of spatiotemporal continuity that enabled the founding of a consistent production-line aesthetic so crucial to the development of a film industry. But they also seem to me to capture the violence of the technology: it is, by technical necessity, on the exact point of the edit that the dismembering violence occurs, as if the cutting of the filmstrip *is* the cutting of flesh, and the disposal of the elided frames *is* the disappearance of the body. Is there, then, embedded in Méliès' exuberant conjuring tricks, a premonitory critique of the capacity of the cinematic apparatus for redefining representations of the body to the point of abstraction?

As Alison McMahan points out, 'the history of cinema can be seen as part of a broad industrial drive to mechanisation, the drive to measure, quantify and ultimately automate every aspect of life'.[41] Méliès' films are utterly ambivalent about technology, and his mutable bodies, while engaging the spectacular potential of the cinematic apparatus, are envisioned as ephemeral, barely controllable: they resist quantification by the machine. Méliès' on-screen persona tells us parables about media avatars: if he was pre-empting the development of a fantastic cinema, he was just as likely implicating the camera in the production of surrogate on-screen selves, perhaps accidentally warning that the camera may not reflect reality back at us, but may distort, fragment and reconstruct it in unwarranted ways.

Towards the end of *Hugo*, Méliès recounts his first encounter with the Cinématographe, and the audience is shown recoiling as a train approaches on the screen in front of them. The oft-cited myth of the panicking audience is a convenient way to stress the culturally irruptive nature of the medium with which spectators were apperceptively ill equipped to deal, but it is likely to be apocryphal, and at least exaggerated.[42] For Scorsese, the sequence is a tribute to the wonder years of cinema, as well as a note of commonality between an early 'attractionist' aesthetic and his first contact with the dimensionality of 3D. Paul Young reminds us that the way cinema represents itself is important, and *Hugo* is certainly a fine example of self-regarding cinema. As well as being connected to the mechanisation of everyday life, the history of cinema can be seen not as the development of machines or narrative conventions, but as the inculcation of viewing practices to create a primed, receptive audience of biddable consumers.[43] Filmic representations of Méliès have often fallen back on this image of his audience as passive receptors of his simple wonders, at the expense of more nuanced engagement with the contexts and sentiments that may have fostered the work. Hugo, who spends much of his time watching the activity of the train station, can only fix the machines and people who depend on him by learning how to *look*, and how to interpret the clues in his environment that will unlock, and thus heal, the history of Méliès/cinema.

Notes

1. Kim Newman, 'Hugo', *EmpireOnline.com*, December 2011, http://www.empireonline.com/reviews/reviewcomplete.asp?FID=136891.
2. Todd McCarthy, '*Hugo*: Film Review', *Hollywood Reporter*, 17 November 2011, http://www.hollywoodreporter.com/movie/hugo/review/263209.
3. Kristin Thompson, '*Hugo*: Scorsese's Birthday Present to Georges Méliès', *David Bordwell.net*, 7 December 2011, http://www.davidbordwell.net/blog/2011/12/07/hugo-scorseses-birthday-present-to-georges-Méliès/.
4. See, for example, Mark Savage, 'Can Martin Scorsese's *Hugo* Save 3-D?' *BBC*, 2 December 2011, http://www.bbc.co.uk/news/entertainment-arts-15967276; Andrew O'Hehir, 'Scorsese's Spectacular 3-D *Hugo*', *Salon.com*, 24 November 2011, http://www.salon.com/2011/11/24/scorseses_spectacular_3_d_hugo/singleton/. For more on *Hugo*'s use of 3D, see Chuck Tryon's essay in this collection.
5. Peter Bradshaw, 'Hugo – Review', *Guardian*, 1 December 2011, http://www.guardian.co.uk/film/2011/dec/01/hugo-scorsese-film-review.
6. McCarthy, '*Hugo*'.
7. Roger Ebert, '*Hugo*', *RogerEbert.com*, 21 November 2011, http://www.rogerebert.com/apps/pbcs.dll/article?AID=/20111121/REVIEWS/111119982/-1/RSS.
8. David Sexton, '*Hugo* – Review', *London Evening Standard*, 2 December 2011.
9. Ibid. The Lumières did their own experiments with stereoscopic films, including a remake of their train film. See Louis Lumière, 'Stereoscopy on the Screen', *Society of Motion Picture Engineers Journal* no. 27 (September 1936), pp. 315, 318; referenced in Ray Zone, *Stereoscopic Cinema and the Origins of 3-D Film* (Lexington: University Press of Kentucky, 2007), pp. 141–3.
10. Robbie Collin, '*Hugo*, Review', *Daily Telegraph*, 1 December 2011, http://www.telegraph.co.uk/culture/film/filmreviews/8929152/Hugo-review.html.

11. For more on the reception of *Hugo*, see Chuck Tryon's essay in this collection. There is also an extensive discussion of the film's visual technologies in Lisa Purse, *Digital Imagery in Contemporary Cinema* (Edinburgh: University of Edinburgh Press, 2013), pp. 129–51.
12. Scorsese sits on the board of directors of preservation advocacy group the Film Foundation; is a founding member of both the National Film Preservation Foundation and the World Cinema Foundation; and co-chair of the American Film Institute's National Center for Film and Video Preservation.
13. See, for example, Christina Silva, 'Scorsese Says All His Future Films Will Be 3-D', *Associated Press*, 26 April 2012; http://news.yahoo.com/scorsese-says-future-movies-3-d-221344262.html.
14. Michael Temple and Michael Witt, 'Introduction 1890–1930: Hello Cinema!', in Temple and Witt (eds), *The French Cinema Book* (London: BFI, 2004), p. 10.
15. See, for example, *The Wonderful Living Fan* (1904), *Cartes Vivantes* (1905) and *The Hilarious Posters* (1905).
16. For more on this dialogic relationship between magician and audience, see Dan North, 'Illusory Bodies: Magical Performance on Stage and Screen', *Early Popular Visual Culture* vol. 5 no. 2 (July 2007), pp. 175–88.
17. *Hugo* glosses over this adulterous arrangement: there is no mention of Méliès' first wife nor of his children.
18. See, for example, Lucy Fischer, 'The Lady Vanishes: Women, Magic and the Movies', in John L. Fell (ed.), *Film before Griffith* (Berkeley: University of California Press, 1983), pp. 339–54; Linda Williams, 'Film Body: An Implantation of Perversions', in Philip Rosen (ed.), *Narrative, Apparatus, Ideology: A Film Theory Reader* (New York: Columbia University Press, 1986), pp. 507–34; Victoria Duckett, 'The Stars Might Be Smiling: A Feminist Forage into a Famous Film', in Matthew Solomon (ed.), *Fantastic Voyages of the Cinematic Imagination: Georges Méliès's Trip to the Moon* (Albany, NY: SUNY Press, 2011), pp. 161–81; Karen Beckman, *Vanishing Women: Magic, Film, and Feminism* (Durham, NC: Duke University Press, 2003).
19. Stan Brakhage, *The Brakhage Lectures*, http://www.ubu.com/historical/brakhage.index.html (Chicago, IL: The GoodLion, at the School of the Art Institute of Chicago, 1972), p. 8.
20. Susan Daitch, *The Paper Conspiracies* (San Francisco, CA: City Lights Books, 2011), p. 40.
21. Georges Méliès, 'Mes Mémoirs', in Maurice Bessy and Lo Duca (eds), *Georges Méliès, Mage* (Paris: Prisma, 1961), pp. 168–217.
22. Frank Kessler, 'Georges Méliès', in Richard Abel (ed.), *Encyclopedia of Early Cinema* (London: Routledge, 2005), pp. 601–2.
23. Adam Lowenstein, 'History without a Face: Surrealism, Modernity, and the Holocaust in the Cinema of Georges Franju', in *Shocking Representation: Historical Trauma, National Cinema, and the Modern Horror Film* (New York: Columbia University Press, 2005), p. 18. Franju devoted another short film to Méliès, namely 'Méliès père et fils' (1977), episode #136 of the TV series *Chroniques de France*. See Philippe Rège, *Encyclopedia of French Film Directors, Volume 1* (Plymouth: Scarecrow Press, 2010), p. 415.
24. The Théâtre Robert-Houdin, which Méliès owned from 1888, had already been demolished in 1924 to make way for the Boulevard Haussman at this point, so an alternative location had to be found.
25. In reality, Méliès was invited to the first public screening Lumière Cinématographe shows at Salon Indien, Grand Café in Paris, 28 December 1895.

26. Other directors involved were Jean-Louis Bertucelli, Marc Caro, Philippe Gautier, Aline Isserman, Gérard Krawczyk, Jean-Pierre Mocky and Zbigniew Rybczynski. A ninth film was directed by Maurizio Nichetti, but not included in the final broadcast.
27. This is a reference to Méliès' *L'Homme à la tête en caoutchouc* (1901), in which he uses a set of bellows to inflate a disembodied version of his own head until it explodes.
28. Kentridge accompanied these short films with a more extensive homage to Melies, *Journey to the Moon* (2003).
29. William Kentridge quoted in Cheryl Kaplan, 'The Time-image: William Kentridge interviewed by Cheryl Kaplan', *PAJ: A Journal of Performance and Art* vol. 27 no. 2 (2005), p. 37.
30. See, for example, *The 400 Million* (1938), with photography by Robert Capa of the Second Sino-Japanese War, or *How Yukong Moved the Mountains* (1971–7), a twelve-hour document of the Cultural Revolution for which his personal friendships with Zhou Enlai and Mao Zedong gave him privileged access to the country.
31. Sylvain de Bleeckere, 'A Key to the Metaphysics of the Wind', in Kees Bakker (ed.), *Joris Ivens and the Documentary Context* (Amsterdam: Amsterdam University Press, 1999), p. 218.
32. André Stufkens, 'The Song of Movement', in Bakker, *Joris Ivens and the Documentary Context*, p. 70.
33. Tom Gunning, 'Shooting into Outer Space: Reframing Modern Vision', in Solomon, *Fantastic Voyages of the Cinematic Imagination*, p. 109.
34. Jonathan Rosenbaum, '*A Tale of the Wind*: Joris Ivens's Last Testament', in *Essential Cinema: On the Necessity of Film Canons* (Baltimore, MD and London: Johns Hopkins University Press, 2004), p. 42 [originally published in *Chicago Reader*, 29 May 1992].
35. Ibid., p. 40.
36. Frank Kessler has tackled the perception that Méliès' films were slavishly tied to a theatrical perspective (e.g. by framing full-body shots of actors, and keeping self-contained sets bordered by the edges of the frame). He suggests that this was not out of artistic inertia or aesthetic timidity, but was a conscious decision to mimic, then subvert, the kinds of continuity possible in theatrical performance. See Frank Kessler, 'The Gentleman in the Stalls: Georges Méliès and Spectatorship in Early Cinema', in Ian Christie (ed.), *Audiences: Defining and Researching Screen Entertainment Reception* (Amsterdam: Amsterdam University Press, 2012), pp. 35–44.
37. In episode 21 of Season 21, 'Moe Letter Blues', in the Itchy and Scratchy cat-and-mouse-cartoon segment (*La Mort d'un chat sur la lune*), a rocket is fired into the eye of Scratchy the Cat's decapitated head; in the Season 13 episode 'Blame It on Lisa', in the cartoon segment *Par for the Corpse*, Itchy uses Scratchy's head as a golfball and drives it into the Moon.
38. Teresa Rizzo, '*YouTube*: The New Cinema of Attractions', *Scan: Journal of Media Arts Culture* vol. 5 no. 1 (May 2008), http://scan.net.au/scan/journal/display.php?journal_id=109; see also Andrew Clay, 'BMW Films and the Star Wars Kid: "Early Web Cinema" and Technology', in Bruce Bennett, Marc Furstenau and Adrian Mackenzie (eds), *Cinema and Technology: Cultures, Theories, Practices* (Basingstoke: Palgrave Macmillan, 2008), pp. 37–52.
39. *A Trip to the Moon Back in Color* (Groupama Gan Foundation for Cinema/Technicolor Foundation for Cinema Heritage, 2011), p. 183.
40. Jack Zipes, *The Enchanted Screen: The Unknown History of Fairy-tale Films* (London: Routledge, 2011), pp. 31–48.

41. Alison McMahan, 'Technology 1890–1930: The Drive to Mechanisation and Digitisation', in Temple and Witt, *The French Cinema Book*, p. 42.
42. For discussions of the panicking audience and early cinema, see Stephen Bottomore, 'The Panicking Audience? Early Cinema and the "Train Effect"', *Historical Journal of Film, Radio and Television* vol. 19 no. 2 (1999), pp. 177–216; Martin Loiperdinger, 'Lumière's Arrival of a Train: Cinema's Founding Myth', *Moving Image* vol. 4 no. 1 (2004), pp. 89–118.
43. Paul Young, *The Cinema Dreams Its Rivals: Media Fantasy Films from Radio to the Internet* (Minneapolis: Minnesota University Press, 2006).

THE BATTLEFIELD FOR THE SOUL
SPECIAL EFFECTS AND THE POSSESSED BODY

STACEY ABBOTT

While the notion of demonic possession suggests a battle for the soul, eyewitness accounts of supposed cases from the sixteenth through to the twentieth and twenty-first centuries repeatedly describe possession as the manifestation of a physical attack upon the body. According to possession lore, symptoms usually include physical scratches, convulsions, bodily contortions, all of which are supposedly pushed to extremes during the process of exorcism as the demon is forced to come forward and identify itself. Theologian and popular author Malachi Martin asserts that

> it is as though an invisible manhole opens, and out of it pours the unmentionably inhuman and the humanly unacceptable. There is a stream of filth and unrestrained abuse, accompanied often by physical violence, writhing, gnashing of teeth, jumping around, sometimes physical attacks on the exorcist.[1]

Significantly, some believe that the soul is in fact never at risk during possession. It is simply the body that comes under attack, as argued by Fr Jose Antonio Fortea:

> Only the body is susceptible to demonic possession. A demon does not reside in – or in any other way 'possess' – the *soul* of the person. In all circumstances, the soul continues to be free and incapable of being possessed.[2]

These accounts of supposedly 'real' cases of possession and documented examples of exorcism have provided a stylistic template for cinematic possession and established a discourse that continues to pervade the genre, in which the body is presented as the site of a battle between good and evil. For instance, Philip C. Almond recounts one reported case of supposed demonic possession, dating from the sixteenth century, in which the body of the victim, Alexander Nyndge, was described as undergoing extreme physical contortion and torment, as his

> chest and body began to swell and his eyes to stare. He beat his head against the ground. He was often seen, we are informed, to have a lump running up and down his body between the flesh and the skin. He gnashed his teeth and foamed at the mouth. He shrieked with pain, and wept and laughed. He had the strength of four or five men, and his features were horribly disfigured.[3]

This description calls to mind numerous cinematic images of demonic possession – *The Exorcist* (1973), *Amityville 2: The Possession* (1982), *The Exorcism of Emily Rose* (2005) – as well as other bodily invasion imagery such as the sexually transmitted parasites that ripple just beneath the skin in David Cronenberg's *Shivers* (1975), the contorted and disfigured bodies in John Carpenter's *The Thing* (1982) and the transforming werewolf imagery of Joe Dante's *The Howling* (1981) and John Landis's *An American Werewolf in London* (1981). Technological developments within special effects – practical, optical and digital – have provided a visual language for the representation of possession and its visceral impact upon the body.

In 1973, many of the aesthetic parameters for the demonic-possession film were established by William Friedkin's *The Exorcist*, based upon the book by William Peter Blatty that was itself inspired by a newspaper story about the reported exorcism of a fourteen-year-old boy in Maryland.[4] In Friedkin's film, the body of thirteen-year-old Regan MacNeil (Linda Blair) became the location for a tug of war between science, religion and demonic influence, represented graphically through Dick Smith's and Marcel Vercoutere's combined special effects. Through Vercoutere's profilmic mechanical effects, Regan is made to levitate, her bed to shake and her bedroom walls to crack, while Smith's special makeup effects graphically depict her skin being repeatedly lacerated, her body contorted and her neck rotated 360 degrees.[5] While the effects are lavish and spectacular, the horror emerges from their physicality. Prior to *The Exorcist*, the possession movie, a subgenre that largely emerged in full force in the 1960s, was preoccupied with anxieties about demonic influence upon the innocent, concerns also expressed in Blatty's novel.[6] Following in the New Hollywood tradition of *The Wild Bunch* (1969), *Bonnie and Clyde* (1967) and *The Godfather* (1972), in which the conventional shootouts of the Western, outlaw and gangster films respectively were reworked to emphasise the bloody penetration of the body by bullets, Friedkin's *The Exorcist* focused the satanic or demonic film genre away from fears for the damnation of the soul – as illustrated in *Faust* (1926), *Night of the Demon* (1957) and *The Devil Rides Out* (1968) – toward an emphasis upon the destruction of the body through possession. In so doing, the film showcases the extent to which the body is vulnerable to attack.

The critical and box-office success of this film contributed to the legitimisation of the work of the special makeup-effects artist within the film industry, marking the beginning of a 'golden age' for this craft as the horror genre became increasingly preoccupied with the body. Philip Brophy argues that the contemporary horror film of the 1970s and 80s 'play[ed] not so much on the broad fear of Death, but more precisely on the fear of one's own body, of how one controls and relates to it'.[7] I would argue that, more precisely, these films captured the horror of the *loss of control* of one's own body, embodying a range of anxieties surrounding the impact of violence against the body at war, the risks of unleashed sexuality or fears of the diseased body culminating in the AIDS crisis of the 1980s. These genre preoccupations enabled special makeup-effects artists like Tom Savini, Rick Baker and Rob Bottin to extend the boundaries of their artistry with each film they made and as a result there grew a symbiotic relationship between the horror genre and the makeup artist. Their particular skills and techniques clearly influenced developments within the horror genre in the 1970s and 80s but cultural preoccupations around the body as expressed in the genre also pushed their work in a particular direction.

The development of increasingly sophisticated computer-generated imagery (CGI) in the 1990s and beyond, however, has led to a reduction in the use of practical effects within cinema. While CGI is largely defined by its hyperrealism, it still lacks the physicality that Brophy argued was the essence of modern horror, 'accentuating the very presence of the body on the screen', making CGI more compatible with speculative genres such as the science-fiction film that present imagined technologies, worlds and futures, than with the torture horror of *Saw* (2004) or *Hostel* (2005).[8] Therefore, while CGI is seemingly more ubiquitous across mainstream cinema – often showcased within blockbuster films and their 'discursive surround'[9] (behind-the-scenes featurettes, audio commentaries and marketing materials) as the pinnacle of technical prowess – practical effects are still used alongside digital effects. Within the bodily possession movie, in particular, both play a significant role in conveying the physicality and horror of possession, albeit in new ways.

This chapter will explore the continuing relationship, established in *The Exorcist*, between special effects and the representation of bodily possession, which for my purposes can extend to the possession of a human body by a spirit, demon or infecting agent that attacks from within, wrests control of the body from the individual and incites physical transformation – such as in the haunted-house and vampire films. Through my analysis, I will consider how special effects have been used within the genre to express shifting anxieties and discourses surrounding the body and its cinematic representation.

The Uncanniness of the Possessed Body

The notion of a possessed body is by its very nature inherently uncanny as it suggests a breakdown of individual identity when the body is made to house a multiplicity of personalities, making the familiar unfamiliar. In the cinema, special effects have played a significant role in presenting this multiplicity and in so doing, conforming to Noël Carroll's argument that feelings of horror are generated by a confrontation with something that 'is categorically interstitial, categorically contradictory, incomplete or formless'.[10] Carroll's conception of the 'categorically interstitial' is something that challenges physical, social or spiritual boundaries, linking Carroll's argument to Julia Kristeva's concept of abjection, that which 'disturbs identity, system, order. What does not respect borders, positions, rules. The in-between, the ambiguous, the composite.'[11] The possessed body in cinema is by definition categorically interstitial, and if not formless, its boundaries are blurred as the body contorts, pulsates and extends beyond its traditional shape. Elsewhere I have argued that digital effects in the science-fiction genre serve 'not to rupture the boundaries of the body but rather to stretch and extend the body beyond its usual limits', to cinematically construct a futurist post-humanism, in which the body becomes a CG cyborg.[12] In contrast, special effects in the possession movie contort and damage the body as a means of reducing humanity to the flesh, into which a multitude of souls and/or spirits are thrust.

The manner in which Regan is presented in *The Exorcist* through a combination of special effects conveys the uncanniness and the abjection of the possessed body in a multitude of ways. For instance, Regan's possessed body is created through the combined performances of the child actor Linda Blair, the actress Eileen Dietz, who doubled for Blair in some of Regan's more physically traumatic moments and Mercedes McCambridge, who provided the vocal performance during the exorcism scenes.[13] McCambridge's voice lends Regan a more gender-neutral quality, blurring the line between the female host and the male demon within. The voice is also older and more weathered, suggesting through the dubbing a form of ventriloquism in which the demon speaks through Regan.

Double exposure of the possessed Regan in *The Exorcist* (1973)

Dick Smith constructed a dummy of Regan as a stand-in for the movie's iconic head-rotation sequence and one shot in particular evokes Carroll's notion of the categorically interstitial and Kristeva's abjection.[14] Immediately after Regan's head had turned 360 degrees on her neck, Friedkin inserted a shot, apparently from the point of view of Father Karras (Jason Miller). It is a close-up of the inanimate Regan dummy over which the image of Dietz in heavy demonic makeup is superimposed, suggesting the duality of possession in which more than one soul or spirit inhabits a single body. The combination of practical effect and optical superimposition brings together the physical (makeup, dummy) and the spectral (the dissolve in which two images merge together as one). This shot captures the composite of brutalised body and evil spirit, the innocent Regan buried beneath the layers of effects. Mark Kermode suggests that 'the overlap brings to life Smith's dummy which, despite its moving eyes and eerily condensing breath, retains an otherwise frozen leer', and further argues that this shot lends an authenticity to the sequence following the ostentatious head rotation, 'moving back from the ridiculous to the sublime'.[15] It is the combined optical and physical special effects that embody the horror of possession, highlighting the internal conflict between the body and soul.

Other demonic-possession films have used different techniques and effects to suggest the presence of multiple souls within the possessed body. In *The Exorcism of Emily Rose*, it is achieved through a series of jump cuts with the overlapping sound of multiple voices naming the six demons residing within Emily (Jennifer Carpenter). The discordance of the editing, mixed with Carpenter's highly physical performance and the strained articulation of this dialogue, once again highlights the physicality of possession but this time it is an invisible battle being waged within the body. The invisibility of the battle emphasises Emily's internal struggle to maintain control and retain the sanctity of her soul despite the horror being done to and through her body. Possession is here presented as a physical violation of body and soul.

In contrast, digital effects are engaged in *The Rite* (2011) when the exorcist, Father Lucas Trevant (Anthony Hopkins), becomes possessed by a demon. Throughout his own exorcism by trainee Michael Kovak (Colin O'Donoghue), as the demon is pushed to identify itself (a pivotal moment in the ritual), black veins are made to appear across Trevant's face and head, particularly around the eyes. In these moments, the digital effects are used to create an almost translucent layer of darkness over the priest's face that appears and disappears as he loses and regains control of his body. While the use of CGI in these moments lacks the physicality of Smith's makeup for *The Exorcist*, it serves to suggest the emergence of the demonic presence from within the priest's body as his own personality becomes buried within. But the ethereal manner, intrinsic to CGI, in which the darkness appears and disappears on his face with little damage to the body, emphasises a spiritual, rather than a physical, battle between priest and demon. Here the battle is not *for* the soul but *between* souls, each vying for control of the body.

Special effects have similarly been enlisted to present the duality that blurs physical and spiritual boundaries within other forms of possession movies. Ghost stories most often deploy sound to convey the intermingling of souls as mediums communicate with the dead. In *The Others* (2001), a haunted-house movie that tells the story of a family of ghosts who are unaware that they are dead, mother Grace Stewart (Nicole Kidman) is terrified when she sees the face of an old woman speaking to her with the voice of her daughter. It is later revealed that the old woman is a medium brought to the house to exorcise its spirits. But it is the contrast between the old, withered face and the child's voice emanating from it that is unnerving.

In *What Lies Beneath* (2001), very subtle digital effects are used to suggest the coexistence of two souls in one body.[16] After performing a seance to communicate with the spirit of the murder victim she believes is haunting her house, Claire Spencer (Michelle Pfeiffer) is framed in close-up, emphasising her blue eyes, before the camera pans to her reflection in the mirror in which she has distinctive green eyes, their colour digitally altered. Later as Claire, now possessed by Madison Frank (Amber Valletta), begins to seduce her husband Norman (Harrison Ford), Claire looks at him as she sits astride his chest, informing him 'I think she is starting to suspect something.' When he asks 'Who?', she leans forward and, as she says 'Your wife', her face subtly morphs into the face of Madison. Later, a similar digital dissolve is used to show the transition between living body and possessing spirit when Norman drugs his wife and positions her in the bath to fake a suicide. As he lifts her paralysed body up to look at the necklace around her neck, her head falls backward to reveal the face of the corpse of Madison, staring up at him with grey, shrivelled skin and hollowed eyes. These subtle digital effects, presented in single shots (but actually composited from multiple elements) are designed to elicit a sudden scare, but also to convey the fluid coexistence of two spirits in one body, united by their shared anger at Norman's betrayal of them.

Let the Right One In (2008) relies on a combination of traditional and digital techniques to suggest a similar duality in the vampire-child Eli (Lina Leandersson), as evidenced in the possession film, in this case not possessed by a demon, but instead containing an old soul within a young body – reminiscent of the scene from *The Others* described above. Like Regan, Eli is a special-effects construct that blurs lines between male and female, young and old, human and monster. Numerous other vampire films and television series have also showcased the dual nature of the vampire. While in many early adaptations of *Dracula*, this was constructed through performance and makeup (*Nosferatu* [1922], *Dracula* [1931)] and *Dracula* [1958]), vampire films increasingly began to present this duality through the spectacle of digital and special makeup effects. For instance, in *Fright Night* (1985), when attractive and youthful vampire Jerry Dandridge (Chris Sarandon) is stabbed through the hand with a wooden pencil, he loses control of his façade and reveals the monster within, represented through elaborate prosthetics on his face, teeth and hands to present him as a human/bat hybrid. When Dracula (Gary Oldman) appears as a human/wolf hybrid in *Bram Stoker's Dracula* (1992), the sequence entails elaborate prosthetic makeup, enhanced by a very brief superimposition of a close-up of Oldman over the wolf face. *From Dusk till Dawn* (1996) showcases the transition of a night-club stripper into a hideous, reptilian monster by digitally morphing through the different stages of Salma Hayek's facial prosthetics, suggesting a fluid and seamless transformation. In the mythology of television series *Buffy the Vampire Slayer* (1997–2003) and *Angel* (1999–2004), vampirism is overtly equated with demonic possession. When a person is 'turned' by a vampire, the demon takes over the body while the victim's soul is released. This possession is visualised by digitally morphing back and forth between the vampire's human and vamp faces, presented by the prosthetics of distorted and monstrous forehead and fangs. The use of special effects in these texts not only highlights this duality but also serves to visualise the struggle within the vampire to maintain control of the self. The monstrous visage emerging at points when the vampire is overcome by bloodlust or anger presents the vampire body as a site of conflict.

In all these cases, the vampires are presented as either evil or physically and spiritually damned, while Eli in *Let the Right One In* is, physically and morally, a more ambiguous character.[17] This ambiguity is suggested through the subtlety of the film's special effects. In contrast to more graphic and spectacular traditions within contemporary vampire films, Alfredson's film deliberately downplays special effects.[18] As Alfredson explains, 'the film is really complicated and it's really stuffed with CGI (for Swedish standards), though nobody seems to notice'.[19] Eli's physical ambiguity is therefore presented through a combination of dialogue dubbing, sound effects, digital manipulation of her image and simple jump cuts. For instance in two scenes, shots of child-actor Leandersson as Eli are very briefly replaced by a single shot of an older woman in Eli's place: first, when Eli reveals her vampire hunger to new friend Oskar (Kare Hedebrant) as she laps up blood from the floor and then looks up and tells him to go away; and later, when she invites him to look into her eyes and be her for just a moment. Unlike *The Others*, where a similar moment suggests the presence of a medium speaking to Grace through the ghostly voice and body of her daughter, in *Let the Right One In* these shots appear as a glimpse of Eli's alternative self, providing an impression of the old soul housed within her young body.

Eli's physical ambiguity is further enhanced by the film's use of sound. As in *The Exorcist*, her voice is dubbed by another actress with an older and more 'abrasive and boyish' voice, suggesting that she is potentially older than she looks while also blurring gender lines.[20] Eli repeatedly tells Oskar that she 'is not a girl' and the specific meaning of this statement is unclear. Is she raising questions about her age, her vampiric nature or, perhaps, her gender? Furthermore, the scenes of her attacking her victims are accompanied by sounds of animals screeching and mewling, emphasising her more feral qualities. Finally, after revealing her bloodlust to Oskar, Eli runs away and climbs a tree to hide from him but also to hunt, now that her thirst has been awakened. In this shot, as Eli scans the neighbourhood for potential victims, her face, filmed in medium long shot, undergoes a subtle transformation, highlighting her otherness, with her eyes made to appear wider, her cheeks hollow and shadows to flit across her face, suggesting layers of facial imagery. This shot does not leap out as spectacle in the manner of *The Exorcist*'s double exposure but instead achieves a disturbing sense of the uncanny through its subtlety. Eli is presented throughout the film as a form of technological abjection, blurring the lines between high- and low-tech effects so that she appears as a physically and morally ambiguous character, possessing a multitude of interlinked, sometimes contradictory, identities.

In contrast, the American remake, *Let Me In* (2010), uses CGI to mark a clear transition of the vampire, renamed Abbey (Chloë Grace Moretz), from an outwardly normal girl to an animalistic monster. When her friend, renamed Owen (Kodi Smit-McPhee), cuts his thumb to propose a blood pact, thus forcing her vampiric nature to the surface, Abbey's eyes turn white, her pupils become abnormally dilated and black veins appear beneath the surface of her skin, alluding to the monster within (reminiscent of the possession in *The Rite*). When she runs away from Owen, her scramble up the tree to look for a new victim is achieved through full digital animation of her body, now thin, elongated and inhuman. Unlike the layering of identities in the image from *The Exorcist* or the representation of Eli in the Swedish film, here the actress is replaced by a digital character that evokes her monstrosity. This is reinforced by two additional scenes where the full digital animation of Abbey's form is repeated as her bloodlust overwhelms her and she is forced to hunt. In both scenes, the first when she attacks a man in an underpass and the second when she attacks the police officer who has tracked her to her apartment, Abbey is transformed into a feral monster who lunges upon and clings to the bodies of her victims as she drinks their blood, despite their attempts to extricate themselves from her. In these scenes, Abbey appears more like Gollum from *The Lord of the Rings* (2001–3) than the young girl who befriends Owen. Digital effects here remove the ambiguity of the vampire's physical form as expressed through the combination of low-tech effects adopted in *Let the Right One In*, and render her clearly as a monster, making Owen's decision to stay with her all the more disturbing. In this manner, the utilisation of computer-generated effects and, in particular, full-character digital animation, removes much of the humanity from the possessed and presents her as a monstrous 'other'. Where the composite nature of most possession effects (whether demonic, spirit or vampiric), from *The Exorcist* to *What Lies Beneath* to *Let the Right One In*, highlights the internal conflict of the possessed, Abbey evokes the fear of an external threat – fear of the possessed monster – not the familiar made unfamiliar but the body made unknowable. In contrast, another group of possession films, discussed below, deliberately capitalise upon familiarity with the limitations of the body in the generation of horror.

The Spectacle of the Grotesque Body – Performance as Special Effect

According to Mark Kermode, when making *The Exorcist*, 'Friedkin decreed that all the supernatural goings-on of the exorcism sequence should be achieved mechanically, on-set, producing a sense of verisimilitude often lacking in post-production effects.' Friedkin's aim was to generate horror through the implied realism of his profilmic techniques, suggesting that these events could happen.[21] The intense physicality of the special effects, where objects move, bodies are struck or thrown about, and skin tears, contributes to the conception of photographic realism he sought. Over the years, however, *The Exorcist* has become less well known for its 'realism' than for its spectacle. Set-pieces like the vomiting of green bile, the levitation and the head-spinning have become iconic moments, often evoking cheers at midnight screenings of the film, where once they might have elicited screams of fear. The effects, while still impressive as examples of their craft, stand out more obviously as the generations pass and new techniques and approaches are introduced, particularly compared to the hyperrealism of computer-generated imagery in films like Paul Verhoeven's *Hollow Man* (2000) or James Cameron's *Terminator 2: Judgment Day* (1991). As a result, a series of recent demonic-possession movies, such as *The Exorcism of Emily Rose* and *The Last Exorcism* (2010), have turned away from special effects to convey the horrors of possession. In these films, the physical performance of the grotesque body, with some digital and aural enhancement, serves as a special effect in itself.

While Friedkin's film approaches the genre through the prism of faith, these demonic-possession films, along with *The Rite*, *Paranormal Activity* (2007), *An American Haunting* (2005), *The Devil* (2010) and *The Devil Inside* (2012), to name a few, emerged within a post-millennial context, influenced by anxieties around religious fundamentalism. In this period, the Catholic Church demonstrated a renewed interest in demonic exorcism, a fact that has captured media interest in the form of newspaper articles, nonfiction books, television series and feature films.[22] The period is, however, also marked by an increased scepticism about religion as argued by Kevin J. Wetmore:

> [A]fter September 11, the fear of religion and of those who hold fundamentalist beliefs again rose to dominance in horror cinema. There are two streams of religiously based horror that emerge in the last decade. In the first, fear is generated because the religious teachings about evil are correct . . . . In the second, the fear is of religion itself, especially fundamentalism. In other words, religion itself is the problem.[23]

A stream of post-millennial demonic-possession movies, best exemplified by *The Exorcism of Emily Rose* and *The Last Exorcism*, deliberately evoke this ambivalence toward religion and the supernatural by walking a line between these two horror traditions in their representation of the possessed body.

The Exorcism of Emily Rose was inspired by the true story of Anneliese Michel, a German Catholic student who died after a series of 'failed' exorcisms and whose parents and priests were tried for negligent homicide. The film, relocating the events to the US, presents the story as a courtroom drama in which the prosecution advances a scientifically accepted explanation for Emily's condition, namely that she suffered from epilepsy and mental illness, while the defence attempts to cast doubt on this argument by encouraging the jury to consider the possibility of possession. Both sides of the argument are proffered and while the film privileges the supernatural explanation over the scientific, partly by telling Emily's story from the point of view of the defence, the extreme physical performance of Carpenter in the possession and exorcism scenes positions the narrative within the realm of the possible as well as the supernatural. This is particularly evident when comparing the film to the German-made *Requiem* (2006), similarly inspired by the Michel case but presenting the notion of 'possession' as the delusion of a disturbed young woman struggling with the symptoms of epilepsy, magnified by religious guilt and repression. Where Carpenter's performance emphasises extreme physical contortion and abuse, Sandra Hüller's performance as Michaela highlights psychological trauma.

Taking a different approach, *The Last Exorcism* falls within the popular horror tradition of the faux documentary or found-footage horror film, a cycle that includes *The Blair Witch Project* (1999), *Paranormal Activity* and *REC* (2007). While a fiction film, *The Last Exorcism* conforms to the conventions of the documentary, with handheld camera, natural lighting and direct address, as it chronicles a minister's collaboration with a film crew to expose the fraudulence of demonic exorcisms. In so doing, the film explores the dichotomy between illusion and reality, by confronting a phony exorcist with a 'real' possession.

The emphasis on questions of truth and reality in both *The Exorcism of Emily Rose* and *The Last Exorcism* requires a more restrained presentation of possession than is evidenced in the prequels to *The Exorcist*, *Dominion: Prequel to the Exorcist* (2005) and *Exorcist: The Beginning* (2004) in which the possessed victims defy laws of gravity by floating in the air and crawling up walls like a spider, conveyed through digital effects. In these climactic moments, there is no doubt that these characters are possessed by demons. In *The Exorcism of Emily Rose* and *The Last Exorcism*, however, the horror is focused upon the damage and abuse done to the body but the cause of the damage is called into question. Is this the product of demonic possession or a damaged mind and body? In this manner, a notion of realism is the product of the actor's performance, in which she twists and contorts her body in extreme and disturbing ways, but ways that could be the result of psychosis, as in *Requiem*. In *The Last Exorcism*, the supposedly possessed girl, Nell (Ashley Bell), begins to suggest that her body is no longer under her own control through the contrast between her absolute stillness, staring blankly at the film crew outside her bedroom or later standing posed in the position of a crucifix, and her sudden, violent bursts of movement and fury as she attacks the exorcist.

Similarly, in *The Exorcism of Emily Rose*, Emily's boyfriend describes how he once woke up to find Emily lying on the floor, her eyes open but blank with her pupils fully dilated, her body rigid and contorted with her back arched, neck twisted and hands gnarled. With the exception of the eyes, which were digitally altered to dilate the pupils, this pose is an extreme physical contortion of the body performed by the actress. These performances call to mind the work of silent-cinema actor Lon Chaney in *The Penalty* (1920), *The Blackbird* (1926) and *The Unknown* (1927), in which he repeatedly contorted and manipulated his body to create a series of disfigured and disabled characters, presenting the grotesqueness of his body as an object of horror. As with the work of Chaney, what makes these sequences so effective and disturbing is that the actresses are actually performing this bodily manipulation – a fact reinforced by the inclusion of the Ashley Bell audition footage on the DVD of *The Last Exorcism*. These scenes convey real pain and discomfort in the body; through these and other extreme examples of body contortion, the genre returns to an aesthetic that once again, 'accentuat[es] the very presence of the body on the screen', as Brophy argued for body horror of the 1980s.[24]

These body contortions are clearly based on real-life accounts of possession and exorcism as well as medical cases of severe epilepsy, schizophrenia and post-traumatic stress disorder as explored in *Requiem*. Aesthetically, they also evoke a now infamous deleted scene from *The Exorcist*, Regan's spider-walk. In the original novel, William Peter Blatty captures the dehumanisation of Regan through her possession in one particular passage:

> Gliding spider-like, rapidly, close behind Sharon, her body arched backward in a bow with her head almost touching her feet, was Regan, her tongue flicking quickly in and out of her mouth while she hissed sibilantly like a serpent.[25]

This passage presents Regan's movements as defying the normal limitations of the body, with her 'body arched backward in a bow', while equating Regan with spiders and snakes to visceral effect. This scene was shot by Friedkin for the film, using a harness, rig and piano wire constructed by Vercoutere. The shot was, however, eventually cut from the completed film. Unavailable for many years, the scene eventually resurfaced on the DVD, reaffirming Mark Kermode's suspicions that its exclusion from the film was because, with the harness and wires still visible within the shot, 'the scene simply didn't work on a technical level'.[26] While the mechanics of the effect are obvious, the scene still presents an unsettling and alien image of the child, more lizardlike than human. Her arched back as she descends the stairs is unnatural and her body is made to move in a way that is physically impossible.

The Exorcism of Emily Rose and *The Last Exorcism* each contain scenes that capture unnatural movements to suggest demonic intervention. In *The Exorcism of Emily Rose*, Emily's boyfriend recounts seeing her struggling to reach out toward the crucifix in a church as her body was pulled backward away from the cross into a backbreaking bend. This shot was achieved largely through Carpenter's performance, with some minor digital enhancement to force her back further than is physically possible.[27] During the second exorcism in *The Last Exorcism*, Nell, asked by the minister to allow the demon to come forward, lies on the ground crying until finally her body becomes rigid and then her neck twists with a bone-crunching jolt to the right. The sound-effects work here accentuates the discomfort and unnaturalness of this position. Later in the scene she also performs an uncomfortably realistic back extension, with her hair dropping to the floor as she bounces on her heels to accentuate the extremity of this position. The climax of the body distortion comes after she dares the exorcist to stay silent for ten seconds so that the demon can release the girl. As she counts to ten, she begins to break her fingers, presented in close-up and punctuated with the precise sound effects of the bones breaking and matched by the girl's screams, causing the exorcist to intervene. Everything in this scene is performed by the actress – although one assumes that the bones were not broken, simply bent. The effects are viscerally enhanced by sound effects, and by the roving camera that repeatedly films Nell at angles that emphasise the distortion of her body and facial expressions.

The use of the back extension in both films evokes the spider-walk from *The Exorcist*, novel and film, but presented in a way that showcases the contorted bodies of the actresses. In this manner these films present the body itself as a special effect put under extreme physical stress and abuse, more disturbing than makeup or CGI. While on the surface, this approach ties into the films' engagement with debates about the validity of demonic possession, it also highlights the genre's preoccupation with the boundaries and limitations that define the human body. If Dick Smith's physical makeup effects in *The Exorcist* highlight the fragility of the body, while the digitally animated body in *Let Me In* serves as a distortion of the body, in these performance-led horror films, the horror is within the body itself, capable of suffering extreme contortion and abuse – whether at the hands of the devil, psychosis or the demands of cinematic performance.

Physical performance of possession in *The Last Exorcism* (2010)

It is clear that one of the primary sources of anxiety that unites films of possession, whether demonic, spiritual or vampiric, is the fear of loss of control of the body. This loss of control raises questions about the relationship between identity and the body, as the 'self' appears lost to possession. Lost to demons attacking and reducing the body to monstrous flesh; ghostly possession in which individual agency is sacrificed as the body becomes a medium of communication with the spirit world; or vampirism where the body is hijacked by a bloodlust that overwhelms reason, a loss of control made all the more poignant as the vampire has become more sympathetic and ambiguous.

These anxieties, emerging in full force in the 1970s out of the growing secularisation of Western society, have in recent years been reignited by a growing ambivalence toward spiritualism in the face of bodily violence. As Wetmore argues, since 9/11 there has been a resurgence of religion within popular culture, which has also generated increasing suspicion, alongside a culture of terrorism and war highlighting a constant threat to the body.[28] This has manifested within the horror genre, dominated in recent years by subgenres such as 'torture porn' and the zombie film, which present the body itself as an object of horror, and supernatural horror, exploring the world of spirits, vengeful ghosts and demons. Possession films unite these two traditions, utilising special effects – practical, optical, auditory and digital – which embody through their composite nature the disjuncture between body and spirit. While special effects are usually associated with pure spectacle, in the possession genre they overtly link the spectacle of the body in disarray with questions of identity. In this manner they articulate one of the genre's primary aims: to undermine the boundaries between the human and nonhuman, the self and other, and in so doing question the nature of humanity.

Notes

1. Malachi Martin, *Hostage to the Devil: The Possession and Exorcism of Five Contemporary Americans* (San Francisco, CA: Harper One, 1992), p. 19.

2. Fr Jose Antonio Fortea, *Interview with an Exorcist* (West Chester, PA: Ascension Press, 2006), p. 72.
3. Philip C. Almond, *Demonic Possession and Exorcism in Early Modern England: Contemporary Texts and Their Cultural Contexts* (Cambridge: Cambridge University Press, 2004), p. 1.
4. See Mark Kermode, *The Exorcist* (London: BFI, 1997) for details about the writing of the novel and its adaptation for the cinema and Thomas B. Allen, *Possessed: The True Story of an Exorcism* (Lincoln, NE; iUniverse.com, Inc., 2000) for a detailed account of the Maryland possession and exorcism.
5. See Don Shay, 'Dick Smith – 50 Years in Makeup', *Cinefex* vol. 62 (June 1995), p. 120 for discussion of Smith's makeup effects in this film.
6. Charles Derry, *Dark Dreams: The Horror Films from Psycho to Jaws* (London: Thomas Yoseloff Ltd, 1977), pp. 85–106.
7. Philip Brophy, 'Horrality – The Textuality of Contemporary Horror Films', *Screen* vol. 27 no. 1 (January/February 1986), p. 8.
8. Brophy, 'Horrality', p. 8.
9. Barbara Klinger, 'Film History Terminable and Interminable: Recovering the Past in Reception Studies', *Screen* vol. 38 no. 2 (1997), p. 107–28.
10. Noël Carroll, *The Philosophy of Horror: Or Paradoxes of the Heart* (New York and London: Routledge, 1990), p. 32.
11. Julia Kristeva, *Power of Horror: An Essay on Abjection*, trans. Leon S. Roudiez (New York: Columbia University Press, 1982), p. 4.
12. Stacey Abbott, 'Final Frontiers: Computer-generated Imagery and the Science Fiction Film', *Science Fiction Studies* vol. 33 (March 2006), p. 97.
13. Animal noises were also integrated into the sound mix.
14. Shay, 'Dick Smith', p. 120; Kermode, *The Exorcist*, p. 65.
15. Ibid., p. 67.
16. Anon, 'What Lies Beneath', *3D Graphic FX* (2000), available at http://candles2.tripod.com/index.htm.
17. Good vampires Angel (David Boreanaz) and Spike (James Marsters) (on *Buffy* and *Angel*) are in fact doubly possessed as they each have their original souls forced back into their bodies, housed alongside the demon.
18. See Stacey Abbott, *Celluloid Vampires* (Austin: University of Texas Press, 2007) for a discussion of special effects in the vampire film.
19. Alfredson quoted in Blake, 'NIFFF 2008 – *Let the Right One In* Interview', *Twitch*, 25 July 2008, http://twitchfilm.com/interviews/2008/07/nifff-2008-let-the-right-one-in-interview.php.
20. Alfredson, quoted in Blake, 'NIFFF 2008'.
21. Kermode, *The Exorcist*, p. 67.
22. As evidence of the popular attention gained by contemporary stories of possession and/or exorcism, see media articles by Pullela, Wilkinson, McCarthy and popular nonfiction publications by Allen, Baglio, Fortea and Martin. See also BBC serial *Apparitions* (2008) and Showtime original motion picture *Possessed* (2000).
23. Kevin J. Wetmore, *Post-9/11 Horror in American Cinema* (New York and London: Continuum, 2012), p. 140–1.
24. Brophy, 'Horrality', p. 8.
25. William Peter Blatty, *The Exorcist/Legion* (Baltimore, MD: Cemetery Dance, 2010), p. 108.

26. Kermode, *The Exorcist*, p. 61.
27. See 'Keith Vanderlaan's Captive Audience Project Gallery: Exorcism of Emily Rose', available at http://radarla.com/CAP/, accessed 1 June 2012 for an illustration of the digital manipulation used in this scene.
28. Wetmore, *Post-9/11 Horror in American Cinema*, p. 140–1.

BAROQUE FAÇADES
JEFF BRIDGES'S FACE AND *TRON: LEGACY*

ANGELA NDALIANIS

Science Fiction and Science Fictionality

One of the most successful vehicles of technological virtuosity in the cinema is the science-fiction film. Since 1968, when Stanley Kubrick's *2001: A Space Odyssey* was released, science-fiction films have invited audiences to contemplate the future impact of technology on humanity while simultaneously displaying the latest advances in current audiovisual-effects technologies. In their own way, science-fiction films attempt to come to grips with the radically changing world around us, and the effects that technological mediation will have on human identity in the distant – but not too distant – future. This essay is concerned with the ways in which science-fiction themes make themselves felt through special effects and the technologies that produce them. My interest is in how science-fiction films articulate what Brooks Landon calls 'science fiction thinking',[1] and what Istvan Csicsery-Ronay labels 'science-fictionality, a mode of response that frames and tests experiences as if they were aspects of a work of science fiction'. [2] Yet it is the software technology itself – and not a science-fiction narrative – that prompts the audience to ponder the science-fictional nature of these entertaining effects; the science-fictional is contained in the very technology used to create the special effects. As Csicsery-Ronay explains: 'SF has become a form of discourse that directly engages contemporary language and culture, and that has, in this moment, a generic interest in the intersections of technology, scientific theory, and social practice.'[3] It's precisely this notion of science fictionality or science-fiction thinking that's at the core of this essay. Focusing on *Tron: Legacy* (2010), I will explore how the film's special effects parallel the concerns of the narrative by asking their audience to ponder the nature of the human–machine interface. I characterise this as an effects-driven metaphysical question that exits the diegetic world of the film to generate its own science-fictional narrative – one that escapes the control of the film-makers, but which is, nevertheless, integral to the film-making process.

Over the last decade, motion capture has become a common computer-generated (CG) effects tool used to 'capture' the actions and movements of actors and objects and then translate their motions into a digital world on screen. The characters in *Final Fantasy: The Spirits Within* (2001), the Mummy in *The Mummy* trilogy (1999–2008), Gollum in the *The Lord of the Rings* films (2001–3), the main characters in *The Polar Express* (2004), King Kong in *King Kong* (2005), Davy Jones in *Pirates of the Caribbean: Dead Man's Chest* (2006), the characters in *Beowulf* (2007), the Na'vi in *Avatar* (2009), Tintin, Captain Haddock and Ivanovitch Sakharine in *The Adventures of Tintin* (2011), among many others, all contributed to advancing motion-capture effects in ways that heightened the 'reality effect' of fantastic, fictional characters in the on-screen film world. Whereas motion capture records the movement of actors (and objects), performance capture – also known as e-motion and facial motion capture – took the detailing of movements and expressions further still by concentrating on capturing the more intricate, micro movements involving facial expressions. The films *The Curious Case of Benjamin Button* (2008) and *Avatar* are, perhaps, most paradigmatic of the advances made in performance-capture techniques over the last decade. Whether using the Mova Contour® Reality Capture system (as in *Benjamin Button*)[4] or mobile cameras mounted on a head cap worn by the actor (as in *Avatar*),[5] one thing is certain: mainstream cinema has created many CG faces that rely on cutting-edge developments in visual-effects software and hardware.

In his book *Performing Illusions: Cinema, Special Effects and the Virtual Actor*, Dan North begins with an analysis of the final minutes of *King Kong* where 'the mortally wounded giant ape shares a tender moment with Ann Darrow (Naomi Watts) at the top of the Empire State Building'.[6] Referring to the contact that is made between the live actor, Watts, and the synthetic actor Kong – who was modelled on the live-action acting of Andy Serkis and whose actions and expressions were translated digitally into the computer – North explains that 'This moment of trans-photographic contact, with a live actress reaching out to touch a computer-generated co-star, challenges the spectator to spot the join between the two worlds.' North's book is concerned with this 'join' and 'the relationship between the real and its technological mediation', which, when coming together in the same scene trigger a dialogue between the spectacle and its methods of construction.[7] Later in the book he refers to the writings of the animator Norman McLaren, who argued, 'what happens between frames is more important than what is on each frame'. Animation is thus 'the art of manipulating the invisible interstices that lie between frames'.[8] I am more concerned with exploring the journey of 'science fictionality' that travels between the frames (which contain the diegetic world and the special effects that give it expression) and the live-action world that gives shape to it. In exploring this journey, the conceptual framework of the 'frame' will be replaced by the metaphor of the façade, specifically the allegory of the baroque house and baroque façade as theorised by Gilles Deleuze in his book *The Fold: Leibniz and the Baroque* (1993). I'm less interested in the baroque façade as a stylistic category and more as a philosophical exploration that applies Deleuze's theoretical ruminations about the nature of subjectivity and the soul, exteriority and interiority, surface and depth to digital special effects. In doing so, my aim is to untangle the science-fictional concepts that *Tron: Legacy* articulates through its use of special effects. It's Jeff Bridges's face that I'm especially interested in. Unlike Andy Serkis, who was converted into the CG giant ape Kong, the Stoor hobbit Gollum and the intelligent chimp Caesar (*Rise of the Planet of the Apes* [2011]); Zoe Saldana, Sam Worthington and Sigourney Weaver, who were transformed into the tall, blue-skinned aliens, the Na'vi; or Brad Pitt who was aged into a shrivelled and shrinking old man barely recognisable as Pitt, Jeff Bridges performed as and appeared on screen with a younger version of himself – the CG character Clu. The construction of the two Bridges – the digitised 1980s version and the 'real' twenty-first-century version – opens up a baroque dialogue about the slippery nature of what it means to be human as a result of technological mediation. I will follow a baroque philosophical journey that explores the nature of the dialogue created between the two Jeff Bridges' faces: the face belonging to the reality of the twenty-first century, and the other being the digitally reconstructed face of versions of Jeff Bridges that extend back to the 1980s.

The Baroque Façade, and Digital Skins

Tron: Legacy picks up a few years after the events of the first *Tron* (1982). In that earlier film, Kevin Flynn (Jeff Bridges) – one of the masterminds behind ENCOM, the successful computer technology corporation – is caught up in a struggle with the Master Control Program (MCP), an artificial intelligence that controls the ENCOM mainframe and that – like any good villain – has higher aspirations for controlling the world. The MCP uses experimental teleportation technology to transfer Kevin Flynn into the mainframe where he exists as a virtual character, but Flynn eventually escapes and is reconstructed as living flesh back in 'reality'. *Tron: Legacy* opens with a backstory informing us how, after his escape, Flynn set up a secret lab beneath an arcade where he continued to experiment with teleportation, until, one day, he disappeared. The film then focuses on Flynn's now twenty-seven-year-old son Sam (Garrett Hedlund), who traces his father's steps back to the arcade and there, like his father, soon finds himself in the digital world known as the Grid where he discovers that his father has been trapped for the last two decades. A cult classic, *Tron* was ground-breaking in its use of computer graphics in film, creating a CG *mise en scène* that was populated by live actors. Similarly pushing digital-effects technology to its limits, *Tron: Legacy* bargains on 'anthropomorphising the computer's operations' and, in doing so, makes 'ontological connections between the electronic and real worlds'.[9] Director Joseph Kosinski, who has a degree in architecture from Columbia University, took an architectural approach to constructing the film's digital world populated by virtual humans. Kosinski relates how he 'gathered around him artists from diverse disciplines, including architects and automotive designers, and the result [was] … a complicated blend of techniques that melded together the film narrative's virtual and real worlds'.[10] Kosinki's architect's eye clearly impacts on the spectacle that is the world of the Grid – its architectural exteriors, its lavish interiors, its high-tech vehicles and weaponry; but the architect's eye also informs the virtual flesh of 'living' beings who exist in this realm. Both virtual inanimate and animate objects succumb to a gridding system that is made visible at numerous points in the film, a system that echoes the AutoCAD Architectural software used in current architectural design. At the same time, the visible gridding performing for the viewer in the Grid also reflects the 3D modelling that operates in a gridding system in order to map the faces and bodies of actors into the computer during the motion- and performance-capture process. Like the role served by the building façade, the 'skinning' of humans and architecture alike simultaneously signals a relationship to a space that surrounds and to a space within. All are visibly interconnected in the space of the Grid, and the labyrinthine connectedness of and between surfaces is driven by a baroque logic.

The baroque façade has been understood as functioning independently of the building it often encases. It is a surface that evokes dynamism, movement and plasticity both stylistically and metaphorically, in that its aesthetic properties generate a dialogue between spaces. In the context of the baroque city, as Christian Norberg Schultz explains, 'the single [façade of a] building [also] loses its plastic individuality and becomes part of a superior system … an organic part of the urban system'.[11] Fluid interactions are created between inside and outside: the façade that merges with the urban exterior and the sacred space of the church inside; the façade as emblematic of the sacred interior, and the public realm of the city space it looks out onto; the façade as physical embodiment of the materiality that makes up everyday life, and the interior which operates as mysterious link to the wonders of the sacred and immaterial.

Fragments and wholes converge and fold into one another, in the process altering signification as inside becomes outside and outside becomes inside. For example, in the *Chiesa di San Carlo alle Quattro Fontane* by architect Francesco Borromini (Rome, 1638–46), the serpentine façade with its convex and concave motions suggests this dynamic interplay. While its vertical lines connect the lower, street level of the façade to the lighter upper levels, decorated with floating putti, the façade also bends and curves to meet the city (a motion represented in the way the façade literally folds around the corner to meet one of the four fountains depicting a River God); it then inverts this movement by retreating back into, while simultaneously signalling, the space of the sacred interior whose undulating rhythms and flowing lines further echo this fluid logic but which, in this instance, service the more sacred and personal function of the church interior. For Deleuze, such movements are emblematic of the baroque 'fold', which 'differentiates its folds in two ways, by moving along two infinities, as if infinity were composed of two stages or floors: the pleats of matter, and the folds in the soul'. This is Deleuze's allegory of the baroque house:

> the lower level is assigned to the facade, which is elongated by being punctured and bent back according to the folds determined by a heavy matter … . The upper level is closed, as a pure inside without an outside, a weightless, closed interiority, its walls hung with spontaneous folds that are now only those of a soul or a mind.[12]

The baroque façade becomes a point of mediation that folds between and articulates the complex, metaphysical relationship that exists between matter and spirit, which is represented not only in the body and mind of the human being, but which can also find expression in artistic objects like paintings and sculptures, in architectural structures such as *San Carlo alle Quattro Fontane* and in films like *Tron: Legacy* – keeping in mind, of course, that all of these cultural objects fold back to the humanity that creates and admires them.

Discussing architecture through a Deleuzian lens, Patrizia Magli states that both faces (*facce*) and façades (*facciate*) involve a dialogic relationship between the inside and outside, the material and the metaphysical, the visible and the invisible. Referring to Deleuze, she places emphasis on architecture as body; in turn, this body engages in a dialogue about existence, the spiritual and the soul. She continues:

> An example of this is the Baroque façade, which, being divided in two, *a lower level and an upper level*, reproduces the physiognomic axiology and its correlation between the opposites high/low, spiritual/material … . The fact that one is metaphysical and concerns souls while the other is physical and pertains to bodies does not prevent the two vectors making up a single world-building face.[13]

I want to take up this idea of the 'single, world-building face', the inside and the outside; but I'd like to instead investigate it in alternative architectural terms. I'd like to explore the digital architecture employed to create the world of *Tron: Legacy*; in particular, the façade that is Jeff Bridges's face, which is reproduced as a digital skin that wraps itself onto his virtual dark double, Clu. Using chroma-key compositing, Bridges was filmed against a bluescreen background, allowing his body and performance to be fluently composited into the virtual environment of the Grid. His (and his body double's) movements were motion captured and this data mapped into a 3D model that duplicated the actor's animations in digital form. In addition, in order to capture the minute expressions of Bridges's face, using the performance of the real Bridges of 2009–10, the visual-effects team built a helmet rig with four infrared cameras for him to wear on set while performing, which recorded his expressions from four angles. The captured data were transferred into the computer, and a façade of Bridges's body and face came into virtual existence. The film represents an alternate expression of the baroque façade but, like the façade of *San Carlo alle Quattro Fontane*, Bridges's face-as-façade functions as a porous barrier that connects the exterior to the interior, and the interior to the exterior. The lower and the upper, the material and the spiritual are articulated through an interplay that folds: the materiality of the narrative 'real' world into the transcendent, technological and spiritual-like space of the narrative world's virtuality; and the materiality of the technology employed to give life to the fictional world that is the film *Tron: Legacy* – a special-effects technology that attempts to wield its own transcendent, wondrous power for the spectator.

Pushing the boundaries of computer-generated imagery and, in particular, motion capture and 3D technology, the film represents – both within its diegesis and beyond, through its use of special effects – a fluid, shifting and porous relationship between the virtual and the real. Diegetically, the film collides the 'real' world of the main character Sam Flynn, and the virtual world of the Grid (a digital world created by his father Kevin Flynn). The façade that mediates and defines the relationship between the two is performed by the game arcade called 'Flynn's Arcade' – which has both 'real' and virtual manifestations. Non-diegetically, however, the special effects and computer-generated architecture that construct these realms also generate a labyrinthine interplay between layers of reality and give shape to new forms of subjectivity.

Conceptually, the film mirrors the convex/concave motions of Borromini's church as its narrative and special effects untangle sets of shifting relationships about outside and inside, façade and interior, façade and exterior, the realm of matter and the realm of the soul or mind. On the level of the final product experienced in 3D on grand-scale IMAX-sized screens, the audience reaction was one of wonder that mirrored an almost spiritual fervour.[14] The intention of the film's creators was to immerse viewers both in a story that depicted the possibilities of science and technology as states that mirror religious experience and worship, and into a special-effects spectacle that triggered worshipful awe on the part of the spectator akin to a believer praying before an altar. Yet, as I've argued elsewhere,[15] the success of many similar special effects in blockbuster-film experiences also relies on an awareness of the materiality of the medium (the computer hardware, software programming, the new 3D cameras and viewing systems, etc.). The special effects become a virtuoso performance about the technology that makes possible these wondrous illusions.[16]

Before the film's release, great fanfare surrounded the fact that *Tron: Legacy* was the first 3D movie to integrate a digital head and body onto an existing actor to create a younger version of a character, using performance-capture or e-motion-capture technology developed by the special-effects house Digital Domain. In watching a film like *Tron: Legacy*, we may not know the technological details that conjure the final illusions; nevertheless, most viewers were aware that this was a mediated process because of the hyperreal status of the visual effects, and because of the media hype about the technological advances that accompanied the film's release. The greatest media buzz revolved aound the process involved in creating Clu. As mentioned earlier, there were more cutting-edge precedents to this visual effect: Andy Serkis's performances in *The Lord of the Rings: The Two Towers* (2002), *Rise of the Planet of the Apes* and *King Kong* captured bodily and facial expressions that were then inserted into the fantastic bodies of Gollum, Caesar and Kong respectively; Brad Pitt's performance and expressions were used to age and de-age his body and face in *Benjamin Button*; and Jamie Bell, Andy Serkis and Daniel Craig's performances in *Tintin* were translated into an animated reality that bore minimal resemblance to their 'human' faces. The challenge that confronted *Tron: Legacy*'s effects team was one of resemblance – specifically, resemblance to Jeff Bridges. Most people who saw the film were aware of how Bridges looked almost thirty years ago, and fans of the *Tron* franchise definitely knew what he looked like when he played Kevin Flynn in the 1982 film. To create Clu (and the younger version of Flynn who appears in the film), computers had to be programmed to generate digital skin – a façade – of Bridges circa 1982. The team then had to wrap a CG mask around Bridges's face, making him look young again. Because of the issue of resemblance, Bridges's face and its digitisation lends itself to a baroque interpretation. He is both *facce* and *facciate* – face and façade – a membrane or surface through which a dialogue between the real and the virtual takes place.

Digital Domain took images of Bridges from his early films[17] and then ran everything – the 2010 Bridges and the 1980s Bridges – through sophisticated software that rebuilt his performance as Clu onto his younger face until the effect created an amalgam of an idealised and de-aged Jeff Bridges from around the early 1980s.[18] Bridges operates like a cyborg: he is part man (the actor) and part machine (the technology he connects to), and his cyborgification becomes a threshold that fluidly traverses layers of the baroque house as science-fiction narrative that is simultaneously science fictional in the meanings it produces. Clu is presented in the film as pure, digital matter brought to life by computer hardware and software. He is a virtual being whose artificial materiality asks the viewer to ponder both on the nature of humanity (in light of its reliance on and interface with the technological), and on the possibilities of machine-beings created by humans that develop human-like identities. As is typical of science fiction, the narrative is driven by the creation myth. The first layer of this myth is found in the implied presence of *Tron* embedded in the film, that recalls the players who created versions of themselves – their avatars – in the 'game' space of the Grid. In *Tron: Legacy*, the creator is more explicitly Kevin Flynn who is god-in-the-machine and outside it (the memory of the corporeal Flynn of *Tron*). Kevin Flynn is presented as living matter that happens to reside in digital form in the virtual world of the Grid. As a scientist in *Tron*, his hubris makes him turn his back on the metaphysical and spiritual unknown: like many scientists in science-fiction films, through science, everything – even creation – is within the grasp of human knowledge. In *Tron: Legacy*, however, his imprisonment in the Grid has taught him a great deal about the relationship between matter and the soul. His spiritual identity is reflected both in the austere, priest-like robes he first appears in, and in the Buddhist garb he favours for most of the film. He is creator of the Grid, he is creator of his digital double Clu, and he has nurtured an environment that has given birth to the Isoes, truly sentient beings whose last survivor is Quorra (Olivia Wilde). The mystery of the machine-as-creator that gave birth to these artificial creatures is echoed further in the enigmatic, shadowy and chaotic space known as the Outlands, which exists beyond the architectural and regimented spaces of the Grid, and which is where the Isoes fled (unsuccessfully) to escape Clu. Flynn refers to their creation as a 'miracle' that is informed by a supernatural, transcendent power beyond even his reach. In attaining that 'life', don't the Isoes, like Flynn, have access to the upper levels of the baroque house?

In his book *The Return of the Baroque in Modern Culture*, Gregg Lambert provides an overview of Heinrich Wölfflin's list of attributes that identify the baroque style. Some of these include: 'a heightened sense of transience', an emphasis on monumentality and the sublime, the 'multiplication of surfaces, contours, and folds' (which include layers of reality). While not discussing the baroque – or what he calls the digital baroque – in Deleuzian terms, Norman Klein has similarly stressed the transcendent and sublime nature of baroque spectacle.[19] Above all, experiences of the baroque

> bear an important element for reading the cause of the spectator's anxiety before the baroque facade, a feeling of anxiety that underlines an apprehension of the power of the artwork which the baroque, at this stage of its conception, places to the foreground.[20]

The emphasis on the transcendent and the sublime; on the multiple levels of reality that fold into each other obscuring where one ends and the other begins; and on the monumental and wondrous spectacle of creation are all experienced by the viewer of *Tron: Legacy*. These themes are present within the diegesis and beyond it. In addition to the awe-inspiring 3D visual effects, and the colossal spectacle that is the Grid and the avatars that occupy it, the film also opens up the possibility of a Deleuzian, philosophical reading that evaluates the nature of subjectivity through the articulation of Jeff Bridges's digital skin. In addition to performing a science-fiction story premise that relies on a form of time travel that goes back in time to claim Bridges's thirty-five-year-old face, the film's effects also pose another question: which is the real Jeff Bridges?

Chimeras of Similitude

Deliberating on the potential of digital design and effects programs in his article 'CyberBaroque and Other DigiTales', the architect and architectural theorist Marjan Colletti considers this move towards digital design as one that has baroque potentiality. He characterises the baroque as 'remarkably contemporary because it discovered and also shattered a plethora of binary conditions, boundaries and frames that provide an analogy to today's actuality-digitality feedback system'.[21] In his manifesto-like prose, he emphasises the importance of engaging both with the actuality or materiality and virtuality of computer-aided architectural design (CAD); virtual realities and cyber realities can't exist without the material software and hardware that drive them. It's in unison that they can give shape to expressive forms that encompass baroque sensibilities. Calling upon Deleuze, his CyberBaroque call-to-arms demands designers redress the independence of 'façade (expression, reception, materiality) and interior (effect, action, space), [and] the separation of below (matter, function) and above (manner, vision)'.[22] Adopting a CyberBaroque approach to design allows the creator to deny the materiality and rationality of the computer, allowing it to 'perform a sensorial task' by targeting 'purely sensual neural experiences'; digital spectacle speaks to aesthetics and performance.[23] In the world of *Tron: Legacy*, the digital architecture becomes a CyberBaroque – or what I have elsewhere called a neo-baroque – performance that is about virtuosity: a virtuosity of the medium and the advances made since its predecessor *Tron* took the first steps in creating digital spaces as part of the cinematic experience; a virtuosity that, within the diegesis, pits the virtualised human against the sentient digital creation Clu; and a virtuosity that, on the level of narrative and special effects, ponders the relationship between reality and illusion in light of how digital realities have imprinted themselves firmly onto the human world and on human identity, in the process forcing a rethinking of binaries of inside/outside, digital skin/human skin, matter/soul. While appearing to belong purely in the realm of matter and rationality, the computer gives shape to sensorially provocative and fantastic spaces. Its creations take us past the façade's exterior, and give us access to abstract journeys that makes us deliberate on the nature of life itself. Echoing Deleuze's words, the CyberBaroque connects two realms: 'one is metaphysical, dealing with souls ... the other is physical, entailing bodies', but both occupy the domain of the baroque house and ultimately transform 'the cosmos into a "mundus"'.[24] The baroque engages in a total unity of the arts that is, at its core, theatrical in nature: Jeff Bridges's acting folds into a performance captured on film, then another captured by the computer, which, in turn, gives shape to a digital avatar that is an amalgam of two Jeff Bridgeses – one that existed in the 1980s and another in the 2000s. This baroque theatre is a performance about effects technology that is capable of creating a version of science-fictional time travel: it playfully engages in a theatre that allows multiple versions of Jeff Bridges from across time appear to perform in the same space.

Sarah Garland discusses the phenomenon of 'chimeras of similitude', explaining that

> there are those resemblances that imply they have another life ... those that imply that their life is a mere resemblance, the creation of another ... and those ideas that either melancholically or triumphantly read resemblance as artifice – namely the suggestions that the world is a stage, that there is an art to behaviour and a truth to disguise.[25]

Citing Henri Focillon's analysis of baroque form in *The Life of Forms*, she agrees that such resemblances are maniacally obsessed with representation and 'similism'. What makes such 'maniacal similism' baroque is the performative and self-reflexive nature of these chimeras of similitude. The Jeff Bridges narrative parallels the metaphysical concepts that the film raises through the Kevin Flynn/Clu doppelgänger. Which version of Jeff Bridges that appears in the film is the real Bridges? Is it the actor who plays Kevin Flynn and who bears an indexical relationship to the person Jeff Bridges as he appears today? Is Clu any less a version of Jeff Bridges, given that his face is sampled from images of Bridges's 'real' face as it appeared in the 1980s? And, in capturing versions of the actor across time, do those versions maintain an essence – the spirit – of the human Jeff Bridges who shares a space in our world? The technological virtuosity behind the reconstruction of Jeff Bridges's early 1980s face, speaks not just to the capacity of computer-generated imagery to mimic the face of Jeff Bridges, but it also engages with the nature of Jeff Bridges – as star and as human being. Which, if any, of these performances is real?

Many scholars have discussed the inherent theatricality of the baroque, especially in relation to the blurring of boundaries between illusion and reality.[26] On the level of its narrative and special effects, *Tron: Legacy* presents and represents the theatricalisation of existence in philosophical terms, especially in its focus on chimeras of similitude as embodied by Sam and Kevin Flynn in the virtual world of the Grid. William Eggington, in his book *Theater of Truth*, argues that a baroque vision approaches

> the world through a veil of appearances; truth is defined as the adequation of our knowledge to the world thus veiled; hence, inquiry of any kind must be guided by the reduction of whatever difference exists between the appearances and the world as it is.[27]

He continues by stating that the baroque tests reality by creating a performance about the deceptive nature of appearances: 'the Baroque makes a theater out of truth' by drawing attention to its chimera-like nature.[28] The slippery and theatrical nature of appearance – and of existence as appearance – is at the core of *Tron: Legacy*.

Eggington argues that there are two strategies of the baroque. The first is the 'major strategy', which 'assumes the existence of a veil of appearances, and then suggests the possibility of a space opening just beyond those appearances where truth resides'.[29] On the level of the narrative, the world of *Tron: Legacy* can be interpreted as succumbing to this major baroque strategy. The digital spectacle that is the architecture of the Grid represents a false truth, which is demarcated by both the 'real' and virtual façades of Flynn's Arcade. These are the liminal spaces that represent where inside and outside, virtual and real blur. Beyond that, the digital flesh that replaces the bodies of Sam and Kevin Flynn – and which operates as reminder of their digital conversion in the Grid – also functions as a digital façade that articulates a difference between their virtual bodies and their actual bodies which had corporeal presence in the real world. Further reflecting Eggington's major strategy, the synthetic bodies of artificial beings like Clu, who reigns over the Grid and insists that this false reality is the superior reality, are exposed as false ones that must be escaped. Spectators are invited both to immerse themselves in the wondrous spectacle that is the fictional world of the Grid, but to also identify with the human protagonists who strive to exit this world and the dangers its deceptive artificiality throws their way.

Eggington also insists on a 'minor strategy' of the baroque, stating that, whereas the major strategy sets up a difference between reality and illusion, the minor strategy blurs the distinction, therefore questioning the nature of reality. In doing so, the minor baroque strategy 'remind[s] us that we are always, at any level, involved with mediation'.[30] For Eggington, it is the minor strategy that reveals a truer baroque experience in that it engages in a complex relationship with its status as representation and truth. One of the problems, however, is that Eggington comes at the issue of two baroque strategies from an elitist perspective, often reserving a more radical possibility of the baroque (minor baroque) for high-culture examples, while denying the possibilities of a self-aware baroque within the domain of 'commercialized culture'. In addition, he fails to consider the possibility that his minor and major categories can coexist within the same work, and can express themselves through avenues he hasn't considered.

Films like *Tron: Legacy* do precisely this. On the level of its science-fiction narrative, the film does, in part, succumb to the strategies of the 'major' baroque. There are clear demarcations between reality and representation. However, as discussed, the virtual society that is the Grid (through Kevin Flynn's tampering with its methods of creation) has also given birth to sentient digital beings who escaped beyond the 'official' walls and entered the Outlands, which appear to represent a 'more authentic' virtual-natural landscape that is visually depicted in ways that evoke a sublime and transcendent space. This is a landscape that has attained a soul. Escaping the world of matter ruled by Clu, and rising to the metaphysical heights of Deleuze's baroque house, its quasi-religious status is mirrored in the religious motifs that wrap themselves across the creator Kevin Flynn's digital body. Are these beings, the film asks its audience, any less 'real' or any less lacking in human-like subjectivity? And what of Quorra who further blurs the boundaries between the human/artificial, the soul/pure matter and exits into the world of the human real? Furthermore, on the level of the special effect, the 'minor' strategy's obsession with drawing attention to processes of mediation through representational media is at the forefront – as is evident in the complex layers of reality generated by Jeff Bridges's performances as Kevin Flynn and Clu. Both Kevin Flynn and Jeff Bridges literally confront versions of themselves: Flynn confronts Clu in the Grid, and a 2000s version of Bridges confronts his 1980s self on screen. Clu and young Jeff are reborn, technological beings that perform the role of sacred monsters. Science fiction succumbs to the science fictional and both are imbued with a baroque logic.

In 'Pits, Pores, Scratches: The Skin of Things', Patrizia Magli states that:

> the material/spiritual opposition, in the planning of façades, often involves [a] deeper opposition, the one between matter and form . . . . But the matter that background is made of, *like the skin of our face seen close up*, comes across as an infinitely porous texture, sometimes pierced by holes. . . . Like our skin, the surfaces of façades are relational borders, allowing separation, but also exchange between what is internal and private and what we recognise as external and public. And as such, they express the pressure both of internal and external forces . . . [that not] only exist in space but also in time . . . . Holes point to an interruption on the surface of a wall . . . . A hole is a fracture that breaks a spatial continuum. Holes, like windows and doors, signal a dialectic between interior and exterior.[31]

As Magli explains, the presence of holes in the façade initiates a dialogue. Jeff Bridges's face, with its actual marked holes that allow the computer to triangulate his features, is at once dead and alive. The thing that was his face and had become frozen in time in the 1980s is reanimated and forced to exist in the present. The dialectic that emerges is one that Kenneth Gross gives expression to in his analysis of fictions about animated statues. 'The life of the statue often turns out to be that of a ghost or a galvanized corpse. The animated statue thus becomes as much a form of ruin as of resurrection'[32] in that it arrests time and 'represents a stopping point; it represents the reification of something once living and mutable, its death as it were'.[33] The uncanny presence of a young Jeff Bridges mapped across the face of Clu is a reminder of Jeff Bridges's mortality – a fact made all the more potent when the young and old confront one another. 'Like an archive', the holes on Jeff Bridges's skin become passageways that allow the computer to 'map out and preserve the marks of his history'.[34]

Bridges's face is a performance – a theatre – about the iconic impact of the cult film *Tron*; about *Tron: Legacy*'s virtuosic updating of that history and an even grander staged event; and about the role performed by Jeff Bridges – and his face –as façade that opens up a time-travel passageway between past and present, but also about the nature of mortality and the soul in light of the virtual. In travelling a journey through the holes on this digital skin, the façade that allows access to Bridges's past and present also confronts us with a metaphysical question about reality, identity, representation and life. It is the science fictionality that opens up a passage through which to explore the baroque nature of *Tron: Legacy*. The effects technology makes Jeff Bridges's face into a theatre, one that invites questions about the relationship between the virtual and the real, the virtual as real and the real as virtual. Faced with the skin that is Bridges's face/façade, what is needed is a 'cryptographer',[35] as Deleuze says, who can decipher the puzzles that are laid before us as Bridges's face folds and unfolds onscreen.

Notes

1. Brooks Landon, *Science Fiction after 1900: From the Steam Man to the Stars* (New York and London: Routledge, 2002), pp. 6–7.
2. Istvan Csicsery-Ronay, *The Seven Beauties of Science Fiction* (Middletown, CT: Wesleyan University Press, 2008), p. 2.
3. Ibid., p. 4.
4. See Mova Contour company website for further information: http://www.mova.com/.
5. For information about the visual effects and motion and performance capture in *Tron: Legacy*, see Jody Duncan, 'Legacy System', *Cinefex* vol. 124 (January 2011), pp. 28–57; for *Avatar*, see Jody Duncan, 'The Seduction of Reality', *Cinefex* vol. 120 (January 2010), pp. 68–146.
6. Dan North, *Performing Illusions: Cinema, Special Effects and the Virtual Actor* (London and New York: Wallflower Press, 2008), p. 1.
7. Ibid.
8. Ibid., p. 81.
9. For further information about the effects in *Tron*, see ibid., pp. 129–30.
10. 'Tron: Legacy', *Computer Graphics World*, 4 January 2011, n.p., http://www.cgw.com/Press-Center/Web-Exclusives/2011/Tron-Legacy.aspx.
11. Christian Norberg Schultz, *Baroque Architecture* (Rome: Electa/Rizzoli, 1991), p. 12.
12. Gilles Deleuze, *The Fold: Leibniz and the Baroque* (Minneapolis and London: University of Minnesota Press, 1993), p. 3.
13. Patrizia Magli, 'Pits, Pores, Scratches: The Skin of Things', *Barcelona Metropolis: City, Information, Thoughts*, April–June 2011, n.p., http://www.barcelonametropolis.cat/en/page.asp?id=23&ui=537.
14. For more on the spiritual-like nature of special effects, see Angela Ndalianis, *Neo-Baroque Aesthetics and Contemporary Entertainment* (Cambridge, MA: MIT Press, 2004), ch. 5.
15. See ibid., ch. 4.
16. Dan North makes a similar point in *Performing Illusions*.
17. 'Tron: Legacy'.
18. See Duncan, 'Legacy System', pp. 28–57; and Mike Seymour, 'Tron: Legacy, Face Off', *FX Guide*, December 2010, http://www.fxguide.com/featured/tron_legacy_face_off/.
19. Norman M. Klein, *The Vatican to Vegas: The History of Special Effects* (New York: New Press, 2004).
20. Gregg Lambert, *The Return of the Baroque in Modern Culture* (New York and London: Continuum, 2004), p. 18.

21. Marjan Colletti, 'CyberBaroque and Other DigiTales', *Nordic Talking: 4 1/2 Years in Studio with Kjetil Thorsen* (Vienna and New York: Springer, 2009), n.p., online version: <http://marjan-colletti.blogspot.com.au/2009/10/cyberbaroque-and-other-digitales-marjan.html.
22. Ibid.
23. Ibid.
24. Deleuze, *The Fold*, p. 29.
25. Sarah Garland, 'Second Sight: Reading Twentieth-century Self-reflexivity through the Baroque', *EnterText* vol. 7 no. 3 (Winter 2007), http://arts.brunel.ac.uk/gate/entertext/7_3/ET73GarlandED.doc.
26. See, for example, Klein, *The Vatican to Vegas*; Deleuze, *The Fold*; Norberg Schultz, *Baroque Architecture*; Lambert, *The Return of the Baroque in Modern Culture*; Ndalianis, *Neo-Baroque Aesthetics*; William Eggington, *Theater of Truth: The Ideology of (Neo)baroque Aesthetics* (Stanford, CT: Stanford University Press, 2009).
27. Eggington, *Theater of Truth*, p. 2.
28. Ibid.
29. Ibid., p. 3.
30. Ibid., p. 6.
31. Magli, 'Pits, Pores, Scratches'.
32 Kenneth Gross, *The Dream of the Moving Statue* (Ithaca, NY and London: Cornell University Press, 1992), p. 10.
33. Ibid., p. 16.
34. Magli, 'Pits, Pores, Scratches'.
35. Deleuze, *The Fold*, p. 3.

GUILLERMO DEL TORO'S PRACTICAL AND DIGITAL NATURE

MICHAEL S. DUFFY

One can easily overlook film-makers like Mexican-born Guillermo del Toro, who emerged with 1993's quiet, unusual vampire feature *Cronos* (budget: roughly $2 million) and in 2013 embraced grand spectacle with *Pacific Rim* (approximate cost: $190 million),[1] which posits an international – rather than American-led – solution to a globally threatening menace of monsters from another dimension. While del Toro often claims to have developed his career independently of business concerns, he is best defined as a gifted director who nonetheless 'plays the Hollywood game' when it suits him, forging a successful career by splitting time equally between studio work 'for hire' and lower-budget 'personal' projects.[2] However, the real intrigue in del Toro's career comes not just from how he's been able to navigate an ever more complex investment structure that governs both studio and independent film-making, but in how he has been able to maintain and manage a strong, consistent artistic personality and aesthetic across the increasingly multiple venues and platforms of contemporary entertainment media.

Skirting the borders between 'serious' cinema (*The Devil's Backbone*, *Pan's Labyrinth*) and more mechanised spectacles (*Blade II*, *Hellboy*), del Toro's career reflects the aesthetic trajectory of his work as it moves toward global blockbuster aesthetics with *Pacific Rim*. Del Toro embraces the genre of 'the fantastic' (periodically melding it with historical narratives) because it allows him to utilise images that have no 'real-world' referent, yet he consistently endeavours to make his images 'mean' as powerfully as any of his film's human characters seemingly do.[3] In his 'display' of fantastic moving images, del Toro attempts to avoid the 'hallucinatory excess'[4] of many digitally rendered special-effects sequences – though one could argue that certain sequences in *Pacific Rim* veer into this realm. Del Toro is passionate about 'meaningful' images, whether moving or static, and how the astute application of such images can entice viewers to reach for more. 'I think there is power to visual rhyming', he's said in an aesthetic self-assessment, and in del Toro's films, the 'spectacular' is arguably *not* fetishised. Del Toro claims to be interested in more than just special effects 'for spectacle's sake', and in interviews, he discusses his and others' artistic work in sincere and humorous terms, often referring to visual 'quotes' of the poetics of film-makers he admires. Del Toro also dismisses the notion that audiences of 'popular' cinema can't distinguish between special/visual effects that 'work' and ones that merely fill space as a genre requirement.[5] He frequently mentions that he strives to make sure that every image he directs has an impact on the viewer, however subtle: 'Very often, people try to make [visual effects] perfect and take all the edges off. What I worry about is not how perfect they are, but how expressive they are. I worry about the visual effect.'[6]

Guillermo del Toro seems acutely aware of the potential that digital applications and spaces have to overwhelm film-making's visual texture. More interestingly, he excels at using 'effects' to

Liz displays her power in *Hellboy* (2004)

display moments of characterised *uncertainty*, such as Liz Sherman's (Selma Blair) first scene in *Hellboy* (2004), which serves to reveal both the first indication of her extraordinary fire-powered ability and how she is learning to control it; the scene triples its meaning by using Liz's 'gift' to convey an unbalanced psychology and an existing love for her horn-headed paramour, Hellboy (who is brought to life through makeup, prosthetics and actor Ron Perlman – his unique visage remains perhaps the film's greatest visual 'effect').[7] Later in the film, Hellboy counters Liz's psychological and physical uncertainty with his own; in a private conversation, he leans into her and gently waves his hand up and down his deep red, horned face, quietly emoting 'I wish I could do something about … this.' For del Toro, the best visual effects 'display' the raw realities of our emotional frailties.[8] When del Toro conveys these moments of characterised, cinematic change and uncertainty, he is *making fantasy a reality* for the audience, and in his own way, giving special effects meaning beyond just 'something to look at'. As Hellboy and Liz embrace in the film's final moments, Liz's blue flame (a digital enhancement) merges with Hellboy's practical red prosthetics on screen in a magical moment of cinematic bliss (the logic being that Hellboy doesn't burn, because he's a demon).

In illuminating some of the techniques del Toro has applied and interpreted throughout his career, I am of course dissecting the very things that might be more magical if they remained a mystery; as more than a few visual-effects practitioners have said, the best visual effects are 'the ones you don't notice', or rather the ones that *don't* cause the film's characters to pause with you and gaze at what is going on in front of them. It is not that simple, of course; most attempts at creating special effects are indeed 'complex assemblages', noted Michele Pierson, and 'the finished artefact has often passed through a number of different stages of assembly'.[9] It seems only proper to explore del Toro's film-making career as one whose individual obsessions and proclivities encourage this exploration of 'complex assemblages' not only in technique, but in theme and aesthetic value.

When observing del Toro's career, we see that his catalogue of works is in fact steeped in historical periods or contexts; even those set in modern or futuristic times have significant ties to either real, fantastic or 'alternative' histories – thus primarily reflecting or reinterpreting elements of the past, rather than 'predicting' possible futures. In his first feature, *Cronos*, an ageing antique shopowner is transfixed by and becomes addicted to a vampiric bio-organic device originally created by an alchemist in the fifteenth century to give its owner eternal life. In *Mimic* (1997), scientists in New York genetically formulate a hybrid insect to wipe out an infected cockroach population that is poisoning local children, and five years later, wonder where their 'cure' went wrong, as the species mutate aggressively into human size in the subways beneath the city. In *The Devil's Backbone* (2001), the ghost of a dead child haunts a small school/orphanage that is more concerned about covering up its past than embracing the future. In *Blade II* (2002), the members of an ages-old vampire race that Blade (Wesley Snipes) himself has pledged to wipe out are themselves threatened by a new genetic strain of their species created by one of their own. In *Hellboy*, a conflicted demon is brought into this world with an instinct to help, but a destiny to destroy, and is pursued by an ancient force of evil that resurfaces in the present. In *Pan's Labyrinth* (2006), haunted by personal horrors following the Spanish Civil War, an eleven-year-old girl becomes torn between her own stark reality and the riddles that she is compelled to answer in an equally threatening fantasy world. *Hellboy II: The Golden Army* (2008) showcases a revolt by nature itself, its ancient leaders and their mecha-organic machines, as the title character further questions his own destiny. For a major director working within an increasingly technology-oriented franchise film-making of the 2000s, there is a distinct – and I would argue, deliberate – lack of contemporary (or 'advanced') technological conceits and themes that sets del Toro's films apart from many major studio releases. Further, the mechanised nature of many clockwork-like motifs and images throughout his films most often represent antagonistic elements of history, society and culture, while the positive forces in his films do everything they can to overcome their obstacles in a more fluid manner that refuses to be defined by one particular approach. There is, therefore, a distinct metaphorical push and pull between practical and digital effects and applications in all of the director's films, and I will argue that the interplay between different generations of effects approach and technique has manifested itself visually and aesthetically throughout his body of work.

Mark Kermode notes the overarching theme of the 'triumph of sympathy and melancholia over terror' in del Toro's films, and how 'the ghosts of history, the freedom of fantasy, the imperative of choice, [and] the relationship between the "real" and the "imagined"'[10] all manifest themselves in del Toro's work. Born and raised in Mexico, del Toro had an early interest in makeup and special effects, and learned techniques from Dick Smith, makeup supervisor for many of the most notable American films of the 1970s, including *The Exorcist* (1973), *The Godfather* (1972), *Taxi Driver* (1976) and *Marathon Man* (1976). Del Toro perfected his own approaches for many years before forming his own production company, Necropia, in the early 1980s, making short films and working on a well-known Mexican television show before finally gaining the opportunity to helm his first feature-length film, *Cronos*. In interviews, del Toro has made some of his central iconic interests very clear: 'I have a sort of a fetish for insects, clockwork, monsters, dark places, and unborn things.' In fact, Del Toro's fascination with monsters is 'almost anthropological', according to the man himself – 'I study them, I dissect them in many of my movies: I want to know how they work, what the inside of them looks like, [and] what their sociology is.'[11]

In *Cronos*, del Toro approaches vampirism as a 'homeopathic, alchemical idea',[12] opening his film with a short prologue detailing the creation of the gold-plated Cronos device by an alchemist in 1536. The opening shot of the film pans over a desk filled with oversize bug fossils, surgical gears and mechanical devices, and del Toro notes that alchemy 'wasn't just a process where some inventors were trying to obtain gold', it was 'searching for the ultimate in bio-matter – to take bio-matter, be it lead or flesh, and turn it into the ultimate expression of itself, in terms of the metals, and in terms of the flesh', thus equating to 'eternal life/eternal flesh'.[13] From the outset, del Toro's hybridised sensibilities between the organic and the mechanical are made evident, both in his first feature and in his discussion about it. The 'cronos device' itself, roughly resembling a gold beetle, is discovered in an angelic statue by an elderly antique shopowner in modern-day Mexico, who upon first use, becomes transfixed and addicted to

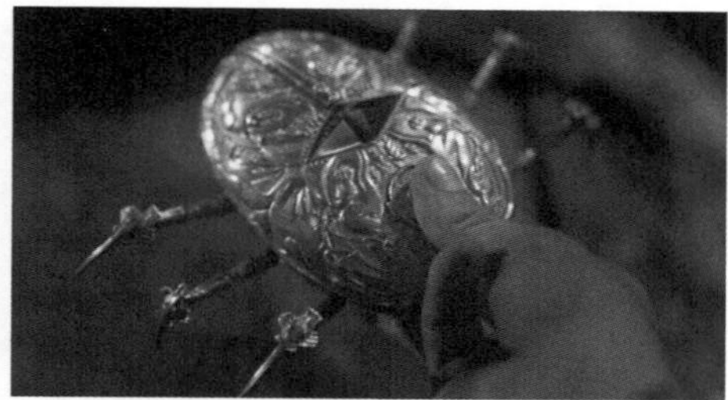

Cronos (1992): the 'Cronos' device and innards

the device's particular flesh-piercing qualities, and its ability to grant eternal life, which in turn creates a vampiric thirst for blood. For del Toro, the film was truly a 'hand-crafted' family affair – thirteen practical 'cronos' devices were mechanised by del Toro's father-in-law for external shots throughout the film. The interior of the device is only glimpsed for a few brief moments, which reveal that it is operated by an insect and a set of clockwork-like gears that transfuse the blood of their host. Conceived and shot as an outsized (table-length) practical bug and device, del Toro purchased old gears from a nineteenth-century textile machine and painted them gold … and the insect was filled with real cow innards.[14]

As I noted earlier, del Toro admires 'the grotesque' as a film-maker primarily because 'the fantastic is the generic license to indulge in those [unbelievable, unreal] things without shame'.[15] *Cronos* displays these tendencies not only in its effects use and implementation, but also in the characterisation of its protagonist. At one point, a vampirised Jesus Gris (Federico Luppi; the name Jesus, of course, conjures its own allusions to flesh being pierced by metal) begins to rip off his outer layer of skin, revealing a white, pasty layer underneath, the first stage in what could be called del Toro's chronology of organic and synthetic transformation, change and metamorphosis through complex character-driven special/visual effects. Another long-running theme in del Toro's work is 'the power of choice', though it is usually tied to tragedy. Characters in del Toro's films will often die of their own will, their self-sacrifice an attempt to convey del Toro's assertion that 'choice is the essence of the human soul'.[16] This kind of character change and metamorphosis is often inherently tied to what 'happens' through special/visual effects.

Mimic also opens with a prologue, this time set in contemporary Manhattan and detailing the development and release by an entomologist of a 'Judas breed' of genetically modified cockroaches into the subways beneath the city; they are combating an infection that is paralysing and killing local children. Del Toro here 'mimics' his own 'cronos device' effects, and expands them: as the scientist sets down the bio-container and prepares to release the insects, a brief extreme close-up of the interior of the mini-pods (and the insect within each) is followed by close-ups of the pods being opened. This scene serves as the 'next step in evolution' – one of the taglines in the film's preview trailer[17] – in del Toro's effects approach and development. Thematically, we've seen this story before, of course; developed as an antidote to the disease, this attempt to meddle with DNA has dire consequences for all involved. Five years later, giant human-sized – and human-mimicking – insects are discovered in the subway tunnels under the city. *Mimic* illustrates how nature can take back its own destiny when it is infringed upon by another species – a theme del Toro frequently visualises in future films.

Mimic also introduces a play–counterplay between special-effects approaches – before fully introducing digitally rendered giant insects in the film, del Toro focuses on the discovery of a gruesomely detailed, human-sized creature cadaver, which the main characters promptly proceed to dissect with great interest. Meanwhile, in another part of the city, a humble immigrant shoemaker gradually gets drawn into the film's climactic underground narrative, as he discovers that his autistic grandson has followed the giant bugs underground – the boy's spoon-playing communicates with the mutated breed because it resembles their own 'voice', and his wire-constructed miniature figurines represent a clue for his grandfather. The film features the first appearance of del Toro's patented 'fetus-in-a-jar', an iconographic trope that has cropped up in nearly every one of his movies since. Just as our protagonist, who created the genetic breed, begins to piece together the true nature of the threat, she encounters one of the most advanced 'breed' in a subway terminal, and it snatches her in spectacular flying fashion. Though the rest of the film presents digitally rendered insects chasing down characters in more familiar Hollywood-horror style (and it must be noted that the director was engaged in creative struggles with Miramax throughout the production), del Toro concocts an intense sequence which again turns the focus back on the physical anatomy of the creatures. The scientists, and a cop who has accompanied them underground, are trapped in an old subway car; the cop's leg is bleeding after a 'hybrid' has attacked him, and digitally rendered bugs, attracted to the human blood, are attacking the car from all sides. The characters must inoculate themselves against the threat by completely covering their clothes/bodies with the organic slime from a dead bug's intestines, so that their scent will match the bugs. Perhaps we could read into this sequence del Toro's positioning of himself as a director who is staking his claim in the industrial battle between physical- and digital-effects technologies.

Del Toro's followup, *The Devil's Backbone*, illustrates the deeply personal impact that war can have on children. An unexploded bomb sits in the courtyard of Santa Lucia School, in Spain, 1939, during the final year of the Spanish Civil War. The building's makeshift function – sheltering war orphans – and the bomb's presence, are an active reminder that the possibilities of death lurk around every corner. *The Devil's Backbone* is a story of greed, corruption and loss of innocence, but the film, like all del Toro's works, contains an otherworldly component, the ghost of a boy named Santi (Junio Valverde), who haunts the school, seeking retribution for his own murder. Santi is, in del Toro's words, 'a ghost that is romantic [and] evokes the past'.[18] The visual portrayal of the undead Santi is distinctly different to many Hollywood productions featuring 'ghosts'. Del Toro notes:

> The normal procedure for the ghost would be to hang the poor kid on wires, shoot him against green screen, probably put an aura of glow around him, make him transparent all the time, and make the whole presence of the ghost digital. The ghost then becomes an abstraction … something that doesn't coexist with the character in the same frame. I wanted to avoid that, so I approached the ghost as a kid in makeup, physically there in the frame, then enhanced later by digital effects. … We have 3-D animated particles around his forehead for the blood and diffusion … . So ultimately when we composite these elements together, the presence of the ghost becomes both physical and beautifully ethereal.[19]

The Devil's Backbone (2001): Santi the ghost

Del Toro worked with DDT,[20] a prosthetics/makeup collective whose members exchanged concepts with the director until they agreed on 'a frequency of cracks' for Santi's skull and the precise colour and intensity of his 'tears of oxide'.[21] Santi's character traits are also proof of how budgetary limitations can inspire creativity in characterisation: because there wasn't enough money to pay for a completely visible skeleton in Santi's ghostly figure, del Toro arrived at the conceit that Santi's skeleton would only be visible when the ghost walked under moonlight. In one pivotal scene, Santi is reciting to Carlos the name of the man who murdered him, so that his living counterpart will be able to lead the guilty man to Santi's final resting place. As Santi touches Carlos's face, the spirit disappears into the ether (this aesthetic will be revisited in del Toro's next film, *Blade II*). Though Santi seems to gain closure in his quest by the end of the film, the final shot of his character reveals that his spirit has not been redeemed, transformed or otherwise beautifully restored, as ghosts so often are in other films; Santi's body remains in the water underneath his apparition, and his soul seems damned for eternity due to the cruel nature of fate and broken humanity. The film's technical credits also reflect the filmmaker's hybrid sensibilities – there are separate credit titles for 'special mechanical effects', 'special make-up effects' and 'special digital effects'.

Blade II is perhaps del Toro's most outrageous and uproarious cinematic statement, simultaneously a mainstream franchise sequel and a further exploration and expansion of del Toro's propensities for bloody flesh, anatomical indulgence and increasingly complex digital character enhancements that seamlessly blend with practical and prosthetic applications. This adaptation of the black vampire hunter originally created for Marvel Comics in the 1970s lightens up its central hero while conversely conceiving more aggressive and psychologically unstable villains. Blade's mission in life is simply to wipe out all vampires, but – as in all great sequels – the tables are turned when they come to him for help after the emergence of the Reaper strain, a violent genetic mutation of their species that threatens to wipe out not only the original vampire race, but all of humanity. Del Toro's fascination with creature anatomy is explored here in graphic detail, as Blade and the vampires perform an autopsy on a dead Reaper. Del Toro has said of the film: 'I said to (producer Peter) Frankfurt and [writer David] Goyer that if I had my way, the movie would be called *Blade II: The Anatomy Lesson*. I really wanted to show you how things work from the inside.'[22] As the vampires drop a sample of blood into the dead Reaper's stomach, the organs convulse one last time in hypertension – even though the creature is dead, its anatomy defies its nature in gasping one last time for an addictive fix. During the autopsy, Blade and his reluctant vampire allies discover a way of defeating the Reapers through a flaw in their anatomy.

At the film's conclusion, Blade battles Nomak (Luke Goss), the original – and now last – of the Reapers, and as Blade delivers the fatal blow telegraphed in the autopsy scene, del Toro takes the camera inside Nomak's anatomy for a close-up, showing in anatomical detail just how precisely Blade's sword pierces the villain's undead heart. As Nomak resigns to his fate ('the power of choice') and disintegrates in flames, del Toro references Hammer Studios' classic technique of

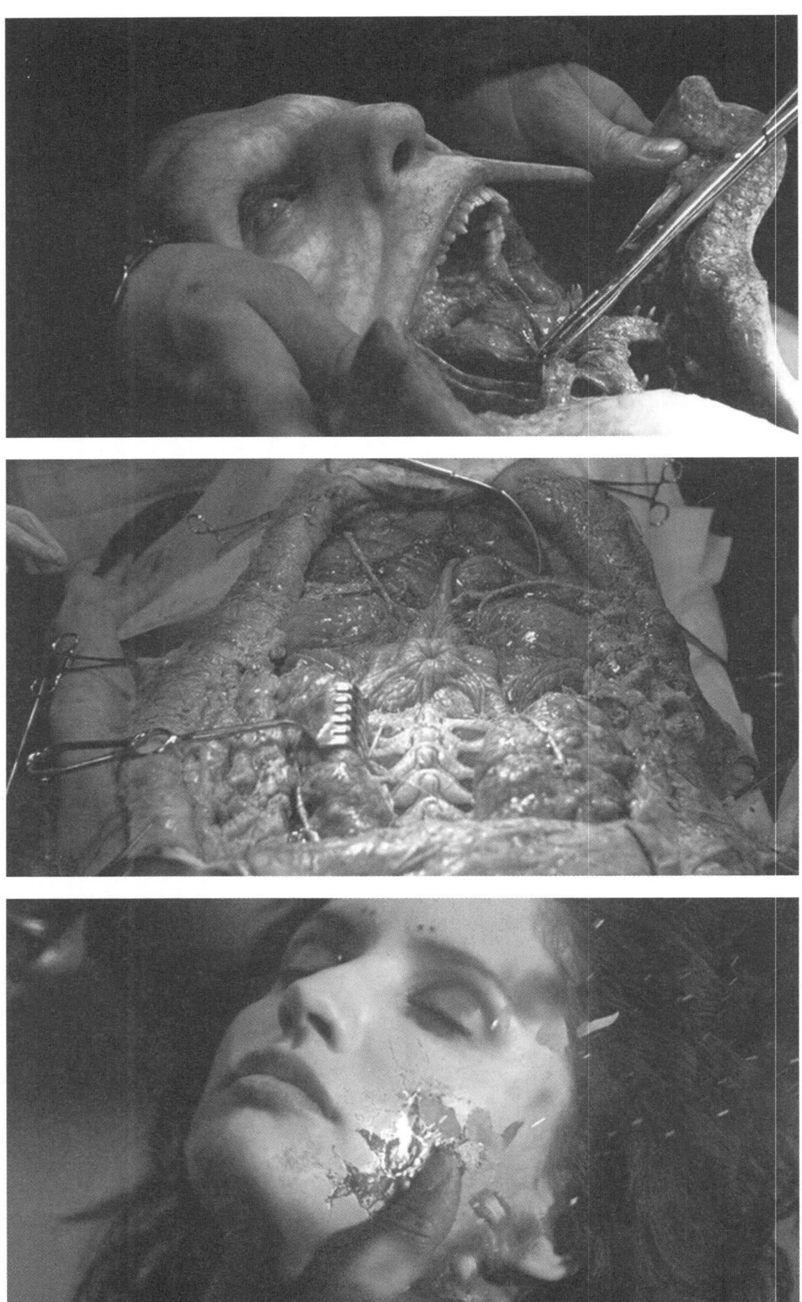

Blade II (2002): the Reaper cadaver; Reaper autopsy; Nyssa ashes away

destroying Dracula, as flames and ash fall to the ground.[23] This is followed by the death of female vampire Nyssa (Leonor Varela), whom Blade has gotten close to throughout the film. Blade honours her request to see the sunlight for the first and last time in her life, and as he holds her in his arms, her body disintegrates into ash in the face of the rising sun. For me, this moment gives a positive filmic answer to Scott McCloud's question for the comics medium in his book *Understanding Comics: The Invisible Act*: 'Can emotions be made visible?'[24]

Pan's Labyrinth has a myriad of literal and potential meanings that can be derived from its complex weaving of history, fantasy and beautifully detailed visual texture. Paul Julian Smith wrote in *Film Quarterly* that *Pan's* displays 'an extraordinary fluidity of movement between fantasy and reality', but also – and perhaps more importantly for del Toro's reputation – the film 'reinforces, rather than reduces the horrors of history'.[25] Del Toro increasingly calculates his methodology of visual-effects assemblages like clockwork as well. There are digital fairies and stickbugs veering back and forth between Ofelia's (Ivana Baquero) painful reality and equally disturbing fantasy-state, and Vidal's (Sergi López) pocketwatch and the mill wheel in the background of his makeshift office both of course reflect not only del Toro's obsessions, but also the 'fantasy of mechanical Fascism'.[26] What's rather extraordinary about *Pan's* is that it does this not by abandoning del Toro's signature visual aesthetic and interests, but rather by enhancing them in more threadlike ways throughout the narrative. While Kristine Kotecki has argued that *Pan's* situates itself within a dynamic that plays with 'hypertextual' and 'metafictional' themes of narrative, the constructed nature of special-effects content, and viewers' parallel Oz-like return to a reality we know and understand,[27] I would argue that the conclusion to *Pan's Labyrinth* is neither one of submission to a 'sane' reality nor the full embrace of a 'fantasy' existence – it is a hybrid possibility of both. Is not every film – and viewing – a dream that we eventually wake up from (however many times we go back to it)?

Hellboy II: The Golden Army contains what are perhaps del Toro's most blatant clockwork thematics, with its entire opening credit sequence focused on a construction and transformation of clockwork-like gears to finally assemble the title logo, not only building the visual aesthetics of the Golden Army, the film's ancient mecha-organic soldiers, but also hinting at the film's finale, which features characters fighting on top of giant moving clockwork-like gears.[28] Simultaneously developing and holding back Hellboy's destiny as the destroyer of worlds, the film's main theme involves the rebellion of the now underground, naturalistic world against our contemporary industrialised society. The Golden Army, ancient beings constructed of steampunk-style living mecha-organic gears and joints, transform and shift in ways that are as intimately detailed, if not more so, as the movements of the robots in the live-action *Transformers* films (2007–). *Hellboy II* delivers particularly stylistic approaches to special effects that manifest themselves in narrative, aesthetic and theoretical context. Del Toro explains, 'In film, in my opinion, the text is in the texture',[29] and his wish to always give equal consideration – and thematic weight – to both practical and digital approaches to special effects endows his storytelling with a unique style and sensibility that appeals to global audiences while equally reflecting his artistic and industrial ambitions.

Pacific Rim is perhaps the clearest metaphor yet for del Toro's career, and for Hollywood's reliance on digital spectacle in its bid for international audiences. The shifting and transforming 'bodies' and creatures he had previously dealt with are now supersize – malfunctioning giant mechanical machines losing ground in the battle for survival against increasingly strong and

Hellboy II: The Golden Army (2008): clockwork finale

brutal competition. Ron Perlman pushing his way out of the dead kaiju's stomach in a post-credits bonus scene, asking where his shoe is, is an indicator that del Toro has retained his individualist spirit, but much of *Pacific Rim* feels different to what the film-maker has previously pursued. In interviews, del Toro gushed about what drew him to the project, proclaiming his love for the Japanese genre of storytelling that the film is largely based on, and its production pipeline of 'man-in-suit' monster-making and miniature metropolis destruction:

> There was an implicit code in watching these movies, even as a kid, where I knew they were miniature – they were miniature cities, miniature planes, miniature tanks. So there was no real life impact to me. They became spectacles, almost ballets, of elemental creatures – elementals of nature, going through this sort of destructive opera.[30]

An evolution of del Toro's fascination with the visual aesthetic of clockwork can be seen in the Gipsy Danger jaeger's central nuclear-powered spindle, as it whirs into action and powers up a machine both gear- and mind-controlled by humans. The organic also meets the industrial on a mass scale in the film, with overhead images of giant kaiju skeletons lying still in streets and alleyways between half-destroyed city skyscrapers.

Though Hollywood's attempt to further explore Japanese and international cultures in *Pacific Rim* (as well as in *The Wolverine* and *47 Ronin* that year) was an admirable and much welcomed task, the film displays a distinct problem – nuclear power and 'the bomb' continue to be significant narrative cruxes as both an 'analogue solution' and a cross-cultural legacy that both Eastern and Western cultures seemingly can't escape. In *Pacific Rim*, Sydney, Australia gets trounced; Australian youth is sacrificed; central Hong Kong is devastated; Russian and Chinese jaegers (enormous fighting machines with two human pilots) fall by the wayside; but Japanese–American cooperation is the 'working' relationship. However, it's not without consequences, both literal and allegorical. *Pacific Rim*'s finale makes del Toro's penchant for combining the known and the

Pacific Rim (2013): kaiju skeletons merge with city skyscrapers

unknown alchemical substances among us into a kind of 'world building' of complex and contradictory effects aesthetics. In the film's finale, it is revealed that the dimensional portal at the bottom of the sea that our heroes must close to save the Earth from giant monsters can only be shut by our greatest manmade weapon of destruction – the nuclear bomb.

In a final moment of desperation, members of Earth's resistance think all is lost, as their advanced, digitally powered machines are all failing due to the kaiju's adaptability to our technology. But the film's hero, Beckett (Charlie Hunnam), emerges with a solution – he tells his superior Stacker Pentecost (Idris Elba): 'The Gipsy Danger isn't digital … it's analogue – nuclear!' What could be del Toro's meta-in-joke on cinematic-effects technologies also serves as both a convenient problem solver (and plot saver) but also a somewhat disturbing renege on the director's signature pacifism – nuclear weapons and technology once again become Earth's ultimate saviour. The problem is that this narrative twist inverts the meaning of Japan's post-war Godzilla and kaiju-themed films – they were allegories about the *dangers* of the atomic bomb and its continuing use, not storylines that advocated continuing nuclear solutions to the world's problems.[31] 'The bomb' of course carries its own set of histories and associations, not only with mankind's destructive capacity, but arguably its epochal influence on post-war Japanese history and culture, very much informing themes and visual iconography, narrative and character in manga, anime and film from the 1950s forward.

As with most Hollywood cinema that resorts to an 'atomic solution' to Earth's problems, radiation fallout from the final act is not addressed. However, *Pacific Rim*'s narrative doesn't shy away from the dangers of man playing with big nuclear toys and early experiments that are doomed to failure, as it's revealed that Pentecost, one of the original jaeger pilots, is sick with some kind of cancer (it's not explained which) due to overexposure to a less-perfected fighter construction. This character strand lends an eerie subtext to an otherwise fairly healthy blockbuster conceit; but in traditional gung-ho American fashion, the film allows Pentecost to enact del Toro's 'power of choice' and sacrifice himself by 'stepping into the suit' one last time, carrying a nuclear warhead into the sea and detonating it to distract surrounding kaijus from the crew's main mission – dropping another nuke into their dimensional gateway.[32]

Pacific Rim still contains much meat in terms of del Toro's aesthetic, and in many ways represents the apex of his explorations, as it delves into the boundaries between flesh and steel, liquid and turbine, cinema ... and its possible future. Despite a glossy overall look merely based on its supersize budget, *Pacific Rim* also attempts to 'dirty up' its visual architecture and effects by, as del Toro puts it, 'celebrating imperfection through really perfect images'.[33] An aesthetic conundrum to be sure, but interesting nonetheless. 'I really have a problem with the idea of perfection', he's said, 'I think it's sort of a Fascist ideal, an impossible ideal.' No wonder, then, that many of del Toro's antagonists look, feel, display (and indeed are of) fascist ideals.

Pacific Rim's 'corroded textures,' dented machines, and peeling paint do lend its world a kind of weariness that enhances its verisimilitude, and Rinko Kikuchi's portrayal of Mako Mori, whose childhood trauma of course mirrors Japan's own post-war history, gives historical and aesthetic weight to the film's overall vision. Ultimately, however, as del Toro himself presciently said in 2010, 'The worst thing that can happen to a filmmaker is to be given everything he needs; it destroys the basic hunger; it makes you lose perspective';[34] simultaneously, his long-time director of photography, Guillermo Navarro, argues that 'Everything works like clockwork in his mind.'[35] Perhaps *Pacific Rim* was an equally precise career calculation for del Toro; the question will be how he manages his creative tools from this point forward. He's definitely still very interested, and invested in, innovating the craft and business of special effects in the film industry; in 2010, he formed Mirada, a creative collective, to pursue new avenues in visual-effects production, aesthetics and applications ('Purveyors of handmade storytelling since 2010', their motto reads).[36] As Paul Goldberger has asserted, 'art does not save the world – but it can make the world worth saving'.[37] For their thought-provoking uses of special effects that inspired me to write this chapter, I most definitely consider del Toro's films – and their visually dense effects and worlds – a part of this world worth saving.

David Summers has argued that art has historically provided – and in many cases, created – a focal point for political, cultural and religious belief and connectivity, and therefore, a meaningful existence, giving us the ability to acknowledge and transform our world. In his book *Real Spaces: World Art History and the Rise of Western Modernism*, Summers makes the case that human knowledge and meaning are inherently tied to our three-dimensional spaces and spatial architectures, objects and creations therein.[38] The alignment of bodies and spaces in three-dimensional contexts thus formed our understandable existence, and Summers's contention is that the increasing 'virtuality' of all forms of existence in Western culture has a huge caveat attached in the form of a loss of the originally identifiable concepts of space.[39] This, of course, mirrors the debate in film technology and theory regarding the mechanical creation or reproduction of increasingly digital images. Perhaps the attempts by industry veterans like James Cameron to promote contemporary 3D and 'immersive' technologies are more than just justifiably revenue-inducing enterprises? Could these notions represent an underlying subconscious need to 'make sense' of our increasingly 'open' digital/spatial existence by fashioning it around ourselves in an understandable framework? Or put more simply, is it about diving into new, unknowable spaces, or rather defining a new *controllable* space for ourselves that we can comprehend in identifiable spatial and technological terms?[40] What is the 'future of entertainment'? Will it take us into a new set of spaces, or rather virtual replications (and therefore, as Summers argues, representations) of old ones? Guillermo del Toro's films remind us that in fully considering any kind of future for humanity, we must first make peace with our pasts, and in doing so, we must acknowledge and reconcile our competing methods of industry, technology, thought and creativity so that we may better understand our true natures.

Notes

1. This number doesn't include promotional/marketing costs paid by Warner Bros. (which only funded 25 per cent of *Pacific Rim*'s budget; Legendary Pictures paid the rest), and studios generally don't reveal what they spend on marketing campaigns, but for 'tentpole' productions such as this, it is likely to be in the tens of millions. See *Box Office Mojo*, http://www.boxofficemojo.com/movies/?id=pacificrim.htm. Legendary Pictures' co-production deal with Warner Bros., in place since 2005, ended in 2013; the company formed a new deal with Universal Pictures. Del Toro and Legendary are pursuing a *Pacific Rim* sequel for release in 2017. See Marc Graser, 'Legendary Pictures, Warner Bros. Likely to Split', *Variety*, 14 May 2013, http://variety.com/2013/biz/news/legendary-warner-bros-likely-to-split-exclusive-1200472600/.
2. While nearly all of del Toro's films have been reasonable performers at cinemas, his biggest financial and critical success was the historical fantasy tale *Pan's Labyrinth*, which grossed four times its budget at the box office.
3. Del Toro:

> What appeals to me is that this genre requires the ultimate amount of craftsmanship. To portray reality requires enormous skills, but to portray unreality or imaginary things that never existed requires a different set of skills that I find I'm more attuned with.

In Kimberly Chun, 'What Is a Ghost?: An Interview with Guillermo del Toro,' *Cineaste*, Spring 2002, pp. 28–32.

4. Scott Bukatman, *Matters of Gravity: Special Effects and Supermen in the 20th Century* (Durham, NC: Duke University Press, 2003).
5. 'I think the eye is quicker than the mind.' From Del Toro, interviewed by Henry Sheehan, 'What Makes del Toro Tick?', Directors Guild of America, Spring 2007, http://www.dga.org/Craft/DGAQ/All-Articles/0701-Spring-2007/Director-Profile-Guillermo-del-Toro.aspx. Del Toro has said elsewhere:

> We say that an audience doesn't care whether it's real or CGI, but they do. The average eye of the regular Joe is trained by thousands of hours of TV and visual effects; there's media hitting you all the time. So your eyes know. Sometimes my daughters, who are pretty savvy at the ages of 7 and 12, look at my movies and say, 'That monster is computer-generated.' And I say, 'Nope, it's real.' So it's nice that they are confounded.

In Brent Simon, 'Guillermo del Toro on "*Hellboy II*" and Impressing a Girl on a First Date', *New York Magazine*, 8 July 2008, http://www.vulture.com/2008/07/guillermo_del_toro_on_why_hellboy_ii.html.

6. Bill Gibron, 'DVD Verdict Interviews Guillermo Del Toro, Director of *Blade II*', *DVD Verdict*, 29 July 2002, http://www.dvdverdict.com/interviews/deltoro.php.
7. Ron Perlman came to the role with an already beastly history; he had a cult following from the shortlived American television series *Beauty and the Beast*, which ran on the CBS network from 1987 to 1990. Universal Studios, which produced *Hellboy* and *Hellboy II: The Golden Army*, was apparently initially keen on Vin Diesel to star.
8. Del Toro had long believed in embedding practical effects into his pictures – years before, he had thought that the only way he could bring Hellboy to life was as an eight-foot-tall animatronic creature but, after consulting James Cameron for advice, became convinced that it should definitely be an actor.
9. Michele Pierson, *Special Effects: Still in Search of Wonder* (New York and Chichester: Columbia University Press, 2002), p. 59.
10. Mark Kermode, 'The Past Is Never Dead', *The Devil's Backbone*, Criterion Blu-ray, 2013.
11. Del Toro, interviewed by Leonard Lopate for his 2009 novel cowritten with Chuck Hogan, *The Strain*, WNYC radio, 5 June 2009.
12. Guillermo del Toro audio commentary, *Cronos* DVD, Lionsgate Home Entertainment, 2003.
13. Del Toro, *Cronos* audio commentary, 2003.
14. 'I love anything clockwork', says del Toro.

    > I have an automaton that plays the cello and another that has a little funnel and whistles a tune. I like to open them up and check the mechanisms. And I have, in my day, taken a couple of watches apart.

    In Sheehan, 'What Makes del Toro Tick?' The main animated menu of Criterion's 2010 Blu-ray/DVD release of *Cronos* features the miniature-shot inner clockwork of the Cronos device as displayed in brief but memorable shots in the film.
15. Guillermo del Toro interview, *Cronos* Blu-ray/DVD, Criterion, 2010.
16. Del Toro interview, *Cronos* Blu-ray/DVD.
17. This phrase/theme would be used again in promotion for Twentieth Century-Fox's successful *X-Men* film series, which began in 2000.
18. Del Toro interview, 'Summoning Spirits' (featurette), *The Devil's Backbone*, Criterion Blu-ray, 2013.
19. Adam Blair, 'Interview: Guillermo del Toro', *Films in Review*, 22 November 2001, http://69.195.124.61/~filmsinr/2001/11/22/interview-guillermo-del-toro/.
20. DDT's company and work can be viewed at http://www.ddtsfx.com/ddt_eng/index.html.
21. Del Toro, 'Summoning Spirits'.
22. Gibron, 'DVD Verdict Interviews Guillermo Del Toro, Director of *Blade II*'.
23. Del Toro describes how he directly referenced iconic comic-book panels and aesthetics for *Blade II*'s visual-effects moments:

    > In the breakdowns for special effects shots, they were called 'The Frazetta shot' or 'The Jack Kirby Explosion' or 'The Doctor Manhattan Explosion' from [DC Comics graphic novel] *Watchmen*, and so on and so forth. There is a lot of preparation that goes into these little homages.

    In Gibron, 'DVD Verdict Interviews Guillermo Del Toro, Director of *Blade II*'.

24. Scott McCloud, *Understanding Comics: The Invisible Art* (Northampton, MA: Tundra/William Morrow Paperbacks, 1993).
25. Julian Smith, '*Pan's Labyrinth*' (Review), *Film Quarterly* vol. 60 no. 4 (Summer 2007), pp. 4–9.
26. Richard von Busack, 'Pagan Triumph' (Film Review), *Metroactive*, 10 January 2007, http://www.metroactive.com/metro/01.10.07/pans-labyrinth-0702.html.
27. Kristine Kotecki, 'Approximating the Hypertextual, Replicating the Metafictional: Textual and Sociopolitical Authority in Guillermo del Toro's *Pan's Labyrinth*', *Marvels & Tales* vol. 24 no. 2 (2010), pp. 235–54.
28. This motif goes all the way back to *Cronos*, of course – and del Toro's first *Hellboy* film. In *Hellboy*, one of the film's villains, Kroenen (Ladislav Beran), is composed of sand and gears that hold his physical presence together; as Hellboy finds him in lair in ancient ruins, they battle, and Hellboy and his bureau boss dispatch Kroenen with giant pieces of clockwork.
29. Guillermo del Toro BAFTA interview with Jason Woods, 8 July 2008.
30. 'Guillermo del Toro, On Monsters and Meaning', *All Things Considered, National Public Radio*, 12 July 2013.
31. For more perspective, see J. F. Sargent, 'How *Pacific Rim* Got Kaiju Wrong', *Film School Rejects*, 1 August 2013, http://www.filmschoolrejects.com/opinions/how-pacific-rim-got-kaiju-wrong.php.
32. 2011's triple meltdown and ongoing problems at Fukushima Daichii nuclear power plant in Japan, following a devastating earthquake and tsunami which killed nearly 20,000 people, unfortunately only compounds Japan's post-war 'memory of defeat' and makes more complex a tragic nuclear legacy that's still very hard to overcome. This could be one of the reasons why *Pacific Rim* received a rather muted reception when it was finally released in that country in late summer.
33. Guillermo del Toro interview, Studio Q (podcast), 11 July 2013, http://www.youtube.com/watch?v=qagl76LELI4 or https://twitter.com/jianghomeshi/status/347393426356060160.
34. Del Toro interview, *Cronos* Blu-ray/DVD.
35. Guillermo Navarro interview, *Cronos* Blu-ray/DVD, Criterion, 2010.
36. See 'Purveyors of Handmade Storytelling since 2010' at http://mirada.com/.
37. See http://www.paulgoldberger.com/lectures/does-design-matter-thoughts-at-college-commencement/.
38. David Summers, *Real Spaces: World Art History and the Rise of Western Modernism* (London: Phaidon, 2003).
39. Del Toro's thoughts coincide here, referencing the oft-used term 'handmade' to signify a kind of 'traditional authenticity': 'I think films should be handmade. I have this notion that is perhaps the same thing that leads me to keep the props from my films, because I love that they are tangible things.' See Simon, 'Guillermo del Toro on "*Hellboy II*"'.
40. Robert M. Brain writes in his review of Summers's *Real Spaces*: 'All human knowledge, all meaning, it would seem, begins with making models in three-dimensions. In the age of the ubiquitous flat screen, this claim should invite further investigation.' See Brain, Book Review: *Real Spaces: World Art History and the Rise of Western Modernism*, *Journal of Interdisciplinary History* vol. 38 no. 1 (Summer 2007), pp. 102–3.

3 *SCREENS*

Among the first 'attractions' whose spectacular logic, Tom Gunning argues, comprised the shocks and surprises of early cinema and continues to influence cinema today, special-effects images have always enjoyed a high degree of screen mobility and presence, replicating across displays of all kinds as attention-grabbing stimuli in their own right and through promotional and behind-the-scenes materials that open them up to technophilic appreciation and critique. Special effects are a film's marquee visuals, the aesthetic equivalent of charismatic movie stars: in design and graphic traits, they inflect the viewing experience in a variety of ways. In the past, a film's favoured and expensive imagery might well anchor its advertising campaign and poster art, but in the era of DVD/Blu-ray formats, digital data sharing and social media, special effects spread across the internet in captures, cam rips and YouTube videos. The affinity between special effects and screens ultimately blurs the ontologies of media: through their shared technological base of 3D imaging software, a model of a monster or spaceship built for a narrative feature film can be redeployed in a television series or the interactive arena of a video game. Shaping the itinerary of special effects, then, are questions of visuality, spectacularisation and travel.

This final group of essays focuses on the visual apparatus of display technologies, both as a material framework for film exhibition and as a subject for representation within media. Long part of the preferred imagery of special effects, technologies of visualisation permeate the worlds of science fiction, often as a way of reflecting upon the optical networks in which we, as media subjects, find ourselves. Chuck Tryon, in 'Digital 3D, Technological Auteurism and the Rhetoric of Cinematic Revolution', assesses historical and current innovations in digital 3D, attending simultaneously to scientific principles of perception and the rhetoric by which cinema positions itself as cutting-edge. Tryon finds, in Scorsese's *Hugo* (2011), an auteur-led film that demonstrates the essential debt of cinema's present to its spectacular, sideshow past. The merging of science and art in special-effects practice continues with 'Shooting Stars', in which Bob Rehak traces the history of astronomical visualisation from the 1950s artwork of Chesley Bonestell to contemporary CGI sequences in science documentaries. Julie Turnock's 'Designed for Everyone Who Looks Forward to Tomorrow!' shows how the work of experimental film-makers on the US West Coast in the early 1970s created the conditions that led to the culmination of the 'New Hollywood' cinema in the spectacle-driven commercial narratives exemplified by Spielberg's *Close Encounters of the Third Kind* (1977) and George Lucas's *Star Wars* (1977), in the process examining the overlaps between two aspects of film culture that are often considered to be diametrically opposed. Following a similar historical thread to different ends, Gregory Zinman's essay 'The Right Stuff' considers the migration of avant-garde special effects into mainstream film production, mapping a complex set of exchanges at the level of artisanal labour as experimental artists lend their skills to big-budget film-making. Oliver Gaycken presents a new reading of Spielberg's *Jurassic Park* (1993), showing how the lines of influence between animatronic puppetry and the innovative digital animation used to create the film's dinosaurs are mirrored in the exchanges between the film's designers and the paleontological researchers, who learned much about dinosaur physiology from the motion simulations in the production. Finally, Aylish Wood subjects Christopher Nolan's *Inception* (2010) to an interdisciplinary analysis that bridges science studies, contemporary critical theory and an 'ecological' approach, establishing connections between the stories that emerge in both the moving images and the production-culture disclosures of DVD commentaries and the trade press; the result is a piece of film criticism that shows how various are the ways to discover the many possible meanings of a single text, an instruction manual on how to watch and learn from the technologies used to make the film happen.

There is no special effect without someone to see it, and there is no seeing without some form of screen to mediate the experience. Films and their narratives are vessels that contain effects: it is screens, large or small, that offload them for us. We began by examining what effects do, and *how* they do it. We end by considering the means by which we receive and experience them.

DIGITAL 3D, TECHNOLOGICAL AUTEURISM AND THE RHETORIC OF CINEMATIC REVOLUTION

CHUCK TRYON

On 14 January 2012, moviegoers watching Martin Scorsese's *Hugo* (2011) at the Regal Union Square Theatre in Manhattan were confronted with an unexpected experience. Because the digital projection technology stopped working twice during the screening, extending the screening time by nearly an hour, the final thirty minutes of Scorsese's loving tribute to early cinema played while commercials meant to precede a subsequent showing of the movie appeared on screen. The advertisements ran over the top of the film's dramatic final scenes, in which master film-maker Georges Méliès (Ben Kingsley) is receiving belated recognition for his contributions as a cinematic pioneer. The commercials, which presumably started automatically, went unnoticed by the staff at the theatre, leaving moviegoers to watch, with a mixture of anger and bemusement, what one blogger called a 'mashup' of Scorsese's 'tribute to film preservation' and an assortment of advertisements for cell phones, cars and TV shows, bringing attention to the contrast between our fantasies of theatres as movie palaces and their role as sites of labour and commercialism. Although the event might have otherwise passed unnoticed, a quick-thinking audience member preserved the unplanned mashup on his cell-phone video camera and posted the video to YouTube, if only temporarily. The video then led to an impromptu discussion of how 3D and digital projection were affecting the moviegoing experience, with many observers complaining that digital, and especially 3D, projection in theatres had led to a decline in the quality of theatrical screenings, comments that seemed to stand in stark contrast to celebratory accounts of how digital projection – and 3D in particular – was revolutionising cinematic exhibition.

Initially, the revival of 3D was heralded as being able to transform cinematic storytelling, with *Wired* proclaiming in its typical hype that *Avatar* (2009) director James Cameron 'could change film forever'.[1] Similarly, others within the film industry suggested that 3D could serve to attract audiences – now accustomed to consuming movies on a variety of domestic and mobile screens – back into theatres.[2] James Cameron and other successful Hollywood film-makers, such as Martin Scorsese, Steven Spielberg and Robert Rodriguez, seemed to imply that 3D movies offered a simultaneously more spectacular and immersive experience. This endorsement by Hollywood auteurs helped to legitimise the industry's efforts to promote 3D and, in turn, to facilitate the conversion process. But within just a few months of *Avatar*'s premiere, many journalists were reporting a backlash against the format.[3] A number of film critics and reviewers helped to reinforce that backlash, condemning 3D effects as intrusive, distancing movies from their quest for realism. Perhaps the most strident mainstream critic of 3D was Roger Ebert, who wrote a number of articles mourning the transition away from celluloid and what he called the 'suicidal' reliance on 3D.[4] While Ebert could point to scientific data about eye strain and the pleasures of watching movies without 3D glasses, much of the discussion centred on whether 3D could provide a more immersive – and presumably more realistic – viewing experience, one that many critics identified. In order to combat the perception that 3D effects were, in fact, more intrusive, promotional media sought to instead depict the format as a means of reinventing cinematic storytelling. This was done, in large part, by mobilising the status and reputations of prominent film-makers to redefine blockbuster films, transforming them from industrial artefacts into the individual expressions of talented and innovative individual film-makers. This chapter will look at four examples of this process, examining the marketing and promotion of the 3D films of four prominent directors, James Cameron, Robert Rodriguez, Steven Spielberg and Martin Scorsese. Implied in this examination of the marketing strategies is the idea that what Jonathan Gray describes as 'paratextual features' – the advertising, promotional and commentary texts accompanying the release of any major film – help to establish audiences' interpretations of those films, often well before they actually see the movies themselves, and, more crucially, how those films fit into a wider discourse about the culture of moviegoing.[5] Following Gray, I argue that these paratextual materials help to establish the interpretive frameworks and expectations we bring to the movie theatre, directing how we engage with the movies we watch. Thus, in order to position 3D as an artistic evolution rather than an industrial gimmick, the movie industry identified the format as one that could be used imaginatively by creative and innovative directors.

This use of the concept of the technological auteur – a figure asserted via DVD documentaries, director's commentary tracks, public appearances at cinema trade shows and publicity articles in film and technology magazines – helped to popularise digital 3D and, in turn, the overall transition to digital projection in theatres, a technological change that was a crucial concern for the movie industry.[6] In fact, as David Bordwell surmises, 3D served as a kind of 'Trojan horse' for digital projection, one that allowed theatre owners to enjoy a temporary 3D gold rush, even while the new projection technologies provided the studios with even greater control over the distribution process.[7] In order to make 3D movies more attractive, a number of them were promoted as the products of skilled film-makers who supposedly approached movies in terms of individual craftsmanship or artistry. This updated version of auteurism is consistent with the repackaging of film culture most commonly associated with the popularisation of DVDs. Catherine Grant aligns this process with the perception, reinforced through these paratextual features, that an individual film-maker can corral the collective efforts of film crews to express a personal vision.[8] As Grant surmises, building upon an earlier argument by Timothy Corrigan on the commercialisation of the auteur, this form of authorship can be enlisted to promote and market Hollywood films and the wider film experience. Such discourses can help create the perception that audiences are not merely watching another sterile, industrial piece of entertainment. They are instead, as Barbara Klinger suggests, tapping into the desire to consume a 'personalised product'.[9] Although Grant and Klinger are primarily discussing the role of auteurism in selling DVDs (and the related practice of using DVDs to sell auteurism), this process of commercialisation also sought to characterise 3D effects as an individualised form of expression, one that fit neatly into existing personas associated with the directors, such as Cameron's reputation as a 'visionary' and Scorsese's status as a film historian. This depiction of the technologically aided auteur is consistent with the production discourses that John

Thornton Caldwell has identified within DVD extras, with Caldwell noting that film-makers who work with digital effects are often portrayed as 'talented artists driven by intuition and personal vision', often to the point of obscuring more mundane, but utterly crucial, forms of film production and post-production labour.[10]

3D movies were promoted through appeals to auteurism in order to revive the activity of moviegoing, which was often regarded with a sense of nostalgia as something that was on the verge of being lost. Discussions of the failed *Hugo* screening focused not just on the film's nostalgic content (a 'mashup' of Scorsese's 'tribute to film preservation') but on the desire for better theatrical experiences that featured professional projectionists. Although reports about steep box-office declines have been somewhat exaggerated, many entertainment reporters tend to accept this idea uncritically, leading to changed assumptions about the cultural role of movie theatres in everyday life. David Poland, in particular, has countered the notion that the frequency of moviegoing is declining significantly, pointing out that box-office totals remained relatively steady between 2010 and 2011, despite a steady drumbeat of articles suggesting otherwise.[11] Poland also complicated recent assertions that audience backlash against 3D might be causing a decline in theatrical attendance, pointing out that six of the ten highest-grossing films were in 3D and that 3D movies continued to be a major draw outside North America. I mention these details not in order to stake a claim about whether 3D is positively or negatively affecting box office. Instead, Poland's arguments serve as a reminder that discussions of box office can have a substantial effect on movie culture, shaping audience expectations about the theatrical experience and even about the movie industry itself. As Charles Acland points out, 'discourses of moviegoing have material effects'.[12] Trade press accounts, fan blogs, pre-show advertisements and even DVD extras can help to shape how the activity of moviegoing is perceived, which in turn, may shape decisions about what kinds of movies get made and distributed, as well as where and how new theatres are built. To counter the concerns about how digital projection might be altering the theatrical experience, 3D became aligned not merely with auteurism but also with a sense of nostalgia. In fact, many of the key technological auteurs who produced 3D films made movies that evoked a sense of nostalgia, whether for older genres or modes of film-making. In the sections that follow, I trace out four tendencies of the technological auteur in the era of 3D. First, Cameron's *Avatar* aligns itself not only with a return to nature but also with past cinematic evolutions such as the introduction of colour and sound. Second, Robert Rodriguez's *Spy Kids: All the Time in the World in 4D* (2011) recalls both the gimmicks of the 1950s, such as Smell-O-Vision, and the idea of the carnival worker selling a unique film experience along the lines of a roller-coaster ride. In turn, Spielberg's *The Adventures of Tintin* (2011) evoked nostalgia not only for comic books and the innocent, childlike world they imagined but also for Spielberg's own early-career B-movie aesthetic. Finally, Scorsese's *Hugo* offers a nostalgic retelling of cinema's origin stories, imagining it as a medium with the capacity to astonish us in much the same way that Méliès the magician astounded audiences over a century ago.

Back to the Future: 3D in the 1950s

As most press accounts about *Avatar* acknowledged, 3D projection was not a new phenomenon. Stereoscopic 3D projection existed in the earliest days of cinema, but it was not widely used until the 1950s, when studios were seeking gimmicks to attract audiences back into theatres and to compete with television.[13] Although Robert Sklar argues that these 1950s experiments were meant to exploit cinema's ability to depict movement and often sought to appeal to audience desires for immersion in the world of the motion picture, they are more accurately aligned with what Michele Pierson describes as a desire for textual and aesthetic novelty.[14] These 1950s experiments were launched with the independently produced *Bwana Devil*, a 1952 'African adventure' film starring Robert Stack. The film exploited the sense of depth created by three-dimensionality by depicting trains rushing toward the screen and natives throwing spears toward the audience, causing images from the film to protrude into the visual space of the viewers in the movie theatre.[15] By comparison, many of the 3D films from the 2000s eschew this 'protrusive' aesthetic, instead opting to use 3D to create greater depth.

As Pierson notes, the 3D process in the 1950s was plagued by technological and economic challenges at both the levels of production and exhibition. The illusion of 3D was typically produced by filming a scene simultaneously with two cameras, which would then be synchronised together in post-production, so that two strips would be projected simultaneously. Bulky cameras made production more difficult, while the additional film stock required to create 3D films increased production costs significantly.[16] Eventually 3D became more commonly associated with the sensory thrills of amusement parks and other attractions, including IMAX screens, sensations that Acland perceptively aligns with what he calls a 'tourist gaze'. Acland, drawing from Paul Virilio's characterisation of the format as a kind of 'cataract surgery', points out that the IMAX films reignite the perceptual experience of early cinema, creating in viewers the sense of immersion that had been lost as audiences became more accustomed to watching movies.[17] For Acland, this tourist gaze is further reinforced not only by the location of many IMAX screens – in museums and amusement parks – but also by the subject matter, which tended to favour documentaries and educational films, often focusing on scientific or anthropological topics, although more recently, Hollywood films using IMAX technologies are more often likened to 'thrill rides', roller coasters that turn movies into a more visceral pleasure. In fact, in her review of *Journey to the Centre of the Earth 3D* (2008), one of the early films to exploit digital 3D, Katey Rich pushes the amusement-park metaphor in suggesting that the movie 'feels like a visit to Frontierland, with boat rides, mine carts, and one heck of a log flume'.[18] We are, as it were, transported by our sensory experience of watching movies on the (extra) big IMAX screen.[19]

James Cameron as Cinematic Revolutionary

This transport metaphor played a crucial role in the marketing and promotion of *Avatar*, one of the first high-profile films associated with the emergence of digital 3D. The movie takes us several centuries into the future to a distant planet, which we encounter first from the safety and confines of a spaceship. Gradually, through our identification with paraplegic soldier Jake Sully (Sam Worthington), we are able to enter the world of Pandora, immersing ourselves in its breathtaking landscapes and its bright, multicoloured flora and fauna, in which the tribes of Na'vi creatures live in harmony with nature. The film's plot centres around Sully taking on an assignment involving participation in the Avatar Program, which allows him to control the body of a Na'vi. Thus, in much the same way that IMAX films ostensibly took us to distant lands, reinforcing connections between film and bodily transport, Cameron's use of 3D seemingly carries us into another world, one characterised by exotic flora and fauna but also one in which the film engages advanced technologies in order to promote a narrative that is, in fact, critical of the abuses of these tools.

During the promotion of *Avatar*, assessments of James Cameron tended to place emphasis not only on his role as a film-maker but also on his status as an inventor, someone able to work with engineers and scientists to develop new technologies. Biographies such as Rebecca Keegan's *The Futurist: The Life and Films of James Cameron* portray the director as a kind of restless experimenter and inventor, someone who takes extreme risks, both through his hobbies of deep-sea diving and through his attempts to develop new cinematic technologies.[20] These narratives and other similar press accounts helped to position *Avatar* as a 'game-changing' film, one that would deliver a total immersive experience capable of making us forget that we were watching a movie. In fact, *Avatar's* aesthetic departs considerably from the 'shock effect' typically associated with 3D films of the 1950s. Rather than shocking viewers with the illusion of objects coming directly at them, 3D is often used in *Avatar* to provide what Todd McGowan describes as a sense of 'overwhelming plenitude'.[21] For example, most promotional texts, including the film's official trailer, start with an introduction to the wheelchair-bound Jake Sully before showing his descent into Pandora's tropical landscape, shunning an aesthetic of protrusion and focusing instead on adding depth and extra layering as we fly into that world.

The idea that *Avatar* would prove a completely immersive experience was widely promoted at the time of its release and reinforced through publicity materials that played a crucial role in shaping how the film was interpreted. Press reports highlighted the fact that Cameron hired a linguist to create the language spoken by the Na'vi people and that he employed biologists to help imagine the flora and fauna that might have evolved in Pandora. This heightened sense of immersion was reinforced by a 'guidebook' designed to appear as if it were an actual scientific study of the planet Pandora. While this material promoted a form of immersion that was 'informational' rather than sensory, it helped to underscore the ways in which *Avatar* was meant to be experienced rather than seen, inhabited rather than watched. Although such artefacts might seem peripheral to the actual movie, they are, in fact, central to the process of establishing its meaning and significance. As Gray points out, trailers and other promotional materials are actively involved in 'the process of creating textual meaning, serving as the first outpost of interpretation'.[22] To be sure, these textual artefacts have a long history; however, the marketing of *Avatar* not only served to promote a specific film but also to convey that Cameron – through his skill as a technological auteur – was changing the entire cinematic experience.

In addition, the *Avatar* promotional materials suggested that digital 3D techniques would supposedly create a more fully immersive experience than the 3D films of the 1950s. Cameron attempted to distance *Avatar* from these older 3D films: 'Ideally, the technology is advanced enough to make itself go away. That's how it should work. All of the technology should wave its own wand and make itself disappear.'[23] However, despite these claims that Cameron was making the projection technologies disappear, the effects techniques in *Avatar* actually called attention to themselves and served as a primary source of attraction for audiences curious to see how the 3D experience was accomplished. Advertisements, including one for the

Panasonic VIERA HD television set, even featured Cameron working on the movie's set, operating a camera, while reminding us that the director 'changed cinema'. Thus, although we were promised an immersive experience, many viewers instead found themselves paying attention to the technologies of production and, in some cases, of exhibition as well. These advertisements, as well as the special features on the DVD, also helped to promote the commercialisation of Cameron as a technological auteur, a discourse that was already in place during the promotion of his previous film, *Titanic* (1997), another movie gaining Cameron credit for using visual effects to create a heightened sense of realism.[24] Acland has noted that the *Avatar* DVD works to emphasise 'Cameron's endlessly expanding imagination', one that is expressed through his ability to invent new cinematic technologies.[25] As a result, *Avatar* furnished audiences with a doubled message. On the one hand, technologies are supposed to disappear as viewers 'forget' that they are watching a movie, a theory that seems to reinforce the goal of complete immersion in the world of the film. On the other hand, we are also constantly reminded through a variety of press discourses about the technologies and tools that make that immersive experience possible.

Robert Rodriguez as Playful Showman

Picking up on the desire for novel theatrical experiences, film-maker Robert Rodriguez sought to reactivate his long-dormant *Spy Kids* franchise (2001, 2002 and 2003), not only by using 3D but also by reviving another late-1950s movie attraction: the incorporation of scents into the theatrical experience. *Spy Kids 4* featured not only digital 3D but also scented cards with numbers that viewers could scratch off whenever a corresponding number appeared on screen. In this sense, the film countered contemporary adoptions of 3D to encourage cinematic immersion with a more protrusive aesthetic that engaged 3D to shock and surprise. Thus, Rodriguez sought to engage with a much more active, energised moviegoing audience of young children, conditioned by playing video games and used to active participation in the narratives they encountered. As Rodriguez explains,

> Just watching my own kids with interactive gaming, you ask them to watch a movie, it just feels so passive to them. I thought, this helps bridge the gap. It's an interactive thing, almost like playing a game while you're watching the movie.[26]

Thus, rather than following the lead of Cameron and other directors who focused on the immersive potential of 3D, Rodriguez seemed to revel in the novelty of 3D – and Aromascope – to entice younger audiences to see the movie in theatres.

Like 3D, scents served as a device to lure teenagers back into theatres. The most prominent attempt to exploit this gimmick was 1960's *Scent of Mystery*, produced by Mike Todd, Jr, which used a technology called Smell-O-Vision to augment the movie. Smell-O-Vision involved a complex system in which perfume containers were stored on a rotating belt and, when the appropriate scene in the movie took place, a small needle would pierce the container, releasing the scent, which would then be disseminated by strategically placed fans.[27] Although *Scent of Mystery* was a box-office failure, one that proved costly for its creators, the idea of incorporating scent into the movies continued to recur, often in homage to Todd's very limited experiments, most notably in the 1982 John Waters film, *Polyester*, which used scratch-and-sniff cards, rather than pipes or fans, in part to alleviate the problem of unwanted scents lingering after a scene ended, the technique also chosen by Rodriguez for his Aromascope feature.

However, like *Scent of Mystery*, *Spy Kids 4* received mostly negative reviews, especially from film critics (though younger audiences were somewhat more forgiving), in part because the scented cards were perceived as too intrusive, distracting reviewers from the film itself, a problem reinforced by the fact that the darkened lenses of the 3D glasses made it difficult to see the numbers on the scratch cards clearly. As Mary Ann Johanson complained,

> We're told that at certain points during the movie, when a number pops up on screen, we're meant to scratch that number on the card and inhale deeply. Never mind that between the dark of the theatre and the added darkening factor of the 3D glasses, you won't be able to see anything to do so.

Johanson went on to add that most of the cards simply smelled like 'cardboard'.[28] In this sense, the additional 'dimension' was not designed to create a more realistic world for moviegoers to enter. Instead it intentionally introduced distraction, especially for younger viewers seeking more 'interactive' forms of entertainment, even while nostalgically evoking the gimmick cinema of Smell-O-Vision and its imitators. Further, like the publicity for *Avatar*, the promotional materials for *Spy Kids 4* situated the film within the film-making style of its director. Like Cameron, Robert Rodriguez is often associated with new technologies, and he had already used 3D in his previous *Spy Kids* film in 2003. But with *Spy Kids 4*, the promotional materials instead highlighted the director's affinity for B-movies and his ability to make 'cheesy gimmicks' part of a fun theatrical experience.[29] Thus, like Cameron, Rodriguez was involved in the attempt to redefine filmgoing, in part through the promotion of textual novelty, even if Rodriguez focused on an interactive rather than immersive aesthetic.

Steven Spielberg as Blockbuster Adapter

Perhaps one of the more nostalgic 3D adaptations was Steven Spielberg's reworking of Hergé's classic Belgian comic-book hero, Tintin. Like Cameron and Rodriguez, Spielberg's use of 3D built upon existing aspects of his reputation as an auteur, one that is grounded in both a fascination with film genres and an appreciation of childhood innocence. In fact, Spielberg's *The Adventures of Tintin* engaged digital 3D to reinforce a sense of immersion similar to that offered by Cameron in *Avatar*, even while the movie also seemed to evoke nostalgia not only for the innocence of the character of Tintin but also for the comic books themselves. Thus, the movie presented a significant challenge in that it was working with Hergé's incredibly popular comic books, raising questions about the role of adaptation and authorial influence in transferring a text from one medium into another.

As many reviewers noted, the Tintin books seem unusual candidates for adaptation into a Hollywood blockbuster. Although phenomenally popular outside the US, especially in the Francophone world, they were much less well known in the US, making them more difficult to market.[30] That being said, *The Adventures of Tintin* may have been more unsettling because of the ways in which its style of performance capture seemed to approach what Masahiro Mori called the 'uncanny valley', the line at which computer-generated characters begin to appear almost human, in addition to digital animation tools that allowed Spielberg to create sequences that would have been impossible with normal film technologies. This situation led a reviewer writing for the *Economist* to complain that Spielberg was somehow 'cheating' by automating the animation process through performance capture, rather than using either live action or more traditional forms of (presumably hand-drawn or handcrafted) animation. Such complaints typically emphasise the idea that performance capture is 'distracting', in part because we are seeing a recognisable actor, redrawn with features that don't belong to him or her, with the reviewer for the *Economist* ultimately quipping, 'Spielberg and his colleagues should remember that there's another performance-capturing device which is far more sophisticated than their latest boxes of digital tricks, and it doesn't require lycra unitards. It's called a camera.'[31] Thus, although performance capture seemed like a natural device for depicting nonhuman characters such as Gollum, when applied to more seemingly human, if cartoonish characters, it was seen as unsettling or unwarranted. However, despite these complaints, Spielberg's use of performance capture was directly related to the immersive aesthetic that dominated the film, as well as his commitment to remaining faithful to the Hergé comics. As Spielberg noted in an interview, performance capture allowed him to 'create the same visual panels with a movie frame around them that Hergé had done in exploring his stories'.[32]

Mainstream critics' complaints about the film's lack of realism seem unusual, especially given the original Tintin was an intrepid boy journalist capable of travelling the globe in the space (or time) of a single comic-book frame. In fact, one of the more compelling instances of motion capture and 3D in the film was the bravura sequence in which Tintin, Captain Haddock and company embark on an incredibly involved chase scene rushing through the streets of Bagghar, Morocco and around narrow, cliffside roads all in the course of what appears to be a single shot, although, of course, the concept of the 'shot' is less relevant in the world of digital animation. Such a sequence illustrates one of the key challenges Spielberg faced in making *The Adventures of Tintin*, taking a beloved comic book and reworking it for the big screen. Thus, even though it has been widely reported that Spielberg used the pages of the comic books as virtual storyboards that would influence composition and even the actors' movements, the on-screen images seem both similar to the originals and startlingly different.

At the same time, adaptation and influence haunted *The Adventures of Tintin* in other ways. Hergé decreed just before his death in 1983 that Spielberg should be the Hollywood director who translated his movies to the big screen, in part due to the success of Spielberg's *Raiders of the Lost Ark* (1981) and its narrative similarity to the Tintin stories.[33] Spielberg himself read the comic books in 1981, around the time he was working on his first Indiana Jones film, and many critics suggested initially that *Tintin* appeared to be 'an Indiana Jones for kids'.[34] This relationship opens up questions about the nature of influence, and although many critics faulted Spielberg for his interpretation of *Tintin*, others argued that Hergé's comics might fruitfully be read as precursors to the blockbuster form with which Spielberg has been readily identified.[35] At the same time, the choice to adapt *Tintin* is rooted in Spielberg's history of exploring childhood innocence. As Spielberg himself noted, Tintin, despite his interactions with unsavoury characters such as Captain Haddock and Red Rackham, is a 'kind of Boy Scout', a character who not only remains honest but also proves himself to be capable of handling all of the challenges thrown at him. Thus, although *The Adventures of Tintin* was unfairly seen by some US critics as a box-office and creative failure – after all, its worldwide box-office receipts reached $373 million – the film was still framed and promoted as enabling Spielberg to extend the blockbuster style that he had been cultivating since the beginning of his career.

Martin Scorsese as Nostalgic Historian

Like Spielberg, Martin Scorsese sought to promote 3D as a logical continuation of older forms of cinematic storytelling, both in promotional interviews and at the level of narrative. Also like Spielberg, Scorsese took as source material an innovative graphic text written primarily for younger readers. *Hugo* is an adaptation of Brian Selznick's children's novel, *The Invention of Hugo Cabret*, which tells the story of twelve-year-old orphan Hugo (Asa Butterfield), who befriends and essentially 'rediscovers' pioneering film-maker Georges Méliès, a figure often cited as the 'father' of special-effects cinema.[36] Hugo's father worked in a museum but died in a fire, leaving him to be raised by his uncle, an alcoholic who kept the clocks in a busy Parisian train station before he disappeared, abandoning Hugo, who not only assumes his uncle's duties in the station but also works to complete an automaton his father had been building as a hobby. As the plot unfolds, we learn that the automaton had originally been designed by Méliès, who now works as a shopkeeper in the train station after leaving his film career behind. Hugo, in collaboration with Méliès' goddaughter, gives the film director (and his movies) new life, both by getting the automaton to work and by reminding Méliès – and the audience – about the artistry of his films, many of which were destroyed during World War I, in part to melt the film stock into plastic to be used for the heels of shoes.

This desire to rediscover and redeem one of cinema's popular origin stories animates Scorsese's film and is a continuation of Scorsese's own financial and emotional investments in the practice of film preservation. In this sense, Scorsese was able to take a format that seems hostile to film preservation, digital 3D, and to produce a film that serves as a kind of love letter to the origins of cinema. In fact, Scorsese ended up drawing a connection between the fantasies of perceptual realism and his work in 3D. In an interview with the *Guardian*, Scorsese remarked that he had 'always been obsessed with 3D', adding that he had collected and relished such proto-cinematic visual toys as Viewmasters and Victorian-era stereoscopic devices, and that the toys' 'sense of depth took me into another universe'.[37]

This focus on the history of film's origins serves as a way for Scorsese to rewrite the digital transition by linking it visually to cinema's foundational myths associated with the founding figures, the Lumière brothers and Méliès. In fact, through the character of Rene Tabard (Michael Stuhlbarg), Scorsese reimagines the earliest film screenings, including the Lumières' famous *Arrival of a Train* (1896), which supposedly provoked such fear in audiences that many of them dove for cover as the train seemed to rush toward them. In Scorsese's retelling, the scene is now filmed in 3D, allowing the train to appear to protrude into the world of the spectator, visually reinforcing the shock effect felt by the earliest cinema audiences. In addition, the film devotes one of the climactic scenes to a flashback showing Méliès' studio and the painstaking efforts involved in producing his early trick films. We see acrobats dressed in skeleton costumes, along with crew members building models and setting up puffs of smoke to simulate explosions. While this early history of film has often been discussed in terms of its ability to reinforce the illusionary potential of cinematic images, Scorsese presents these scenes less as moments of deception and more as instances of magical performance. Because these scenes are revealed to us through flashback – and with Méliès as our guide – we are, in a sense, taken behind the curtain and allowed to see how the trick was constructed, in much the same way that DVD extras indulge knowing audiences with a glance 'behind' the camera (or, more recently, in front of the computer monitor) where thrilling effects are produced. To some extent, this sequence precisely resembles a making-of documentary that was never made, taking us back to the origins of cinema in order to recast it as a medium for the production of special effects. Many of these scenes show viewers – Hugo, Isabelle (Chloë Grace Moretz), Mama Jeanne (Helen McCrory) and Tabard – watching movie screens, entranced by the images before them. Thus, like the other digital 3D films, Scorsese's *Hugo* is focused on the movie theatre as the site of breathtaking spectacle, where viewers can be astonished by special effects.

Conclusion

Debates about 3D films have served to highlight some of the complicated feelings surrounding the moviegoing experience in the digital age. While movie theatres have historically been associated with romanticised promises of shared experiences with a wider collective, theatres increasingly compete with convenience technologies such as laptops and mobile devices, which offer alternative screening sites. More crucially, shortened theatrical windows accelerate the lifecycle of Hollywood films, ensuring that they pass through theatres and onto DVD and streaming formats much more quickly than in the recent past. As a result, studios have sought to produce event screenings, presenting large-scale, big-screen spectacles featuring 3D effects in order to entice audiences back into theatres. However, as the screening of Scorsese's *Hugo* shows, movie theatres are also sites of (increasingly non-union) labour, as well as locations where viewers are exposed to (increasingly automated) segments of pre-show advertising, activities that undercut the 'ideal settings' promoted by director James Cameron and others.

To combat this changed perception of moviegoing, 3D has been used simultaneously as a cutting-edge technology and one that is linked to nostalgia for older forms of cinematic storytelling. The role of 3D in creating new forms of cinematic entertainment has been championed by film-makers who are actively involved not only in producing entertaining movies but also in the process of reorienting the theatrical experience. James Cameron, through his status as a technological auteur, posits industrial solutions, eager that film-makers develop new tools to contribute to novel textual and aesthetic experiences, yielding audiences the contradictory pleasures of being completely immersed in the world of a film, even while they may be aware of how it was constructed. Robert Rodriguez, meanwhile, was less focused on producing feelings of immersion than on generating opportunities for interactivity. Although the interactive potential of scented cards may be minimal, they fit neatly into the traditions of gimmickry commonly enlisted to promote the theatrical experience. Like Cameron, Steven Spielberg concentrates on the creative and expressive possibilities of 3D, even while facing the specific challenge of adapting a two-dimensional text, Hergé's comics, into a three-dimensional form. However, despite the stylistic differences, Spielberg employed the motion-capture tools to create a more seamless form of action cinema in the spirit of his prior blockbusters. Finally, Martin Scorsese seeks to redeem 3D by restaging cinema's origins using the format. Not only does he ground the development of cinema – and the theatrical experience – in the work of special-effects pioneer Georges Méliès, but he also reimagines the original movie screening, of the Lumière brothers' *Arrival of a Train*, as a 3D movie in which the train barrels toward frightened viewers, but now with an additional dimension. In all cases, however, these film-makers seek to revive the filmgoing experience, rescuing it from both the aesthetic limitations of past movies and from the individualised, mobile screens that reportedly serve to distract our gaze, both by emphasising the social aspects of moviegoing and by reminding us of the sensual pleasures of watching movies on the big screen.

Notes

1. Joshua Davis, 'James Cameron's New 3-D Epic Could Change Film Forever', *Wired*, 17 November 2009, http://www.wired.com/magazine/2009/11/ff_avatar_cameron/all/1.
2. Mike Fleming, 'MPAA Cites 3D for Fueling Box Office Spike', *Deadline Hollywood Daily*, 10 March 2010, http://www.deadline.com/.
3. See for example, David Poland, 'Pirates & 3D', *Movie City News*, 24 May 2011, http://moviecitynews.com/2011/05/pirates-3d/.
4. Roger Ebert, 'Why I Hate 3-D (and You Should, Too)', *Daily Beast*, 9 May 2010, http://www.thedailybeast.com/.
5. See Jonathan Gray, *Show Sold Separately: Promos, Spoilers, and Other Media Paratexts* (New York: New York University Press, 2010).
6. For a discussion of the transition to digital projection in theatres, see Chuck Tryon, *Reinventing Cinema: Movies in the Age of Media Convergence* (New Brunswick, NJ: Rutgers University Press, 2009), pp. 59–92. See also David Bordwell, *Pandora's Digital Box: Films, Files, and the Future of Movies* (Madison, WI: Irvington Way Press, 2012).
7. Ibid., pp. 74–5.
8. Catherine Grant, 'Auteur Machines? Auteurism and the DVD', in James Bennett and Tom Brown (eds), *Film and Television after DVD* (New York: Routledge, 2008), p. 101.
9. Barbara Klinger, *Beyond the Multiplex: Cinema, New Technologies, and the Home* (Berkeley: University of California Press, 2006), p. 89. See also Timothy Corrigan, *A Cinema without Walls: Movies and Culture after Vietnam* (New Brunswick, NJ: Rutgers University Press, 1991).
10. John Thornton Caldwell, *Production Culture: Industrial Reflexivity and Critical Practice in Film and Television* (Durham, NC: Duke University Press, 2008), p. 22.
11. David Poland, 'The Slump Scam: 2011 Edition', *Movie City News*, 26 December 2011, http://moviecitynews.com/2011/12/the-slump-is-a-scam-2011-edition/. Poland notes, for example, that two of the six major studios were expecting increases in domestic box office between 2010 and 2011, while also pointing out that critics blamed the 2005 box-office 'slump' on similar causes, such as piracy, video games and the Internet.
12. Charles R. Acland, *Screen Traffic: Movies, Multiplexes, and Global Culture* (Durham, NC: Duke University Press, 2003).
13. For more detail on this history, see Ray Zone, *Stereoscopic Cinema and the Origins of 3-D Film, 1838–1952* (Lexington: University of Kentucky Press, 2007).

14. Michele Pierson, *Special Effects: Still in Search of Wonder* (New York: Columbia University Press, 2002) p. 53.
15. Robert Sklar, *Movie-made America: A Cultural History of American Movies* (New York: Vintage, 1994), p. 285.
16. Pierson, *Special Effects*, p. 53.
17. Charles R. Acland, 'Imax Technology and the Tourist Gaze', *Cultural Studies* vol. 12 no. 3 (1998), pp. 429–45. See also Paul Virilio, 'Cataract Surgery: Cinema in the Year 2000', in Annette Kuhn (ed.), *Alien Zone: Cultural Theory and Contemporary Science Fiction Cinema*, trans. Annie Fatet and Annette Kuhn (New York: Verso, 1990), pp. 169–74.
18. Katey Rich, 'Movie Review: *Journey to the Centre of the Earth 3D*', *Cinema Blend*, n.d., http://www.cinemablend.com/reviews/Journey-to-the-Center-of-the-Earth-3D-3199.html.
19. Acland, 'Imax Technology and the Tourist Gaze', p. 433.
20. Rebecca Keegan, *The Futurist: The Life and Films of James Cameron* (New York: Crown, 2009).
21. Todd McGowan, 'Maternity Divided: *Avatar* and the Enjoyment of Nature', *Jump Cut* no. 52 (2010), http://www.ejumpcut.org/archive/jc52.2010/mcGowanAvatar/.
22. Gray, *Show Sold Separately*, p. 48.
23. Eddie Wrenn, '*Avatar*: How James Cameron's 3D Film Could Change the Face of Cinema Forever', *Daily Mail*, 26 August 2009, http://www.dailymail.co.uk/.
24. See, for example, Ron Magid, 'Epic Effects Christen *Titanic*', *American Cinematographer* vol. 78 no. 12 (December 1997), http://www.theasc.com/magazine/dec97/titanic/eect/index.htm.
25. Charles R. Acland, 'You Haven't Seen *Avatar* Yet', *Flow* vol. 13 no. 8 (2011), http://flowtv.org/2011/02/you-havent-seen-avatar/.
26. 'Robert Rodriguez on His *Spy Kids* Stinker', *Deadline Hollywood Daily*, 17 August 2011, http://www.deadline.com/.
27. Scott Kirsner, *Inventing the Movies: Hollywood's Epic Battle between Innovation and the Status Quo: From Thomas Edison to Steve Jobs* (Seattle, WA: CreateSpace, 2008), pp. 45–6.
28. See for example, Mary Ann Johanson, '*Spy Kids 4: All the Time in the World in 4D* (review)', *Flick Filosopher*, 19 August 2011, http://www.flickfilosopher.com/.
29. Ethan Anderton, '*Spy Kids 4* Hitting Theatres with an All-new Form of Smell-O-Vision', *First Showing*, 24 June 2011, http://www.firstshowing.net/.
30. Nathan Heller reports that Tintin books had sold more than 200 million copies and had been translated into over fifty languages. It is also worth noting that, although the film had a comparatively poor box-office performance in the US, its ticket sales in Europe were extremely robust. In fact the combined North American box office of $75 million was only slightly greater than the combined total of $62 million for France and Belgium. See Nathan Heller, 'Tintin: How Hergé's Boy Reporter Invented the Hollywood Blockbuster', *Slate*, 29 December 2011, http://www.slate.com/articles/arts/assessment/2011/12/steven_spielberg_s_tintin_how_herg_s_boy_reporter_invented_the_hollywood_blockbuster_.single.html.
31. 'Tintin and the Dead-eyed Zombies', *Economist*, 31 October 2011, http://www.economist.com/.
32. Mekado Murphy, 'The Adventures of Spielberg: An Interview', *Carpetbagger Blog*, 20 December 2011, http://carpetbagger.blogs.nytimes.com/2011/12/20/the-adventures-of-spielberg-an-interview/.
33. 'Tintin and the Dead-eyed Zombies'.

34. Manohla Dargis, 'Intrepid Boy on the Trail of Mysteries', *New York Times*, 20 December 2011, http://movies.nytimes.com/.
35. Heller, 'Tintin'.
36. For a discussion of this trope, see Dan North, *Performing Illusions: Cinema, Special Effects and the Virtual Actor* (London: Wallflower Press, 2008), p. 7.
37. 'Martin Scorsese on Hugo – "I've Always Been Obsessed with 3D"', *Guardian*, 2 December 2011, http://www.guardian.co.uk/film/video/2011/dec/02/martin-scorsese-hugo-3d.

SHOOTING STARS
CHESLEY BONESTELL AND THE SPECIAL EFFECTS OF OUTER SPACE

BOB REHAK

If Alfonso Cuarón's *Gravity* (2013), with its $716 million worldwide box-office gross and multiple Academy Award, Golden Globe and BAFTA wins, enjoyed a mainstream and critical success unusual for a visual-effects-heavy science-fiction film, it was certainly not the first time the movies had turned to outer space – more specifically, low-earth orbit and the immediate neighbourhood of our solar system – as subject matter and staging area. Indeed, the mutual affinity of cinema and outer space is apparent in one of its earliest and most enduring images, of a rocketship smashing into a pie-faced Moon, which dates back to 1902's *Le Voyage dans la lune*. So iconic is Georges Méliès' Man in the Moon to the history of special effects that it is quoted, as Dan North points out, in the logo and trophy design for the Visual Effects Society[1] – as well as in a cometary fantail of tributes, quotations and parodies that establish this as perhaps the first 'microgenre' of movie magic.[2] But before we explain (or explain away) this image's pedigree as just another instance of the early-cinema 'attraction', we should note its specific identity as a *visualisation of outer space*.[3] Amid the many wonders conjured by Méliès and other pioneers, it is *Le Voyage* we enshrine as *locus classicus* of the SF film – suggesting not just a primordial symbiosis of special effects and genres of the fantastic, but the particular fascination that astronomical settings have always held for that alliance.

The 111 years separating *Le Voyage dans la lune* and *Gravity* comprise a baggy assortment of cinematic excursions into space, realised at wildly different levels of budget, technology and sophistication. They range from the wire-flown and spark-dripping rocketships of the *Flash Gordon* and *Buck Rogers* serials in the 1930s and 40s to the Technicolor and CinemaScope saucer-cruisers of *This Island Earth* (1955) and *Forbidden Planet* (1956); the pristine ballet of satellites, shuttles, moon buses and the Jupiter-exploring *Discovery* in *2001: A Space Odyssey* (1968); the dingier and more lived-in craft of *Silent Running* (1971), *Star Wars* (1977) and *Outland* (1981); the blockbuster pulp of *Total Recall* (1990), *Independence Day* (1996) and *Starship Troopers* (1997); and in the first decade of the twenty-first century a slew of movies set in space or on other planets including *Red Planet* and *Mission to Mars* (both 2000), *Serenity* (2005), *WALL-E* (2008) and *Avatar* (2009). Elastic enough to encompass both horror (*Alien* [1979], *Lifeforce* [1985], *Event Horizon* [1997] and *Supernova* [2000]) and comedy (*Dark Star* [1974], *Spaceballs* [1985], *The Hitchhiker's Guide to the Galaxy* [2005] and *Space Station 76* [2014]), outer space has served as the scenic and narrative foundation for franchises like *Star Trek* (1966 –), *Star Wars* (1977–), the *Alien* series (1979–), and *Battlestar Galactica* (1978–), as well as a means of injecting new life into long-running entertainment brands like James Bond in *Moonraker* (1979) and Jason Vorhees in *Jason X* (2001).

Despite the variety of their manifestations, depictions of space and spaceflight in cinema underwent a rapid and significant transformation in the middle of the twentieth century. In the decades following the end of World War II, visualisations of space became increasingly preoccupied with achieving a 'realism' predicated not just on special effects' traditional concern with perceptual cues allowing the integration of created and captured imagery, but on the relationship between space visuals, engineering and design concepts of the emerging Space Age, and scientific data on the appearance, position and lighting of objects in space. While this modal shift in visualisation practices had many players and participants, one person in particular – Chesley Bonestell (1888–1986) – played a determining and richly interconnected role in the 'realistic turn' that paved the way for more scientifically faithful portrayals of space in key films of the 1960s, 70s and beyond, from *2001: A Space Odyssey* to *Star Trek II: The Wrath of Khan* (1982). Although not associated directly with the latter films, Bonestell's influential work as a designer, painter and illustrator make him, along with the authors and engineers Willy Ley and Wernher von Braun whose concepts he gave visual life to, a forerunner of 'visioneers' such as space-habitat developer Gerard K. O'Neill and nanotechnology pioneer Eric Drexler, who in the 1970s and 80s 'used their training in science and engineering to undertake detailed design and engineering studies', and in doing so, 'built communities and networks that connected their ideas to interested citizens, writers, politicians, and business leaders'.[4]

A Space-age Supergenre

Any genealogy of outer-space imagery in US film, of course, barely scratches the surface, neglecting important traditions in Japanese, Soviet, German and other national cinemas; outer space in electronic and digital media such as television (the various *Star Trek* series, *Babylon 5* [1994–8], *Farscape* [1999–2003] and *Firefly* [2002–3]) ; and the centrality of space to video games (*Elite*, *Wing Commander*, *Freespace*, *Homeworld*, *EVE Online* and many others). More problematically, it leaves out the myriad ways in which outer space has been constructed for the screen in scientific and technical image-making, such as educational documentaries, NASA animations, journalistic coverage and the less publicly visible domain of concept sketches, engineering draftsmanship and prototyping art that subtend any industrial science but may be particularly integral and influential in hugely collective human enterprises focused on the cutting-edge and near future, such as space research and exploration in the twentieth century. As an area of communications practice, outer space can be viewed as a transmedia 'supergenre' of visualisation practices married to changeable functions and meanings but displaying other forms of coherence – two in particular – over time.

First is the dependence of depictions of outer space on special effects. In all cases outside of strict scientific observation (that is, images recorded through telescopes, astronauts' cameras or the lenses of space probes), outer space has always had to be 'faked' on screen, with painted artwork, miniatures and models, and analogue or digital animation stepping in not just to augment but generate outright settings beyond our world's surface. Renderings of planets, moons, asteroids, stars, galaxies, nebulae and the deep blackness of the void around them function as spectacular scenery in their own right and as a *mise en scène* for organic and technological presence: the activity of human beings, alien species, ships, satellites, stations and colonies. This imagery can range from the spatially and temporally local (Earth and other planets of the solar system; our established past and immediate future) to the exotically distant and extrapolative (far reaches of intergalactic space; the singularities of black holes; suns and worlds in primordial birth, cataclysmic destruction and slow heat death).[5]

Second, our ways of conceiving and constructing astronomical vistas has had to contend with a constantly shifting body of knowledge about the physical universe, as well as with the hypothetical and actual feats of engineering required to carry our bodies and instrumentalities off-planet. In the period after World War II, the Space Age – preceding and in many senses laying the groundwork for the 'Space Race' between the United States and Soviet Union in the 1960s – marked a rapid coevolution of government programmes and scientific initiatives whose best-known US institution – the National Aeronautics and Space Administration or NASA – was founded in 1958. Those decades simultaneously saw an explosion of design and illustration activity across multiple media screens and forms, from science-fiction film and television to comic books, children's toys and scale plastic model kits.[6] An imagistic counterpoint to the era's popular-science and SF writing (in particular the work of Isaac Asimov, Arthur C. Clarke and Robert A. Heinlein), this mix of high and low, industrial and popular culture, was knit together by scenes of space and spaceships in which the fanciful contended with the 'factual' in fascinating tension. Disorganised and decentralised in overall structure, yet strictly circumscribed in specific practices, the visual and technological canon of space culture was collectively forged in an arena of circulating and evolving images.

The relationship between this ecology and the reality it purports to describe or forecast has been the subject of several studies. Constance Penley observes that our perceptions of NASA have long been bound up in fantasy: 'We process our knowledge of NASA in a variety of more or less unconscious ways, ranging from simple displacement to outright denial', she writes, going on to note the powerful utopian lure of an always almost-there future. 'A lot of this individual and collective refashioning of NASA's meanings tends to be wish-fulfilling, to produce the NASA we want, not the one we have.'[7] Part of NASA's mission, then, becomes a cultivation of favourable attitudes toward the agency in particular and space exploration in general by associating itself with the popular *Star Trek* franchise, whose fandom was blossoming in the mid-1970s.[8] '*Star Trek* is the theory, NASA the practice', Penley writes, describing the coevolution of the two institutions – one governmental, one cultural – into the 1980s and early 90s.[9]

A deeper, pre-NASA history addresses depictions of outer space as ways of 'dreaming' the future that span centuries, from the epics of Greek and Roman antiquity to the writings of Cyrano de Bergerac, Edgar Allen Poe and Jules Verne.[10] As the Space Age nears in the first half of the twentieth century, however, critical discourse shifts from poetry, fantasy and lyricism to the more modernist vocabulary of design, map and blueprint. Such narratives often enforce a distinction between 'real' and 'imaginary' aspects of their subject even as they assert a mutually determining relationship between the two:

> The history of spaceship design has thus had a dual nature: that of the spaceships of the imagination, and that of the spaceships of reality. Their evolution has not been mutually exclusive; there have been many parallels, overlaps, and cross-breedings.[11]

Another approach stresses the ideological frameworks in which space visualisation took place. In *Space and the American Imagination*, Howard E. McCurdy observes that 1950s 'images and visions' of outer space, whether framed in the nonfiction terms of popular-science publications or the avowed inventions of SF film, television and literature, cohered ideologically despite the variety of their instantiations.

> The spacefaring vision draws upon cultural traditions as forceful as the terrestrial exploration saga and the myth of the frontier. Its allure draws strength from the hope that these traditions will be replayed in a new domain, the realm of outer space. … Space exploration has proved to be one of the most entertaining images of the twentieth century, by definition, holding the interest of its audience and giving pleasure.[12]

The collective imagining of what De Witt Douglas Kilgore terms the 'astrofuturist' vision – with its 'progressive, evolutionist account of physical reality and social history' and its commitment to the liberal tenets of 'individual freedom, equality, and rationality as primary social and political goods'[13] – clearly depended on the production and circulation of images; and histories like McCurdy's and Kilgore's note the importance of science popularisers and science-fiction artists and authors in spreading (and explaining) those images. Yet while individual movies, in particular SF films of the 1950s, appear frequently in histories of space visualisation, their technical and artistic background as special-effects creations has received less attention.

Documentaries of the Near Future: Space on Screen

The earliest films showing space travel, such as the Danish *Himmelskibet* (1918) and the Soviet *Aelita* (1924), envisioned voyages to Mars in airplane-inspired ships and egg-shaped vessels which made little reference to the science of rocketry that was then emerging through the work of theorists and experimenters such as Konstantin Tsiolovsky and Robert H. Goddard. A more rigorous presentation of spaceflight arrived with *Frau im Mond* in 1929. Following up on his 1927 landmark *Metropolis*, director Fritz Lang researched publications on space travel and hired engineer Hermann Oberth and science writer Willy Ley as consultants to ensure scientific accuracy in the film's depictions of spaceflight and the conditions of weightlessness astronauts would experience. The Nazis considered the resulting scenes dangerously realistic, leading the Gestapo to remove Lang's film from distribution and confiscate the miniature rockets used in its production.[14] Brushing up against the reality of German rocket research, the controversy over *Frau im Mond*'s depictions of spaceflight demonstrate the intimate relationship between this area of visual practice and government operations, linked through the pipeline of special-effects design and scientific/military research. (The first V-2 to be launched, in 1942, bore a *Frau im Mond* logo.)[15] Willy Ley, along with Wernher von Braun, emigrated to the US following the end of World War II, and became central figures in space visualisation – Ley through a series of book and journal publications, von Braun as the highly visible face of space design by the US government. But it was within popular film that some of the most prominent conceptions of human space exploration were realised, through the work of Chesley Bonestell.

As one of the most highly paid matte artists of his day, much of Bonestell's work in Hollywood's golden age hid itself in the tradition of 'invisible' special effects. The paintings he executed as a contract player for RKO, Fox and MGM in films such as *The Adventures of Robin Hood* (1938), *The Hunchback of Notre Dame* (1939) and *Only Angels Have Wings* (1939) were mainly 'set extensions'. As his career developed, however, Bonestell's contributions became more technically involved, inviting attention in their own right. The concluding frames of *Rhapsody in Blue* (1945) pull back slowly from a concert pianist, seen in overhead medium close-up, to a viewpoint situated in the clouds. As the pullback continues, Bonestell's artwork becomes increasingly dominant, transitioning from the live-action plate of the musicians to a bird's-eye perspective on the auditorium and finally adding superimposed clouds. The resulting slide along the Z-axis into an increasingly fantastical, semi-animated space is something more than a matte painting: a 'virtual camera' movement *avant la lettre*, anticipating shots such as the opening pullbacks of *Star Trek: First Contact* (1998) and *Fight Club* (1999).

The trend toward integrating Bonestell's art into sequences blurring the lines between captured and created imagery is also evident in a montage in *The Fountainhead* (1949), King Vidor's adaptation of the Ayn Rand novel about the innovative and uncompromising architect Howard Roark, played by Gary Cooper. In a passage dramatising Roark's rise to professional success, architectural drawings dissolve into views of 'finished' houses and buildings that are themselves Bonestell paintings. The montage concludes with a particularly layered assemblage in which live-action actors converse in the foreground with Bonestell artwork of a factory, itself integrated into a background plate with traffic moving in the streets, rear-projected behind them. All of Roark's buildings in *The Fountainhead* were supplied by Bonestell in paintings that did double duty as illusion. First, they had to convince of the physical reality of the imaginary building's presence in a real skyline – stitched into the scene through principles of perspective and lighting, matched to a camera's viewpoint through its interlacing of painted and photographic materials. (Later, match-moving would enable such virtual elements to be tracked into dynamic cameras in long, apparently unbroken takes, but in the heyday of Classical Hollywood matte painting, what was required was more of an embroidery atop a static image.) Second, they had to convince at the level of diegetic truth, that is, they had to pass as plausible products of Roark's genius. Bonestell's work in *The Fountainhead*, which makes us reconsider all of his talents in this light, reflects his training as an architect, where he rendered buildings before they were built, supplying a crucial interstitial stage between design and finished reality.

All of these factors – Bonestell's architectural and drafting skills, his familiarity with the visual storytelling codes of Hollywood, the increasing push of cinematographic technique at the level of the special effect (if not always marked as such) – primed the stage for Bonestell's most lasting impact as a transmedia visualiser of outer space. Bonestell's involvement in space art and the cinematic and televisual elaboration of visions of (American) space presence crossed over into science fiction but rarely left the solar neighbourhood. By supplying artwork that threaded throughout the disparate media of this time, Bonestell provided an integral layer of visualisation and popularisation of the movement. The quartet of films comprising his 'space' work in Hollywood – *Destination Moon* (1950), *When Worlds Collide* (1951), *The War of the Worlds* (1953) and *Conquest of Space* (1955) – covers the tonal gamut of US science-fiction cinema at midcentury, from the high-minded 'space exploration pseudo-documentaries' of *Moon* and *Conquest* to the pulpier spectacles of planetary destruction and alien invasion in *Collide* and *War*.[16] Bridging the four productions was a group of behind-the-scenes figures including producer George Pal, art director Hal Pereira, makeup artist Wally Westmore and 'special photographic effects' cinematographers Irmin Roberts, Gordon Jennings, John P. Fulton and Farciot Edouart. Bonestell's role fell outside existing categories in the Hollywood industrial system; he is credited variously as 'Technical Advisor of Astronomical Art' for *Moon*, 'Technical Advisor' for *Collide* and supplier of 'Astronomical Art' for *War* and *Conquest*. What he brought to the movies, however, was neither precisely artwork nor technical knowledge, but a fusion of the two in special-effects sequences that established the 'reality' of outer space, spaceflight and alien perspectives.

Destination Moon, which Dan North cites as an example of 1950s SF cinema 'inspired by genuine rocket research and concerted efforts to reach and explore outer space … sometimes smuggling in militaristic propaganda', was budgeted at higher levels than its B-movie counterparts and executed at a greater level of sophistication, drawing on special-effects departments and personnel honed by their experience making war films in the 1940s.[17] Making the transition from his matte paintings of the previous decade, Bonestell's contributions to *Moon* continue the 'animation' of his artwork presaged in the montages of *The Fountainhead* but expanded here to long passages of dramatic illustration. The rocketship *Luna* is introduced by a push-in on a physical model – a miniature acknowledged as such within the film – which dissolves on a graphic match to a Bonestell painting of the ship under construction on its launch pad. The next shot moves closer to the launch pad, mating a Bonestell painting to a live-action insert of the crew working at its base; the final shot contains no painted layers, showing only the full-sized lower section of *Luna* built for close-ups. The resulting relay shuttles us between two differently scaled *Luna* mockups by way of process shots combining painted and captured elements – optical manipulations sandwiched between practical 'bread'.

Similar handoffs organise the three effects sequences that occupy the rest of the movie's running time: the *Luna*'s takeoff from Earth, its flight to the Moon and its landing on the lunar surface. The takeoff cuts together live-action footage of the astronauts straining against G-forces on their acceleration couches, shots of the miniature *Luna* gushing flames from its engines and close-ups of portholes into which have been inserted Bonestell paintings of Earth seen from high altitude. As the ship leaves orbit, Bonestell's paintings provide an astronomical clock to measure its journey in cinematic time, Earth shrinking in size while the Moon grows larger. Reversing the sequence's opening, the miniature ship descends into a Bonestell painting of the Moon, while more of his paintings fill the cockpit windows to show the approach of the cratered surface.

If this linkage of shots works to escort us by increments into a specifically Bonestellian outer space, its endpoint – the *Luna* at rest, its passengers opening an airlock midway up the ship's side to gaze out at their surroundings – marks the next logical stage by walking us into the painting itself. Bonestell's panorama of the craggy horizon appears first in a lengthy pan lasting more than a minute – inviting appreciation as a piece of landscape art in its own right – and ends in a tilt downward to the lunar surface. Close-ups before and after establish the shot of the painting as the astronauts' point of view, suturing us into the artificial moonscape like the privileged observers of technological sublimity Scott Bukatman identifies as the addressees of later visual-effects sequences.[18] The astronauts descend from their spaceship to stand on the lunar surface, a full-sized foreground sculpture based on Bonestell's designs with his 200-foot cyclorama providing the moonscape backdrop to the sound stage set.

Author Robert A. Heinlein, who cowrote *Destination Moon*'s screenplay and lent the production his authority as an emerging 'grand master' of science fiction, broke down Bonestell's work on this sequence with a numbered list:

1. A Mount Wilson observatory photograph.
2. Bonestell's tabletop model.
3. A pinhole panorama.
4. A large blowup.
5. A Bonestell oil painting, in his exact detail, about twenty feet long and two feet high, in perspective as seen from the exit of the rocket, one hundred fifteen feet above the lunar surface.
6. A blown-up photograph, about three feet high, of this painting.
7. A scenic painting, about four feet high, based on this photograph and matching the Bonestell colours, but with the perspective geometrically changed to bring the observer down to the lunar floor.
8. A scenic backing, twenty feet high, to go all around a sound stage, based on the one above, but with the perspective distorted to allow for the fact that sound stages are oblong.
9. A floor for the sound stage, curved up to bring the foreground of the scene into correct perspective with the backing.
10. A second backdrop of black velvet and 'stars'.[19]

'The result', Heinlein wrote, 'looks like a Bonestell painting because it *is* a Bonestell painting – in the same sense that a Michelangelo mural is still the work of the master even though a dozen of the master's pupils may have wielded the brushes.'[20] In doing so, he offers a way to understand the peculiar form of authorship that often attends special-effects sequences – and much other Hollywood labour besides – in which a single 'vision' guides the work of multitudes. Chesley Bonestell was not himself a special-effects craftsman or technician but a designer of vistas executed by crew on a sound stage.

Bonestell's interest in astronomy dated back many years – at the age of seventeen he was enraptured by a view of Saturn's rings at Lick Observatory, and at twenty-two he witnessed the 1910 appearance of Halley's Comet[21] – but it was not until the early 1940s that he began to create his pieces of space art. The first work he executed in this vein, 'Saturn as Seen from Titan' (1944), went on to become 'the single most famous space painting ever created'.[22] Showing the ringed planet in crescent against a deep-blue sky framed by craggy, ice-frosted mountains, the painting brought together multiple techniques of rendering and reference, including the calculation of precise visual angles; a command of perspective, colour and composition; and principles of light scattering and refraction. Particularly important to the painting's impression of reality was its dependence on photoreference, for Bonestell first set up a tabletop model with plasticine mountains (it is likely that he also included a model of Saturn), photographed it, then used the resulting image as a foundation to paint over.[23] For Bonestell, 'Saturn as Seen from Titan' marked a fusion of skills developed in Hollywood with the science of optics and discipline of draftsmanship honed through architecture:

> [T]he planets of our Solar System had never been accurately depicted from their satellites, through a definite visual angle. Always before it had been an 'artist's conception' . . . . As my knowledge of the technical side of the motion picture industry broadened I realised I could apply camera angles as used in the motion picture studio to illustrate 'travel' from satellite to satellite, showing Saturn exactly as it would look, and at the same time I could add interest by showing the inner satellites or outer ones on the far side of Saturn, as well as the planet itself in different phases.[24]

The resulting painting and others accomplished through similar techniques

> hit the world of astronomy and science fiction like an atomic bomb. No one had ever before seen such paintings – they looked exactly like snapshots taken by a space-traveling National Geographic photographer. For the first time, renderings of the planets made them look like real places and not mere 'artist's impressions'.[25]

This distinction, between artwork that announces its own illustrative status and artwork posing as photography, is crucial in defining the particular class of imagery produced not only by Bonestell, but matte painters and visual-effects artists more generally. In what would later fall under the rubric of simulation or perceptually realist artifice, the discursive label of 'artwork' is eschewed or deferred, held at bay, until a bracketing moment in the special effect's lifespan. Within the moment of viewing, however, the apparently solid boundary between the real and invented, the scientifically informed and the artistically imaginative, fuses into a pleasurable indeterminism. This uncanniness, which has always been the signature structure of feeling produced by special effects, lubricates the transmedia movement of space art into nonnarrative realms, leveraging the accurate yet artful rendering of outer space as a uniquely boundary-crossing class of imagery.

Bonestell's opening tableaux for *The War of the Worlds* overlaid his trademarks such as Saturn's rings viewed from within the planet's atmosphere with animated elements such as gently moving clouds to present the solar system as seen through the alien eyes of the conquest-driven Martians seeking a new home. Bonestell's contributions also extended to the creation of spacecraft and technology: he designed rocketships such as the Space Ark in *When Worlds Collide* and provided the original version of the *Destination Moon* rocketship.[26] *Conquest of Space* brought to physical life many scenarios out of Bonestell's contributions to a popular 1952–4 *Collier's Magazine* series on humanity's future in space, as well as Willy Ley's book *The Conquest of Space* (1949) – the movie's ostensible source. The commercial and critical failure of *Conquest of Space* put the kibosh on Pal's plans for a sequel to *When Worlds Collide*. But by that point, Disney's 'Man in Space' series had begun to air, with shows broadcast in March 1955, December 1955 and December 1957. The numerous transmedia expansions of 'Man in Space' across comic books, school texts and a recut to run as a theatrical documentary short (for which 'Man in Space' received an Academy Award nomination in 1956) suggest something of the fecundity of Walt Disney's marketing techniques and serve as a testament to the supersaturated environment of outer-space visualisation.[27]

Beyond Bonestell: The Realist Sublime

In the early 1960s, when Stanley Kubrick and Arthur C. Clarke were researching and pre-producing the movie project that would become *2001: A Space Odyssey*, Kubrick's famed perfectionistic impulses and passion for exhaustive research led him to view every science-fiction film he could lay his hands on, but his desire to improve on and outdo earlier special effects led him to the realm of nonnarrative, nonfeature cinema, where he found some of his most important resources. Kubrick was particularly impressed with a Cinerama film called *To the Moon and Beyond* (1964). Both *Universe* (1960) and *To the Moon* were documentary-style shorts employing special effects to portray outer space. From the Los Angeles-based Graphic Films that produced *To the Moon* Kubrick hired Con Pederson, Douglas Trumbull and Richard Yuricich, hoping to draw upon their expertise in shooting outer-space material.[28] As Douglas Trumbull notes:

> Con Pederson and I – Con in particular – had been deeply involved in quite a few NASA projects at Graphic Films ... so we really knew a lot about space hardware and how it worked. We had done a film called *Space in Perspective*, which projected futuristic things that could happen in space – like giant floating hydroponic gardens and guys in little one-man space capsules with mechanical arms. A lot of what we came up with for 2001 grew out of things that we had done previously.[29]

In this sense, the Bonestellian tradition remained very much in play throughout the decades that followed, providing a connection point between the needs of science-fiction cinema storytelling and the educational and scientific realms of visualisation through special effects. If the Cinerama connection suggests a return to the attractions of early cinema, it should not be forgotten that the material within the attraction – its conceptual core – drew in sophisticatedly detailed ways on the store of knowledge and speculation built up over previous decades. The picturing of outer space had a memory and followed precedent, even as it innovated. In certain genres of special effects, content can stay much the same while its rendering, informed by new techniques, increases in sophistication. Just as Bonestell repainted 'Saturn as Seen from Titan' numerous times to get the painting 'right', George Lucas released special editions of the first three *Star Wars* movies (1997) featuring redone special effects, while several different *Star Trek* series 'remastered' their special effects prior to DVD and Blu-ray release. (Was it coincidental that in all of these examples, outer-space imagery received the brunt of the updating?)

The possibilities and visibility of cinematic outer space exploded in the 1970s with the release of *Star Wars*. The pleasurably utopian simplicities of George Lucas's 1977 film have been contrasted to the dark wave of New Hollywood that preceded it, a movement whose science-fiction extensions can clearly be read in the dystopian futuristic visions of *2001: A Space Odyssey* and *Silent Running*. The extraterrestrial threat brought to Earth in *The Andromeda Strain* (1971) and the ecological singularity premised in *Phase IV* (1974) both had their outer-space referents, though little screen time was given over to space imagery specifically – the opening shots of *Phase IV* showing an eclipse recall moments from both *2001* and *Forbidden Planet*. Other dystopias resolutely confined themselves to the Earth's surface and even beneath it: *THX 1138* (1971), *Soylent Green* (1973), *Rollerball* (1975), *A Boy and His Dog* (1975), *Logan's Run* (1976) and *Damnation Alley* (1977). By contrast, *Star Wars* explicitly invoked a 'galaxy far, far away' and featured among its settings a host of planets and moons including Tatooine, Alderaan, Yavin and the Death Star. John Dykstra's Dykstraflex camera was a sophisticated motion-control rig allowing shots to be performed multiple times and, combined with bluescreen travelling mattes, it created a highly dynamic picture of outer space.

The dynamism of this vision and the new fluidity of camera motion are easy to read as a forerunner of the virtual cameras that followed in the digital era, but it is also productive to read them against another history, that of space art and NASA imaging. Space artists such as Bob McCall and Don Davis followed in Bonestell's footsteps, with many contributing work directly to the space programme. NASA's Fine Arts Program was founded in 1962 by James Dean as a means of augmenting the extensive photographic records:

> When a major launch or test flight took place, NASA cameras recorded everything. Yet when we looked at all these photographs something was missing. We were not experiencing the excitement or significance of these events. We came to the conclusion that artists must be asked to help complete this visual record. Machinery can duplicate and preserve the cold facts but the emotional impact of what was going on is within the province of the artist.[30]

While paintings of astronauts suiting up in clean rooms humanised and even sentimentalised the cold facts of engineering, outer-space visualisation also had the advantage of showing vistas and events that scientific instruments – photography – could not for physical reasons portray. Ralph McQuarrie contributed artwork and animations to the CBS broadcast of the Apollo moon landing in July 1969 and, even as Bonestell was collaborating with Clarke on *Beyond Jupiter* (1972), the visualisation of outer space was about to be transformed by two important events, one scientific, the other cinematic.

The Voyager missions launched in August and September 1977 and had close encounters with the planet Jupiter in 1979 and Saturn in 1980. (Later they would encounter Uranus and Neptune in 1986 and 1989 respectively.) The images from the 1970s flybys generated arresting colour images of the distant gas giants, each with its spectacular features such as the Great Red Spot and Saturn's system of rings. Prior to that, the Viking missions had launched in 1975 and landed on Mars in August and September of 1976. The entire decade of the 70s bubbled with American space-exploration activity, in fact, as the Apollo missions continued until 1972 and Skylab orbited the Earth between 1973 and 1979. Even as the Space Shuttle programme, which began in 1981, tamed and limited the actual space-exploration agenda, the 'visioneering' movement continued to map a future in projective, speculative space technologies such as the 'L5' colonies of Gerard K. O'Neill's *The High Frontier* (1976), a book which featured artwork by Bonestell, Don Davis and Rick Guidice. The net result of these manned and unmanned missions was to flood the global media with space imagery that interwove with science-fiction illustration through publications such as *Starlog* (which started publishing in 1976 and ended in 2009), *Future* (1978–81) and *Omni* (1978–95). While all of these were hybrid science/science-fiction publications, at either extreme there were journals such as *Astronomy* and *Popular Science* and *National Geographic*, and in the realm of outright fiction *Heavy Metal* (the American version of France's *Metal Hurlant*, which premiered in 1977).

Arguably, the visual culture of the 1970s drove a certain standardisation of outer-space imagery, informed by scientific data as well as artistic trends – forged collectively by the confluence of film and television entertainment, journalistic coverage of the space programme and traditions of painted and drawn space art in science-fiction publications. The most significant shift in such visualisations, however, occurred during the production of *Star Trek II: The Wrath of Khan* (1982). The script called for a demonstration of the 'Genesis device' – a terraforming tool whose ability to reshape entire worlds held fearsome destructive potential. Industrial Light & Magic's (ILM) fledgling CGI wing, headed by Alvy Ray Smith, turned to digital imaging to generate the brief sequence in which the Genesis device is shown approaching a barren moon, impacting it and transforming its surface into a verdant, living land of oceans and mountainscapes under blue, cloud-studded skies. Drawing on his experience working at the Jet Propulsion Laboratory (JPL) – a federally funded research facility associated with NASA – with computer-graphics pioneer Jim Blinn, Smith envisioned a sequence based on the planetary flyby animations Blinn had created at JPL to illustrate Voyager's encounters with Jupiter and Saturn.[31] Central to Smith's vision was the fluid, unbroken, 'impossible' camera shot characteristic of JPL's space animations, an aesthetic Smith believed would speak to the cinematic eye of ILM's owner:

> [Smith] thought about the way George Lucas seemed to watch a film; he had noticed that Lucas, unlike a mortal moviegoer, paid close attention to camera moves and all the decisions that the director made about the camera.[32]

Committed to the idea that 'the effect they generated needed to have a camera shot in it that no human camera operator could ever have done', Smith worked with Ed Catmull and Jim Veilleux to build fractal mountains and a realistic star field; for the latter, he eventually turned to actual star maps, converting the Yale Bright Star Catalog of 9,100 stellar objects into 3D maps to populate the visible space around the Genesis planet.[33] The resulting shot, which Smith called 'a sixty-second commercial to George Lucas … to show him what he's got',[34] has been enshrined as a milestone in the development of digital imaging in cinema, and a juncture to the world of digital visual effects and the forked path of digital animation that Pixar, then in embryo at ILM, would develop over the next three decades.

Conclusion

Any history of special effects covering the transition from analogue to digital eras risks reiterating the reductive trope that today's special effects are inherently 'better' (as opposed to, say, more numerous, detailed and smoothly integrated) than those of the past. In the case of outer-space special effects, the temptation is multiplied by a quest for 'accuracy' based on current and emerging engineering achievements and up-to-date scientific data. The makers of *Gravity*, for example, describe it less as a story than a painstaking simulation. In the words of Tim Webber, the film's visual-effects supervisor,

> *Gravity* isn't sci-fi … and it's not a space fantasy. It's set a few years into the future, but it features contemporary space technology with a few minor changes. [Director Alfonso Cuarón] wanted it to feel at all times like real space.[35]

As proof of this verisimilitude, coverage of the movie's production emphasised the pipeline through which scientific and engineering information transmuted into convincing imagery: Earth was created as a detailed 'atmospheric rendering based on heights and depths of landmasses, clouds and oceans', the starry backdrop of space drew on a NASA spreadsheet listing the position, colour and intensity of 9,000 stars visible from Earth, and the space shuttle Explorer was digitally generated from 'very high resolution archival images of the orbiters Atlantis and Discovery, as well as blueprints', accurate down to the placement and proportions of 'engines, hinges, doors, thermal coverings and ceramic heat shields'.[36]

Recalling the time of Bonestell reminds us that, in visualising outer space, the realistic and the fanciful have always come together to express a vision whose lure is precisely the promise of a delivered future, as beholden to ideologies of the frontier, the individual and the alien as to cues of perceptual realism and scientific accuracy. Bonestell draws our attention to a deeper tradition of space art that marks the confluence not just of digital and photographic ontologies – concerns of mimesis and simulation – but of the mutually structuring fields of scientific investigation and imaginative speculation and the way in which those areas intersect in the topics of outer space and space exploration. Approaching this field of activity through the lens of special effects enables us to see them as emergent practices of visualisation connected to larger trends in national consciousness and the popular imaginary.

Our cultural image bank of outer space has been mediated by fictional representations of outer space in concert with actual scientific mappings of what is 'really' out there and how we might explore it. Chesley Bonestell's style of painting – or rather, the set of methods his artwork anchored – evoked the overlap between a romanticised and fictionalised conception of human presence in outer space and attempts to capture an objective visualisation of external reality. This play of forces has worked over time to shape our expectations of outer space. For all but a select few, outer space is unattainable, perhaps maddeningly so, and so our representations have filled the gap: everything we see of outer space has come to us through mechanical prostheses of one sort or another, so our representations of outer space speak, perhaps in amplified and concentrated form, to every ambivalence we have about the technological mediation of observable reality.

Notes

1. For an extended discussion of this shot and the other tableaux of *A Trip to the Moon*, see http://drnorth.wordpress.com/2010/06/10/a-trip-to-the-moon-le-voyage-dans-la-lune/.
2. Bob Rehak, 'The Migration of Forms: Bullet Time as Microgenre', *Film Criticism* vol. 32 no. 1 (2007), pp. 26–48.
3. Tom Gunning, 'The Cinema of Attraction: Early Film, Its Spectator, and the Avant-Garde', in Timothy Corrigan and Patricia White with Meta Mazaj (eds), *Critical Visions in Film Theory* (Boston, MA: Bedford/St. Martin's, 2011), pp. 69–76.
4. W. Patrick McCray, *The Visioneers: How a Group of Elite Scientists Pursued Space Colonies, Nanotechnologies, and a Limitless Future* (Princeton, NJ: Princeton University Press, 2013), p. 10.

5. See Samuel H. Vasbinder, 'The Vision of Space: The Artist's View', in Gary Westfahl, George Slusser and Kathleen Church Palmer (eds), *Unearthly Visions: Approaches to Science Fiction and Fantasy Art* (Westport, CT: Greenwood Press, 2002), pp. 67–74; see also Ron Miller, *Space Art: A Starlog Photo Guidebook* (New York: O'Quinn Studios, 1978).
6. See Bob Rehak, 'Materializing Monsters: Aurora Models, Garage Kits and the Object Practices of Horror Fandom', *Journal of Fandom Studies* vol. 1 no. 1 (2012), pp. 27–45; see also S. Mark Young, 'Creating a Sense of Wonder: The Glorious Legacy of Space Opera Toys of the 1950s', in Cynthia J. Miller and A. Bowdoin Van Riper (eds), *1950s 'Rocketman' TV Series and Their Fans* (New York: Palgrave Macmillan, 2012), pp. 149–62.
7. Constance Penley, *NASA/TREK: Popular Science and Sex in America* (London: Verso, 1997), p. 15.
8. Francesca Coppa, 'A Brief History of Media Fandom', in Karen Hellekson and Kristina Busse (eds), *Fan Fiction and Fan Communities in the Age of the Internet* (Jefferson, NC: McFarland & Co., 2006), pp. 41–59.
9. Penley, *NASA/TREK*, pp. 18–19.
10. Frederick I. Ordway III, 'Dreams of Space Travel from Antiquity to Verne,' in Frederick I. Ordway III and Randy Liebermann (eds) *Blueprint for Space: Science Fiction to Science Fact* (Washington, DC: Smithsonian Institution Press, 1992), pp. 35–48.
11. Ron Miller, 'The Spaceship as Icon: Designs from Verne to the Early 1950s', in Ordway and Liebermann, *Blueprint for Space*, p. 49.
12. Howard E. McCurdy, *Space and the American Imagination* (Washington, DC and London: Smithsonian Institution Press, 1997), p. 2.
13. De Witt Douglas Kilgore, *Astrofuturism: Science, Race, and Visions of Utopia in Space* (Philadelphia: University of Pennsylvania Press, 2003), p. 2. See also Sharona Ben-Tov, *The Artificial Paradise: Science Fiction and American Reality* (Ann Arbor: University of Michigan Press, 1995); and John Cheng, *Astounding Wonder: Imagining Science and Science Fiction in Interwar America* (Philadelphia: University of Pennsylvania Press, 2012).
14. Spaceflight in Silent Film, IEEE Global History Network, http://www.ieeeghn.org/wiki/index.php/Spaceflight_in_Silent_Film.
15. Spaceflight in Silent Film.
16. Dan North, *Performing Illusions: Cinema, Special Effects and the Virtual Actor* (London: Wallflower Press, 2008), pp. 106–12.
17. Ibid., p. 107.
18. Scott Bukatman, 'The Artificial Infinite: On Special Effects and the Sublime', in *Matters of Gravity: Special Effects and Supermen in the 20th Century* (Durham, NC: Duke University Press, 2003).
19. Robert A. Heinlein, 'Shooting Destination Moon', in William Johnson (ed.), *Focus on the Science Fiction Film* (Englewood Cliffs, NJ: Prentice-Hall, Inc., 1972), p. 56.
20. Ibid.
21. Ron Miller and Frederick C. Durant III, *The Art of Chesley Bonestell* (London: Paper Tiger, 2001), pp. 13–15.
22. Ibid., p. 42.
23. Ibid.
24. Ibid., p. 41.
25. Ibid., p. 44.

26. Some designs from an earlier version of *Destination Moon* underway in the 1940s, ended up in the 1950 film, including a slightly modified version of Bonestell's ship *Luna* tweaked by art director Ernst Fegté. For more, see 'Sons of Conquest' in Jack Hagery and Jon C. Rogers, *Spaceship Handbook: Rocket and Spacecraft Designs of the 20th Century: Fictional, Factual, and Fantasy* (Livermore, CA: ARA Press, 2006), pp. 194–205.
27. Randy Liebermann, 'The Collier's and Disney Series', in Ordway and Liebermann, *Blueprint for Space*, pp. 135–46. See also J. P. Telotte, 'Animating Space: Disney, Science, and Empowerment', *Science Fiction Studies* vol. 35 (2008), pp. 48–59.
28. Julie Turnock, 'Before Industrial Light and Magic: The Independent Hollywood Special Effects Business, 1968–75', *New Review of Film and Television Studies* vol. 7 no. 2 (June 2009), pp. 143–4.
29. Don Shay and Jody Duncan, '2001: A Time Capsule', *Cinefex* vol. 85 (April 2001), pp. 74–117.
30. 'NASA Fine Arts Program', Facebook page.
31. Michael Rubin, *Droidmaker: George Lucas and the Digital Revolution* (Gainesville, FL: Triad Publishing Co., 2006), pp. 246–7. For technical background, see Jim Blinn, 'Where Am I? What Am I Looking At?', in *Jim Blinn's Corner: A Trip down the Graphics Pipeline* (San Francisco, CA: Morgan Kauffmann Publishers, 1996), pp. 69–82.
32. David A. Price, *The Pixar Touch: The Making of a Company* (New York: Alfred A. Knopf, 2008), p. 39.
33. Rubin, *Droidmaker*, p. 246.
34. Ibid., p. 247.
35. Joe Fordham, 'Extra-Vehicular Activity', *Cinefex* vol. 136 (January 2014), p. 44.
36. Ibid., pp. 51–3.

DESIGNED FOR EVERYONE WHO LOOKS FORWARD TO TOMORROW!

STAR WARS, *CLOSE ENCOUNTERS OF THE THIRD KIND* AND 1970s OPTIMISTIC FUTURISM

JULIE TURNOCK

The special-effects-heavy films of the late 1970s and early 80s, such as *Star Wars* (1977) and *Close Encounters of the Third Kind* (1977), are so familiar to us that we can no longer recognise their strangeness: their hodgepodge, heterogeneous effects techniques, languid immersive sequences and the abstracted representation of mind states are all examples of unusual style and technology that broke with the norms of the time. These kinds of sequences appear at crucial points, such as the jump to light speed in *Star Wars*; the psychedelic light show at the climax of *Close Encounters*; and maybe less familiarly, Spock's exploration of 'V'ger' in *Star Trek: The Motion Picture* (1979) and the entry into the unknown at the end of *The Black Hole* (1979), just to name a few. These special-effects sequences employ the pre-digital techniques of optical printing, rotoscoping, multiplane animation and other methods not to create realistic diegetic spaces, but instead to expand beyond conventional imagery to generate complex, abstract sensations and feelings of mystery, wonder, astonishment and oddity.

If, as Douglas Trumbull, special-effects supervisor on *Close Encounters of the Third Kind* put it, 'It's important to visualize the future for people',[1] then I argue that special-effects production was essential to imagining and picturing a more optimistic future for 1970s moviegoers. Rather than emphasising the nuts-and-bolts technology behind the effects as I do elsewhere, this essay addresses the strong appeal of space and alien-based science fiction in the late 1970s, by exploring popular discourses around science fiction, futurism and technology. Moreover, the special effects in these popular films must be understood as related to popular aesthetic discourses around a more visually impactful, technology-heavy style of popular film-making appropriate to a fast-moving, increasingly technologically savvy society.[2]

While researching a long-term project on 1970s and 80s-era special effects, I bought a great number of vintage film fan magazines on eBay. Included in a large lot with the magazines *Cinefex* and *Cinefantastique* was nearly the entire run of a title I had never encountered before: *Future*, which was published from 1978–81 by the editorial team behind the prominent and long-running science-fiction fan magazine *Starlog*.[3] Like the other magazines started by the *Starlog* Group in the mid to late 1970s, including *Cinemagic* and *Fangoria*, *Future* addressed a readership of science-fiction and fantasy enthusiasts who were curious to explore their favourite films and television shows. Unlike the others, however, *Future* was not just a science-*fiction* magazine. Billing itself as 'The Magazine of Science Adventure', and 'Designed for Everyone Who Looks Forward to Tomorrow!', *Future* included a wider swath of material than the usual fan magazine. Articles from the first several issues included what one might expect from such a publication: an interview with *Close Encounters*' special-effects supervisor Douglas Trumbull; a nostalgia piece on 1950s science-fiction pulp magazines; an interview with *Future Shock* (1970) author Alvin

Toffler. The magazine also covered less predictable territory, such as a critical article about the potential for military presence in space, two pieces on German electronic group Kraftwerk, a multiauthor brainstorming session on the future of gender roles in society (including contributions from women science-fiction writers), African American experimental musician Lenny White's 'audio film' *Adventures of Astral Pirates* (1977) and a defence of gay liberation though the logic of human rights.[4]

What unifies these articles is a surprising combination of the fantastic, hopeful, politically liberal and technophilic. For me – a cinema historian researching the special-effects production and aesthetics of popular 1970s cinema – *Future* opened up an alternative framework for conceptualising the period's trend toward 'space' and 'alien' films thick with special effects typified by *Star Wars* and *Close Encounters*. In the process, the magazine emerged as a site of discourse that brings these films into focus in a broader context, helping to answer the questions: Why science-fiction 'space' movies at this time? And, more specifically, why do so many films of the era end, like *Close Encounters*, with diegetic spectators gaping at a special-effects music and light show? One simple answer is: because they are copying Stanley Kubrick's *2001: A Space Odyssey* (1968). While this explanation may be true up to a point, it allows us to ignore a great deal of cultural, and indeed political, context that made these kinds of films and these kinds of ending sequences so alluring and affecting to audiences.

Future magazine and others like it help us build connections not only to 1970s popular science-fiction film-making and special effects, but also to other techno-optimistic experimental film-making manifestos like Gene Youngblood's 1970 *Expanded Cinema*.[5] With what I will call 'optimistic futurism' in mind, this trend in space and alien films reveals itself as more than simple fantasies of escape from the economic hardships and cultural ambiguities of the 1970s, or proto-Reaganite retreats to conservative politics and Hollywood economic re-entrenchment.[6] While certainly available for conservative readings, these films also tapped into a brief liberal (or perhaps 'liberatory' is a better word) moment that championed the intellectual viability of optimism –a brand of optimism, moreover, that placed technology and imagination in powerful proximity to cultural ethics. And these films did so through visualising alien and future technologies through their ambitious special-effects design and production.

Star Wars and *Close Encounters*, the two giant hits of 1977, are both films that enflame partisan passions. For enthusiasts, these films present worlds of unlimited imagination, enlivened by spectacular technology and fast-paced action. However, in academe and to many established critics, they are more often characterised as marking the demise of mainstream Hollywood's brief period of politically engaged 'adult' and 'sophisticated' film-making, led by directors such as Robert Altman, Hal Ashby, Alan J. Pakula and Sidney Lumet. The charge goes that, instead of addressing their audiences as intelligent adults, providing them with complex, realistic, ambiguous narratives, these later films bypass the intellect, bombarding viewers with spectacular action and cartoonishly simplistic characterisations, infantilising the audience by appealing only to their more basic impulses.[7] Further, instead of making films like *Easy Rider* (1969) or *Klute* (1971) that the discerning studio executives 'would themselves want to see', these films ushered in a mode of 'all things to all people' blockbuster film-making that prioritised formulaic narratives, maximising profit rather than striving for an innovative production.[8] Perhaps most damning to these critics, promising young film-makers such as George Lucas and Steven Spielberg created rapacious entertainment empires of their own, betraying the 1960s rebellious counterculture from which they emerged.[9]

It must be pointed out, however, that these views emerged largely in retrospect, through the lens of post-1980s anti-Reagan polemics. Many respected reviewers at the time gave primarily positive assessments to both *Star Wars* and *Close Encounters*.[10] Too often, we understand these films from a contemporary standpoint of what they begat, rather than within the specific historical context from which they emerged. Reviewers' comments can help tease out the prominent cinematic currents found in these films, which were received as intellectualised plays on genre (developing from popular 'New Hollywood' genre updates as *The Godfather* [1972] and *Chinatown* [1974]) while joining a conversation on the implications of the words 'space' and 'alien' as well as the broader ramifications of science fiction for society at large. Therefore, instead of attempting to rescue these films from either the enthusiasts or the detractors, the goal of this essay is to understand *Star Wars* and *Close Encounters* within the popular rhetorical currents of their time, rather than as byproducts of later political and economic forces or narrative structuring.[11] Whatever their reputations have become, in both cases the films were on the whole well received as representing a fresh new approach to mainstream big-budget film-making, in large part due to their kinetic and spectacular display of 'alien' technology.[12]

It seems indisputable that the blockbusters of 1977 represent a new approach to big-budget Hollywood film-making, diverging both from the traditional studio 'road show' (*Ben-Hur* [1959], *The Sound of Music* [1965]) and the auteur films of New Hollywood. Instead of 'casts of thousands' or gritty naturalism, these films ushered in an era of increasingly elaborate special effects, fantasy and science-fiction subject matter, and open-ended elaborate worlds or environments to explore. With a nod to Youngblood's *Expanded Cinema*, I call this late 1970s approach to mainstream film-making the 'expanded blockbuster'. Strongly inspired by the example of *2001* as well as West Coast experimental film-making such as that of Jordan Belson, John Whitney, Pat O'Neill and others, film-makers like George Lucas sought to make popular films that took advantage of the latest imaging and special-effects technology to create visually dynamic movie spectacles that would appeal to both the senses and the intellect.[13] Elsewhere, I have discussed the expanded blockbuster in terms of the aesthetic history of the crossover between West Coast experimental film-makers and Hollywood, both as labour and inspiration.[14] Here, I will discuss the aspects of these films that sought to create meaning from images in a manner deemed more appropriate to a 'future shocked' society, one accustomed to a fast-paced moving-image culture and its accompanying technologies. Youngblood advocated this approach in *Expanded Cinema*:

> When we say Expanded Cinema, we actually mean expanded consciousness. Expanded Cinema does not mean computer film, video phosphors, atomic light or spherical projections. Expanded Cinema isn't a movie at all: like life, it's a process of becoming, man's on going historical drive to manifest his consciousness outside of his mind, in front of his eyes. ... [an] intermedia network of cinema and television, which now functions as nothing less than the nervous system of mankind.[15]

Although *Star Wars* and *Close Encounters* were presumably too narratively driven for Youngblood's taste, Lucas and Spielberg were successful in marrying these experimental and

UFOs as seen in *Close Encounters of the Third Kind* (1977)

theoretical modes to that of popular entertainment.[16] However, the overwhelming success of the films is rarely attributed to their aesthetic or approach.

A useful sequence to consider is *Close Encounters*' first look at the UFOs. Narratively, this serves as a model for the way many special-effects sequences work, especially in the post-Classical era, where the narrative 'stops' in order for the characters (as audience stand-ins) to gape at the special-effects object.[17] However, in foreshadowing the euphoric climax, it also exemplifies the ways the special-effects object provides a moment of optimistic transcendence by manifesting in the ordinary Indiana setting while remaining independent of it.

The UFOs here behave as if part of the live-action diegesis by strobing out the screen and flaring the lens, as well as maintaining careful lighting consistency on the faces of the actors in the first unit photography. The soft, feathered mattes mean that the edges bleed seamlessly into the night photography as planned.[18] However, the self-contained intensity of the lighting and colours, emphasised by the comparatively weak earthly lights like the police headlights, separate them from the 'main' diegetic area of principal photography. The overall emphasis in the composition within the frame is on the arrangement of lighting, and its pulsating, otherworldly intensity. The smoky atmosphere in which the UFO models were photographed physicalises their glow and lighting effects.[19] By optically printing them into the *mise en scène* with no smoke effects, the UFOs appear to be special, moving microenvironments *within* a 'normal' diegesis. Both the spectators of the film and the characters are gaping at the UFOs as simultaneously beautiful aesthetic objects, spectacular special-effects novelty and stirringly extraterrestrial technology. The special-effects aesthetics suggest that the UFOs are adjacent to our world, yet entice us towards them, as models for new possibilities. Stanley Kauffman recognised the aesthetic allure of the film's special effects in his review of *Close Encounters*:

> Visually, [*Close Encounters of the Third Kind*] is nearly perfect. ... One of the chief attractions of the film form for the Film Generation is, I think, that an art dependent on technology seems the

> most fitting means of expression for an age dominated by technology. ... During [the film's final] forty minutes our technology made us masters of unimaginable cosmic mystery. ... I know that I can go back to that film again and get the feeling again, through technology.[20]

One popular explanation for the late 1970s popularity of *Star Wars* and *Close Encounters* is that audiences had tired of the 'doom and gloom' of late 1960s and early 70s cinema's mistrust of authority, aimless anti-heroes and fatalistic view of the future. Instead, the new films provided hope and optimism for troubled times, or less charitably, rose-coloured glasses to wear while your head was in the sand.[21] What is little remembered about this trend towards optimistic futurism, as articles in *Future* strongly indicate, is the way it also positioned itself as critical and countercultural by brainstorming alternatives to the corrupt and disheartening present that we as a global society could help make happen in the future. Lucas especially – and Spielberg to a degree – saw themselves as participating in an accessible version of countercultural cinema, which they imagined all the more powerful as a vision of popular, not experimental film-making.[22] In contrast to the pessimism of their peers, Lucas and Spielberg embraced the contemporary current of optimistic futurism. For them, presenting a vision of alternative, more hopeful worlds was an important ethical function as well as a motivation for developing special-effects techniques and systems to realise this vision.

Certainly the amorphous (and politically problematic) notions of 'hope' and 'optimism' have long been co-opted for various political purposes.[23] For a while in the 1970s, however, evidence from aesthetic manifestos, popular nonfiction, magazine mastheads, speculative fiction and cinema suggests that optimistic futurism was a viable countercultural and intellectual position. And it is important that this optimistic futurism was strongly based in a hopeful view of technology and media forecasting. It projected a world organised and expanded via networking – a technological field that would combat the post-industrial revolution problems of alienation and atomisation.

Nearly all of the popular futurist publications of the 1970s agreed that technology was pushing humankind toward previously unimagined realms of being, at an unprecedented speed.[24] As this proliferation of imagery across a number of art and entertainment platforms suggests, the tropes of 'space', 'aliens' and 'the future' carried both a hopeful and subversive tinge for countercultural 1970s America that had more to do with a technologised imaginary than any actual space-race politics.

Popular music afforded another context, through David Bowie's persona as a more evolved and idealised alien with Ziggy Stardust (1972), Stevie Wonder singing about a more enlightened life on 'Saturn' (1976) and even the electronic music that promoted a fusion of human and machine in acts such as Devo, the aforementioned Kraftwerk, Gary Numan and the Electric Light Orchestra. The tropes of futurism, space and aliens allowed the consumer the role of self-othering, even if he or she seemed otherwise 'normal' (that is, white, middle class and suburban). While this may read to us now as a form of queer identification (and it arguably was), the popularity of these acts attests to a broader cultural sense of self-alienation. Perhaps the decade's pervasive disillusion with the contemporary earthbound hippie movement meant we would have to look elsewhere for a model of a better society. Identifying with an alien point of view and marking oneself as 'alien' – a being who evolved beyond Earth's petty concerns –

was a way to transcend what seemed unresolvable quagmires of race, gender and sexual orientation. Of course, since these ideas originated on this planet at a particular juncture, it was never wholly possible to escape problematic representation and structures, as both *Star Wars* and *Close Encounters* make clear.[25] However, it remained an expressed ideal.[26]

In contrast to the 1980s highly pessimistic framing of technology in the popular imagination (as in, for example, *Blade Runner* [1982] and *Robocop* [1987]), it is important that optimistic futurism forecast an idealistic view of a new kind of technology. As commentators such as Toffler pointed out, the new technology, with its emphasis on networks and synthesis, would have the potential to avoid the alienating, mass-produced and monetised technology associated with the industrial revolution.[27] Instead, it would connect people on a more profound level, which would be essential in coping with the coming problems of overpopulation and energy and other resource shortage. For Toffler, technology would achieve this on a fairly quotidian, prosaic level. Improved and more extensive communication technology would, it was hoped, lead to better interpersonal understanding. For others, like Youngblood, technology would work together with psychotropic drugs and 'Eastern' meditative states to expand our senses and minds to almost literally merge with those of others. A late 1970s reimagined notion of technologised psychedelia plays an important role as well. Far from just 'blissing us out' on individualistic mind expansion on a personal level, psychotropic drugs, along with media sounds and images, would generate a kind of technologically mediated telepathy. While by the late 1970s, this liberalised view of psychotropic drugs had long passed its late 60s heyday, the mind-expanding potential of technology (sometimes augmented by drug use) held on in the imagination – as we can see in films such as *Brainstorm* (1983), *Altered States* (1980) and even *Tron* (1982), in which 'trippy' special-effects sequences with lurid colors, vortex effects, distorted or phosphorescent shapes, porous character edges, and/or disjointed editing help visualise the technologically augmented mind-states of the characters.

Many theorists of the emerging media topography of the 1960s and 70s probed the social and cultural changes that technological mediation would bring. Prominent voices of what eventually became known as the postmodern, such as Marshall McLuhan and Fredric Jameson, described the emerging abstracted relationship between the human physis and the 'world' as experienced directly. While they and other theorists characterised this 'post'modern phenomenon ambivalently at best and terrifyingly at worst, popular strands of optimistic futurism cast these trends in a more positive light, welcoming freedom from the limitations of individual consciousness. Freeing oneself from the limitations of one's physical body was a powerful fantasy inherent in psychedelia and Eastern-inflected spiritualism including yoga and meditation, which promised merging with others via technological mediation through shared sensations instigated by shared aesthetic experiences.

In the rhetoric of the era, the film-maker emerged as the primary conductor for marshalling these various forces into a popularly accessible form. If Stanley Kauffmann deemed technologised art the most fitting expression for a technologically dominated age, Youngblood agreed that cinema's harnessing of sound and vision to impact the sensorium invested it with major potential for a new kind of art.[28] An artist, most ideally a film-maker or what we might consider a video-installation artist, was now a 'design scientist' who would create 'great films not great for their plots or stories but for their design'.[29] Youngblood went on to observe,

> The artist does not point out new facts so much as he creates a new language of conceptual design information with which we arrive at a new and more complete understanding of old facts, thus expanding our control over the interior and exterior environments.[30]

On a popular psychology level, Toffler and others like architect and futurist John McHale believed that it was the artists who had a vital role in softening the impact of the future, via metaphor.[31] Like Youngblood, however, Toffler believed that the softening process was not primarily about numbing or even acclimatisation, but instead about enhancing and maximising the potential for experiential receptivity.

With this receptivity in mind, many members of the 'Film Generation' and experimental film-makers shared a commitment to collapsing the long-held hierarchy within aesthetic judgment favouring art that stimulates the mind over art that stimulates the senses. They sought not to invert the value system, but to balance it. For film-makers like Lucas and Spielberg, this meant a commitment to developing spectacular special-effects imaging technology. In interviews, both directors held up *2001: A Space Odyssey* as the ultimate in technologised spectacle that was also thrillingly thought-provoking.[32] Moreover, it was exactly the spectacle of technological achievement that provoked the intellectual response. However, the slow pace of Kubrick's realistic renderings (spaceships docking with one another) and abstract display (the Star Gate sequence at the end) represented a model *not* of the expanded blockbuster, but rather the expanded *art house* feature. In interviews, Lucas strongly implied that *Star Wars* would be like *2001*, but faster paced and less tedious.[33]

We can see an example of what Lucas meant by the fast-paced effects in the famous jump to light speed in *Star Wars*. As they had in many of its sequences, *Star Wars* special-effects technicians created a wholly artificial space and sense of movement, combining techniques of motion-control spaceship movements, high-speed photography, rotoscoped laser blasts, multiplane animation elements and bluescreen composites. The jump to light speed combines hand animation, bluescreen and foreground live-action photography. The effect is strongly reminiscent of the West Coast experimental animation of Jordan Belson and the Whitney Brothers as the neon-like beams and points of light produce the feeling of rapid acceleration into depth.[34] As Han Solo (Harrison Ford) eases a lever forward and a humming builds, moving points multiply within the picture plane and then streak towards an illusionistic vanishing point. The animation dynamises the overall composition by mobilising the eye, as do the strobing of the frame and the vibrating darting rays. By this approach, the viewer feels simultaneously bounced about with jolts of light and colour, and pulled bodily into the swift current of hyperspace. And rather than unpleasantly jostled and disoriented, the viewer is meant to experience the glee of bodily stimulation and then the exhilaration of bodily transcendence. And importantly, the viewer undergoes it together with the rest of the audience and the characters.

Indeed, acceleration was Toffler's hook in *Future Shock*, which explored the commonly held idea that technology and civilisation were transforming at an unprecedented pace that humans could not keep up with. As Youngblood put it, with imagery derived from *2001*, we as a society were at 'the Dawn of Man, in transition from the industrial age to the cybernetic age',[35] and

The jump to light speed in *Star Wars* (1977); Jordan Belson's *Allures* (1961)

new imaging technology that emphasises 'synaesthetics and kinaesthetics' would enable this transition.[36]

In an interview five years previously for his then upcoming directorial debut *Silent Running* (1972), *Close Encounters*' special-effects supervisor Douglas Trumbull contributed his own version of optimistic futurism:

> [*Silent Running* is] also about man's relationship to machinery and technology. ... I have a point of view that doesn't look at them in any fear. ... They're always treated as malevolent factors in movies, but we get into very pleasant man-machine relationships.[37]

And even more pointedly, 'I'm future-oriented … . I like the ideas of Toffler's 'Future Shock'.[38] Trumbull's technological futurism was primarily concerned with the brain's capacity to process information: 'The audience today can consume novelty at a fantastic rate and can receive change and be involved in it faster than motion pictures can keep up with them – at least their present state.'[39]

In fact, after his work on *Close Encounters*, Trumbull spent the next several decades developing a high-frame rate camera and projection system, Showscan, that was meant to foment a revolution in cinema exhibition by, as he put it, taking advantage of the brain's ability to absorb large amounts of visual information.[40]

The emergence of a special-effects-intensive cinema alongside a trend toward optimistic futurism cannot be seen as a coincidence. Technophilia and positive associations with technological 'progress' fuelled much of the parallel formation, following the artistic manifestos of writers and artists like Youngblood and Whitney. They believed that the fusion of art and technology would lead to a new plane of sensual experience, and that these experiences should be collective and intellectual. Special effects ended up developing in the direction of more straightforward photorealism through the 1980s. However, late-1970s effects tended to emulate *2001*'s model of expressive sensuality, encouraging what Scott Bukatman calls 'kaleidoscopic perception', or the perceptual unmooring of the body through aesthetic manipulation.[41]

This fusion of psychopharmacology, yogic states and imaging technology as a way past our current problems is of course a fantasy, but a powerful cultural one in the 1970s and into the early 80s. When George Lucas says things like, 'corny as it sounds, the power of positive thinking goes a long way' and 'I discovered making a positive film is exhilarating',[42] it is important to note that it he is not simply expressing naive optimism, but a cultural trend that links science-fiction narratives, fantastic imagery, special effects and imaging technologies in an ethical commitment to finding alternative ways of viewing the world.[43] And in the case of both Lucas and Spielberg in the 1970s, conceiving and developing special-effects technology fit into this ethos. For them, world building did not just mean art directing and set building to enable actors to present a narrative. It meant imagining whole new worlds and ways of being in those worlds, and populating them with life forms that made us see our own humanity differently. This has long been the *raison d'être* of literary science fiction, but film-makers of the 1970s believed that this message would hit home much more powerfully if people could visually experience it. Film-makers went to considerable trouble to develop complex special-effects technology and foreground it in these films in large part to realise a worldview and an environment enabling audiences to see the world's multivalent alternatives.

Of course, it must also be pointed out that this impulse was neither wholly altruistic nor naively conceived. The kind of special-effects-heavy, world-building film-making instigated by *Star Wars* and *Close Encounters* thrived because it also fit snugly into changing Hollywood economics that encouraged sequelisation, ancillary products and accessible, eye-popping spectacle. However, it should also be emphasised that these films were not initially understood as easily monetised commodities by Hollywood, and that it took the success of these films to win this acceptance.[44] Though counterintuitive, the money-making aspect of the expanded blockbuster was an important part of its formula. In the Hollywood economic logic of success, the film-makers needed their films to make a great deal of money to give them the clout to realise their personal film-making freedom. The expanded blockbuster drew on existing positive, hopeful and optimistic associations with space and alien life in order to hook into those aspects of expanded cinema and optimistic futurism that would elicit the response Stanley Kauffman noted at his screening of *Close Encounters*, quoting a fellow moviegoer who walked out of the screening proclaiming, 'I feel good, man.'[45]

Rather than feeling good primarily because the hero vanquished his enemies and the hero and heroine ended in a passionate clinch – the traditional Hollywood 'feelgood' ending – the films I have discussed here made use of the triggers associated with drug taking and sensory expansion to promote a sense of potential alternative universes. Certainly narrative outcomes are rosy there as well: Luke Skywalker (Mark Hamill) and his rebel pals win a tentative victory over the Empire, and Roy Neary (Richard Dreyfus) leaves his Earthbound problems for a journey of wonder and discovery. But *Close Encounters'* musical light show, punctuated by luminescent neon spaceships 'in the disco style',[46] as Vincent Canby put it, takes thirty or so minutes to end the film with an unmistakable hopefulness and feeling of well-being, with its lively melodic tones, radiant soft lights washing over the auditorium and wondrous shining spaceships pulsating in time to the music. More conventionally, *Star Wars*' protracted feelgood ending is also a technological spectacle. Narratively, Luke and his fighter-pilot brethren must make an especially precise hit on the Death Star to exploit a weakness and destroy it. Although patterned after a World War II dogfight, the sequence's reliance on special effects and editing is surprisingly abstracted. Shots that alternate from Luke's face, to his point of view down the narrow canyons, to ships zipping by and sideswiping him, punctuated by the flashing of laser blasts and strobing colourful explosions, all generate exhilarating, fast-paced kineticism.

A retrospective look at *Star Wars* and *Close Encounters* must necessarily occur through the historical lens of 1980s conservative politics. The fact that these films were prototypes of the special-effects-heavy Hollywood blockbuster that is so often politically allied with the business-friendly 1980s has not helped their political reputation. And perhaps they cannot be entirely absolved of their affinity for conservative embrace. But it is also worth remembering that the 1980s conservative rhetoric of 'optimistic futurism' was quite different from the trend that was co-opted.[47] The Reaganite technological imagination was in awe of technology, but it emphasised technology's destructive possibilities rather than its liberatory or connective potential. In other words, Reaganite views of the world would have us fear technology, and furthermore fear the political realities that produced these potentially destructive devices (the so-called 'Star Wars' weapon system is a primary example). It serves up Cold War American exceptionalism and nostalgia for golden age American individualism, rather than the more liberal version's technologies that aid intersubjective and immersive communication. It is primarily through the distorting lens of 1980s politics and criticism of it that *Star Wars* and *Close Encounters* are so easy to misconstrue today. However, optimistic futurism within the context of the expanded blockbuster provides these and other late 1970s films with a more nuanced framework for analysis.

In the 1970s, it was not unusual for special effects to be considered an important and innovative form of artistic expression, and for artists like Douglas Trumbull to be proclaimed as media prophets. For a while, special-effects artists were trumpeted in publications like *Future* and others as fulfilling the important social role of visualising the future and presenting alternative ways of seeing the world. Although often dismissed as cheaply sensational or politically retrograde, the expanded blockbusters of the 1970s sought to visually penetrate the human sensorium and instil complex sensations within their kinetic and eye-catching effects sequences.

Special thanks for help with this essay go to Andrew Johnston, Scott Richmond, Alison Whitney, Bob Rehak and Jonathan Knipp.

Notes

1. Kevin Thomas, 'Technology's Impact on Society Woven into *Silent Running*', *Los Angeles Times*, 14 March 1971.
2. Julie Turnock, *Plastic Reality: Special Effects, Technology, and the Emergence of 1970s Blockbuster Aesthetics* (New York: Columbia University Press, 2015).
3. In March 1979 *Future* was retitled *Future Life*. *Starlog* had a strong emphasis, as the title suggests, on *Star Trek* fandom.
4. On military plans for space: Stella Morris, 'War in Space', *Future Life* no. 10 (1979), p. 23; on Kraftwerk: 'Germany's Music Marches On', *Future* no. 5 (1978), pp. 14–15; on Lenny White: Charles Bogle, 'SF Graphics', *Future* no. 3 (1978), pp. 59–61; on gender roles: 'Future Forum: Do You See a Continuation of Traditional Sex Roles during the Next Fifty Years?', *Future Life* no. 9 (1979), p. 50; on gay rights: David Gerrold, 'Sen. Briggs vs. SF Fandom', *Future* no. 6 (1978), pp. 32–3.
5. I would also include John Whitney's *Digital Harmony* (Peterborough, NH: Byte Books/McGraw Hill, 1980), which combines technology and music theory, how-to computer-graphics instructions and collected interviews, as part of a similar theoretical movement.
6. Perhaps most influentially argued by Robin Wood in *Hollywood from Vietnam to Reagan* (New York: Columbia University Press, 1986), pp. 162–88.
7. See also Peter Biskind's *Easy Riders, Raging Bulls* (New York: Simon & Schuster, 1999), especially the chapter 'Star Bucks', pp. 316–45. Will Brooker provides a thorough roundup of *Star Wars'* academic neglect and dismissal in *Star Wars* (London: BFI/Palgrave Macmillan, 2009), pp. 8–9.
8. A nostalgic position expressed recently by former Paramount executive Peter Bart in *Variety*, 'Hollywood Loses Its Zeal for the Real', 4 June 2011; 'H'wood Combats Franchise Fatigue', 12 March 2011. Further, for discussion of the use of the term 'New Hollywood', the 'Film Generation' and other terminology such as American auteurs, American New Wave directors, see Thomas Elsaesser, Alexander Horwath and Noel King (eds), *The Last Great American Picture Show* (Amsterdam: University of Amsterdam Press, 2004), especially the three introductory essays by the editors. See also Thomas Schatz, 'The New Hollywood', in Jim Collins, Hilary Radner and Ava Preacher Collins (eds), *Film Theory Goes to the Movies* (London: Routledge, 1993), pp. 8–36.
9. For an elaborated articulation of this position, see Michael Pye and Lynda Myles, *The Movie Brats: How the Film Generation Took over Hollywood* (New York: Holt, Rinehart, and Winston, 1979).
10. See reviews, for example, by Vincent Canby, 'Star Wars', *New York Times*, 26 May 1977 and 'Close Encounters of the Third Kind', *New York Times*, 17 November 1977; A. D. Murphy, 'Star Wars', *Daily Variety*, 19 May 1977 and 'Close Encounters of the Third Kind', *Daily Variety*, 8 November 1977; Roger Ebert, 'Star Wars', *Chicago Sun-Times*, 27 May and 'Close Encounters of the Third Kind',

Chicago Sun-Times, 14 December 1977; and Gene Siskel, 'Star Wars', *Chicago Tribune*, 27 May 1977 and 'Close Encounters of the Third Kind', *Chicago Tribune*, 14 December 1977.

11. Generally, these historical issues have been discussed in terms of economics, such as in Schatz, 'The New Hollywood' and Richard Maltby, *Hollywood Cinema: An Introduction* (Oxford: Blackwell, 1995); and '"Nobody Knows Everything": Post-Classical Historiographies and Consolidated Entertainment', in Steve Neale and Murray Smith (eds), *Contemporary Hollywood Cinema* (London: Routledge, 1998) or in terms of narrative structuring and patterning, most influentially by David Bordwell, Janet Staiger and Kristin Thompson, *The Classical Hollywood Cinema: Film Style and Mode of Production to 1960* (New York: Columbia University Press, 1985) and David Bordwell, *The Way Hollywood Tells It* (Berkeley: University of California Press, 2006).
12. See note 10.
13. See Turnock, *Plastic Reality*.
14. Ibid.
15. Gene Youngblood, *Expanded Cinema* (New York: E. P. Dutton and Co., 1970), p. 33.
16. Youngblood, for his part, admired *2001*, but found it unnecessarily 'anti-technology', and bogged down by 'melodrama' (ibid., pp. 59, 151). Youngblood did not think popular film-making as it existed in the late 1960s and early 70s a likely vehicle for the kind of transcendence he proposed. He explicitly criticised 'counterculture' films such as *Easy Rider* and *Bonnie and Clyde* (1967) as too invested in old narrative patterns and programmed responses (ibid., p. 59).
17. As described variously, by Warren Buckland, 'Between Science Fact and Science Fiction: Spielberg's Digital Dinosaurs, Possible Worlds and the New Aesthetic Realism', in Sean Redmond (ed.), *Liquid Metal: The Science Fiction Film Reader* (London: Wallflower Press, 2004); Brooks Landon, *The Aesthetics of Ambivalence: Rethinking the Science Fiction Film in the Age of Electronic (Re)Production* (Westport, CT and London: Greenwood Press, 1992); Michele Pierson, *Special Effects: Still in Search of Wonder* (New York: Columbia University Press, 2002) and Albert LaValley, 'Traditions of Trickery', in George S. Slusser and Eric. S. Rabkin (eds), *Shadows of the Magic Lamp: Fantasy and Science Fiction in Film* (Carbondale: Southern Illinois University Press, 1985). Certainly, the sequence is constructed around looking, where Roy (Richard Dreyfus) serves as the primary point of action, with some attention given to the experience's impact on Jillian (Melinda Dillon) and her son Barry (Cary Guffey). The sequence is bookended by characters looking towards the UFOs, their faces illuminated by light. However, even the narrative function of the special-effects object is not so straightforward. The narrative of the film as a whole is structured around looking, being amazed and having (naive) faith in what you see. In this way, the first look at the UFOs far from 'stops' the narrative. The stopping, looking, gaping of the characters is well within their narrative trajectory.
18. Douglas Trumbull, 'Creating the Photographic Special Effects for CLOSE ENCOUNTERS OF THE THIRD KIND', *American Cinematographer*, January 1979, p. 75.
19. Ibid.
20. Stanley Kauffman, 'Epiphany: *Close Encounters* Review', *New Republic*, 10 December 1977.
21. Furthered by Biskind, *Easy Riders, Raging Bulls* and Pye and Myles, *The Movie Brats* and David Cook, *History of the American Cinema: Lost Illusions, 1970–79* (Berkeley: University of California Press, 2000), among others.
22. Lucas's close partnership with Coppola's 'alternative movie studio/hippie commune' concept American Zoetrope in the early 1970s is evidence of this, as are his experimental student films.

Spielberg's involvement was more tangential, through personal friendships with Lucas, Coppola, de Palma and others associated with New Hollywood.

23. The Frankfurt School theorists, especially Theodor Adorno and Walter Benjamin, have most influentially formulated fear of reification in political rhetoric.
24. Not surprisingly, several prophets of technology appeared in the media they were helping to describe and to a degree, create. Some commented in a popular register, like Ray Bradbury, others more academically, like Marshall McLuhan; all became quote machines on the role of the 'new media'. Alvin Toffler's *Future Shock* (New York: Bantam, 1970) was on the *New York Times* bestseller list by October 1970 ('General List', 11 October 1970), and stayed there for at least two years. Marshall McLuhan's *Understanding Media* and *The Medium Is the Message* appeared regularly on the *New York Times* bestseller lists as well through the late 1960s (*New York Times*, 2 October 1966 and 4 July 1967). Other book sensations like Scottish Pop artist and architect John McHale's *The Future of the Future* (New York: George Braziller, 1969) explored the future of the lived environment.
25. Problematic representation in *Star Wars* could start with the unshaded Proppian fairy-tale adventure structure, with the princess as an object to be rescued and won and the associated Manichean worldview. Moreover, the majority of nonhuman aliens are represented as villains, foes or dangers to the humans. In *Close Encounters*, Roy Neary's nagging wife and bratty kids are encumbrances from which he must escape to depart on his adventure, and huge crowds of non-Western (such as Indian) people react to the presence of alien life as stereotypical naive idol worshippers out of an 'exotic locale' 1930s Hollywood movie.
26. *Future* magazine, for example, used the rubric of futurism to explore a number of controversial issues for a readership they assumed would at the very least entertain contrarian or alternative ways of looking at social problems.
27. Toffler, *Future Shock*, p. 25.
28. This will remind many readers of Benjamin's notion of cinema's potential for new, modern kinds of impact on the human sensorium. However, Benjamin posits this impact as an unconscious byproduct of cinema as an instrument of modernity, that is, that cinema is unconsciously imitating, replicating and thematising the aesthetic of industrialisation. However, for Youngblood and others, the impact on the sensorium should be purposefully and explicitly designed for various kinds of sensory impact. See Walter Benjamin, 'The Work of Art in the Age of Its Technological Reproducibility', in Michael Jannings (ed.), *Walter Benjamin: Selected Writings Volume 3, 1935–1938* (Cambridge, MA: Harvard University Press, 2002), pp. 101–33.
29. Youngblood, *Expanded Cinema*, p. 70.
30. Ibid., p. 71.
31. 'The Future and the Functions of Art: A Conversation between Alvin Toffler and John McHale', *Artnews*, February 1973. For Toffler, 'future shock' was a disease, a 'real sickness' that many suffer from, and many people needed these mediated technologised experiences to cope with the too-rapidly changing experiential field (Toffler, *Future Shock*, p. 2).
32. See interviews in Lester D. Friedman and Brent Notbohn (eds), *Steven Spielberg: Interviews* (Jackson: University of Mississippi Press, 2000); and Sally Kline (ed.), *George Lucas: Interviews* (Jackson: University of Mississippi Press, 1999).
33. Kline, *George Lucas,* p. 50.

34. In films such as Belson's *Allures* (1961) or *Samadhi* (1967) or John Whitney's *Permutations* (1968) and James Whitney's *Lapis* (1966), as discussed more thoroughly in Turnock, *Plastic Reality*.
35. Youngblood, *Expanded Cinema*, p. 41.
36. Ibid., p. 97.
37. Kevin Thomas, 'Technology's Impact on Society Woven into *Silent Running*'.
38. Ibid.
39. Ibid.
40. For more on Trumbull's Showscan, and Peter Jackson and James Cameron's recent experiments with HFR film-making, see Turnock 'Removing the Pane of Glass: *The Hobbit*, 3D High Frame Rate Filmmaking, and the Rhetoric of Cinematic Realism', *Film Criticism*, Spring/Summer 2013, pp. 30–59.
41. Scott Bukatman, 'The Ultimate Trip: Special Effects and Kaleidoscopic Perception', in *Matters of Gravity: Special Effects and Supermen in the 20th Century* (Durham, NC: Duke University Press, 2003), pp. 111–30. See also Scott C. Richmond, 'Resonant Perception: Cinema, Phenomenology, and the Illusion of Bodily Movement' (PhD Dissertation, University of Chicago, 2010). Annette Michelson has influentially understood *2001* in terms of modernist aesthetics thematising cinematic space. Certainly in terms of *Star Wars* and *Close Encounters*, 'modernist' is not the most appropriate descriptor. The term modernist implies a rational engagement through an intellectual 'working through', rather than emphasising the sensations of the experiential. It was the sensational and experiential aspect that special effects exploited in popular film-making. See Annette Michelson, 'Bodies in Space: Film as "Carnal Knowledge"', *Artforum* vol. 8 no. 6 (1969), pp. 54–63.
42. Kline, *George Lucas*, pp. 121, 149.
43. Ibid.
44. See Pye and Myles, *The Movie Brats*.
45. Kauffman, 'Close Encounters review'.
46. Canby, 'Close Encounters review'.
47. Certainly, the political profile of futurism has changed as well. It is interesting to note that the face of futurism has become Newt Gingrich, who frequently calls himself a 'conservative futurist', citing Toffler. However, rather than advocating education and familiarisation with technology to ease the shock, as Toffler does, Gingrich exploits the anxieties associated with technology as a scare tactic. See Paul Gray and Karen Tumulty, 'Inside the Minds of Gingrich's Gurus', *Time Magazine*, 23 January 1995.

THE RIGHT STUFF?
HANDMADE SPECIAL EFFECTS IN COMMERCIAL AND INDUSTRIAL FILM

GREGORY ZINMAN

In 1983, Jordan Belson undertook a job requiring him to construct film sequences that brought together various formal and thematic motifs from his thirty-five-year career as an independent artisanal film-maker. Working with the purposefully rudimentary apparatus of his optical bench – a 'plywood frame around an old X-ray stand with rotating tables, variable speed motors, and variable intensity lights'[1] – Belson built upon the techniques with which he had conjured the shimmering starfields of his *Allures* (1961), the celestial terrascapes featured in *Samadhi* (1967) and the flickering particles of *Light* (1973). Yet this particular film was not intended to be another short contemplative work steeped in the director's hallucinatory drug experiences or Eastern religious practices, nor was it another grant-financed exploration of filmic materials and inner consciousness. Instead, it was a big-budget studio production: *The Right Stuff*, Philip Kaufman's adaptation of Tom Wolfe's account of the origins of the US space programme. Already familiar with Belson's cosmic cinema, Kaufman wanted the avant-garde film-maker to lend his unique sensibilities to creating special effects for the film. Belson shot over 20,000 feet of film for *The Right Stuff* – enough for an entire feature – of which roughly three minutes were shown in the finished work.[2] 'Jordan is a true artist', said Kaufman at the time, 'His studio is like a monastery for film creation. Very few people are ever allowed inside . . . . From there, he creates skies and universes and strange light effects, using his own techniques.'[3]

But what happens when others are 'allowed inside' a deeply personal practice so different in scale and intention from commercial or industrial film-making? That is to say, if the means and ends of artisanal avant-garde film production – as practised by Jordan Belson, Len Lye and John Whitney, Sr – are usually pitted ideologically against those of conventional, commercial film productions, how are we to best understand their intersection? And why do 'handmade' effects, such as those seen alongside their digital counterparts in *The Fountain* (2006) and *The Tree of Life* (2011), persist in the contemporary film-making landscape?

Part of the answer lies in the fact that handmade film processes are steeped in the materiality of their making. By my use of the term 'handmade', I intend to denote the artisanal development and deployment of innovative cinematic techniques designed to create new modalities of vision and new ways of seeing. As I have argued elsewhere, handmade films, which reject cinema's putative indexical relation to reality in favour of abstract form, otherworldly colour, textural richness and sensory depth, function as ideal objects with which to challenge – and subsequently, to reshape – our definition of what constitutes the moving image.[4] In this context, handmade moving images also become ideal subjects to consider under the rubric of special effects: images that similarly bend, extend, or eradicate the limits of the cinematic real. When used as special effects in commercial or industrial film-making, handmade moving images are often employed as markers of the cosmic, the mystical and the inexpressible. At the same time, they are also chosen and valourised for their tactility, as well as for their ineluctable relation to the real that manifests in both aleatory movement and a play of light that cannot yet be replicated by computer-generated imagery. In other words, handmade effects impart a sense of the cinematic real not by virtue of their indexicality, but instead through something closer to Gilles Deleuze's concept of sensation – that which addresses both the viewing subject and the unfolding event while functioning as both a becoming and a happening. Emerging from his consideration of Francis Bacon's paintings, Deleuze's concept of sensation is dependent upon a degree of abstraction, in which an overtly literal or familiar representation draws a viewer's eye too quickly to recognition. This condition of familiarity, when the represented object or experience is immediately identified, understood and processed, softens the possibility for bodily or perceptual shock and diminishes the sensation.[5] The handmade moving-image effect operates in a similar fashion, its strangeness registering as something beyond a film's narrative, and even beyond language – an opening up of perceptual experience.

Such sensations are not produced by happenstance: handmade effects are also, necessarily, linked to the notion of craft, or the way of making things. The word 'craft' connotes a qualitative valence, a level of skill with respect to the tools and materials at hand – the 'well-made-ness' of an object. Here I endorse Alison Pearlman's definition of craft as 'the kind of artistic approach that requires an artist to develop, over time, attention to and respect for a material other than his or her ego, an empathy with another matter's distinct properties, laws, or conventions'.[6] Heidegger's conception of *techné*, not as a 'practical performance' of skill but instead as a 'mode of knowing', also provides a useful heuristic for this approach to moving-image production.[7] It is this 'mode of knowing' that allows the handmade image to act, in Heideggerian terms, as a 'bringing-forth', something that reveals the previously concealed – the cosmic, a glimpse of infinity, or the unutterable. Finally, the rubric of craft helps situate artisanal cinema as an oppositional practice. As James Plaut observes: 'The hand-produced object is different from the industrial product, differently conceived, differently made, differently used.'[8] Constructed with small budgets and preoccupied with formal innovation and abstract imagery, handmade film practices carry economic and even political valences with respect to mainstream film production.

However, when repurposed for commercial and industrial use, whether for a desired aesthetic effect, for cost considerations, for lending a patina of avant-garde credibility to a commercial production or out of genuine enthusiasm and appreciation of a practitioner's work, handmade film-making techniques demonstrate how the avant-garde can operate in a variety of filmic registers and to diverse effects. Belson himself registered this negative view of work for mainstream productions: 'Many fine artists and technicians are doomed to work only on commercial projects that someone else wants, which is not the same thing as producing works of art on your own.'[9] But even if commercial film-making is emphatically 'not the same thing' as artisanal cinema, the question remains as to why so many independent, handmade film-makers would choose to join commercial productions. Some may reason that the promise of increased exposure might balance out the loss of autonomy; others may believe that a change in the mode of production might result in technical and artistic breakthroughs; while still others may suppose they simply do it for the money. These are all possible arguments and outcomes stemming from the linkage of the handmade with the commercial or industrial. An examination of how the work of Belson, Lye, Whitney, Chris and Peter Parks and others have operated in a mainstream setting reveals how craft-based, artisanal film practices indeed transform mainstream cinema – particularly our conception of special effects – and further refine the methods of their practitioners, even as the recontextualised settings of the work threaten to misrepresent or obfuscate its avant-garde origins and meanings.

The use of handmade techniques in commercial and industrial film thus complicates art historian Thomas Crow's oft-repeated assertion that 'the avant-garde serves as a kind of research and development arm of the culture industry'.[10] While it is certainly the case that avant-garde approaches may help develop the overall craft of film-making on a variety of production scales, the appearance of handmade techniques in industrial cinema has also furthered the cause of the avant-garde itself, all while opening up the possibilities of experimental film-makers developing new kinds of special effects. Consider, for example, Len Lye's 1935 film, *A Colour Box*, a startling four-minute work generally regarded as the first widely seen example of direct animation.[11] Lye created *A Colour Box* by eschewing photographic mediation in favour of painting directly on clear celluloid, his geometric patterns – triangles, circles, wavy lines – and vibrant colour fields providing accompaniment and counterpoint to 'La Belle Creole', a beguine by Don Baretto and his Cuban Orchestra.[12] Though he had experimented with scratch films a decade earlier, Lye's subsequent experiences working in traditional frame-by-frame animation had proven frustrating and difficult to fund. Lye was so poor that he could not afford a camera or lights. He brought a sample of his direct-animation technique to John Grierson, an advocate of documentary and experimental film-making who was in charge of the civil-service film unit of Great Britain, which, through various bureaucratic machinations, fell under the jurisdiction of the General Post Office. Grierson encouraged Lye to make a film for him under the auspices of the GPO, giving the artist £30 plus materials. The film would ultimately serve as an advertisement promoting 'cheaper parcel post'.[13]

Lye completed the painting for the film in just five days, but editing, hand-stencilling the relevant GPO information and printing the original painted film via the new three-colour Gasparcolor process, stretched the production to two months. Lye described the process leading up to completing *A Colour Box* as

> dots floating around in a lot of riddling-raddling colour . . . . It made me drool while I was painting . . . . After doing various lengths of my drooling colour sequence of glutinous frog's eggs, spaghetti twangings, colour wriggling and scrapings, I'd select ones that went together.[14]

What to Lye had been an experiment (albeit a highly satisfying one) in film form, 'a simple toy',[15] soon became an avant-garde sensation. Lye's nonobjective film, full of shifting, jittery kinetic shapes and lively musical accompaniment, while technically a state-sponsored advertisement, was nevertheless markedly different from the smoothly realistic efforts of Walt Disney and other commercial animators, as well as the typically 'serious' fare of the filmic avant-garde. The film screened all over Europe,[16] winning a Medal of Honour at the Brussels International Film Festival, at which four other GPO films also received awards.[17] The British press, unsurprisingly, trumpeted its homegrown success and, as David Curtis has pointed out, *A Colour Box* was consequently seen 'by a larger public than any experimental film before it and most since'.[18] Here, then, was a popular new film illustrating a means of movie-making with a remarkably low barrier to entry. It was, as Lye's biographer Roger Horrocks has noted, a style of film-making that could be rendered simply by children with felt-tipped markers, or with staggering complexity by artists who refined their techniques over years of experimentation.[19]

One of Lye's great strengths as a moving-image artist was his inventiveness in adapting tools and techniques to his cameraless animation. In addition to pioneering the use of various colour printing processes, Lye utilised cheap plastic combs and a camel hairbrush on *A Colour Box*, and items such as stencils and a small saw blade to achieve varying textures and effects on other films. For the premiere of *Kaleidoscope* (1935), a promotional film for Churchman's cigarettes that features extensive stencilling, Lye went so far as to cut the shapes of the cigarettes out of the actual filmstrip. These lines perform a charming *pas de deux* at the end of the advertisement, dancing in parallel before leaning toward one another and rotating around the frame. Lye's painstaking efforts represent a kind of proto-Spatialism, which meant that the light from the projector could pass through the film, making the 'cigarettes' even brighter when shown on screen.[20] Lye also achieves an impressive illusion of space in this sequence, as his brushed and combed paints shift from brown to red to blue incredibly quickly in the background of the frame, providing motion and unexpected depth to the cigarettes/lines in the foreground.[21]

With every subsequent film, the industrial production environment of the GPO afforded Lye the opportunity to develop, in his words, 'something not previously done in film technique'.[22] That work opened up 'the possibility of an accessible avant-garde',[23] and demonstrated that the 'paint brush had to be accepted, once and for all, as a viable alternative to the camera'.[24] Furthermore, it directly influenced the efforts of paint-on-film artists such as Norman McLaren,[25] Harry Smith, Stan Brakhage and José Antonio Sistiaga, as well as, as we will see, contemporary media artists. Even Alfred Hitchcock was taken with Lye's films – so much so that he asked Lye to contribute handpainted effects for *Secret Agent* (1936). Lye was to create a painting of fire for a scene involving a train wreck. In a move befitting his impish personality (he had been active among the London Surrealists), Lye made the 'fire' spread from the on-screen action onto the film stock, making it appear as if the entire reel were going up in flames before the image momentarily blacked out. At a preview screening of the film, an alarmed projectionist apparently believed that the combustible celluloid had been set ablaze, and stopped the picture entirely. He screamed that there was a fire, and the audience scrambled for the exits. Needless to say, the studio executives who had gathered to view the film were greatly displeased. Though Hitchcock wanted to keep the sequence in, Gaumont-British made him cut Lye's fire from the film, fearing a spate of accidents, misunderstandings and potential lawsuits.[26]

Hitchcock, it turns out, had an abiding interest in combining elements of the avant-garde with commercial entertainment, as evinced by his inclusion of a Salvador Dali-designed dream sequence in *Spellbound* (1945) and Oskar Sala's electronic sound effects for the score of *The Birds* (1963). Graphic designer Saul Bass accordingly asked John Whitney, Sr to assist him in constructing the title sequence for Hitchcock's *Vertigo* (1958). A pioneer of computer animation, Whitney's work in commercial film opened up new potentialities for image-making in both avant-garde and commercial film-making. The series of hypnotic, multi-hued Lissajous

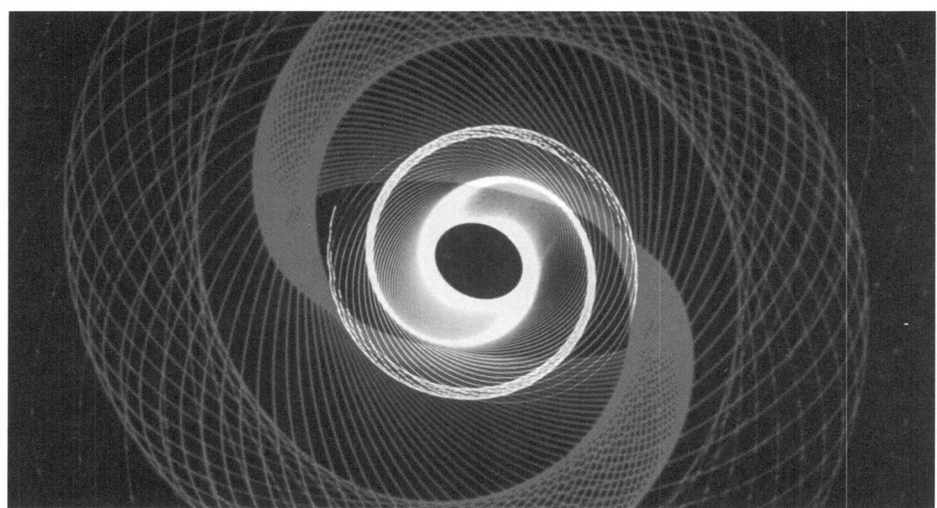

Computer animation pioneer John Whitney, Sr worked with designer Saul Bass to create the spiralling animations for the title sequence of *Vertigo* (1958)

waves spiralling out of a woman's eye towards the camera that Whitney animated for *Vertigo*'s titles spoke to the filmic avant-garde's past – particularly in its evocation of Marcel Duchamp's spinning disks from *Anémic cinéma* (1926)[27] – even as it looked to the machine-assisted nature of cinema's special-effects future. Whitney and his brother James's abstract film collaboration, *Five Film Exercises* (1943–4), for which they had developed their own optical printer as well as a series of pendulums to create a synthetic soundtrack,[28] had been included in Frank Stauffacher's 'Art in Cinema' series at the San Francisco Museum of Art in 1947. In the statement they wrote to accompany their work, they postulated, 'perhaps the abstract film can become the freest and the most significant art form of the cinema. But also, it will be the one most involved in machine technology, an art fundamentally related to the machine'.[29] And yet here was Whitney working for hire a decade later, lending his abstractions to a narrative Hollywood film.

In many ways, Whitney's contribution to *Vertigo* is emblematic of how many handmade filmmakers' work is incorporated into commercial productions. Handmade images in these films are often set apart from the – or presented as operating in a heightened state of – reality from the diegetic world of the film. The otherworldly quality of handmade images relegates these contributions to extradiegetic sequences (such as title sequences), visionary ruptures in the ostensible setting of the narrative (dreams, meditations, hallucinations) or the heretofore unseen (outer space, other worlds). These handmade images thus act as special effects that expressly delineate new modes of vision.[30]

For *Vertigo*, Whitney was able to realise the title-sequence spirals by modifying another device, one connected to a rotating base that produced sine waves without tangling its wires. This device, which he called a 'cam machine', had a series of independently rotating tables, camera operations, variable shooting speeds and myriad surfaces for readying sequences to be shot across multiple axes.[31] Whitney attached a drawing stylus to the cam machine to execute his designs. The resulting apparatus was a 'precursor of computer animation stands developed nearly twenty years later'.[32] Whitney's interest in developing new technologies for abstract film-making led him to design computer-controlled optical printing machines as well as the slitscan technique that Douglas Trumbull later adapted for the 'stargate' sequence in Stanley Kubrick's *2001: A Space Odyssey* (1968). With assistance and funding from IBM in the mid-to-late 1960s, Whitney's experiments in digital computer animation paved the way for increased recourse to computers to generate imagery for commercial films.[33] What's more, John's work with the cam machine on *Vertigo* allowed James to use an updated version of the same technology to realise his own marvellously complex abstract film of kaleidoscopic mandalas, *Lapis* (1963–6).[34]

Though appearing only briefly in the film, Whitney's abstractions resonate on a variety of cinematic levels. In terms of *Vertigo* itself, the inclusion of Whitney's designs can be considered in keeping with Hitchcock's aforementioned applications of the avant-garde in his oeuvre. The spiralling waves of the sequence simultaneously vouchsafe an abstract graphic representation of the film's title and anticipate *Vertigo*'s themes of mental disorientation and fractured psychology. They also provide an example of the Whitneys' intentions to develop 'a truer vision of reality by destroying the particular representation' via a process of mechanical abstraction.[35] Furthermore, the fact that Whitney's device was made up of salvaged antiaircraft technology from World War II – which he later modified with surplus M-5 and M-7 Anti-aircraft Gun Directors – repurposed to produce highly associative moving images echoes the historical avant-garde's concern with bringing art into everyday life. Indeed, the sword-into-ploughshare implications of war machines being turned into art machines are profound and far reaching, an inversion of Paul Virilio's assertion of 'the eye's function being the function of a weapon'.[36] Contra Virilio, Whitney's example serves as a reminder that, while there may be inherent spectacle in war and in many kinds of cinema, spectacle takes on different forms, meanings and reception. Here, Whitney's modification of weaponry into an instrument not of surveillance or even documentation, but one that expresses radically new abstractions, rhymes with his later statements regarding the intrinsic relationships between mathematics and Indian mandalas, and puts forward a vision that dissolves barriers between the spiritual and the scientific, between natural and machine-made forms, between the interiority of meditation and the exteriority of the natural world.[37]

As much as revealed or inner truth, the issue of economics also factors into whether handmade effects are used in commercial and industrial film. Compared to present-day computer-generated effects, which can require dozens of technicians and animators at a cost that can easily spiral into tens of millions of dollars, handmade techniques are comparatively inexpensive. Director Darren Aronofsky hired the father-and-son team of Chris and Peter Parks to create special effects for *The Fountain*, a nonlinear, metaphysical meditation on love and the fear of dying; they were able to realise the required psychedelic imagery for $140,000 in six weeks of work. The Parks specialise in microphotography, a close-up picture-making method originally developed by Peter to photograph marine biology invisible to the naked eye. By combining clear liquids, paint, inks and dyes with tiny brushes and palette knives in a Pyrex dish, the Parks were able to create 'fluid paintings' of astonishing depth and complexity, characterised by an organic randomness that cannot yet be matched by computer technology, and that can be magnified over 500,000 times their initial size.[38]

Chris and Peter Parks' 'fluid paintings' provided fantastic visuals for *The Fountain* (2006)

While financial cost was certainly a factor in Aronofsky's decision to engage the Parks' artistry, the director also expressed an antagonism towards computer-generated effects. The technology of CGI, Aronofsky argued, develops with such rapidity that effects often end up hopelessly dating the films in which they are featured. Although he did indeed employ some digital effects in the film, Aronofsky sought something 'timeless' that he found in the Parks' water-based microphotography. He saw in their handmade visions 'a way to use a lot of these old techniques to do some new and really neat stuff'.[39]

The film revolves around a man's (Hugh Jackman) attempts to save his lover's (Rachel Weisz) life in three different yet interrelated timelines: first as a sixteenth-century conquistador seeking to spare her from the Spanish Inquisition, next as a modern-day scientist seeking to cure her cancer and finally, as a futuristic wanderer chasing eternal life while transporting a leafless, ageing Tree of Life (which contains the spirit-essence of the woman) through deep space. The Parks' water-based microphotography is extensively featured in this final timeline, appearing both as a perpetually raining, golden miasma surrounding the protagonist's spaceship-cum-biosphere, and most significantly as a magnificent, rippling supernova that results in the main character's ascension/passage beyond spacetime, and the tree's blooming rebirth. Once again, handmade effects are used to stand in for the cosmic or the previously unimagined. Here, also, the indexical, representational qualities of the Parks' work, indicative of actual physical forces such as gravity and the aleatory realities of waveformation and the refraction of light, are granted an aesthetic value over the manufactured imagery of CGI.

While handmade film effects may represent significant savings for a well-known director such as Aronofsky, the occasion to supply effects for a feature film often offers handmade artists the most lucrative opportunity they may ever encounter. For instance, until Grierson commissioned *A Colour Box* with a production budget of a mere £400, Len Lye had been plagued by what he called 'capitalist film things'[40] – the constant struggle to secure funding, and the heady cost of the traditional animation form he had been pursuing prior to that point. Pat O'Neill, who has supported his sculpture, collage drawing, and short and feature-length experimental film works by taking on effects work for such films as *The Empire Strikes Back* (1980) and *Return of the Jedi* (1983),[41] has described the avant-garde conundrum of 'the necessity of making a living and paying the costs of an art process that has turned out not to be entirely self-sustaining'.[42] While often an economic necessity, O'Neill and other artists have noted that taking on commissioned commercial work is rarely satisfying in an artistic sense, and often diverts energy from their own projects. This sentiment is echoed by Belson, who was delighted to be well compensated for his work on *The Right Stuff*, but wary of commercial film-making's artistic limitations:

> I made more money than I'd ever made in my life – eventually, a thousand dollars a week ... for me, making the money was one of the most exciting parts of the whole experience, and I imagine this is true for most people working in commercial film, because in other ways the process is very frustrating.[43]

While Belson was fortunate enough to have struck an agreement with Kaufman whereby he retained ownership of the extensive unused footage he shot for the film, what was used can be understood both on a creative continuum with his earlier work and as a divergence from its previous applications.

Commercialism aside, Belson was well suited to work on a film about space exploration. In the late 1950s, he had collaborated with sound engineer Henry Jacobs on the expanded cinema Vortex Concerts at San Francisco's Morrison Planetarium, where Belson, according to scholar and archivist Cindy Keefer, operated up to thirty different projection devices that displayed on the planetarium's sixty-five-foot dome. His mix of intensely layered real-time imagery comprised slide projectors, a kaleidoscope, rotating and zoom projectors, various prisms, a stroboscope, a spiral generator, four interference pattern projectors, 16mm projectors and the planetarium's sophisticated starfield projector. This last item, called the Academy Projector, was a unique device capable of projecting a realistic field of nearly 4,000 stars.[44] This machine was, like Whitney's cam machine, fashioned from surplus World War II materials. Indeed, it seems fitting that the starfield projector that made thousands of spectators look toward the heavens was built, as Keefer points out, from lenses designed for aerial photography.[45] What is more, Belson's 1964 film *Re-entry* was inspired by astronaut John Glenn's return to Earth in February 1962, and even incorporated snippets of Glenn's radio communications.[46] The otherworldly beauty of Belson's hermetic spectacle eventually caught the eye of Hollywood film-makers looking to imbue their productions with the spectre of the metaphysical. Indeed, as Pauline Kael wrote in 1966,

> Little is heard about Bruce Baillie or Carroll Ballard whose camera skills expose how inept, inefficient, and unimaginative much of Hollywood's self-praised work is, or about the elegance and grandeur of Jordan Belson's short abstract films, like *Allures*, that demonstrate that one man working in a basement can make Hollywood's vaunted special effects departments look archaic.[47]

Stripped of their original contexts, however, Belson's transcendental explorations transmuted into sci-fi-effects fodder when repurposed for other narratives, such as Robert Parish's *Journey to the Far Side of the Sun* (1969), and Donald Cammell's *Demon Seed* (1977), in which Belson's imagery, excerpted from his earlier films, stands in for the 'brain' of the lusty AI super computer Proteus IV.

For *The Right Stuff*, Belson was tasked with creating new images of Chuck Yeager's breaking of the sound barrier, the Earth seen from space, and starfields. He was also asked to recreate the mysterious shimmering 'fireflies' that Glenn reported seeing outside the cockpit of his Apollo spacecraft. Belson had developed a technique to create flickering light particles for his 1973 film, *Light*, and used it again here, probably augmenting his original methods with new techniques. Before he was hired to work on *The Right Stuff*, Belson first prepared the seven-minute, 16mm *The Astronaut's Dream* (1981) over a period of two months. He later told Scott MacDonald that he had composed that film's sequences as a kind of demo reel to show Kaufman, who loved what he saw.[48] Belson would spend the next two years battling with Kaufman and against himself to achieve new wonders in his visuals:

> Over a period of two years, he asked me to try some things more than fifteen times. Even though I might have given up out of frustration after the first time, he pushed me way past the limit which I would have had no reason to go beyond myself; and every time I did, it led me to make new discoveries. I don't know how he knew I could do it.[49]

These 'new discoveries' were put to use in several sequences for *The Right Stuff*. Early in the film, as Chuck Yeager (Sam Shepard) attempts to break the sound barrier in 1947, Kaufman cuts from shots of a model of the Bell X-1 jet soaring among the clouds, approaching supersonic speed, to a Belson shot of the heavens briefly opening up – a deep blue haze of smoky mist. In another shot shortly thereafter, the blue gives way to a white light through which the X-1 flies, and then a shot seen through Yeager's cockpit shows a dark field streaked with yellow light. Kaufman explained that he employed Belson's imagery at this juncture in order to illustrate Yeager's triumph over the unknown, of 'going through the membrane, in a way, to the other side of man's experience'.[50] Here again, handmade techniques offer a means of representing the bounds – and the boundlessness – of human perception.

Belson created other signature abstractions to heighten the drama of the film's depiction of John Glenn's (Ed Harris) orbital flight around the Earth in February 1962. In one shot, outside the porthole of Glenn's Mercury-Atlas 6 craft, blue light streaks by. In another, we see a hazy representation of Earth, not readily recognisable as such, a swirl of rich blue with a deeper blue atmospheric halo. Then Glenn's ship swings around the planet, heading into night, the capsule silhouetted in front of a deep azure sphere, before rounding into

One of Jordan Belson's effects shots for *The Right Stuff* (1983)

daylight, as a sliver of curving orange-yellow cuts against the blue 'sky' of earth. There is a shot of rippling, almost wavelike cloud forms below Glenn's craft bursting slowly in shades of purple and blue-grey, and then we see inside the cabin, as the unreal light reflects off Glenn's helmet, as well as the mirror placed on his chest. As in the Yeager sequence, Belson's handmade effects are used here as mysterious spectacle, and as a delivery vehicle for the Deleuzian sensation probably overwhelming Glenn's apperceptive faculties as he takes in these strange sights for the first time. Equally mysterious were Belson's methods for obtaining such oddly beautiful visuals. Gary Gutierrez, *The Right Stuff*'s special-effects supervisor, said, 'I was just sort of in awe of the effects he was creating, and I have no idea how he created them. We pumped him for information, but he wouldn't give.'[51] Belson similarly stonewalled the *New York Times* when queried about his techniques, saying, 'I don't want people thinking about it when they are looking at the movie. It destroys the illusion.'[52]

While much of Belson's effects work in *The Right Stuff* is stunning, some of it was deployed in questionable ways. Just as it could be argued that Kaufman's foregrounding of his subjects' individual bravery and valour obscures the historical and political context of the space race's role in extending and exacerbating the Cold War arms race between the US and the USSR, the film's use of Belson's imagery to aestheticise the new vistas opened up by space exploration similarly threatens to obscure real-world considerations. For the 'fireflies' sequence, for example, Kaufman intercuts medium close-up shots of a bewildered Glenn surrounded by Belson's glowing fireflies with scenes of aborigines singing and dancing around a sparking fire. The camera follows the blaze's embers as they lift into the night air. The resulting edits create the impression that the primitive ritual being enacted on terra firma is aiding Glenn's journey in the heavens. Regardless of the fact that the film never mentions that 'fireflies' were later determined by NASA to be light-reflecting ice particles outside Glenn's MA-6 capsule,[53] the invocation of a primitive mysticism via a questionable portrayal of indigenous practices is far removed from Belson's subjective investigations of human consciousness and perception in his own work.

Although he acknowledged the hallucinatory qualities of some of his 1960s films, Belson also held fast to the idea that the flaming, spinning mandalas and spacescapes of those works were representations of an inner consciousness, claiming, 'I first have to see the images somewhere, within or without or somewhere. I mean I don't make them up.'[54] His work on *The Right Stuff* may have answered his own question, as posed in an earlier interview: 'In a regular film, when do you see the screen light up, turn all golden, and then break down into shimmering particles?'[55] Here, however, the contemplative and spiritual qualities characterising his earlier work have become narrative and been given specious symbolic value. So while his effects work on *The Right Stuff* resembles elements of a number of his previous films, its meaning and use-value are far different. In contrast to Chris Parks, who disavows any distinction between the various applications of his microphotography – short films, static photographic prints or special-effects work – saying, 'I have never really drawn a line between "art" and anything else creative as they are just different ways in which I express or communicate',[56] it is very difficult to conceive of Belson's work-for-hire sequences on *The Right Stuff* as of a piece with his self-directed work. At the same time, it seems important to recognise that the experience allowed Belson the resources to further develop his craft and to fund future projects.

Terrence Malick's *The Tree of Life* is a more recent commercial production that expresses a particular sensitivity to the work of avant-garde moving-image artists, particularly in the spectacular 'creation' sequence of the film's first half. Malick hired Douglas Trumbull, the special-effects maestro responsible for refining and extending Whitney's slitscan photography techniques for the revelatory 'Jupiter and beyond the Infinite' passage in Stanley Kubrick's *2001: A Space Odyssey*, to oversee the visual effects for *The Tree of Life*. The film slides fluidly between time and space, stretching from the present, in which an architect (Sean Penn) ponders his past, to scenes of his childhood in Waco, Texas, in the 1950s, to the beginning of life and time itself. The most dramatic of these shifts occurs roughly twenty minutes into *The Tree of Life*, when the camera follows the film's unnamed matriarch (Jessica Chastain) as she wanders through a forest after receiving the news that one of her sons has died. In the next shot, we see her in close-up, raising her wet eyes skyward. As she closes them, the screen goes black and we hear her ask in whispered voiceover, 'Lord. Why? Where were you?' What follows is a twenty-minute-long series of abstract and representational images detailing the birth of the world, the emergence of the dinosaurs (brought to life here with CGI) and their extinction via a meteor crashing into the Earth.

To compose the sequence, Malick reached out to the avant-garde film community, and Los Angeles' Centre for Visual Music (CVM) in particular. CVM is the organisation currently responsible for preserving and digitising Belson's films, and Malick approached them regarding the possibility of locating independent experimental film-makers to generate imagery for some sequences, as well as Belson creating new work for the project. CVM sent out a request throughout the experimental film community for 'segments of abstract and experimental film' for a 'major motion picture'. The call, posted on the Frameworks listserve and elsewhere, asked for:

a) Abstract, non-representational work with mysterious, suggestive elements
b) Experimental or abstract work suggesting organic processes
c) Abstract, non-representational imagery that metaphorically suggests molecular, subatomic, natural and/or cosmological processes and phenomena
d) Spiritually inspired abstract imagery, such as that which is inspired by Buddhist or Taoist beliefs or using sacred imagery
e) Abstract Visualisations of music in which the visuals have an organic, mysterious, spiritual or suggestive element.[57]

Malick was thus specifically looking for 'spiritually inspired' and 'mysterious' abstractions that relied on chance operations, or at least represented the unpredictable, incommunicable qualities of 'organic processes'. This in turn, resulted in the film-makers overwhelmingly favouring abstractions made by analogue techniques rather than computer-generated imagery. Trumbull and Malick experimented with 'photographing paints and liquids (like Fluorescein dyes and Half-and-Half) in tanks of water at high speeds, which produced images that could be digitally composited to resemble astronomical phenomena like interstellar clouds'.[58] As Trumbull told the *New York Times*, 'With computer graphics everything is based on some algorithm and there's often a predictability to it ... Terry and I wanted randomness and irregularity that seemed truly natural.'

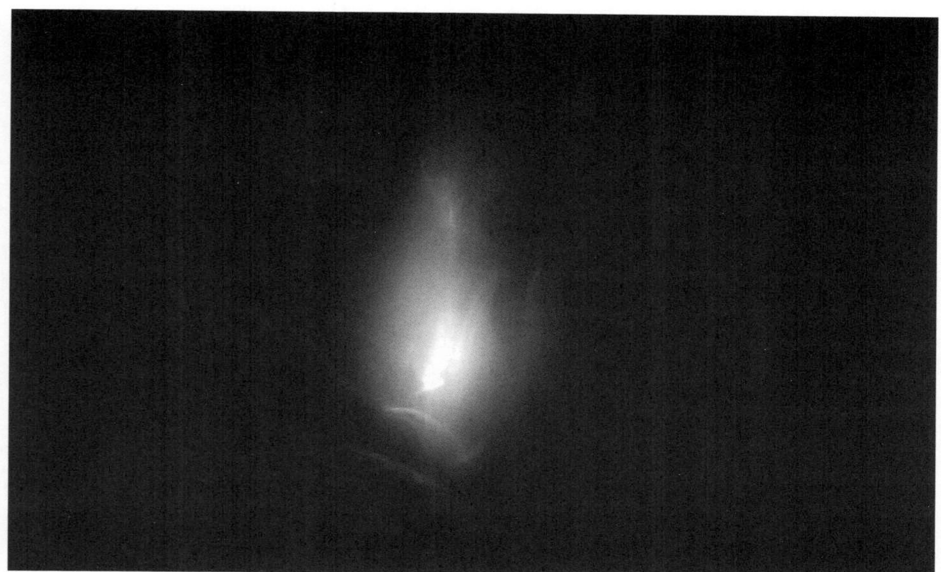

Director Terrence Malick made use of lumia artist Thomas Wilfred's 'Op. 161' (1965–6) in *The Tree of Life* (2011)

The film's extraordinary imagery of transcendence was thus fashioned from the most everyday and Earthbound of materials at hand – a technical approach that mirrors *The Tree of Life*'s insistent thematic belief in the alchemical transformation of the quotidian into the wondrous.[59]

While Belson would seem to have been a good fit for the film, he did not end up working on *The Tree of Life*. Malick nevertheless made use of 'natural' cosmic images from sources such as the Hubble telescope, as well as fragments of handmade films and even more obscure artworks. Indeed, the creation sequence of *The Tree of Life* begins with a mysterious image of a slowly shifting flame of red-yellow light. This 'light before the light' also bookends the film, as the first and last images seen. The fire of creation, it turns out, is actually a work by light artist Thomas Wilfred, 'Op. 161' (1965–6). Now largely forgotten, Wilfred's 'lumia compositions', as he called them, are feats of bric-a-brac engineering and ethereal works of art. He employed reflective mirrors, handpainted glass discs and bent pieces of metal – all housed in a screened wooden cabinet, or, in one case, mounted on a walnut 'tea wagon' – to transform beams of light produced by a series of lamps and lenses. To look inside a lumia device is to see an apparent scrapheap put to near-magical use. Wilfred began honing his materials and techniques in the 1920s, and by the 40s and 50s, his work was exhibited by the Metropolitan Museum of Art, the Whitney Museum of American Art and the Museum of Modern Art. MoMA's director, Alfred H. Barr, wrote to Wilfred in 1959, 'I think it would please you to know that we receive more letters and telephone calls asking for information about Lumia than about any other single work in the Museum's collection.'[60]

An unorthodox transcendentalist, Wilfred sought to represent 'the universal rhythmic flow', in his art, and produced roughly forty works before his death in 1968. At present, only eighteen of his lumia survive, and even fewer are operational. One of the few working pieces is 'Luccata, Op. 162', currently on display at the Los Angeles County Museum of Art. That piece is on loan from the collection of retired radio astronomer Eugene Epstein and his wife Carol, who own nearly half of the extant Wilfreds, including the one featured so prominently in *The Tree of Life*. 'These are rarely seen', explains Epstein, 'if you haven't seen one in person, you're totally unaware of it'.[61] This is largely due to the fact that Wilfred resisted attempts to record lumia's intensely vibrant colours and deliquescent motion. 'I have never permitted any of my works to be filmed', he wrote in 1962: 'We have experimented with the process here and the results have been too poor to be considered.'[62]

Malick's crew spent nearly four years, on and off, filming 'Op. 161', both while it was at LACMA and in the Epsteins' Los Angeles, California, home. The piece runs without repeating itself for one year, 315 days and twelve hours, although it occupies only about a minute or two of screentime in *The Tree of Life*. Epstein recalls that he was contacted by one of Malick's assistants, and that 'they were trying to capture something about creation and so on, and wondering somehow if they could use lumia'.[63] Here again is an example of a commercial (albeit a very artistically minded) film-maker searching for a means of transmitting new visual effects via experimental moving images, and locating that power in the handmade.

The handmade image's persistence can be read, in part, as a rebuke to the perceived coldness and alienation wrought by the digital mediascape, as a challenge to the idea that the 'new' is always synonymous with 'better', and as a refusal to accept that what is old must be continually discarded and dismissed as irrelevant. One might criticise this claim as nostalgic, reactionary, technophobic or essentialist. And yet it is difficult to deny that some qualities of handmade analogue moving images simply cannot (yet) be made or replicated by digital technologies. New-media scholars Jay David Bolter and Richard Grusin's concept of 'remediation', wherein new media borrow from or encompass older media forms, reshaping and energising our understandings of both, pushes media toward what the authors term 'transparency', or the erasure of the medium in order to move the perceiver closer to the object represented. Though Bolter and Grusin assign a 'double-logic' to remediation, made up of, on the one hand, 'immediacy', or the result of that medium-based erasure and, on the other, 'hypermediacy', or the deliberate foregrounding of the medium's material or graphic properties,[64] the handmade cinema is largely unconcerned with realistic representation in the conventional sense, and, by nature of its construction, is hyperconscious of the materiality of its making. Its foregrounding of materiality, in fact, provides its telltale characteristics: textures, patterns and imagery that result from the marriage of the human hand and the mechanical apparatus.

Furthermore, certain formal characteristics of older media do not always make the leap in the transition to newer media forms, and are consequently left behind, ignored by or excised from their new-media iterations. The handmade recurs as both a protest against the perceived artificiality of digital imagery and as an attempt to reinscribe the human amid (or within) a field of machines. The notion of craft, however tied to material 'reality' it may seem, lives on in the digital, as ideas about trial and error, personal style, aesthetics, collaboration, prosthetics (light pens and Wacom tablets rather than brushes and stencils) and problem-solving remain as vital to understanding the techniques and underpinnings of computer-generated imagery as handmade cinema.

A consideration of handmade techniques and effects in mainstream cinema reminds us that avant-garde and mainstream culture rarely remain in discrete camps that go unvisited by one another. As such, the relationship of the artisanal avant-garde to commercial and industrial cinema should not be seen as strictly oppositional, but rather as a network of intertwined aesthetic and economic interests. The result is a feedback loop wherein mainstream films draw upon the individualised aesthetics of avant-garde practitioners when the realist visual language of mainstream cinema proves inadequate to the task of expressing abstract or transcendent thoughts, feelings and experiences while those practitioners take advantage of the resources of larger film productions to further their craft. This is not to say that the avant-garde is not at times exploited or misused by mainstream cinema, or that credit is always given where credit is due, but that both fields can potentially gain from the interaction. A broader study of avant-garde work in mainstream cinema, one that considers everything from Dali's aforementioned contributions to *Spellbound* to the Joshua Light Show's party sequence for John Schlesinger's *Midnight Cowboy* (1969) to Paul Thomas Anderson's interstitial use of video artist Jeremy Blake's 'moving paintings' in *Punch-Drunk Love* (2002), may prove fruitful in developing a more comprehensive history and theorisation of the interpenetration of the avant-garde and commercial film.

Notes

1. Gene Youngblood, *Expanded Cinema* (Vancouver: Clarke, Irwin & Company Limited, 1970), p. 158. Belson told Scott MacDonald, 'High-tech image-making equipment is so outrageously expensive and goes out of date so quickly that you have to be part of a commercial enterprise to use it at all.' In Scott MacDonald, *A Critical Cinema 3: Interviews with Independent Filmmakers* (Los Angeles: University of California Press, 1998), p. 78. It is also likely that Belson incorporated some traditional animation techniques into his films, and had developed other techniques by the time of *The Right Stuff*. The extreme secrecy surrounding Belson's working methods and technical innovations precludes a more updated and detailed accounting of his processes. He told MacDonald (ibid., pp. 77–8):

   > When I was working on the films, I was always experimenting with anything I thought might produce the kind of imagery I was interested in, anything from lasers, optical printing, liquid crystals to the facilities of an entire TV broadcasting studio. ... I didn't want the viewer to be more aware of the process than of the event taking place on screen.

2. Ibid., p. 82.
3. Adam Eisenberg, 'Low Tech Effects: The Right Stuff', *Cinefex* no. 14 (October 1983), excerpted at http://www.centerforvisualmusic.org/JBcinefex.htm. Throughout his life, Belson let slip few fragments of information regarding his film-making process. He was careful to distinguish his work from animation, for instance – even though his earliest films were made via traditional animation methods – insisting to Eisenberg, 'I don't use liquids or models. ... I use mechanical and optical effects; and instead of using an animating table, I call my setup an optical bench.' Belson may have, in fact, used animation techniques on *Allures*, though this is nearly impossible to verify.
4. See Gregory Zinman, 'Analog Circuit Palettes, Cathode Ray Canvases: Digital's Analog, Experimental Past', *Film History* vol. 24 no. 2 (Spring 2012), pp. 135–57.
5. Gilles Deleuze, *Francis Bacon: The Logic of Sensation*, trans. Daniel W. Smith (Minneapolis: University of Minnesota Press, 2003), p. 32.
6. Alison Pearlman, 'Craft Matters', *Afterimage* no. 32 (July/August 2004), p. 6.

7. Martin Heidegger, 'The Origin of the Work of Art', in *Poetry, Language, Thought*, trans. Albert Hofstadter (New York: Harper & Row, 1971), p. 27.
8. James S. Plaut, 'A World Family', in *In Praise of Hands: Contemporary Crafts of the World* (Toronto: McClelland and Stewart Limited, 1974), p. 10.
9. MacDonald, *A Critical Cinema 3*, p. 78.
10. Thomas Crow, 'Modernism and Mass Culture in the Visual Arts', in *Modern Art in the Common Culture* (New Haven, CT: Yale University Press, 1996), p. 35.
11. Roger Horrocks, *Len Lye: A Biography* (Auckland: Auckland University Press, 2001), p. 141.
12. Ibid., p. 137.
13. Ibid., pp. 135–6.
14. Len Lye, 'The Tusalava Model of How I Learnt the Genetic Language of Art', March 1972, unpublished manuscript.
15. Horrocks, *Len Lye*, p. 137.
16. Horrocks notes that some British theatres supportive of the avant-garde were initially wary of screening an advertisement, but made an exception for *A Colour Box*. See Horrocks, *Len Lye*, pp. 138–40.
17. Ibid., p. 140.
18. David Curtis, *Experimental Cinema* (London: Studio Vista, 1971), p. 36.
19. Horrocks, *Len Lye*, p. 141.
20. Horrocks, *Art That Moves: The Work of Len Lye* (Auckland: Auckland University Press, 2009), p. 150.
21. While Lye found some success making *Kaleidoscope* and *Colour Flight* (1937), an advertisement for Imperial Airways, as well as with his films for the GPO, by 1957 he had announced that he would go 'on strike' from film-making due to financial frustrations, and that he would be dedicating himself to his more lucrative kinetic sculptures. His frustrations had been compounded by the fact that *Rhythm* (1957), a one-minute mix of automobile-factory assembly-line footage and clusters of white dots, hand-drawn titles and vertical lines, went unused as a Chrysler advertisement. See Horrocks, *Len Lye*, p. 262.
22. Ibid., p. 148.
23. Brett Kashmere, 'Len Lye', *Senses of Cinema*, www.sensesofcinema.com/contents/directors/07/lye.html.
24. Horrocks, *Len Lye*, p. 141.
25. McLaren joined the GPO in 1937, and watched *A Colour Box* several times a day for weeks on end. See Horrocks, *Len Lye*, pp. 144–5. McLaren went on to head up the animation department of the National Film Board of Canada at the invitation of Grierson.
26. Horrocks, *Len Lye*, p. 153. Similar hand-scratched 'fire' effects were utilised by Fritz Lang to show a barrel exploding into flames in the opening sequence of *The Testament of Dr. Mabuse* (1933).
27. John Conomos, 'The Vertigo of Time', *Senses of Cinema*, June 2000, http://www.sensesofcinema.com/contents/00/6/time.html.
28. For a fuller description of the handmade apparatus used in *Five Film Exercises*, please refer to my essay, 'Eradicating the Psychic Space between Eye and Ear: Synthetic Film Sound's Challenge to the Index', *Animation Journal* vol. 20 (2012), pp. 51–85.
29. John and James Whitney, 'Audio-visual Music', in Frank Stauffacher (ed.), *Art in Cinema* (New York: Arno Press, 1947), pp. 31–4.

30. For a thorough consideration of how special effects are employed to represent subjective transcendence, see Scott Bukatman, 'The Artificial Infinite: On Special Effects and the Sublime', in Lynne Cook and Peter Wollen (eds), *Visual Displays: Culture beyond Appearances* (Seattle, WA: Bay Press, 1995), pp. 255–89.
31. Youngblood, *Expanded Cinema*, pp. 209–10.
32. Dan Auiler, *Vertigo: The Making of a Hitchcock Classic* (New York: St. Martin's Press, 1998), p. 153.
33. In 1961, John Whitney produced a compendium of effects with his analog 'cam machine' in a demonstration reel titled *Catalog*. Cindy Keefer at the Center for Visual Music points out that two versions of *Catalog* exist. The one most frequently seen is shorter, and does not contain the slitscan sequence. Andrew Johnston notes that Whitney was frustrated with the results of the stylus attachment used for *Vertigo*, and that said frustration provided the catalyst for later further computer-based innovations. At IBM, Whitney worked with FORTRAN programmer Jack Citron and used the company's System/360 computers to produce some of the first digital computer films. See Andrew Robert Johnston, *Pulses of Abstraction: Episodes from a History of Animation* (Minneapolis: University of Minnesota Press, forthcoming).
34. Auiler, *Vertigo*, p. 153.
35. Whitney and Whitney, 'Audio-visual Music', pp. 31–4.
36. See Paul Virilio, *War and Cinema: The Logistics of Perception*, trans. Patrick Camillier (London: Verso, 1989), p. 3.
37. 'John Whitney 2' discussion moderated by Standish Lawder, 1969, at the Flaherty Film Seminar in Lakevill, Connecticut, *Film Comment* vol. 6 no. 3 (Fall 1970), p. 36.
38. See Steve Silberman, 'The Outsider', *Wired* vol. 14 no. 11 (November 2006), http://www.wired.com/wired/archive/14.11/outsider.html; and Alastair Smart, 'Insider: Chris Parks Interview', *Telegraph*, 28 January 2007, http://www.telegraph.co.uk/culture/3662845/The-insider.html.
39. Tasha Robinson, 'Darren Aronofsky', The A.V. Club, 21 November 2006, available at http://www.avclub.com/content/node/55490.
40. Horrocks, *Len Lye*, p. 133.
41. Branden W. Joseph, 'Pat O'Neill at Santa Monica Museum of Art,' *ArtForum*, January 2005, p. 176.
42. David E. James, 'An Interview with Pat O'Neill', *Millennium Film Journal* nos 30–1 (Fall 1997), http://www.mfj-online.org/journalPages/MFJ30,31/DJamesInterview.html.
43. MacDonald, *A Critical Cinema 3*, p. 83.
44. Cindy Keefer, 'Cosmic Cinema and the Vortex Concerts', in Arnauld Pierre (ed.), *Cosmos: En Busca de los Orígenes de Kupka a Kubrick* (San Sebastian: TEA Tenerife Espacio de las Artes, 2008), pp. 360–71.
45. Ibid.
46. Robert A. Haller, 'Galaxy: Avant-garde Film-Makers Look across Space and Time', catalog for a film series, 4–7 September 2001, http://www.roberthaller.com/galaxy/galaxy.html.
47. Pauline Kael, 'Movie Brutalists', *New Republic*, 24 September 1966.
48. MacDonald, *A Critical Cinema 3*, p. 83.
49. Eisenberg, 'Low Tech Effects'. p. 24. For *The Right Stuff*, Belson shot on 35mm for the first time. While the larger format film caused disruptive vibrations on his optical bench, Belson said that through his use of 35mm, 'I discovered far more subtlety in my work than I had ever noticed before with 16mm.'

50. Quoted in 'The Journey and the Mission', feature, *The Right Stuff*, DVD, directed by Philip Kaufman (1983, Burbank, CA: Warner Home Video, 2003).
51. Quoted in 'T-20 Years and Counting' feature, *The Right Stuff*, DVD.
52. John Noble Wilford, '"The Right Stuff": From Space to Screen', *New York Times*, 16 October 1983, http://movies.nytimes.com/movie/review?_r=3&res=9C0DE5DB143BF935A25753C1A965948260&scp=73&sq=%22The+Right+Stuff%22&st=nyt.
53. 'Scott Carpenter and the Flight of *Aurora 7*', available at http://www.scottcarpenter.com/aurora7.html.
54. William C. Wees, *Light Moving in Time: Studies in the Visual Aesthetics of Avant-garde Film* (Berkeley: University of California Press, 1992), p. 130.
55. Haller, 'Galaxy'.
56. Brian Sherwin, 'Art Space Talk: Chris Parks', Myartspace>Blog, 22 November 2006, available at http://www.myartspace.com/blog/2006/11/art-space-talk-chris-parks.html.
57. 'CVM's Call for Work: Abstract and Experimental Moving Images (Fall 2006),' http://www.centerforvisualmusic.org/CallforWork06.htm.
58. Dennis Lim, 'Pursuing Imperfection in Malick's Eden', *New York Times*, 22 March 2011, p. AR12.
59. Ibid.
60. Alfred H. Barr, letter to Thomas Wilfred, 26 February 1959, Thomas Wilfred Papers, Yale University Manuscripts and Archives, box 4, folder 3.
61. Eugene Epstein, interview with the author, 2 June 2011.
62. In a letter to MoMA's Dorothy Miller, 19 January 1962, Wilfred explained himself regarding a request to make a film of 'Opus 145' (in Thomas Wilfred Papers):

    > I have never permitted any of my works to be filmed. We have experimented with the process here and the results have been too poor to be considered. Here are the two main reasons: 1. 24 frames persecond [*sic*] can't reproduce one of lumia's main features: absolute continuity of motion at any velocity. The restless flicker of the film destroys the quality of the repose. 2. The intensity range of a lumia composition is too wide for any known colour reproduction process … .

63. Epstein, interview with the author.
64. Jay David Bolter and Richard Grusin, *Remediation: Understanding New Media* (Cambridge, MA: MIT Press, 1999), pp. 5, 24.

'DON'T YOU MEAN EXTINCT?'
ON THE CIRCULATION OF KNOWLEDGE IN *JURASSIC PARK*

OLIVER GAYCKEN

> *Jurassic Park* heralded a revolution in movies as profound as the coming of sound in 1927.[1]

This pronouncement belongs to a bevy of declarations that locate *Jurassic Park* (1993) as a Hollywood milestone; 'the film which established CGI as the dominant force in mainstream moviemaking'.[2] Cinema scholars have refined this contention, on the one hand by pointing out how the film's revolutionary qualities were amplified by its powerful marketing campaign. As Michele Pierson has noted, 'In the buildup to *Jurassic Park*'s release, speculation about the film's computer-generated dinosaurs generated far and away the most publicity for the film.'[3] On the other hand, scholars have also observed how the emphasis on the film as a watershed moment for Hollywood's incorporation of CGI obscures the extent to which its visualisations of dinosaurs relied on traditional visual-effects methods. As Stephen Prince has pointed out,

> Although it is now and forever branded as a CGI film, there are only about fifty computer graphics shots in the movie. Critics and scholars tend to describe the film as if every dinosaur seen on screen came out of a computer, but most scenes involving dinosaurs feature a blend of traditional effects elements and digital ones.[4]

Jurassic Park was remarkable, then, not only for its CGI but also for the seamlessness with which these effects were integrated into a wide range of effects technologies. What distinguishes *Jurassic Park* is both its virtuosic employment of an emerging technology as well as its integration of this new representational option with such existing state-of-the-art techniques as stop-motion miniatures, prosthetics and large-scale animatronics.

This essay will elaborate on the transitional, hybrid nature of the special effects in *Jurassic Park*, first by considering a particular technology created especially for the film, the so-called 'dinosaur input device', which allowed traditional stop-motion animators to control a digital model. Related to this particular technological emblem of the film's transitional nature is how computing pervades the film. In other words, the role of computers in the generation of the film's special effects was not restricted to the relatively limited (and extraordinarily expensive) CGI dinosaur shots; computers permeate the film's effects in ways that a dichotomy of old vs new effects obscures. A more careful parsing of the effects technologies utilised in the film reveals a pervasive use of computer-aided methods that goes well beyond the hallmark CGI shots, as well as a thematisation of computer discourse within the film's narrative. The essay concludes by extending the notion of the transitional to the question of the dinosaur effects'

The dinosaur input device, as demonstrated by Randal Dutra; stop-motion armature in the foreground, whose movements are optically encoded and fed to the wireframe model on the SGI Indigo station in the background (from *The Making of* Jurassic Park [1995])

scientific realism, situating them between the film-makers' claims for authenticity and the palaeontological tendency to dismiss them as appealing but unscientific spectacle.

The Dinosaur Input Device

An anecdote from the film's pre-production provides an exemplary instance of the interpenetration of computer-aided visualisation with traditional effects work. Originally, Steven Spielberg had decided to give the full-body dinosaur scenes to Phil Tippett's group, which would use 'go-motion', a refinement of stop-motion animation. After watching a CGI test animation scene of a *Tyrannosaurus rex* chasing a herd of *Gallimimus*, however, Spielberg reportedly turned to Tippett and said, 'You're out of a job.' Tippett responded, 'Don't you mean extinct?', an exchange that subsequently made its way into the film's dialogue. But as catchy as this banter is, it exaggerates the impact of the CGI animation, rhetorically implying a sharp division where in reality a subtle interpenetration carried the day. On the one hand, go motion was itself a computer-aided refinement of stop-motion techniques. In go motion, puppets articulated by rods are attached to computer-controlled stepper motors, which allows for movements to be stored in computer memory and repeated, with modifications if desired. The motors' precision enabled the introduction of subtle motion blur, the absence of which was seen as stop motion's major drawback.[5] So while the role for CGI did dramatically increase over the course of production, it was not simply a matter of computer technology replacing an older effects method.

Furthermore, far from being out of a job, Tippett's stop-motion animators went on to advise Dennis Muren's CGI team at Industrial Light & Magic, since the stop-motion animators' knowledge of animation proved an invaluable aid to the CGI team's development of realistic movement. The most tangible product of this teamwork was the creation of a new technology, the 'dinosaur input device', which materialised the symbiosis between traditional and emergent special-effects techniques. The DID was an armature that allowed the stop-motion animators to input movement data into the CGI program using traditional stop-motion manual manipulation. Dennis Muren recounted the advantages of this technology: 'So instead of forcing stop-motion animators to learn computers, we came up with this hybrid device which was something they could grab and move.'[6] The new device also brought benefits to stop-motion practice; as the technical team behind the DID wrote in their SIGCHI paper,

> Animators with stop-motion experience are able to start animating immediately, and usually prefer the setup over the traditional setup because they don't have to work around cameras,

lights, and props, and because they can see how the motion looks in the shot right away, instead of having to wait for film to return from a lab.[7]

Pervasive Computing

Tippett's animators were not the only people on *Jurassic Park* to use computer-controlled models. Impressed by the animatronic King Kong at the Universal Studios theme-park ride in Florida, Spielberg initially thought the film's effects breakthrough would be full-sized robotic dinosaurs, and he worked with the creator of that ride, Robert Gurr, to experiment with initial concepts.[8] When he realised that large, free-standing robotic dinosaurs were not viable, Spielberg nevertheless continued to pursue large-scale models, turning to Stan Winston, whose shop ended up creating many animatronic dinosaurs for the film. The largest of these was the full-size *T. rex*, which was mounted on a flight-simulator pedestal adapted by McFadden Systems, a company specialised in flight-simulator programming. In addition to the modified flight-simulator pedestal, other components of the full-size *T. rex* rig were controlled by fifth-size armatures dubbed 'dino simulators', an idea that came to Winston after seeing a telemetry suit controlling robots at Disney World.[9] This rig provided not just precise manual control over the movements but also reproducibility, since the computer responsible for the interlocking of the two devices could also record moves for precise playback of scenes requiring such capability. So, for instance, for the stunt where the *T. rex* pushes Jeff Goldblum's character through the wall of the restroom hut, the Winston team logged the movements during rehearsal and then replayed them for the final shot.[10]

The film's narrative thematises pervasive computing as well. A particularly visible aspect of this tendency is the park's thoroughly networked nature: the electric tour vehicles, with their now charmingly outmoded CD-ROM drives, are controlled from a command centre replete with CRT screens that track visitors, dinosaurs and security systems. Nedry's (Wayne Knight) treachery is only possible because of his intimate knowledge of the park, which is overwhelmingly tethered to computer-controlled systems. The reliance on these systems means vulnerability to systems failure, a point that is tied to Michael Crichton's thesis of the impossibility of total control in the source novel (and which Spielberg refashions into the more conventional theme of 'man usurping God's place'). And a concern with computational realism accompanied the interest in how computers undergird modern life. So not only were the screens that periodically supply crucial bits of narrative data actual contemporary computers, on loan from Apple and Silicon Graphics, these machines were also programmed by a four-person crew headed by Michael Backes: 'Responding to cues received via radio from the set, Backes and his team were able to feed their graphics directly to the appropriate monitors on stage, making it seem as though the actors involved were actually calling up the imagery.'[11] This realism extended to the representation of a computer system that has been singled out for ridicule as an example of Hollywood's typically nonsensical representations of programming. When Lex (Ariana Richards) rearms the security system, the quasi-3D file navigation interface she uses was in fact a demo system tool for Silicon Graphics' IRIX system called the 'file system navigator' or fsn.

Another aspect of the film's treatment of computers relates to how Alan Grant's (Sam Neill) character is introduced. Beginning with an overhead shot of a palaeontological dig in the Badlands of Montana, a team of researchers is excavating a velociraptor fossil. The tools involved in this excavation – brushes, breath, etc. – contrast sharply with the new, digital technique that

Jurassic Park's (1993) version of fsn (left) versus screen grab of actual fsn interface (right)

pulls Grant away from his digging. Indeed, Grant's first line, 'I hate computers', immediately establishes an opposition between digging and imaging. The dialogue spoken by the unnamed dig technician underscores this tension: 'This new program's incredible; a few more years' development and we won't even have to dig any more.' The implication is that Grant's expertise will also be rendered obsolete or 'extinct', which is what Dr Malcolm (Jeff Goldblum) suggests to Grant later. Here, then, the story within the film echoes the story of the pre-production process, as digital techniques threaten established traditions. But here, too, as with the story of the dinosaur input device, the new school finds itself needing the old school; Grant does not simply dismiss computers, rather, he engages with them in a variety of ways.

Shortly after the image is displayed on the screen, Grant begins to read it, pointing out anatomical details that resemble avian features. As he does so, he comes close to the monitor, which momentarily loses the image. Dr Sattler (Laura Dern) comments, 'Dr Grant's not machine compatible.' But what is more important to note here is less that Grant and (digital) machines do not get along, but rather that this disturbance is the first instance of a chain of similar occurrences (e.g. his escape from the laboratory tour, his exit from the tour vehicle) where curiosity leads to unexpected events that thwart the computerised security systems. Grant's intense interest in dinosaurs is what ultimately allows him to survive his encounters with them, but it is also what jeopardises his safety in the first place.

The scene concludes with Grant vivifying the fossil that has been displayed on the screen using a raptor claw and traditional storytelling techniques. Grant's scary story about raptors' hunting behaviour pre-visualises the later raptor hunting scenes. Grant's verbal evocation of dinosaur behaviour juxtaposes the power of traditional techniques (palaeontology as the unearthing and interpretation of evidence) with new-fangled imaging techniques. Grant performs a procedure similar to that of a film-maker, employing a new technology to tell a more powerful version of an established story.

Another instance of the pervasiveness of computing in *Jurassic Park* is the depiction of genetic research and its reliance on computational methods. As Mr DNA makes clear, genetic engineering is primarily a matter of computer-aided number crunching; the secret of life lies in the ability to decode and parse genetic information, an idea that is emblematised near the end of the film in a shot of a raptor onto which a DNA sequence is projected. *Jurassic Park*, in other words, is as much about computers as it is about dinosaurs. And, of course, the dinosaurs in *Jurassic Park* are unthinkable without computers.

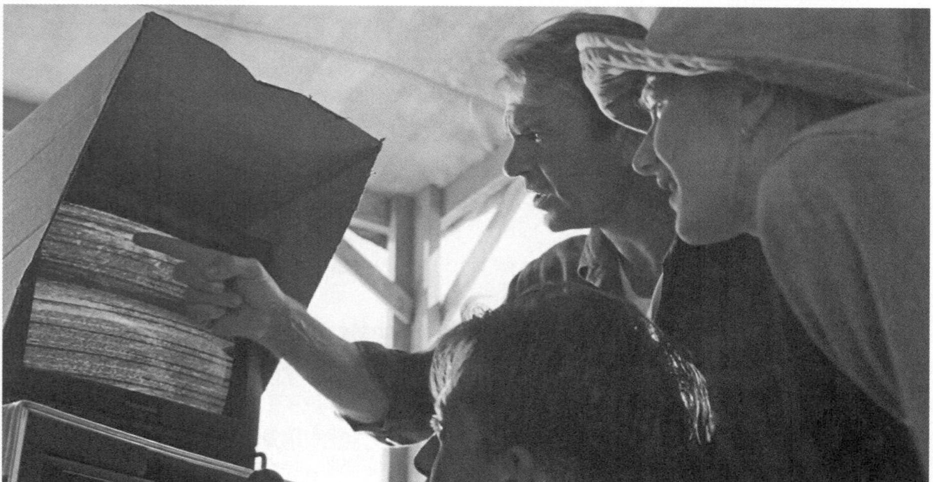

'Digging' versus 'imaging' in *Jurassic Park*

Constance Balides has focused on the film's relationship with post-Fordist economic practices, while Peter Wollen has isolated the film-as-theme-park-(ride) analogy.[12] And psychoanalytic and cultural-studies interpretations have posited that the monsters, i.e. the dinosaurs, are excessive and thus stand in for primal fears or other cultural processes.[13] What has received less attention is how the film is also imbricated in other knowledge economies. As Brooks Landon has noted, the

> nearly traditional complaint about privileging of special effects over story … takes a fascinating new turn when the special effect actually generates the story itself, actually becomes an important, if not determining, factor in the discovery and generation of scientific data and, by extension, of science fiction thinking driven by that data. … computer simulation and

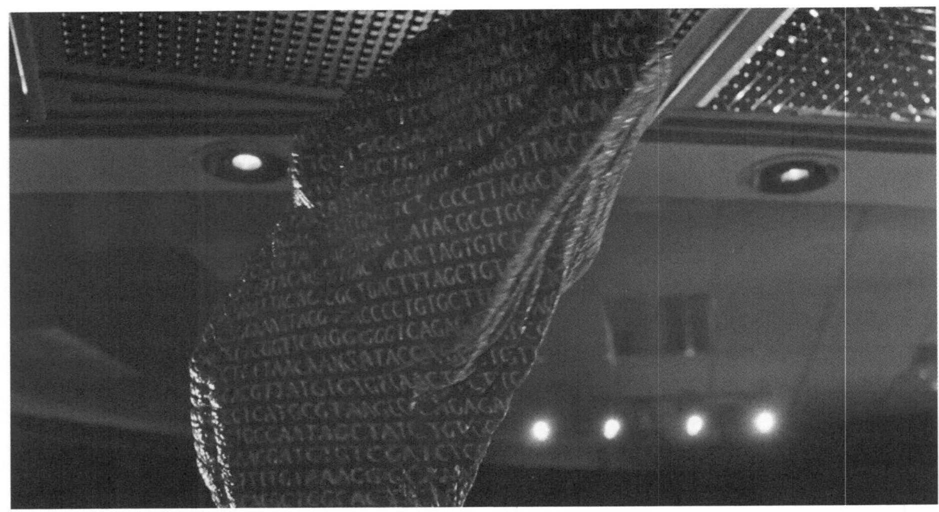

Velociraptor as genetic code in *Jurassic Park*

> visualisation technology now generate a new kind of scientific information that is more and more the focus of science fiction thinking.[14]

If, as Landon suggests, contemporary special effects have a recursive tendency, then out of what kind of data are the digital dinosaurs in *Jurassic Park* constructed? And did *Jurassic Park*'s use of new visualisation effects either constitute or lead to new scientific knowledge?

Living, Breathing *Dinosaurs*? Or, Monsters Nonetheless?

> I never thought I wanted to do a dinosaur movie better than anyone else's, but I did want my dinosaur movie to be the most realistic of them all. … I wanted my dinosaurs to be animals. I wouldn't even let anyone call them monsters or creatures. What I was after was kind of like *Nova* meets *Explorer*, with a little bit of *Raiders of the Lost Ark* and *Jaws* mixed in. But if I had to aspire to a particular movie, it would be *Hatari*. To me that was the high-water mark of man versus the natural in a feature film.[15]

Steven Spielberg's invocation of *Hatari!* (1962) reveals a somewhat surprising generic lineage. On the one hand, it shows Spielberg's consistent veneration of 'invisible' Hollywood craftsmen – his stated admiration for Howard Hawks, or Victor Fleming. On the other hand, Spielberg's characterisation of Hawks's film about professional game catchers as 'the high-water mark of man versus the natural' indicates a particular interest in dramatising the struggle between humans and the natural world. And while paying homage to previous 'dinosaur movies', which he later enumerates as Willis O'Brien's stop-motion animation work in *King Kong* (1933) and Ray Harryhausen's animation for *The Beast from 20,000 Fathoms* (1953) and *One Million Years B.C.* (1966), Spielberg primarily situates his film in relation to documentary genres by invoking two of television's most prominent natural-history franchises, *Nova* (1974–) and *National Geographic Explorer* (1985–).

To what extent, however, can the dinosaurs in *Jurassic Park* be considered 'nature'? By insisting that his dinosaurs be seen as animals, Spielberg sought to update the dinosaur film by incorporating developments in the field of palaeontology that offered a different vision of the kind of animals dinosaurs were. And, of course, the issue of the nature of these 'animals' is inextricably bound up with their technological provenance as state-of-the-art special effects, the most advanced expression of Hollywood's powers of visualisation. So while the importance of computers to *Jurassic Park* goes beyond the CGI shots, the question of how these celebrated landmarks of special effects might be thought of as examples of scientific visualisation has received limited consideration. As work by Michele Pierson, Eric Faden and Kristen Whissel has indicated, digital special effects have manifold and profound links to scientific visualisation.[16] In this sense the film's CGI scenes exhibit a dynamic similar to the circulation of knowledge that the dinosaur input device introduced, where the success of the film's special effects has to do with the blending of traditions, both old and new. Similarly, the quality of the film's animation of dinosaurs was due to the blending of palaeontological knowledge with animation knowledge. A more nuanced understanding of the CGI in *Jurassic Park*, both in terms of the aforementioned overlapping effects traditions as well as the interface with scientific-visualisation processes, can lead to a better understanding both of the multifarious role of computers in contemporary film-making and the links between entertainment and scientific imaging cultures.

In particular, the phenomenological qualities of dinosaur movement in the film, which constitute their 'realism', might be reconsidered. How credible, in other words, is the film-makers' repeated insistence that these are real, realistic, authentic dinosaurs?[17] The effects teams did rely on palaeontological knowledge of dinosaur anatomy and behaviour to create their dinosaurs. The most prominent source of scientific knowledge for the project was the palaeontologist Jack Horner, who worked as the primary science advisor for the entire *Jurassic Park* franchise, as well as serving as the model for the Alan Grant character.[18] As Steven Spielberg said in a discussion of the authenticity of the dinosaurs, 'Jack Horner became our credibility.'[19]

The process of making the animal models did not exactly conform to standards of scientific exactitude, however. The first stage was to generate illustrations based on scholarly texts:

> Working from anatomical breakdowns found in scholarly texts by respected palaeontologists such as Robert Bakker and Gregory Paul, [Paul 'Crash'] McCreery [a conceptual artist at Stan Winston's studio] spent anywhere from two to four weeks on each rendering, working and reworking the forms and action until he was fully satisfied with the results.[20]

These drawings then served as the basis for the maquettes, the detailed small-scale sculptures that served as reference models for the various other forms of effects, whether physical or digital. The digital models were then based on the Winston maquettes.

> Most of the CG models were scratch built by hand in the computer. The CG team scanned in the *T. rex* and raptor model dinosaurs that had been designed and sculpted by the art department at Stan Winston Studio, and then – working with the basic data obtained from the scan – fleshed out the digital models with additional patch-meshes as needed.[21]

The resulting images were startlingly different from previous screen incarnations in their verisimilar detail and speed, but the kinds of animals they resembled were not necessarily dinosaurs.

As Robert Baird has argued, an important cognitive schema that *Jurassic Park* deploys is that of 'animalisation', which is to say that its dinosaurs were modelled on known animal movements, which enhanced their believability.[22] And the dinosaurs did not necessarily resemble a single animal model. As Phil Tippett pointed out, 'In terms of movement, the brachiosaur was kind of a combination of an elephant and a giraffe – it had the long strides and grace of the giraffe, but the weight and mass of the elephant.'[23] This chimerical construction is perhaps even more pronounced in the domain of sound effects.[24] The *T. rex*'s roar is mixture of a lion, a baby elephant and a sound engineer's dog playing with a rope toy; the raptors combine dolphin and rhino noises. Gary Rydstrom made the following observations on the film's dinosaur sounds:

> I found out that there are many things scientists just don't know. For instance, with the brachiosaurs, it would make a tremendous difference in the way they sounded depending on whether their vocal box was located at the top of their necks or at the bottom of their necks. But palaeontologists don't know *where* it was located. The input I got from Spielberg was just to make all the dinosaur sounds believably animalistic – something people could relate to. The line we had to walk was to come up with something that was new and different, yet also familiar enough so that people would believe these things actually exist. We couldn't go too far out with the dinosaur sounds – even if there was scientific evidence to support that – because the audience had to be able to connect with an animal.[25]

One way to characterise the realism of the film's dinosaurs, then, would be to say that they are amateur approximations based on a patchwork appropriation of scientific data. Underlying this kind of interpretation is a particular notion about who generates scientific information (scientists) and the way it flows (from scientists to the public). A version of this attitude is present in the novel, where a guiding premise is that only an entertainment application could justify the expense of the park, which Crichton yokes to his critique of the commercialisation of genetic research; 'all this amazing technology is being used for commercial and frivolous purposes'. [26] The film's other screenwriter, David Koepp, made a similar observation:

> It was funny, but it was really getting into a pretty weird area. Here I was writing about these greedy people who are creating a fabulous theme park just so they can exploit all these dinosaurs and make silly little films and sell stupid plastic plates and things. And I'm writing it for a company that's eventually going to put this in their theme parks and make these silly little films and sell stupid plastic plates. I was really chasing my tail there for a while trying to figure out who was virtuous in this whole scenario – and eventually gave up.[27]

This critique could extend to the film's visualisations of dinosaurs as well, where tens of millions of dollars were spent on creating dinosaurs whose primary goal was not the dissemination of new knowledge but rather the commercial and frivolous aim of entertaining and maximising profits.

It is helpful to recall here David Kirby's differentiation among levels of realism, however. As Kirby writes, 'Film realism has three distinct components incorporating naturalism (visual realism), narrative integration (dramatic realism), and authenticity (scientific realism).'[28] *Jurassic Park*'s concern for realism can be located primarily with naturalism and narrative integration although, as we will see, the matter of whether it attained some measure of 'authenticity' is perhaps an open question. And furthermore, while *Jurassic Park*'s dinosaur recreations do not meet the standards of rigorous scientific evidence, many of these issues remain unresolved even within the field of palaeontological expertise. This aspect of the film's visualisations of dinosaur movement constitutes what David Kirby calls film's deployment as a 'modelling space', where film serves as a venue to demonstrate possibilities that have not yet attained the status of matters of fact.[29]

A juxtaposition of two animators can help to elaborate on this point. Richard Landon, who worked with the DID armatures on *Jurassic Park*, said of the experience, 'It was almost like sculpting motion rather than sculpting clay. We could readily put the big *T. rex* through its paces by moving the miniature motion base and by puppeteering the small armature manually.'[30] Two palaeontologists researching dinosaur locomotion more recently explored recreating how a dinosaur moved in a scientifically accurate manner, in an article that implicitly critiques the kind of dinosaur simulation exemplified by *Jurassic Park*.

> Having previously avoided complete reconstructions in our own research, we wondered whether we could legitimately present our 'result' as a scientific hypothesis rather than just a pretty moving picture. We found the process humbling – not because creating a walking stride for the model was difficult, but because (with the aid of the museum's animator, Scott Harris) inventing motion was all too easy.[31]

In this case, frivolity and inconsequentiality are linked to the misleading ease with which animation can make a dinosaur move.

This sense of something frivolous or playful about the dinosaurs is also a potential source of insight, however. No less a palaeontological authority than Stephen Jay Gould wrote of *Jurassic Park*:

> The dinosaur scenes are spectacular. Intellectuals too often either pay no attention to such technical wizardry or, even worse, actually disdain special effects with such dismissive epithets as 'merely mechanical'. I find such small-minded parochialism outrageous. Nothing can be more complex than a living organism, with all the fractal geometry of its form and behaviour (compared with the almost childishly simple lines of our buildings, and of almost anything else in the realm of human construction). The use of technology to render accurate and believable animals therefore becomes one of the greatest all-time challenges to human ingenuity.[32]

In Gould's view, ingenuity flourishes most strongly in times of 'play', and he concluded this facet of his appreciation by arguing,

> Yes, *Jurassic Park* is 'just' a movie – but for this very reason, it had freedom (and money) to develop techniques of reconstruction, particularly computer generation or CG, to new heights of astonishing realism. And yes, it matters – for immediately aesthetic reasons, and for all manner of practical possibilities in the future.[33]

This assertion of the film's potential to shed light on and open the door to future 'practical possibilities' suggests further questions, such as whether and to what extent the intuitive knowledge of the stop-motion team spurred new palaeontological knowledge. The animators' dinosaur models drew on their craft skillset and understanding of how dinosaurs, as animals, 'should' move. This material extrapolation was based in part on exercises where the animators enacted some of the dinosaur movements, using a form of introjective mimicry to guide their work. The animators possess what H. M. Collins would call 'tacit knowledge', a kind of expertise that is largely undervalued and often difficult to convey directly.[34]

A prominent point of contention related to *Jurassic Park*'s depiction of dinosaur movement is the scene where the *T. rex* runs. Before this scene, Attenborough's character states, 'we've clocked the *T. rex* at 35 mph', a detail taken from Crichton's novel.[35] A number of scientists have investigated this supposition, and these analyses conclude that it is unlikely *T. rex* was a fast runner.[36] But this conclusion is, in an oblique way, already present in the film itself. As lead animator on this sequence, Steve 'Spaz' Williams, pointed out, showing the *T. rex* running that fast did not look realistic. Williams commented, 'A real dinosaur like T. Rex would not be able to run fast and catch a running animal. But the bottom line for the movie was: "It has to chase a Jeep and eat a guy."'[37] And the scene contains the marks of this tension; speed is implied but not directly shown. Indeed, Spielberg's usually clear exposition is strategically muddled, as he masks the relative slowness of the *T. rex* run with the business of Dr Malcolm disengaging the stick shift (and the scene's sense of space is further sacrificed in order to make the rearview-mirror joke). The scene's spatial logic is distorted between, on the one hand, the desire to show *T. rex* as a fast runner and on the other hand, the animator's intuition that an animal of that size did not look right at that speed.

The effects in *Jurassic Park* constitute an example of what historian of science James Secord has termed 'knowledge in transit', a phrase that is meant to circumvent the persistent hierarchy that inevitably arises with the distinction between professional and popular science.[38] This notion of transit, of the necessary, inevitable movement that accompanies all instances of knowledge production, seems useful in this context as well, highlighting how these moving images function. In other words, instead of thinking about the film's dinosaur effects solely in terms of scientific accuracy, it is more interesting to consider how knowledge travels among communities of actors. The notion of evolution, whether in terms of animals or effects technologies, can serve as an emblem for this circulatory model of knowledge. Evolution is not solely punctual nor straightforward, since fragments or components of organisms and technology live on in descendants. The dinosaurs of *Jurassic Park* are more evolutionary than revolutionary, amalgams of previous effects combined with a novel imaging modality. And while certain effects may go extinct, the special-effects dinosaur remains as lively as ever.

I would like to thank the organisers of the Maryland Colloquium on Technology, Science, and Environment for inviting me to present an early version of this essay, which benefited from the group's feedback. I am also indebted to conversations with Tom Holtz and Matthew Carrano about palaeontological perspectives on Jurassic Park, and to Gina Wesley for putting me in touch with Matthew. And thanks, finally, to the editors whose careful attention resulted in substantial improvements.

Notes

1. Tom Shone, *Blockbuster: How Hollywood Learned to Stop Worrying and Love the Summer* (New York: Simon & Schuster, 2004), p. 213.
2. Tom Huddleston, '*Jurassic Park*', capsule review, *Time Out London*, http://www.timeout.com/london/film/jurassic-park.
3. Michele Pierson, *Special Effects: Still in Search of Wonder* (New York: Columbia University Press, 2002), p. 120. Stephen Prince, writing about the film's 'digital aura', makes a similar point: 'A carefully orchestrated marketing campaign promoted the film's use of digital images and promised viewers they would see dinosaurs that were more vivid and lifelike than any they had seen before in movies.' See *Digital Visual Effects in Cinema: The Seduction of Reality* (New Brunswick, NJ: Rutgers University Press, 2012), p. 25.
4. Ibid., p. 26.
5. Don Shay and Jody Duncan, *The Making of* Jurassic Park (New York: Ballantine, 1993), p. 37.
6. Ibid., p. 133.
7. Brian Knep, Craig Hayes, Rick Sayre, Tom Williams, 'Dinosaur Input Device', *Proceedings of the SIGCHI Conference on Human Factors in Computing Systems* (New York: ACM Press, 1995), pp. 304–9.
8. Shay and Duncan, *The Making of* Jurassic Park, p. 19.
9. Ibid., p. 28.

> While the giant hydraulic armature was being constructed, a fifth-scale version was fabricated so that its axes of motion could be interlocked with the big one via the computer. Motion in the full-size T. rex could then be produced by manually moving the scaled-down armature into desired positions.
>
> (ibid., p. 31)

10. See ibid., pp. 108–10. 'Waldo' is a term for remote manipulators, which comes from a Robert A. Heinlein short story. Remote manipulators came into use after World War II in nuclear and biohazard environments to allow manual control over dangerous substances.
11. Ibid., p. 101.
12. See Peter Wollen, 'Theme Park and Variations', *Sight and Sound* vol. 3 no. 7 (July 1993), pp. 7–9; and Constance Balides, 'Jurassic Post-Fordism: Tall Tales of Economics in the Theme Park', *Screen* vol. 41 no. 2 (2000), pp. 139–60.
13. See, for instance, Les Friedman, *The Films of Stephen Spielberg* (Cambridge: Cambridge University Press, 2004); and W. J. T. Mitchell, *The Last Dinosaur Book: The Life and Times of a Cultural Icon* (Chicago, IL: University of Chicago Press, 1998).
14, Brooks Landon, 'Rethinking Science Fiction Film in the Age of Electronic (Re)production: On a Clear Day You Can See the Horizon of Invisibility', *Post Script*, vol. 10 no. 1 (1990), pp. 60–71.
15. Steven Spielberg, quoted in Shay and Duncan, *The Making of* Jurassic Park, pp. 15–16.
16. See Pierson, *Special Effects*; Kristin Whissel, 'The Digital Multitude', *Cinema Journal* vol. 49 no. 4 (Summer 2010), pp. 90–110; and Eric Faden, 'Crowd Control: Early Cinema, Sound, and Digital Images', *Journal of Film and Video* vol. 53 nos 2/3 (Summer/Fall 2001), pp. 93–106.
17. 'Utterly authentic movements' is how Spielberg characterises his aspirations for the effects in the making-of material on the recent rerelease of the *Jurassic Park* trilogy on Blu-ray. Certain scenes in the

film thematise the concern for authenticity. When Hammond (Richard Attenborough) and Ellie Sattler talk over melting ice cream, he provides a brief biography of himself as a showman and offers his overriding rationale for the park, namely, that he wants to offer something other than the illusionism of his first show, a flea circus. 'Something real ... that they can touch', he says. This scene represents one of the strongest instances of Hammond's character speaking as a directorial surrogate.

18. For a discussion of Horner's role, see David Kirby, *Lab Coats in Hollywood: Science, Scientists, and Cinema* (Cambridge, MA: MIT University Press, 2011). The development of the effects over the life of the franchise and beyond (the *Walking with Dinosaurs* series [1999–], etc.) is, of course, relevant to the current argument but goes beyond the limits of this essay.
19. Blu-ray extras. One of the most frequently mentioned examples of the desire for authenticity involves how Tippett's crew initially had the raptors flicking their tongues, in the manner of snakes. Horner, concerned that this detail would undermine his dinosaurs-as-birds thesis, protested, and the tongues disappeared. The explanation for the decision, in Tippett's words, was that 'We all wanted to be as authentic with these things as possible, so we got rid of the tongue movement.' See Shay and Duncan, *The Making of* Jurassic Park, p. 137.
20. Ibid., p. 21.
21. Ibid., p. 134.
22. See Robert Baird, 'Animalizing *Jurassic Park*'s Dinosaurs: Blockbuster Schemata and Cross-Cultural Cognition in the Threat Scene', *Cinema Journal* vol. 37 no. 4 (Summer 1998), pp. 82–103.
23. Shay and Duncan, *The Making of* Jurassic Park, pp. 134–5.
24. *Jurassic Park*'s claim to represent a milestone in the use of digital technologies in cinema history has not received nearly as much attention from the perspective of sound studies as is warranted; it was, after all, the first film released in DTS.
25. Shay and Duncan, *The Making of* Jurassic Park, pp. 142–3.
26. Michael Crichton, quoted in ibid., p. 4.
27. David Koepp, quoted in ibid., p. 56. I foresee linking this recursive tendency in the film to the Crichton novel's underlying engagement with chaos theory and fractal geometry. This argument will form the basis for a future iteration of this essay, where I will pursue how the computational mathematics that the novel thematises, which can itself be traced back to such scientific computer tasks as weather simulation, undergird the film's CGI.
28. Kirby, *Lab Coats in Hollywood*, p. 16.
29. Ibid., p. 35. See also in this regard his citation of Jack Horner's comments on using *Jurassic Park III* as a way to model spinosaurus (pp. 35–6).
30. Shay and Duncan, *The Making of* Jurassic Park, p. 31.
31. John R. Hutchinson and Steve Gatesy, 'Dinosaur Locomotion: Beyond the Bones', *Nature* no. 440 (16 March 2006), p. 292.
32. Stephen Jay Gould, 'Dinomania', in Charles L. P. Silet (ed.), *The Films of Steven Spielberg: Critical Essays* (Lanham, MD: Scarecrow Press, 2002), p. 180. This essay originally appeared as 'Dinomania', *New York Review of Books*, 12 August 1993, pp. 51–6.
33. Ibid.
34. H. M. Collins, *Changing Order: Replication and Induction in Scientific Practice* (Chicago, IL: University of Chicago Press, 1992). The questions that arise at this point, which I hope to address in a future article, concern whether the animation software used in the film – both Sock, originally

implemented for *T2*, which joined the individual networks of points (the 'patch-mesh') that made up the major anatomical segments of the dinosaur computer model, and Envelope, which enabled the computer animators to move points in the *interior* of the patch-mesh to simulate the bulging and compressing of muscles – impacted scientific investigations of dinosaur movement.

35. Crichton's source for this speculative detail was Robert Bakker, *The Dinosaur Heresies: New Theories Unlocking the Mystery of the Dinosaurs and Their Extinction* (New York: William Morrow, 1986).
36. See J. R. Hutchinson and M. Garcia, 'Tyrannosaurus Was Not a Fast Runner', *Nature* vol. 415 (28 February 2002), pp. 1018–21; and 'Tyrannosaurus Was Not a Fast Runner', http://www.rvc.ac.uk/research/research-centres-and-facilities/structure-and-motion/projects/tyrannosaurus-was-not-a-fast-runner. See also Derek Turner, 'Beyond Detective Work: Empirical Testing in Paleontology', in David Sepkoski and Michael Ruse (eds), *The Paleobiological Revolution: Essays on the Growth of Modern Paleontology* (Chicago, IL: University of Chicago Press, 2009), pp. 201–10, which treats the *T. rex* running speed question as a case study. For another investigation sparked by the film's portrayal of *T. rex*, see Kent A. Stevens, 'Binocular Vision in Theropod Dinosaurs', *Journal of Vertebrate Paleontology* vol. 26 no. 2 (2006), pp. 321–30. Stevens was interested in the film's depiction of *T. rex* as unable to see immobile objects, and he concludes that, contra *Jurassic Park*, *T. rex* probably had excellent vision.
37. Steve Williams and Joe Letteri, '*Jurassic Park*: The Illusion of Life', SIGGRAPH presentation, 25 January 1994, archived at https://web.archive.org/web/20011104115221/http://www.silicon-valley.siggraph.org/MeetingNotes/ILM.html. In another version of this anecdote, Williams is quoted (Shone, *Blockbuster*, p. 218) as saying,

   > We had a zillion arguments about it. Some people argued that it was probably like a lion: it never ran unless it had to, and if it ran, it would do so for a very short period of time and move very fast. Using that logic, I had to throw physics out the window and create a T. rex that moved at sixty miles an hour, even though its hollow bones would have busted if it ran that fast.

   In a closing of the circuit, Hutchinson and Garcia, the palaeontologists cited in the previous footnote, apparently contacted some of the animators involved in *Jurassic Park*, as indicated in the question-and-answer portion of the internet supplements to their *Nature* paper:

   > Do the producers/writers of *Jurassic Park* agree with your theory that *T. rex* was probably not a fast runner?
   > JRH: I don't know any of the head honchos personally, so I am not sure. But from my conversations with animators at Industrial Light & Magic, I've learned that they do agree with this idea. They tried animating *Tyrannosaurus* at 50mph or so, and it 'just didn't look right' to them, so they had to pull movie tricks. This was very interesting to me, how movies and science did arrive at similar conclusions independently. They didn't do biomechanics; they just went with their gut feeling.

   See http://www.rvc.ac.uk/research/research-centres-and-facilities/structure-and-motion/projects/tyrannosaurus-was-not-a-fast-runner#tab-q-a-s.
38. James A. Secord, 'Knowledge in Transit', *Isis* vol. 95 (2004), pp. 654–72.

INCEPTION'S TIMESPACES
AN ECOLOGY OF TECHNOLOGY

AYLISH WOOD

In a short dream sequence in *Inception*, the central character Dom Cobb (Leonardo DiCaprio) is seen kneeling at the edge of the sea with Mal (Marion Cotillard), the woman to whom he was married until her suicide. As this scene occurs roughly halfway through the film, the audience is already familiar with the rationale of the story-world (diegesis). The place is limbo, the shore of Cobb and Mal's unconscious minds, accessed as they have gone deeper into dream levels. The two kneel in the sand behind a row of low sand castles and, smiling at their power to 'build their own world', push one over. Behind Cobb and Mal, a line of tall structures is just visible as silhouettes in a haze. At the moment they sweep a sand castle forward, one of these background buildings topples. Not only does it topple, the cascading debris follows the same pattern of collapse as the sand castle. The echoing of both event and movement in the foreground and background suggests everything is connected. The sound design establishes another line of connectivity, one that runs between the past and present. The distant rumble of the falling high-rise building counterpoints the tumble of waves on the beach. The mix also includes the sound of rainfall from the present of Cobb's narration, and links the now and then as it carries across the images.

Connectivity is central in this discussion of *Inception*. Special and visual effects hold a vital place in cinematic visualisations of technologies, especially within the science-fiction genre. But special and visual effects not only visualise technologies, they are themselves mediating technologies. These mediating technologies in turn generate stories, especially in paratexts that accompany the release of a film, including production-culture disclosures, 'making-of' materials (later also released with DVDs and Blu-rays), as well as online interviews and even production notes concerned with describing visual effects. Exploring the connections between these two ways of thinking involves not only thinking *about* special and visual effects, but also thinking *through* them.

Thinking *about* special and visual effects entails exploring their impact on aesthetics, narrative devices, performances, imagined spaces as well as their use in visualising technologies, discussions whose detail is often supported by information found in paratexts. Thinking *through* special effects makes use of paratexts in a different way. For instance, in each of two sequences discussed more fully later (the crumbling of limbo and the collapse of Ariadne's [Ellen Page] dream in Paris), paratexts reveal the hybrid materiality of the imagery. When thinking *about* the special and visual effects involved, the unusual aesthetics of these images can be made sense of as a consequence of the mediations of particular film-making practices. While the imagery is understood to have a hybrid materiality, this insight tends primarily to support rather than inform ways of thinking about figures within a story-world. In contrast, thinking *through* special effects by being mindful of the hybrid materialities in which Ariadne's actions occur, connects her unusual spatio-temporal experiences to a technologically mediated environment, and not just the dreams explicit with the story-world of *Inception*.

The approach of discussing a film in relation to its paratexts is an ecological one, in the sense that there are productive connections running between a story-world and related texts that augment its discursive themes. They are not only parallel texts, offering different kinds of stories within different domains; they also have the potential to inform one another. The following essay explores paratexts that reveal the mediating possibilities of technologies, and establishes connections between these and the experiences of characters in *Inception*. The discussion first outlines the essay's critical framework and then addresses specific special- and visual-effects sequences. An ecological approach is especially useful in a film such as *Inception*, where technological objects are presented as rather mundane and everyday. Though special and visual effects ensure the audiovisual coherence of the twisting and multilayered plot, they are not involved in creating a special device. The lack of a spectacular technology enables an emphasis on *Inception*'s dilemmas of guilt, loss, relationships between parents and children, as well as human imagination and dreaming. Reading paratexts for what they reveal about technologically mediated space brings back into focus the ways in which technology is also central to the actions of characters within the story-world of *Inception*.

Ecological Approaches and Performing Technologies

The last decade has seen an expanding terrain of materials released as part of the marketing strategy of feature films. Interviews and articles are easily available online, while DVD extras package such materials more directly for viewers, constituting an informative resource for anyone wanting to get at the detail and be accurate in their descriptions of film-making practices, especially in relation to special and visual effects.[1] These paratexts, however, are not only explanations for how things were done. They offer additional insights into the ways in which we understand technologies, ones that connect to the overt stories found in the diegesis of films, games and animations.

Donna Haraway's use of the term 'figuration' is helpful in clarifying the ways in which narrative connections form ecologies of technology. For Haraway, technologies are a particular instance of materialised figurations, which she describes as 'condensed maps of contestable worlds'.[2] Ecologies of technology too have the potential to be contestable worlds. By following through connections that run counter to the conventional order of things, new figurations begin to emerge. Haraway suggests that a figure is one who 'collects up people; a figure embodies shared meanings in stories that inhabit the audience'.[3] When teased apart, some of these stories reveal meanings that coexist, yielding insights into how connections work with or against each other. For instance, beginning with *The Dark Knight* (2008), Christopher Nolan has been promoted as a director who resists an overreliance on CGI when other, practical techniques are available. The ostensible basis of this claim is that Nolan wants his audience to anticipate that the images on the screen were created in-camera, as far as possible. Paul Franklin, visual-effects supervisor at Double Negative, says: 'Chris Nolan was keen to ground the world of *Inception* in observed reality.'[4] Despite this emphasis, Nolan is clear he is operating in a cinematic world:

> Well, I think for me when you look at the idea of being able to create a limitless world and use it almost as a playground for action and adventure and so forth, I naturally gravitate towards cinematic worlds … I certainly allowed my mind to wander where it would naturally [go] and I think a lot of the tropes from different genres of movies – heist films, spy films, that kind of thing – they therefore sort of naturally sit in that world.[5]

Where an emphasis on in-camera work quickly reaches something of a dead end, discussions closed off with claims about observed reality, the highlighting of cinematic reality more easily opens into questions about mediated realities. Connecting cinematic and mediated reality leads to an interesting series of new connections between technologies and their place in mediated reality.

Connections that accumulate around technology move between visible effects, the plot themes and actions of characters, and also the paratextual disclosures surrounding technologies. Each of these offers a different narrative mode in *Inception*. One narrative is embedded in the film's story-world, a second is found in its aesthetics and the third is comprised of production-culture disclosures. Narrative in a story-world is familiar, as are aesthetic conventions. Thinking of production-culture disclosures as narratives is less familiar, and takes its cue from John Caldwell's observation that the cultural practices of media production are an important site of analysis. Production communities generate cultural expressions 'involving all of the symbolic processes and collective practices that other cultures use: to gain and reinforce identity, to forge consensus and order, to perpetuate themselves and their interests, and to interpret the media *as* audience members'.[6] Disclosures are not only active within production communities and their related media industry;[7] they are also a source of additional insight, meaning and debate for a wider viewing audience. Historically, these have been consumed through magazine-based publications, which continue to exist alongside the expanding terrain of multimedia paratexts.[8] Though typically used as a descriptive narrative, production-culture disclosures are also expressive of something. Turning to John Law and Vicky Singleton's writing on narratives of techno-science provides a way of thinking through disclosures as active expressions of technology. Law and Singleton explain their approach: 'We take it that to tell technoscience stories is, in some measure or other, to perform technoscience realities.'[9] When taken as narratives, disclosures can be understood to act as performances of particular realities, both generally and specifically, about special- and visual-effects technology. Law and Singleton continue:

> So our argument is that technological storytelling makes a difference, and it is important to understand how this happens, how our descriptions interfere with other performances of technoscience to prop these up, extend them, undermine them, celebrate them, or some combination of these … no description is ever entirely innocent.[10]

Like Haraway's figurations, the combined technological storytelling of the diegesis, aesthetics and paratexts offers connections that have the potential to act as contestations as well as reiterations of ideas about technologies.

Law and Singleton's use of the term 'performance' benefits from some further explanation. The idea that technology performs a function is familiar, but what does it mean to say it performs and, furthermore, that it performs through narrative? In the action-finale of *Inception*, which includes an exploding fortress on dream level three, technology can be described as performing across several different layers of narrative. The story-world of *Inception* is centred on building the edifice of multiple dream levels. A team works together to create a dreamworld in which someone is lured into revealing secrets about themselves. Cobb is the leader of such a team, which includes an architect (Ariadne) who designs the space. A speciality of Cobb's team is complex dreamworlds, constructed around several layers of dream space and dream time. These multiple levels can be destroyed by a kick, some kind of literal collapse introducing the pull of gravity. In the finale, the composition of the imagery visually plays out this verticality, with events across all of the levels showing something falling: a lift plummeting down its shaft, the snowbound fortress collapsing downwards, taking everyone inside down too, Ariadne leaping backwards from the top of Mal and Cobb's house in limbo and dropping towards the ground. Ian Hunter, New Deal Studio's effects supervisor describes the effects and design work behind the collapsing fortress. Though at first sight, this seems to be simply rather mundane details about building materials, it also gives insight into the elements involved in creating the imagery:

> For surface areas like floors or roofs, sheets of urethane foam were pre-cut in different thicknesses and plastered with a trowel. 'In one of the shots,' recalled Hunter, 'the floor comes down and shatters into a million pieces. That was just by virtue of that material being very weak. We tested a lot of materials and some are durable enough that they just flex and bounce. The urethane has a failure point. Once it bends enough it just shatters or splinters along a seam.'[11]

The three narratives each offer different performances of technologies. In the narrative of the story-world, the ability of technologies to take people into shared dreams is stated and inferred by the different scenarios encountered by the characters as they awaken in different spatial and temporal organisations. Time expands across dream levels: five minutes in reality can translate to sixty minutes of a dream. The performance of technology is given in its capacity to relocate people in time and space. In the narrative found in the imagery, both audio and visual, the technological performances combine connectivity and verticality. The sound design connects dreams; for instance, the sound of a building rumbling as its shakes turns into the noise of a riot in the visual shift between levels. The content and framing of the visual imagery is the primary indicator of verticality, which literally establishes connections between the different spaces of the dream levels. Production-culture disclosures concerned with the destruction of the scale model of the fortress draw attention to the materiality of its structure. Referring to 3D modelling, the computer-aided, careful design and construction of the set, these disclosures reveal how the materiality of the structure enables the choreographed illusion of a coordinated collapse of the fortress, echoing the images reverberating across the other dream levels.

While each of these narratives, especially those of the story-world and the aesthetics of the sound and image, are performances in and of themselves, taken together they offer an expanded performance of technology. The performances are connected through their emphasis on technologically mediated reconfigurations of time and space. Drawing out the potential for these performances to inform one another involves thinking in a more ecological way about their productive connections. Within a technologically mediated context, ecological approaches understand performance to occur in relation to complicated interdependencies between 'every element of a performance and its environment'.[12] Through these complicated interdependencies, the contributions of individual elements to a performance become enmeshed. Any figure, whether a technological object, human or nonhuman actor, is a part of a figuration, contributing to a map of a contestable world. Extending this idea, each narrative performance contributes to a figuration of technology, and this expands the terrain through which technology gains meaning. For instance, the relative absence of sophisticated technology in the story-world appears to enhance the idea that *Inception* does not rely on computer-generated technology to create its version of reality. Instead, the ability to relocate involves a human imagining of the observed reality of dreams. But the story-world narrative is expanded by its connections to paratexts, drawing attention to the hybrid materialities from which the realities of *Inception* are constructed. The sound and images of the fortress collapse combine effects produced in-camera with CGI enhancements establishing a mixed reality, though that may pass a viewer by in the heightened pacing of the action. The paratextual details not only describe how the imagery was made, as the emphasis on the substance of the model in the narrative of the fortress demolition highlights materiality and gestures towards mediations of technology that rely on material as well as human elements.[13] This kind of thinking provides an avenue for connecting the environments of dream levels to technological mediations. It is a way of not only thinking *about* special and digital effects, but also of thinking *through* them.

Drawing out connections between individual elements is a feature of ecological approaches. For Gregory Bateson, it is impossible to reduce a description of an ecology to instances of isolated participating elements, to humans or nature or animals or machines.[14] Rather, they participate in combination, generating actions from transversal relations between the heterogeneous domains. Transversality is explicit in Felíx Guattari's *The Three Ecologies* (2008), where complex relations are understood as combinations of elements from all the participating influences. There is no cut between the points of mutuality, or intersection. In her ecology of things, Jane Bennett's emphasis on materiality extends this understanding of transversal relations. Bennett argues for a way of thinking that recognises humans to be co-participants in a materiality comprised of both human and nonhuman objects: 'We *are* vital materiality and we are surrounded by it, though we do not always see it that way.'[15]

Paying attention to the materiality of transversal relations revealed in each of *Inception*'s narrative performances of technology provides another way of thinking about what is seen and heard on the screen. The previous discussion foregrounded the ways in which technologies have the capacity to reconfigure time and space. In the following, I uncover the nonhuman vitalities of two sequences from *Inception*: the crumbing architecture of limbo and the Paris sequence when Ariadne discovers the possibilities of shared dreaming. The vitalities of these effects-based sequences are concerned with the materialities of time and space, in which the mediations of moving-image technologies combine in the mixed realities of the story-world. Within the story-world of *Inception*, reality at first seems to be clear enough. It is the world inhabited in a waking state. For most of the film's characters this distinction apparently remains intact. For Cobb, however, reality is in question through his relationship with Mal. Mal is dead but still exists for Cobb as a projection inside his mind, from where she disrupts his plans and taunts him about the status of his reality. Almost at the end of the film, she explicitly poses the question with which the film has been toying throughout: which construction of reality are we seeing?

Mediated Realities of Time and Space

In the reality of *Inception*'s story-world, time and space are mutable, their constructedness explicit. Within dream levels an architect can transform space, and a dreamscape is shared, based on a reality generated from more than one person. Time changes too, minutes in reality becoming hours, days and months the further someone goes into dream levels. The story of *Inception* develops through two main arcs. One is the heist involving Cobb and his team's attempt to 'incept' Robert Fischer (Cillian Murphy) with the idea of breaking up the monopolistic company he has inherited following the death of his father. The second concerns Cobb coming to terms with his guilt over the death of Mal, which occurred because of an idea he had planted in her mind. Both of these arcs introduce the possibilities of shared dreams that exist on multiple levels. The shared dreams are created through the interventions of the various members of the team: Ariadne is the architect who designs the space, Cobb the leader, Arthur (Joseph Gordon-Levitt) the fixer, Eames (Tom Hardy) the thief and Saito (Ken Watanabe) the bankroller. Through the mediation of a drug, administered via an infusion pump unobtrusively carried in a metal suitcase, team members are able to enter and intervene in people's dreams. The effectiveness of their team is such that they are able to work in nested dream levels, each of which has its own distinct reality. In the case of Fischer's heist, the team works across three levels.

One of the key narrative devices of *Inception* is that dream levels connect; what happens in one carries with it the potential to have implications in others. Mal kills herself because Cobb's insinuation of an idea in one reality gains traction in another; the whole purpose of the planned inception is to implant an idea in Robert Fischer's subconscious while he is dreaming, one that will have ramifications in the real world. Events in dreams have consequences: everything is connected. In the story-world narrative, *Inception* is full of commonplace technological objects with the potential to mediate these connections. Mediation is understood here in the sense meant by Bruno Latour, who defines mediators as objects, including technological ones, which transform, and in doing so leave a trace, evidence of a contributing influence: 'A mediator ... is an original event and creates what it translates as well as the entities between which it plays the mediating role.'[16] Mediators alter an input as they modify the meaning or the elements they are supposed to carry: 'In addition to being "determining" and serving as a "backdrop for human action", things might authorise, allow, afford, encourage, permit, suggest, influence, block, render possible, forbid and so on.'[17] What is curious in an SF film such as *Inception* is no one piece of technology really stands out. The device that renders possible shared dreaming is carried in a metallic suitcase, to which little significant attention is drawn. The device is not constructed using special effects, but is simply a circular infusion pump nestling within the padding of its case, the tubing stretched out to each of the dreamers. The lack of any emphasis signalling this device as special carries over to the diverse possibilities for technological mediations within the film's story-world. This positioning resonates with disclosures emphasising the importance of observed reality, which obscures the amount of mediating technology involved in making *Inception*. But technology *is* present and mediating in all kinds of ways within the story-world of the film: clocks, iPods and earphones, vehicles (cars, vans and even runaway trains), lifts, safes and all of the weaponry on display. In their different ways, these technologies offer instances of the various modes of mediation suggested in Latour's definition. For example, the runaway train blocks Cobb, clocks influence by exerting temporal pressure, while the safe permits the inception of an idea into Fischer's mind.

The idea of mediation can be taken further by thinking through how traces of mediated moments reveal more about what Jane Bennett calls a vital materiality. That is, the ways in which the materiality of both human and nonhuman objects generate actions, rather than the vitality of things being simply seen as vehicles for human actions. Take, for instance, the lift in the hotel on dream level two encountered in the playing out of Fischer's inception. Within level two it mediates by allowing people to go up and down the floors of the hotel building; it is literally a vehicle. But in the finale of the film the lift mediates in a more complex way. It generates the materiality necessary for the connections between the dream levels: gravity. At this point in *Inception*, because the levels are connected and the van in level one is in freefall, level two has no gravity. The construction of gravity by Arthur is not simply about allowing a lift's downward movement on level two, as it is the action of moving that produces the substance through which characters within the story-world are able to move across the time and space of the different dream levels. The performance of technology shifts from acting as a vehicle to one in which it actively generates the materiality that surrounds the characters within the story-world.

Other aspects of the technologically mediated environments of dream levels become apparent through paratexts describing the hybrid imagery of special- and visual-effects sequences. Consider another brief moment of building collapse when, at the end of the film, Cobb and Ariadne return to limbo to seek Saito, their injured and near-dead team member. Though brief, the sequence was constructed by visual-effects teams using a complicated process of digital modelling. Visited earlier in *Inception* through Cobb's recollection of his time with Mal, the rows upon rows of buildings were the pinnacle of their life together in the deepest of dream levels. When we see Cobb and Ariadne wash up on the shore of Cobb's unconscious, the architecture is falling into the sea. The sequence can be interpreted as a visualisation of Cobb's crumbling grasp on reality, and on the intrusions of Mal into his sense of self. When Cobb and Ariadne wash up on the shore of limbo, and as Cobb pulls Ariadne to her feet, a resonant musical note exceeds the tumbling sounds of the waves. This is superseded in turn by a creaking noise accompanied by the image of the section of building shearing off and cascading into the sea. A small chunk of material falls away from the bottom, battered by the wave. When the rest collapses, its sound is mixed into the crashing of the sea. The sequence continues with a 'fly-by' shot of the digitally modelled shoreline of buildings. The pace of the movement is picked up in the score, which then merges with the sound of a building's collapse into the waves. There is something unusual in this brief scene of falling buildings. Though it might be hard to locate what is unusual when first watching, the sound is important, as is the quality of the motion given to the crumbling façades. Production-culture disclosures reveal the scene to be a hybrid entity, its CG imagery created to mimic both architecture and shards of ice that shear off on the cracking edges of a glacier. The sound design also echoes this influence, the cascades of debris sounding like falling ice as well as architecture. The CG artists

Ariadne and Cobb on the shores of limbo surrounded by collapsing buildings in *Inception* (2010). The CG modelling of the building was informed by the dynamics of collapsing glaciers as well as architecture

developed the final images using a modelling routine based on rules about architectural blocks and glaciers:

> In this way, we arrived at a city layout that had familiar features such as squares, streets and intersections, but which also had a totally unique structure that felt more like a natural landform – a cliff being washed into the waves with architectural 'icebergs' floating out to sea … the collapsing architecture … was primarily referenced from natural history footage of glaciers rather than from building demolitions, adding giant splashes with Double Negative's proprietary Squirt fluids system.[18]

This disclosure gives a sense of the elements that combined in creating the distinctive materiality of the imagery: architecture, glaciers and modelling software. The imagery does not simply show the crumbling grasp of a human agent, but a complex and technologically mediated materiality. The spectacle of the collapsing architecture becomes a showcase for the possibilities of generating hybrid spaces.

The complex materiality of hybrid spaces can be explored further in the sequence when Ariadne learns about shared dreaming. Understanding the materiality allows Ariadne to emerge not just as the architect, but also as a character around which figurations of technology are contested. The sight of Paris folded over itself has become one of the iconic images of *Inception*. The scene occurs after Cobb introduces Ariadne to shared dreaming and she realises that she can alter space. Walking along the Parisian streets, Ariadne reconfigures space by causing the squares, intersections and streets to curve over. Ariadne and Cobb continue their journey by stepping upwards along the street. Richard King describes the sound design of the moment of transformation as conjuring the impression of a giant machine slowly locking into place: 'Imagine a machine that would be massive enough to move a city like that. That's the sound that I tried to make.'[19] Later in the sequence, Ariadne extends the view of a series of bridge arches using two mirrors. Unlike the similar reflection of a mirror and archway in *Citizen Kane* (1941), the bridge illusion lengthens into infinity in both directions, Ariadne and Cobb's reflections multiplying too. The edifice is literally shattered when Ariadne rests her hand on the surface of the glass.

If the figure of Ariadne orients a viewer's perspective in space, such a moment might be interpreted as the architect breaking through the surface spectacle of her constructions. Not only is there the illusion of an infinity of reflections, Ariadne and Cobb can actually walk towards it. Just as they could walk vertically onto the folded over streets of Paris, they can enter into the extended spaces created by Ariadne. Taking into account the other narratives surrounding this moment in *Inception* extends the idea that Ariadne breaks through the surface of spectacle. The audiovisual stylisations are designed to render these extraordinary images somehow ordinary by making them both familiar and apparently accessible. A sense of familiarity stabilises the figuration of space, and CG technology seems to mediate only to the extent that created space is apparently objectively real. This figuration is evident in a discussion of the lighting of the curved streets of Paris: 'The lighting had to be so seamless that you never question it', Franklin says.

> It's a dream that has to feel real. This sequence exemplified the key challenge in all the work: No matter how outlandish the imagery – folding streets or a café blowing up – we had to ground it with convincing, absolute reality.[20]

Such an emphasis on grounding the imagery in something called 'absolute reality' obscures the materiality introduced by CG technologies. Interviews and commentaries reveal the extensive digital work involved,[21] but these often reiterate a focus on reality. There is, however, an interesting contradiction destabilising the connections running through this figuration. The sound and images in which Paris is spatially extended are instances of spectacle, but at the same time both Cobb and their creator Ariadne can walk into them. The extensions of familiar space within the story-world of *Inception* expose the extent to which this space is not simply to be looked at, but entered into, colonisable as extensions of the existing orders of a world. Technologies mediate in generating a materiality accessible to the control of human figures, where their battles for dominance continue to ebb and flow, much like the battles for dominance also occurring in the dream levels of *Inception*.

The figuration of a mediated space in which technologies extend the known order of things, involves space as a singular and familiar entity. A contrasting figuration of space also occurs in the Paris sequence, when Ariadne first becomes aware of the existence of shared dreams. Sitting at a table with Cobb, she has been placed within a cliché of Paris, a pavement café on a street corner where she sips coffee. As Cobb speaks, Ariadne comes to the realisation that she is actually between two organisations of time and two different spaces, and in this moment the dream collapses. Exploring the explosion sequence through its ecology allows the mixed reality of this moment to emerge, one in which technology mediates by constituting a space constructed around multiple times. Within the story-world of *Inception*, it is quickly apparent that we are watching a dream, as Cobb tells Ariadne so, but she is unable to control her panic and the dream collapses. It is straightforward to interpret the aesthetics of the shot as an attempt to make this dream reality 'seem strange', and there are several ways in which this strangeness is evident. First, there is the conceptual framing of a shared dream. In *Inception*, dreams seen by an audience are shared ones, constructions designed by an architect, and inhabited by role-playing co-dreamers who take over the dream of an unsuspecting mark such as Fischer.

Once Ariadne realises she is in a dream the integrity of the Parisian café scene disintegrates. The sequence was constructed using special and visual effects: cameras shooting at different speeds; air cannons throwing debris into the air; post-production compositing techniques adding further debris

The constructedness of space and time is also overt in the accumulation of strangeness in the aesthetics of the imagery. Anyone familiar with explosions in films would have an expectation of loud noise, bangs and the sound of debris hitting objects before crashing down. In *Inception* the explosion is different. The world is coming apart, but the series of explosions are without fire. The sound might be described as *pocpocpoc*, an exaggeration of boxes being punched out, which matches well with the images of boxes flung into the air and disintegrating. As the sequence continues, the strangeness of these explosions becomes increasingly noticeable. They start in real time, bursts of debris flung outwards in a widening trajectory, but this widening trajectory slows down so that the debris almost hangs in a gravity-defying hesitation before falling. The sequence has a specific cinematic origin:

> For reference, the film-makers examined the final scene in Michelangelo Antonioni's 1970 film *Zabriskie Point* in which Daria, a main character, imagines blowing up her boss's home . . . . 'We wanted to create the same complexity,' Franklin says, 'all the tiny fragments you get when you blow up something. But, the practical effects team couldn't destroy things to the extent Chris [Nolan] wanted. He wanted cobblestones flying in the air, buildings exploding and shattering. So, we did a lot of CG dynamics. We added levels of detail and complexity to the sequence.'[22]

As the above quotation continues beyond the immediate reference to *Zabriskie Point*, the mediation of moving-image technologies also becomes apparent, in turn revealing more about the materiality of the sequence.

Making sense of the materiality of the explosion entails negotiating a way through the connections across the different narratives. Paul Franklin, visual-effects supervisor at Double Negative, comments that the explosions are a consequence of Ariadne's panic. As the dream's architect, when she panics, the 'fabric of the dream-world starts to unravel, disintegrating violently and flying apart in all directions'.[23] This kind of commentary connects the reality of the dream level to the terrain of Ariadne's dream, making it a consequence of humanness. Other disclosures offer a contested mapping out of connections, revealing how the sequences were filmed and then subjected to post-production manipulations. The sequences involved air cannon blasting materials into the air, which were filmed with high-speed film and digital cameras, and then composited to add debris and slow-motion speed ramps to give the progression of the explosions the feeling of almost hanging in the air. As Franklin says:

> Starting with a rough cut of the live action, the Double Negative VFX animation team used the in-house Dynamite dynamics toolset to extend the destruction to encompass the whole street. The compositors retimed the high-speed photography to create speed ramps so that all explosive events started in real-time before ramping down to slow motion which further extended the idea of abnormal physics.[24]

These disclosures deliver a stronger sense of the mediated materiality from which the explosions arise. At times there are overlapping images of both the fast and slow phases of explosions, the space of the event constituted around a sliding scale of temporalities.

The explosion sequence of *Inception* offers, then, a different kind of timespace. Understood through paratextual narratives, it is a microcosm of complex and technologically mediated times within a space. Since time is both on a small and large scale, *Inception*'s temporality exists on a multiplicity of scales, created by employing various kinds of cameras and digital manipulations. The sequence was shot using several cameras, including one that recorded at a frame rate of around 1000fps. When rerun at normal speed these enabled the generation of the ultra slow-motion imagery. Using speed ramps, created by compositing, multiple scales of timespace coexist within a shot. Unlike the spatial expansions of the later sections of the Paris sequence, the mediations of technology are foregrounded. Technology gives a mixed reality at which to look, to experience and to see experienced. In such a profusion of temporalities, Ariadne's control over her spatial environment breaks down. This breakdown can be explained not only in terms of her panic, but also as an experience of a complex and technologically mediated mix of temporalities. In the scene of the explosion, technology is performed as a complicating and potentially destabilising element in an environment, its capacity to transform the temporal scale of events troublesome.

The Paris sequence is interesting in terms of its status as spectacle, its referencing of other films (*Citizen Kane* and *Zabriskie Point*) and also as an ecology of narratives about mediating technologies. By looking at the mapping of connections between the three kinds of narrative, the images move away from objective reality and become instead explorations of technologically mediated environments. These explorations allow a revisiting of the events of the storyworld. Instead of seeing Ariadne as an architect who designs and reimagines space in the mutable reality of dream levels, she is a figure around whom narratives of technology connect with and contest one another. The performance of technology emerging from the connections is one that transforms time and space, and the experience of time and space. Ariadne is comfortable with a timespace defined only by spatial expansion; this is one she is able to enter and control. By contrast, a timespace defined by an active temporal expansion through a sliding scale of temporalities is too disconcerting. Such a discomfort resonates with critiques in which technology has too greatly increased the pace of living, leading to a dissolution of traditional coordinates. The outcome of the contested mapping of technologically mediated timespace offered by *Inception* is in the end a positive one; Ariadne is able to find her way through and stabilise her experience of space. However, while the physics of the space may be stabilised, the narrative of the story-world continues to play out the difficulties of its territorialisation. At the end of *Inception*, the status of reality remains uncertain.

Conclusion

The approach described in this discussion of *Inception* relies on thinking in a more expanded way about connections between a feature film and its paratexts. It starts from the claim that there are several kinds of narrative surrounding *Inception*. Together, these narratives generate an ecology of connections allowing events in the story-world to be explored through special and visual effects. The individual narratives are drawn from the story-world of shared dreams and the aesthetics of the visual and audio imagery. They are also drawn from paratexts such as production-culture disclosures, which focus more fully on the mediations of technologies, and reveal the roles technologies play in co-constituting the materiality of the realities of *Inception*. These narratives can be dealt with separately, a strategy that is familiar within cinema studies. But there is more to be learnt through connections between the narratives, and in looking at how they inform one another.

The critical framework developed in this essay has the specific task of exposing the extensiveness of the technologically mediated realities of *Inception*. Making connections between feature films, or animations and games, and their paratexts is not limited to questions about technologies. Disclosures around special and visual effects are widely available, and already inform discussions of many different aspects of film culture. An ecological approach offers a distinct way of bringing together the many narratives that circulate in relation to any film, television, animation or game. Though paratexts may at times have the purpose of supporting other stories, they too are narratives and their connections with a story-world offer many opportunities for thinking about the ways in which meaning emerges at an intersection of influences.

Notes

1. See James Bennett and Tom Brown, *Film and Television after DVD* (London: Routledge, 2008).
2. Donna Haraway, *Modest_Witness@Second_Millennium.FemaleMan©_Meets_OncoMouse™: Feminism and Technoscience* (New York: Routledge, 1997), p. 8.
3. Ibid., p. 23.
4. Paul Franklin, quoted in Mark London Williams, 'Contender – Visual Effects Artist Paul Franklin, *Inception*', *Below the Line*, 12 January 2011, http://www.btlnews.com/awards/contender-visual-effects-artist-paul-franklin-inception/.
5. Christopher Nolan, quoted in Cole Haddon, 'Interview: Christopher Nolan Talks *Inception*', *Film.com*, 12 July 2010, http://www.film.com/movies/interview-christopher-nolan-talks-inception.
6. John T. Caldwell, *Production Culture: Industrial Reflexivity and Cultural Practice in Film and Television* (Durham, NC: Duke University Press, 2008), p. 2.
7. See, for example, Vicky Mayer, Miranda M. Banks and John T. Caldwell, *Production Studies: Cultural Studies of Media Industries* (New York: Routledge, 2009).
8. See, for example, Jonathan Gray, *Show Sold Separately: Promos, Spoilers, and Other Media Paratexts* (New York: New York University Press, 2010); Barbara Klinger, *Beyond the Multiplex: Cinema, New*

Technologies, and the Home (Berkeley: University of California Press, 2006); Michele Pierson, *Special Effects: Still in Search of Wonder* (New York: Columbia University Press, 2002).

9. John Law and Vicky Singleton, 'Performing Technology's Stories: On Social Constructivism, Performance and Performativity', *Technology and Culture* vol. 41 no. 4 (October 2000), p. 767.
10. Ibid., pp. 769–70.
11. Ian Failes, 'Inception', *fxguide*, 31 July 2010, http://www.fxguide.com/featured/inception/.
12. David Cameron and John Carroll, 'Encoding Liveness: Performance and Real-time Rendering in Machinima', in Henry Lowood and Michel Nitsche (eds), *The Machinima Reader* (Cambridge, MA: MIT Press, 2011), p. 133.
13. Failes, 'Inception'.
14. Gregory Bateson, *Steps to an Ecology of Mind* (Chicago, IL: Chicago University Press, 1972), p. 491.
15. Jane Bennett, *Vibrant Matter: A Political Ecology of Things* (Durham, NC: Duke University Press, 2010), p. 14.
16. Bruno Latour, *We Have Never Been Modern* (Boston, MA: Harvard University Press, 1993), pp. 77–8.
17. Bruno Latour, *Reassembling the Social: An Introduction to Actor-Network-Theory* (Oxford: Oxford University Press, 2007), p. 72.
18. Bill Desowitz, 'VFX from Inception', *Animation World Network*, 21 July 2010, http://www.awn.com/articles/article/vfx-inception, p. 2.
19. Richard King, quoted in Blair Jackson, 'Christopher Nolan's Inception', *Mix Online*, 9 July 2010, http://mixonline.com/post/features/christopher_nolan_inception/, p. 2.
20. Paul Franklin, quoted in Barbara Robertson, 'In Your Dreams', *Computer Graphics World* vol. 33 no. 8 (August–September 2010), http://www.cgw.com/Publications/CGW/2010/Volume-33-Issue-8-Aug-Sep-2010-/In-Your-Dreams.aspx.
21. See Renee Dunlap, 'Immaculate Inception: Giving Birth to a Dream', *CG Society*, 7 October 2010, http://www.cgsociety.org/index.php/CGSFeatures/CGSFeatureSpecial/inception; Erin McCarthy, 'Inception's Spinning Room Special FX', *Popular Mechanics*, 16 July 2010, http://www.popularmechanics.com/technology/digital/visual-effects/inceptions-spinning-room-vfx; Terrence Russell, 'How *Inception's* Astonishing Visuals Came to Life', *Wired*, 20 July 2010, http://www.wired.co.uk/ news/archive/2010-07/21/inception-visual-effects.
22. Robertson, 'In Your Dreams'.
23. Desowitz, ' VFX from Inception', p. 3.
24. Paul Franklin, quoted in Vincent Frei, 'Inception Paul Franklin VFX Supervisor', *Art of VFX*, 11 August 2010, http://www.artofvfx.com.

AFTERWORD
A CONVERSATION WITH LEV MANOVICH

DAN NORTH

In this new interview, Lev Manovich discusses the difficulties in defining special effects, and the role of software in shaping the aesthetics of digital imagery. He makes the case for 'a new real', an aesthetic of perfection that is a byproduct of digital workflows, and which represents a significant shift in the appearance and meaning of the moving image.

Dan North: One of the problems with talking about special and visual effects is how we define and delimit the subject and be clear about what we're discussing, and what, if anything, should be excluded from that discussion.

Lev Manovich: I feel that answering, or trying to answer that question also means addressing the identity of the moving image for the last twenty years. This is *the* central question: do we have *cinema*, or is it *all* special effects. And what is 'special effects'?

DN: The sticking point is the word 'special'. It assumes that somehow certain processes are to be considered 'exceptional', and all other filmic techniques are 'ordinary' or 'default'. That doesn't help us to think about the part played by effects in the formal schema of film.

LM: I think one way to think about it is not just to focus on how images look, but how they're produced, which means looking at workflows, and the industrialisation of production. In the 80s, film-makers would designate certain shots as *special-effects* shots, and these would be given to specialist companies who would work on them. So, from the point of view of production, they were handled by different people, which made them, in a way, 'special'. Starting in the 90s (and it's still in progress today), you have software that, on the one hand, is geared more towards compositing, like Fusion, or Nuke, and on the other hand, editing software, like Avid or Final Cut. They all use different interfaces; Final Cut or Premiere will still emulate traditional film editing within its interface. With AfterEffects you really have a different paradigm: you have a canvas which is modelled on graphic design, and you can put layers onto this canvas. In the node-based compositing software, such as Nuke, where you have a network of nodes, there is no assumption in the software that some elements are 2D or 3D, and there is no assumption about the size of the nodes. What you've also seen over the last few years is, very gradually, different types of software – editing, animation, compositing – are slowly merging, even if they haven't merged yet.

When you think about film production, it's very similar. Today, you can basically do *everything* in Final Cut, or something similar, but if you want to do something like colour correction, that process is handled by specific people, and they use different software. You can see these things have merged, but in terms of production, it's still kind of separate: the key thing is that before digital, the editor was working on cutting shots in time, but the editor couldn't really interfere with the texture or content of shots. Previously, if you wanted to change the content of a shot, you had to go to a visual-effects house, but if you are using even the most simple editing software, you can already start changing the colour, the hue, the texture, so we can say that, conceptually, special effects and film editing have already merged. But practically, they still operate separately in terms of skills, job descriptions and software packages.

The industry itself has been trying to figure out how to conceptualise this. So they come out with a name like 'invisible effects', and already in the late 90s, if you look at the kinds of awards they have for technical jobs, there are already awards given for these invisible effects. And in the 2000s you have another term emerging, which is 'visual effects', which has become the dominant term.

I've been trying to write about motion graphics because I can see that in the academy in the last five years there have been a few books about special effects but they're about the kinds of effects you see in feature films. There hasn't been much attention paid to shorter forms, TV ads, titles, Flash etc., where you have a new visual language that I've been trying to analyse. It's been said that the term 'motion graphics' has the potential to be a much better description of twenty-first-century moving-image culture than the term 'film' or 'cinema', precisely because of the historical baggage.

DN: Is your primary interest now in the operations of particular kinds of software?

LM: Well, software, but also the job organisation or 'workflow', because at the industry level, it doesn't matter what software is available, what really matters is how production is organised. Especially in the context of commercial production, the most important thing is workflow. The companies might be given nine days to do an incredibly complex commercial, and if they can't do it, it goes to Singapore or Korea or somewhere else.

DN: 'Workflow' is one of those terms that helps us to knit together all of the different processes, but it might suggest that you end up with creative processes that are facilitated rather than proscribed by technology. I wonder, for instance, if we need to start considering the authorial input of software, and the way it imposes restrictions, just as often as it enables people to perform creative tasks. It limits what people can do to an extent.

LM: In theory, computer software doesn't limit anything. It's a machine that can simulate the operations of another machine, and you can program it. In the last few years, I've been trying to speculate about what we might call these *affordances* of software. They are affordances not only in the sense of what software helps you to do, but also in the sense that there is a kind of skill required. Some things are very easy to do, and you're kind of *asked* to do it, because that's what the interface offers you, whereas other things are more difficult, and you basically have to start writing scripts. For example, in AfterEffects, if you're a professional user you can write instructions, but casual users wouldn't know how to do that. It's not like a binary switch where software prevents you from doing certain things. It's a continuous dimension. I've been trying to think about how this kind of structure of software authorship is built into the visual aesthetics of media, and I've been pointing out what I see as certain common features, such as motion graphics in the 2000s, where you have issues like hybridity, which is the aesthetics around mixtures of 2D, 3D, video and so on. In 2D animation in the twentieth century, you had the backgrounds, and the cels that move on top of them, but the colours couldn't be changed, for example. But if you use software like AfterEffects, when you add objects to a canvas, each object has its own channel, and then you click on the object, and it gives you a list of properties. The animation interface works the same way; it takes three clicks to animate the line, it takes three clicks to change the colour, it takes three clicks to move an object, and the result is that we have this new aesthetics of the moving image emerging in the late 90s where there's constant movement, and lots of things are changing at the same time.

This is different from nineteenth- and twentieth-century electronic or mechanical media where, because it was hard work, it had certain physical limits. For example, you were shooting things through a lens onto photographic film. A lens is a physical system where there are certain limits to what it can capture. But designing things in 3D in virtual space, there are no physical limits. The limits come from how much labour I have to put in creating objects, or how many hours it will take to render a frame. So, every medium has some affordances, and every medium has some limits.

DN: At the point of reception, the audience tends to have some sense of the level of effort, the level of technical expertise that has gone in to making the images that they're watching. Disney animation was always about the amount of time and effort that went into it – how many individual frames they had to hand-paint – and I suppose what people are having greater trouble with these days is how to attribute effort to something that has been rendered using software. They have a greater sense with something that has been hand-drawn. They're less familiar with ways to brand what they're seeing today as artistic or as effortful.

LM: My sense is the opposite, especially with the younger generations. Because everybody uses software, everybody uses Photoshop, they're actually much more familiar with how a scene's been done. Every DVD has a 'making-of' documentary. I've been visiting websites of some famous media design companies, MK12 or Imaginary Forces, where they will usually have a 'making-of' video for every commercial. In the old days of the Avid Studios and other software nobody had ever seen anything like it: now people use the same laptops to make movies that everybody has, so there's this pleasure in understanding and knowing the answers of how it's made. I think it becomes a big part of the cultural experience for consumers.

DN: The more sophisticated visual effects get, the more skilled spectators become at that kind of analysis. What struck me was that several of the contributors to this book have

described the effects that they're talking about as 'handmade'. They could have used a word like 'analogue' or 'practical' or 'profilmic' to describe this: they're usually referring to a sort of artisanal effects process that's carried out by singular artists, often in a workshop, using photochemical processes. I suspect that what they're often doing when they talk about 'handmade' is trying to differentiate these processes from what they might see as the lack of hands-on residue in digital effects. Is this just nostalgia? Is this something that people need to get over?

LM: Maybe they don't understand how production works. If you go to a design studio, you'll see storyboards, you'll see sets, you'll see models in bamboo, you'll see digital: I think we're just misinformed about how people actually make things. All of it is handmade, all of it is visual, it's all combined, it's hybrid. We can't view 'digital' technology as some kind of uniform, monolithic thing.

Another thing we need to talk about is aesthetics, because I don't see any writing about it. Look at TV, look at any commercial or music video. Every single image that you see is very perfectly designed, it's very beautiful, and enhanced. The enhancement can be as simple as changing the hue and brightness or, some very lightly visible particle systems, or you have extreme close-ups where you see tears or water. It's a kind of *spectacularisation* of reality, which affects every photograph, but especially every moving image that we see around us, and in commercial media. There's no name for it. Media history doesn't have a name for it, and I haven't seen any academic writing about it. The visual texture, and the emotional, communicative appeal of every image has changed. Until around 2004, computers were not fast enough to do this kind of enhancement on every frame. In digital cinema, there are all these films which are specifically trying *not* to do it (Dogme, for example), but when I think about television aesthetics, every image has been through plastic surgery, so to speak. We have no theoretical framework to write about it, because it's not visual effects: it's on every image. But you also can't call it cinematography because cinematography was all about arranging things in reality, with camera movement, composition and lighting. This all of course happens, including editing, in post-production. Just switch on TV. You're going to see very fast camera moves, you're going to see extreme close-ups of textures, you're going to see advertising with these microscopic shots of raindrops, you're going to see horses galloping around at high speed, and in close-ups of the horses' feet there are these particle systems. It's all these different techniques which make the image incredibly visually appealing and perfect in a way it never was before in the history of human visual culture. This is much bigger than 3D. It affects every single moving image we see being professionally produced. Obviously, all the models in magazines today have been through Photoshop, but with moving images, people can create the strongest effects; first of all, there's some excitement because the visual field is changing all the time, and secondly, we're always seeing micro-movements, with water drops on the skin, close-ups of water drops, or little random particle clouds in the background. The moving image becomes a seductive mechanism in our culture in a way with which still photographs, architecture, can't really compete. We can't call it hyperreal, we can't call it superreal, because all these terms have been used already. Also, this is normal, this is the new real. There is *this*, and there's the raw footage that you see on YouTube, and there's nothing in between.

DN: I certainly know what you're referring to with that pristine nature of the image. It must be a product of the enhanced technological capabilities of even lower-end digital cameras and the relative manipulability of the images they shoot. But I want to go back to your description of hybridity. It once felt paradoxical or even contradictory when you said that digital film-making is characterised by hybridity, yet new media production runs every aspect of a production through the same computer workstations. Hybridity depends on preserving the individual characteristics of each composited component. You see both a kind of hybridity where you preserve those discrete elements, and a processing of everything through a singular workflow.

LM: Yes, I think the two things are connected. The reason this kind of hybridity became possible is because you are using the single digital workflow, and you have what were previously techniques and effects which were only possible in completely separate media machines that now have been simulated, so between three or four or five software applications you have everything: you have printing, you have 3D, you have 2D, you have cinematography, you can have anything you want. At first, these programs couldn't talk to each other, and then they were made more compatible, so the idea was that when you worked on a project you could move it around between different programs and in every program you could add particular effects or particular content which simulates the different media, and at the end you have this hybrid product. The idea was that, not only because they were digital code, but also because all these programs shared the same file formats, you could import any 3D model into AfterEffects, or into Photoshop. I was wondering what the effect was of this hybridity, and how people were excited about this ability to combine the content and the effects.

I think in the late 90s and the first part of the 2000s, you could really see this aesthetic in lots of motion graphics and other short moving-image sequences. I'm not sure it's still true. The other day I was watching the titles from *Mad Men* [2007–]. On the one hand, you can say that these titles also belong to the hybridity aesthetic because there are the silhouettes that lay flat, and then there is a three-dimensional space that forms the backdrop. The three-dimensional space doesn't really come from any existing media: it's visibly a computer artefact because it has a strong perspective, and then there are these building-like surfaces from texture maps which are composed from photographs of Manhattan, and some ads, and the whole thing has been simulated. You can say that the hybridity aesthetics is about foregrounding or exaggerating the looks, the surfaces of different media. For example, you use the look of old film, or video or something else, but sometimes it's about playing with perception and making a contrast between silhouettes and deep space, for example, 2D and 3D. I think the *Mad Men* title sequence is a good example, because it is like a simulated combination of graphic design and 2D animation, so hybridity is really about combining types of presentation, which somehow stimulate perception. When your brain sees some 2D forms next to deep 3D space, something happens, and somehow the brain has to do some extra processing, because it's a kind of perceptual illusion, a special effect. In reality, in 3D space everything would cast shadows. You're not going to have these perfect 2D cutouts.

DN: However, one of the main goals of visual effects, whether achievable or not, has been to erase the boundaries between elements and create seamless composites and hide the hybrid sources of those composited elements.

LM: That's absolutely true; dozens of different technologies might be used in a single action sequence. Maybe we can say that that's the contemporary meaning of 'special effect': this perfect whole where everything looks like it belongs to a similar three-dimensional space. This is different from the superreal look of TV images, or just motion graphics, that I was trying to describe earlier, which is still not animation, and it's not cinematography, because the idea is not to create a completely seamless whole, but instead to show you that the image has been enhanced. On the one hand, you have old-style spectacular special effects in action movies like *Superman* [1978], but in shorter forms you have a little bit more of a celebration of hybridity, of enhancement and of artifice.

DN: Talking about the perfection of simulated imagery always makes me uneasy. In trying to construct a history of special effects, we've always had to try and counter the commonsense assumption that special effects now are 'better' than they used to be. To some people's minds that's very true – 2005 *King Kong* looks more 'realistic' than 1933 *King Kong* – it's just not an interesting point to have to make, because people in 1933 weren't complaining that Kong was a defective, primitive illusion. Rather than tracing a teleological narrative of perfection, we should see 'flaws' in the image as active properties of a visual effect rather than judging old films as inadequate gestures towards what we end up with today.

LM: This 'perfection' of images in the twenty-first century is damaging the meaning and the value of cultural heritage. Sometimes I find it difficult to watch films from the 90s simply because of their visual texture and because they don't have enough contrast when things are not colour-enhanced, and I'm supposed to be more of a sophisticated viewer, right? Maybe I'm just paying too much attention, and everything I watch today is perfect, so things that haven't been perfected are going to stand out.

DN: I often feel that there's something very old-fashioned about visual effects in cinema. They're using very advanced technologies and sometimes they're demonstrating them in very spectacular and innovative ways, but they're still subsuming all of the potentialities of those technologies beneath linear narrative. We take all the radical potential of this technology and we boil it down to decoration for narratives that we've seen before.

LM: I would say that, in the opposite direction, in the last decade people have been talking about a new cultural formula in new media, in this very expansive three-dimensional world of spaces which you navigate or fly through, which exists in both video games and in films (*Avatar* [2009] is one example). In the twentieth century, we *didn't* have the technology to create these elaborate, navigable virtual worlds. It's not like building some cyborg character, as in *Terminator 2: Judgment Day* [1991], it's about constructing miles and miles of a virtual world. This changes how studios work. We have these assets, which may be characters, but also these worlds, and then they build films around them. We don't get that from narrative.

I keep coming back to this super-enhanced image. Of course it's not a new thing because, when you think about twentieth-century photography, by the 30s you had this standardised, Hollywood-style portraiture in cinematography, which is about using fill lights, sometimes five lights to create this separation with a backlight. That already is a very enhanced image, because I don't think this system of five lights existed in portrait photography. I think to audiences of the period that look was hyperreal. Now, you have these new possibilities, and the difference is the degree to which you can do compositing. In addition to lighting a three-dimensional digital scene to get silhouettes and highlights, or to enhance the image, you can alter textures and surfaces and add more layers and elements. Historically, this is a different kind of image.

I think in the 90s when this process started, you had a strong separation between 2D and 3D. Film scanning was very expensive, so it was only about five years ago that it became possible to scan a whole film into the computer. Now the whole film can be edited digitally, and even the special effects break down because the whole thing is a set of pixels. This starts in the early 80s, but it takes about twenty years before it becomes really inexpensive. In the 90s we still talked about the film medium as separate from 3D animation, or from 2D animated cartoons for children. In industrial terms, and in terms of the marketing and reception, you still have these separate worlds. In the 2000s, none of the terms we used in the twentieth century work any more, meaning that if you talk about how things are produced, and if you want to talk about the differences in what the images represent and how they look, the terms cinema, animation, 3D animation, cartoons, special effects, all became completely meaningless. Most forms of image production now use all these technologies together. So in a feature film you might have more shots focused on the live action, whereas in motion graphics, often the live action is not the focus, but the difference became purely quantitative of which layers are foregrounded. We've reached the point in film studies where we're talking about marketing and theatrical distribution, and we can still talk about the different films and genres, but in terms of the aesthetics, poetics, semiotics and technology, we don't have a single term which has a meaning any more. It has all merged. It's wonderful, but it's also troubling, because it's impossible to argue that any of these terms has distinct boundaries.

DN: It *is* troubling when you reach the limits of the vocabulary that you've spent years learning how to use. I wonder if what you're seeing in this perfect image is the 'visual-effects-isation' of the image, the transformation of the image into something spectacular for its own identity. In itself, it carries the same properties that we used to attach to visual-effects imagery.

LM: That's a good way to put it, but another way might be to say that it's not about visual effects becoming the norm, but it's really about twentieth-century traditions of cinematography. The directors and the actors were about the space, and the action, the theatrical aspects of the film. Cinematography was about the camera, movement and lighting.

The difference is that special effects were in their own separate shots, and cinematography was something presiding over every image. What you have now is the cinematography with visual possibilities greatly enhanced with 3D, compositing, camera editing and motion capture, which logically we can think of as cinematography rather than special effects, because it affects every single image as opposed to just some shots. That's another way to go.

Let's think about different kinds of special effects, where it's still possible to make distinctions. Take *Jurassic Park* [1993]. You have this integration, this hybridity between background plates, CGI, animatronic dinosaurs, and all this creates something believable and plausible. Statistically, it's very unlikely that I will walk down a street and see dinosaurs, but physically they would look how they do in the movie. Then you have another kind of visual effects where the idea is to create something that is physically purely impossible. But what happens in contemporary media culture is not that the distinctions disappear, it's that all of these things coexist in the time and space of, for instance, a thirty-second commercial. Many effects are combined sometimes in the same shot, or at least in the space of a thirty-second spot, in such a way that I don't know if the brain has time to make the distinctions. This is not necessarily to question the idea of special effects, but just to say that it's hard to know what they are any more.

DN: That description of the thing that is unlikely but looks possible is what Stephen Prince calls 'perceptual realism': if dinosaurs walked the earth, this is what they would look like. They would cast shadows, and interact in this plausible way with their environments. There's another thing that your visual effects might be doing, and that is showing something impossible but using the same processes of visual simulation that make it *look* perceptually realistic.

LM: Another example is what you see a few years ago where you have this 3D compositing and virtual cameras used in lots of films where the camera starts in one place, flies through a city, goes through a keyhole, then it goes underground. We can say that physically, we can imagine somebody constructing a camera that could do that, but it's unlikely using present technology. In this case there's nothing special about the spaces. What's impossible is the movement. That's maybe 30 per cent or 50 per cent of visual effects today – these impossible camera movements, impossible spatial journeys.

DN: There's certainly an acceleration of that sort of thing. But historically we can find examples of, for instance, Hitchcock doing impossible camera moves where he's used miniatures or moveable walls.

LM: Traditionally, special effects are about inserting one thing into something else, like with King Kong climbing the Empire State Building. You still have it, especially in big-budget films, with cyborgs or starships or aliens, but you also have a lot of statistically impossible or incredibly fast spatial navigations, where in three seconds you move from the pupil of an eye, or the camera travels inside a person's body. People no longer just make visual effects where everything looks photorealistic like *Jurassic Park*. You also have this exaggerated visual look. You have these two things combined. This makes it more conceptually difficult to think about.

DN: I think the image of King Kong climbing the Empire State Building with a woman in his hand might serve the same symbolic function no matter what process they had used to achieve it on screen, but the effect is altered by the mechanics of that technique. They could have used a man in a monkey suit, but instead they've chosen to animate a miniature model. How does that choice of process inflect the symbolic meaning of this image of Kong climbing a skyscraper?

LM: Well, it obviously *does*, but we don't know how. I was studying neuroscience, but I gave it up in the 80s because I realised it would be another thirty or forty years before we would actually know how it works in the brain. So, we can only speculate about how your brain processes it, but it affects very deep processing because 70 per cent of the brain is devoted to visual analysis, so these things affect very big mechanisms.

DN: Anyone who deals with technology is always asked what is coming next. Is there a next phase of image production? Are we going to 'get over' narrative cinema?

LM: When you go to technology trade shows and conferences such as SIGGRAPH, for years and years what you've seen is 3D projection. Not the 3D projection where you need to wear glasses, but where you walk around the space and see 3D objects. The technology is very primitive so far. You can barely even get wireframe objects, so forget about the rendering. You have hundreds of years of traditional image-making, from Renaissance painting to 3D compositing, where people developed incredible skills to make these seductive, believable but unlikely super-images. But if entertainment is going to achieve an illusion of 3D things in space, you'll have to start all over again. What we can do in three-dimensional space in trying to compete with the image is very primitive. Physical space gives you a lot of constraints that you don't have with the image. Visual culture and communication is going to turn at some point towards the real 3D. Something which actually exists in space as opposed to just in the image. Then it's going to be a huge shift and maybe we'll get a new form of realism. We're talking about ten or fifteen years down the line. We can say that special effects began with the Renaissance, with perspective, and we're still operating with the same paradigm. We're just doing it with digital tools. If we go towards this augmented reality, we have to start all over again. One way to get away from cinematography is to give up the image. The image has been poisoned.

INDEX

Page numbers in **bold** indicate detailed analysis; those in *italics* denote illustrations; *n* = endnote; entries for films carry dates whenever a well-known remake is in circulation.

List of Illustrations

While considerable effort has been made to correctly identify the copyright holders, this has not been possible in all cases. We apologise for any apparent negligence and any omissions or corrections brought to our attention will be remedied in any future editions.

Three Kings, © Warner Bros./© Village Roadshow Films Limited; *Jarhead*, © Motion Picture KAPPA Produktionsgesellschaft MbH/Universal Studios; *Ghostbusters*, © Columbia Pictures Industries Inc.; *Ghostbusters II*, Columbia Pictures Corporation; *Gremlins*, © Warner Bros. Inc.; *There Will Be Blood*, © Paramount Vantage/Miramax Film Corp.; *Coraline*, © Laika Inc.; *The Curse of the Were-Rabbit*, © Aardman Animations Limited; *The Boxtrolls*, © Boxtrolls LLC; *James and the Giant Peach*, Disney Enterprises Inc./Allied Film-makers; *Fantastic Mr. Fox*, © Twentieth Century-Fox Film Corporation/Indian Paintbrush/Monarchy Enterprises S.a.r.l.; *Metropolis*, Ufa; *Die Nibelungen: Siegfried*, Decla-Bioscop/Ufa; *Princess Nicotine*, Vitagraph Company of America; *Blackmail*, British International Pictures; *Darby O'Gill and the Little People*, © Walt Disney Productions; *Moulin Rouge!*, © Twentieth Century-Fox Film Corporation; *Terra Incognita*, RECK Film; *Wall-E*, Disney Enterprises Inc/Pixar; *The Matrix*, © Warner Bros./© Village Roadshow Films Ltd; *Fight Club*, Twentieth Century-Fox Film Corporation/Monarchy Enterprises B.V./Regency Enterprises/Fox 2000 Pictures/Linson Films/Taurus Film; *Blonde Venus*, Paramount Publix Corporation; *Sky Captain and the World of Tomorrow*, © Brooklyn Films II/© Filmauro/Riff Raff Productions; *Das Cabinet des Dr. Caligari*, Decla Filmgesellschaft; *War of the Worlds*, © Paramount Pictures/DreamWorks Pictures; *300*, © Warner Bros. Entertainment Inc./Virtual Studios; *300* (book), Frank Miller and Lynn Varley (Milwaukie, OR: Dark Horse Books, 1999); *Happy Feet*, © Village Roadshow Pictures; *Impossible Balancing Feat*, Star-Film; *A Tale of the Wind*, La Sept/CAPI; *The Exorcist*, © Warner Bros./Hoya Productions; *The Last Exorcism*, © StudioCanal S.A./Strike Entertainment Inc.; *Hellboy*, © Revolution Studios; *Cronos*, © Iguana Producciones; *The Devil's Backbone*, El Deseo/Tequila Gang/Sogepaq/Canal+ España; *Blade II*, © Linovo Productions GmbH & Co. KG/New Line Cinema/Amen Ra Films; *Hellboy II*, © Universal Studios/© Internationale Filmproduktion/Eagle Filmproduktion; *Pacific Rim*, Legendary Pictures/DDY; *Close Encounters of the Third Kind*, © Columbia Pictures Industries Inc.; *Star Wars*, Lucasfilm Ltd; *Allures*, Jordan Belson; *Vertigo*, © Alfred J. Hitchcock Productions/Paramount Pictures Corporation; *The Fountain*, © Warner Bros. Entertainment Inc./Regency Entertainment Inc./Monarchy Enterprises S.a.r.l.; *The Right Stuff*, © The Ladd Company; *The Tree of Life*, © Cottonwood Pictures LLC; *The Making of Jurassic Park*, Amblin Entertainment/ZM Productions; *Jurassic Park*, © Universal City Studios Inc/Amblin Entertainment; *Inception*, © Warner Bros. Entertainment Inc./Legendary Pictures.